THE NEW
Bostonians

THE NEW
Bostonians

HOW IMMIGRANTS HAVE

TRANSFORMED THE METRO AREA

SINCE THE 1960S

Marilynn S. Johnson

UNIVERSITY OF MASSACHUSETTS PRESS

Amherst and Boston

ISBN 978-1-62534-147-1 (paperback); 146-4 (hardcover)

Designed by Sally Nichols
Set in Adobe Minion Pro
Printed and bound by Sheridan Books, Inc.

Library of Congress Cataloging-in-Publication Data

Johnson, Marilynn S.
The new Bostonians : how immigrants have transformed the metro area since the 1960s /
Marilynn S. Johnson.
    pages cm
Includes bibliographical references and index.
ISBN 978-1-62534-147-1 (pbk. : alk. paper) — ISBN 978-1-62534-146-4 (hardcover : alk. paper)
1. Immigrants—Massachusetts—Boston—History—20th century. 2. Boston (Mass.—Emigration
and immigration—History—20th century. 3. Boston (Mass.)—Social conditions. 4. Boston
(Mass.)—Ethnic relations. I. Title.
F73.9.A1J64 2015
305.8009744´61—dc23
                        2015009305

British Library Cataloguing-in-Publication Data
A catalogue record for this book is available from the British Library.

For my parents,
Thomas C. Johnson and
Mary W. Johnson
(1925–2005)

Contents

Acknowledgments   ix

Acknowledgments

As I've worked on this book over the past seven years, I've come to understand just how profoundly immigrants have shaped my world and the Boston metro area where I live. On a typical day I interact with immigrants and their children—coworkers, students, service workers, caregivers, and small business owners—from morning till night, at home and at work. First and foremost, then, I thank my immigrant friends, colleagues, neighbors, coworkers, and those who were willing to be interviewed for this book for helping me learn the deeper story of immigration history in greater Boston.

Since *The New Bostonians* is largely a work of synthesis, I am indebted to a host of scholars and journalists who have done pioneering research and writing about immigration in the region. The University of Massachusetts, Boston, has been the most important center of this scholarship, particularly Miren Uriarte and other researchers at the Mauricio Gastón Institute for Latino Community Development and Public Policy, and Paul Watanabe and his collaborators at the Institute for Asian American Studies. Journalists at the *Boston Globe,* the *MetroWest Daily News,* and the *Patriot Ledger* also offered frontline accounts of life in the region's immigrant communities.

A special shout-out goes to those who have done extraordinary work covering the immigration beat: Yvonne Abraham, Maria Sacchetti, and Irene Sege at the *Globe,* and Liz Mineo at the *MetroWest Daily News,* among others. The *Globe's* librarian, Lisa Tuite, was a terrific guide to the paper's photographic resources, helping me locate images for the book.

In digging into some of the lesser-known facets of the new immigration history, I have found local repositories and archivists to be an invaluable asset. One of the most exciting collections on Boston's urban communities is the Documenting Diversity Project at Northeastern University Archives, which has collected the records of many black, Latino, Asian American, and other community-based groups in the city. Thanks to Michelle Romero, who helped me navigate those collections and retrieve key documents and images. In the area of religion, I'm grateful to Robert Johnson-Lally, who led me to the parish visitation reports in the archives of the Boston Archdiocese, and to Rudy Mitchell at the Emanuel Gospel Center, who introduced me to the center's prodigious amount of research and number of publications. The Immigrant Learning Center in Malden has become a leading source on immigrant labor and entrepreneurship in Massachusetts, and it provided very useful material for chapter 4. Finally, I am indebted to Professor Deborah Pacini Hernandez and her extraordinary undergraduate students at Tufts University who canvassed the streets, housing projects, and soccer fields of Cambridge and Somerville to interview Latinos and other newcomers to those communities. The fruits of their work are available online and at the Tufts Digital Collections and Archives.

Colleagues and staff at Boston College have aided this project in innumerable ways. At O'Neill Library, I received expert support from the history librarian Elliot Brandow, while Barbara Mento helped me track down hard-to-find census data. Krastina Dzhambova, a graduate research assistant, worked magic with GIS and IPUMs data extraction, providing the content for many of the maps and charts in the book. Another graduate researcher, Allison Vander Broek, combed through several archival collections on immigrant politics, while the undergraduate assistants Danielle Kidd and Michael Stork retrieved and summarized hundreds of newspaper articles and government reports. Finally, some of my former students—Llana Barber, Lake Coreth, and Yejin Lee—produced first-rate scholarship in local immigration history that helped me understand some of the complexities of the new immigrant communities in greater Boston. Providing the most precious of commodities, Dean David Quigley and the College of Arts and Sciences granted me a full year's sabbatical leave that gave me much-needed time for research and writing.

Colleagues across the region have generously listened to, read, and commented on my work over the years. The Boston Area Immigration and Urban History Seminar at the Massachusetts Historical Society, which I cochair, has been a wonderful source of inspiration and intellectual stimulation, and I am grateful for the feedback its members have offered on this project. The 2010 conference, "What's New about the New Immigration," was especially helpful, and I thank Marilyn Halter, Kate Viens, and Conrad Wright for their editorial input on my work for that project. Members of my Boston area writing group—Bruce Schulman, David Engerman, Brooke Blower, Julie Reuben, Chris Capozzola, Dan Horowitz, Helen Horowitz, and Sarah Phillips—gave consistently helpful criticism and smart writing advice on several chapters. On several occasions Susan Zeiger at Primary Source arranged for me to speak about immigration history with Boston area teachers, who offered much food for thought about immigrant families and children.

I have also benefited from interactions with and feedback from my colleagues in the History Department and the interdisciplinary Diaspora Seminar at Boston College, especially Deborah Levenson, Robin Fleming, Kevin Kenny, Prasannan Parthasarathi, Ginny Reinburg, Lynn Lyerly, Martin Summer, Arissa Oh, Sarah Ross, Dana Sajdi, Grainne McEvoy, John Spiers, Brinton Lykes, Rhonda Frederick, Sarah Beckjord, Carlo Rotella, and Westy Egmont. I offer a particularly big thank-you to those who graciously agreed to read and critique the entire manuscript, including Susan Ware, Dave Reimers, and another anonymous reader. Tom Sugrue, Michael Ebner, Dominic Vitello, Carl Abbott, Paul Watanabe, and Chia Youvee Vang read portions of the manuscript and offered helpful advice as well.

My sponsoring editor at the University of Massachusetts Press, Brian Halley, was an enthusiastic supporter of the book who gave sage advice on the manuscript and ushered me through the editing process. Other folks at the press carefully shepherded the project through the final stages: Carol Betsch, Mary Bellino, and Martin Hanft on the editorial side, Sally Nichols, who designed the book and its striking cover, and Karen Fisk, who coordinated promotion and publicity. It seems fitting that UMass Press became the publisher of *The New Bostonians,* since so much of the research on recent immigration in New England began with scholars at UMass Boston and other branches of the state university system.

Like the immigrants I write about, I have benefited from the love and support of my family in a multitude of ways. Rosa and Jacob Zedek have endured my obsession with this project over the years and have kept me company on excursions to ethnic neighborhoods, restaurants, churches, mosques, and many other Boston-area destinations. Seeing them grow up to be so comfortable in the world and with people from across the world has been a joy. As always, my debt to my husband, Dan Zedek, goes beyond words. An insightful reader, an expert at data visualization and mapmaking, and a superb designer, he offered support for this project in innumerable ways. Most important, though, he has tolerated my endless musings on immigration and many other matters, while offering his constant love, support, wisdom, and optimism. After thirty-five years, I couldn't be luckier.

Portions of chapter 6 appeared in different form in " 'The Quiet Revival': New Immigrants and the Transformation of Christianity in Greater Boston," *Religion and American Culture* 24.2 (Summer 2014): 231–58. Portions of chapter 3 were published in different form in "The Metropolitan Diaspora: New Immigrants in Greater Boston," in *What's New about the "New" Immigration? Traditions and Transformations in the United States since 1965,* ed. Marilyn Halter, Marilynn S. Johnson, Katheryn P. Viens, and Conrad Edick Wright (Palgrave MacMillan, 2014), 23–50. I thank the editors for permission to reprint here.

Introduction

first visited Boston in 1975, a summer trip following my high school graduation. It was, I later realized, a low point in the city's history. That year, Boston was riven over the turmoil of the busing crisis, a violent conflict sparked by a court-ordered desegregation plan following years of unsuccessful efforts to integrate the public schools. Several times that fall, scenes of racial mayhem in Boston topped the evening news, giving the city an ugly reputation that would endure for decades.

The city's tense racial standoff was just one indication of its deepening malaise. Like many older cities of the Northeast, Boston had been steadily losing industry, jobs, and residents since the 1950s. Over the past two decades, the city's population had plummeted, from 801,444 in 1950 to 641,071 in 1970—a 20 percent drop. By the 1970s, the city bore the telltale signs of this decline: a shrinking tax base, run-down housing, deteriorating schools, vacant storefronts, and neighborhoods scarred by urban renewal. As the crime rate surged upward and racial tensions grew, many middle- and working-class whites fled to the suburbs. But not all suburbs were immune from the downturn; older inner-ring communities such as Chelsea, Revere, and Lynn faced similar problems and losses.

By the time I moved to the area, twenty years later, Boston was a very different city. In the intervening years, changes in the global economy had largely succeeded in bringing about the "New Boston" that planners had long envisioned. Experiencing an astonishing turnaround beginning in the 1980s, the city's ailing economy bounced back as its high-tech, medical, and scientific sectors blossomed. Although great inequities remained, new investment and a growing job market had helped to stop the hemorrhaging of population, and a new vitality had appeared downtown and in several Boston neighborhoods. Nearby Cambridge followed suit, as did a number of suburbs that soon shared in the revival.

Boston's renaissance has by now become a familiar story. Similar trans-formations characterized life in New York, San Francisco, and other US cities rejuvenated by the postindustrial economy. Although often told as a story of corporate restructuring, technological innovation, and elite-led gentrification, Boston's metropolitan transformation required a far broader cast of characters. Indeed, just as the larger global economy drove the market for computers, software, and medical devices, new immigrant residents drawn from a global market of workers and entrepreneurs were helping to bring about these changes. Amid the tense black-and-white-defined society of the 1970s, though, few had been aware of the latest new-comers in their midst, or the vital role they would play in the city's future.

This book turns the spotlight on those new Bostonians—immigrants who have arrived since the 1960s. Prior to that, the immigrant share of the US population had been declining for more than forty years, the result of restrictive immigration policies dating back to the 1920s. In the city of Boston, the foreign-born share of the population had fallen to just 13 per-cent by 1970. But the passage of the Immigration Act of 1965 once again reformed the nation's immigration system, accelerating a new migrant stream that would boost Boston's foreign-born population to 27 percent by 2010 (fig. 1). Such numbers approach the record levels set a century earlier, when the foreign born made up more than a third of Boston's population. Like the old immigrants, whose labor powered the region's industrial econ-omy, Boston's newer migrants have been crucial in *re*-building the popula-tion, labor force, and metropolitan landscape of the New Boston.[1]

Although we know much about the Irish and other earlier immigrants to the region, historians have largely ignored these new Bostonians. A quick survey of the library catalog reveals numerous works on the city's old

Foreign-born and native-born population in City of Boston, 1880–2010

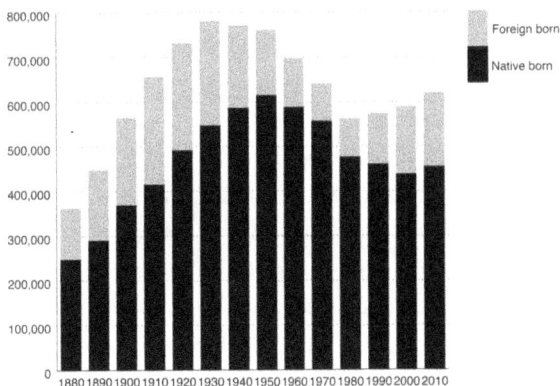

FIGURE 1. Foreign-born and native-born population in City of Boston, 1880–2010. Source: US Census Bureau, *Census of Population and Housing*, 1880–2010.

immigrants, beginning with Oscar Handlin's pioneering 1941 classic *Boston's Immigrants,* chronicling the saga of the hub's Irish newcomers.[2] While in many ways the new Bostonians resemble the European immigrants that Handlin first described, the recent arrivals have been far more diverse, with origins mainly in Asia, Latin America, and the Caribbean. They have gravitated to similar workplaces and neighborhoods as the earlier migrants—but also to jobs that simply did not exist fifty years ago and to communities that rarely in the past housed immigrants. Moreover, the new migration has occurred amid a fast-paced global economy that has produced strikingly different social, cultural, and political arrangements, some of which have fostered new inequalities in a city that has become increasingly unaffordable. *The New Bostonians* explores the old and new immigrant terrain of the metro area to understand just how much the newcomers have in common with their predecessors and how the process of immigrant incorporation has changed in the late twentieth and early twenty-first centuries.

Boston is an excellent vantage point for studying these issues. To date, most scholarly work on post-1965 immigrants has focused on the three largest gateways—New York, Los Angeles, and Miami. More recently, however, scholars have begun to look at the impact of new immigrants on areas that were not historical immigration centers, such as the Sunbelt cities of Dallas and Atlanta. But much remains to be done. As immigrants have settled throughout the country since the 1980s, they have transformed some of the older gateway cities of the Northeast and Midwest, bringing new life to declining industrial neighborhoods and mill towns. The Boston area, with its history of industrial decline and rapid rebirth as a center of the new knowledge economy, is an ideal place to examine this postindustrial transformation and the newcomers' role in it. Boston's long-standing history as an immigrant gateway also offers a good case study of how new and old ethnic groups have encountered one another. As immigrant groups have struggled to adapt to a restructured economy and a changing urban landscape, these encounters have been marked at times by great compassion and understanding, but on other occasions by bitter resentment and violent resistance.

Although this latest wave of immigration is now more than fifty years old, historians have barely begun to develop a historical perspective on it. Since the 1960s, the changing dynamics of migration, settlement, and labor—as well as the evolution of new immigrant religious and political institutions—have transformed immigrant experiences, along with the greater Boston region itself. Analyzing this history helps us put the new immigration into a broader historical frame. The region's newcomers do share a good deal with the Irish, Italian, Jewish, and other immigrants who arrived a century earlier. But there have also been critical differences, most of which stemmed from the sweeping changes in the global economy, the shifting role of the state in American life, and the emergence of new cultural beliefs and political practices in the wake of the civil rights movement of the 1960s. Such changes have brought people together in new and unexpected ways—in neighborhoods, workplaces, churches, and political groups. In its postindustrial rebirth, greater Boston provides an excellent setting for seeing these new relationships at ground level.

While certain migrant groups in Massachusetts have attracted considerable scholarly attention, there is no general history of Boston's new immigrants, and there are very few city- or metropolitan-level studies of the new immigration.[3] This book builds on the important work done by social scientists who have studied immigrants in the Boston region, but it also takes a more explicitly historical approach, not just comparing old and new immigrants but also describing the evolution of the new immigration as it has unfolded since the 1960s. Moreover, *The New Bostonians* is also a work of urban history that looks at how new immigrants and their children have shaped metropolitan development, religion, and politics—subjects that are essential for understanding how newcomers have been incorporated into a historically Irish-Catholic city.

To place Boston's new immigrants within a broader historical trajectory, the book begins by surveying the experiences of previous immigrant groups—mainly the Irish, Jewish, and Italian immigrants who made up the largest numbers of earlier immigrants. The story then moves to the post–World War II years and the changes facilitated by the 1965 Immigration Act, examining the new immigrants' origins and patterns of settlement in greater Boston as well as their role in the region's workforce. The last three chapters look at the process of immigrant incorporation by chronicling the effects of nativism and racism, the development of ethnic churches and religious organizations, and the political mobilization of immigrants and ethnic identities. Although each chapter takes up different subjects and questions, there are common themes that highlight the changing nature and context of the new immigration.

The first such theme is diversity: compared with previous immigrant groups, the new immigrants have been strikingly more diverse in terms of race, nationality, class, and areas of settlement. Unlike the older immigrants, who came mainly from Europe and Canada, newcomers to the region since the 1960s have arrived from countries across the globe. Some of the largest new groups have come from Haiti, the Dominican Republic, China, Brazil, Vietnam, India, and El Salvador; by the twenty-first century, there were growing numbers from Africa and the Middle East as well (fig. 2). Unlike the Europeans, who were at least legally accorded white racial status, many of the new immigrants have generally been considered nonwhite by native-born Bostonians. As such, they have faced entrenched patterns of racial discrimination and segregation, and at times their presence has stirred racial resentment and even violence.

The new immigrants, however, came with a broader range of educational backgrounds and skills. While many were confined to poor immigrant neighborhoods, others had access to professional jobs and business opportunities and were able to settle in wealthier neighborhoods and suburbs that had generally been closed to earlier immigrants. Rich or poor, this diverse group of newcomers brought new cultural and religious traditions to greater Boston, introducing religions such as Buddhism, Hinduism, and Islam, religions that had little prior institutional presence in the region.

Composition of Foreign-born Population in City of Boston, 1910

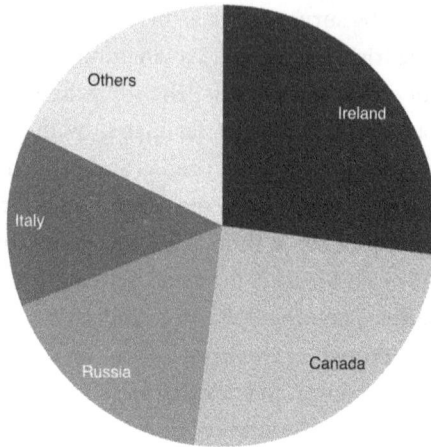

Composition of Foreign-born Population in City of Boston, 2010

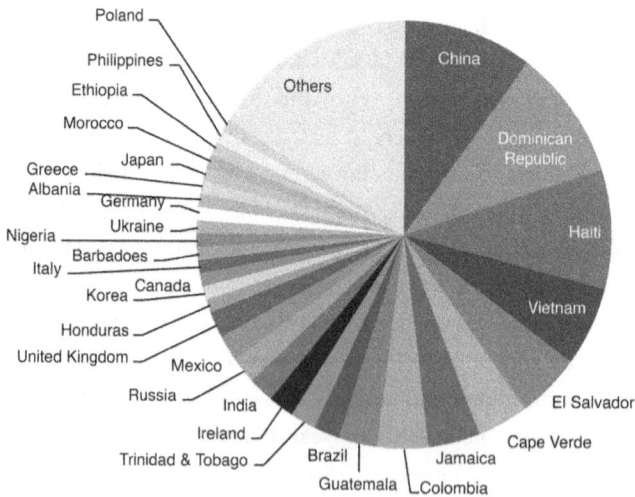

FIGURE 2. Composition of foreign-born population in City of Boston, 1910 and 2010. Source: US Census Bureau, *Census of Population and Housing,* 1910 and 2010.

The increasing diversity of new migrant populations not only affected the dominant society; it also posed a challenge to religious and political institutions within immigrant communities that have had to incorporate newcomers who might share a common language or religion but have distinct cultural styles and practices.

One factor that helps explain this tremendous diversity among new immigrants is the global economic restructuring that has affected greater Boston, as well as the migrants' home countries. In many areas of the globe, rapid but uneven development and urbanization have displaced rural dwellers, left urban workers impoverished or unemployed, and, in some areas, produced educated technical and professional workers with few employment options at home. In the United States, the shift from a manufacturing to a service economy also transformed the opportunity structure for newcomers. In the late nineteenth and early twentieth centuries, European immigrants were mainly working-class families who found work in a booming manufacturing sector that would become increasingly unionized. Some of the earliest post-1965 immigrants did so as well, but as those jobs disappeared, by the 1970s and 1980s newcomers moved into the rising service sector of the region's knowledge economy. That economy has not only transformed work and the potential for mobility but has also reconfigured the metropolitan landscape and local political culture.

The revitalization of Boston's economy since the 1960s has profoundly affected immigrants, but they have also been key movers in that process. Like Italians and Jews who moved into formerly Irish areas, more recent newcomers have settled in an urban landscape long dominated by immigrants. Indeed, many have moved into some of the same homes and neighborhoods and have helped spur a revitalization of declining areas. Their presence in older churches has likewise transformed those institutions as newcomers brought their own distinctive religious styles and practices, which have overtaken the declining congregations of old. But the much-heralded theme of immigrant revitalization is sometimes overstated. For some, particularly poorer black and Latino migrants, settlement in old immigrant communities has often been a dead end—a segregated existence in economically marginalized areas with little opportunity or potential for upward mobility. The persistent influence of racial segregation combined with the restructuring of the metropolitan economy has led to a struggling existence for some while creating greater income and opportunity for others.

Just as the economic framework for immigration has evolved across the twentieth century, the political context has also changed dramatically. Compared with European arrivals at the turn of the last century, new immigrants have been more directly affected by the state through federal and local policymaking around immigration, social welfare, and civil rights. The state's impact, however, has not been a static one. From the 1960s to the 1980s, federal and local policies were generally supportive of immigrants by eliminating discriminatory immigration quotas, facilitating refugee resettlement, protecting civil rights, and fostering multiculturalism. By the end of the 1980s, however, federal and state governments began to retreat from such policies as budgets were cut, social programs eliminated, and more restrictive immigration laws passed. Moreover, the end of the Cold War led to a smaller but more diverse refugee population, while the crisis of 9/11, in which Boston area residents were among the victims, produced a flurry of repressive practices and an anti-immigrant backlash. Although greater Boston has long enjoyed a reputation as an immigrant-friendly destination, global forces and national and state policies since the 1990s have resulted in a chillier welcome.

Finally, globalization has played a dynamic role in the lives of new immigrants. The impact of free trade and global economic restructuring is the most obvious example, but new forms of transportation, communication, and economic and political integration have allowed immigrants to live lives across national borders in ways that were not possible earlier. As historians have often noted, however, globalization has a long history, particularly among immigrants. Earlier groups helped transform their homelands through circular and return migration, sending money to support families back home and raising funds for nationalist political causes. New immigrants continue these practices, but with even greater facility thanks to air travel, cell phones, and the Internet. Transnational behavior has thus intensified among more recent immigrants, particularly among the first generation. How important such global connections will be to the second and subsequent generations remains to be seen.

In recounting the story of immigrant Boston, I have benefited from a wealth of scholarly and journalistic works on specific ethnic groups in the area, including books, articles, dissertations, government reports, oral histories, and extensive coverage of immigration issues by the *Boston Globe,* the *Patriot Ledger,* the *MetroWest Daily News,* and the local ethnic press.

This study also relies on archival research on immigrant community and political organizations, church records, and records and reports by state and federal agencies dealing with immigrants and refugees. Finally, I draw on oral histories conducted by students at Tufts University and by researchers at the Immigrant Learning Center, as well as my own interviews with several key figures in local immigrant communities and organizations.

The wealth of source material on some topics, as well as the dearth of it in others, has forced me to make choices about what to include here. Indeed, there are several important topics—labor organization, education, gender relations, and the coming of age of the second generation—that are not featured prominently in *The New Bostonians*. Such issues are essential to understanding the immigrant experience, but I will leave it to others to explore those questions. Nor does the book probe the extensive transnational networks that have left their mark on immigrants' home countries around the world. Indeed, immigrant-led transformation is hardly limited to Boston; newcomers' efforts to improve and revitalize their communities can be seen not only in their cash remittances but also in new businesses, churches, health clinics, and water systems in towns and cities from Haiti to India. This too is a fascinating and crucial subject that I refer to periodically, but the current study focuses mainly on the immigrant experience in metro Boston and how it has affected this urban community over time. As such it is a hybrid study of immigration and urban history, seeking to do for Boston what other scholars have done for Los Angeles, New York, and Miami.

In tackling such a study, I find that there are a few issues that require further definition. The first involves the boundaries of the region under study. Because of the rapid diffusion of migrants into the suburbs in recent years, any study of new immigrants in Boston must encompass the larger metropolitan area—a region I refer to interchangeably as "metro Boston" or "greater Boston." Defining this area, however, is a tricky business. Census definitions of the metro area have changed several times since the 1960s, from a relatively tight semicircle of towns to a vast commuting region running from the Cape Cod Canal to parts of southern New Hampshire. (For this reason, many of the statistical charts in the book are based on the City of Boston because its boundaries have remained consistent over time.) The changing metropolitan designations reflect how much the Boston region has grown since World War II, but they also make for an unmanageable study area that moves well beyond Boston and its surrounding suburbs. Instead, I have chosen a definition of greater Boston used by the Metropolitan Area Planning Council (MAPC), a regional planning agency established by the Massachusetts legislature in 1963. The number of suburban communities represented by MAPC has grown over the years and by 2014 constituted 101 towns and cities surrounding Boston (fig. 3). These include all the communities within Route 128 / Interstate 95 and a majority of those within the outer beltway of Interstate 495.[4] Following the MAPC definition, I have not generally included the older outlying industrial cities of Lawrence, Lowell, and Brockton (and their suburbs), but I do occasionally discuss them as part of broader regional migration patterns and their consequences.[5]

The experiences of the foreign born in Boston and its suburbs have varied dramatically over time and space, making it is impossible to do justice to this complex terrain. To understand at least part of it, I have focused on certain suburbs in more depth, particularly the immigrant-friendly communities of Quincy, Framingham, and Malden. In the realm of politics, however, most suburbs have barely begun to incorporate immigrants into their governance. In chapter 7, I concentrate on politics in the city of Boston itself, where immigrant activism and electoral participation has a much longer and more developed history.

Finally, I discuss a number of groups in this study who were not actually immigrants but whose experiences and interactions with the foreign born were critical to the story. These include refugees (technically not immigrants under some legal definitions), Puerto Ricans, and certain second-generation ethnics. The latter two groups are clearly not immigrants but American citizens who, unlike non-naturalized or undocumented immigrants, enjoy the rights and responsibilities of citizenship. Such rights have been critical to political empowerment and have become increasingly important for entering the country, accessing social welfare benefits, and avoiding deportation. While I in no way minimize these differences, one cannot understand the evolution of many of the region's Latino communities without investigating the earlier settlement patterns and religious institutions of Puerto Rican migrants. Likewise, second-generation Chinese Americans and Puerto Ricans helped forge the political foundations of the Asian American and Latino communities of Boston, discussed in chapters 5 and 7.

Finally, the new immigrants that I discuss should not be confused with

Selected suburbs

FIGURE 3. Map of metro Boston study area showing selected suburbs.

the term "new immigrants" often employed by historians of second-wave immigration, a term used to distinguish southern and eastern European immigrants of the late nineteenth and early twentieth centuries from earlier groups from northern and western Europe. I refer to those migrants collectively as older or earlier immigrant groups; in the Boston area, they included the Irish, Jews, Italians, Portuguese, and Chinese, among others. The descendants of these earlier migrants have figured prominently in shaping the reception of new immigrants. Many of those who responded most generously, as well as some who lashed out in anger and violence, had family origins in the earlier waves of migration. To gain some insight into why Boston's immigrant descendants both sympathized with and scorned new migrants, we begin in chapter 1 with a short introduction to the city's deeper immigrant past.

CHAPTER 1

Boston's "Old" Immigrants

n colonial Boston, no one was more than half a mile from the sea. Ringed by docks, wharves, warehouses, and taverns, the waterfront was truly the lifeblood of the city. As one historian put it, the port was "the gateway between land and sea," the point of contact between foreign lands and the American interior.[1] Perched as Boston is on the northwestern edge of the Atlantic world, the city's location and early maritime history would shape its economic and social development for centuries.

With hundreds of ships plying the Atlantic, Boston's trade in sugar, rum, slaves, and codfish helped build the port in the seventeenth and eighteenth centuries. Its connection to the Caribbean was especially strong, with sugar and rum distilling emerging as one of the city's key industries. Although its economy and population suffered during the Revolution, the city bounded back rapidly after 1780, its population expanding along with its footprint, as wetlands were filled in to make room for homes, businesses, and workshops. During these years, a new trade with China in tea and hides expanded Boston's commercial reach from the Atlantic to the Pacific. The fortunes earned from this profitable trade helped build new industries, both inside and outside of Boston, most notably in textiles.

The city's role in the maritime economy thus established the ground-work for much of the dramatic social and economic transformation to come. The profits of its commerce subsidized the region's burgeoning industries, while the city's extensive network of ships, business agents, and labor provided the early infrastructure for the mass movement of peoples that would follow. Boston had long been a portal for seamen, sailors, merchants, and foreign visitors from around the Atlantic. But it was not until the 1830s that large-scale immigration from outside Britain would begin to transform the city in previously unimagined ways. From the mid-nineteenth century through the 1920s, the rise of powerful European and American economies beckoned new workers and indus-tries while destabilizing the rural economies and home industries of other regions. In these latter areas, population pressures, agricultural cri-ses, and economic dislocations growing out of capitalist incorporation served to propel millions out of their homelands.

These disruptions occurred across more than a century, but their man-ifestations in Boston—and the United States more generally—appeared in two major surges of migration. The first, from the 1840s to the 1860s, con-sisted of migrants predominantly from northern and western Europe, and most significantly from Ireland. The second wave, spanning the 1880s to the 1920s, brought new foreign-born populations from southern and east-ern Europe—Italians and Jews most notably—as well as smaller numbers from Asia and the Caribbean.

This chapter looks back on the experiences of the city's three largest immigrant groups—the Irish, Jews, and Italians—which collectively made up more than half of the city's foreign-born population at the turn of the twentieth century. We will also look at some of the smaller groups of the second wave—the Chinese, Portuguese, and West Indians—whose settle-ment in the Boston area laid some important groundwork for those who followed in the late twentieth century. Collectively, these earlier groups defined the immigrant experience in greater Boston, shaping popular thinking about immigration and ethnicity to the present day.

FROM WHENCE THEY CAME

During the first great migration era, immigrants from Ireland, Germany, Sweden, the British Isles, and Canada streamed into Boston and its neighboring towns. The city's foreign-born population jumped from roughly 27,000 in 1845 to nearly 66,000 in 1865. Many of these newcomers—espe-cially the English-speaking, from Britain and Canada—blended easily into the urban population. Germans and Swedes, many of them skilled workers, often settled together in small clusters around woodworking shops, brew-eries, and other workplaces. Ultimately, their gainful employment and dif-fusion into different trades and neighborhoods facilitated their integration.[2]

But by far the largest and most visible group of newcomers was Irish Catholics who arrived in growing numbers after 1820 and would have a pro-found impact on the city and its future. Irish immigrants had been settling in Massachusetts since colonial times, although prior to the 1830s, the major-ity were Protestants from Ulster whose artisan livelihoods had suffered as British products displaced the native linen and woolen industries. By the 1830s, however, the bulk of Irish newcomers were rural Catholics whose agricultural prospects at home had soured under British rule. Sustained population growth had led to a fourfold increase in the Irish population between 1732 and 1840, creating extreme land pressures and subdivision into ever-smaller parcels. Falling grain prices after 1815 only aggravated the situation as landholders evicted their tenants to make way for livestock grazing. By 1841, more than half the rural population was left landless, many of them scraping by as bound laborers or tenants on tiny plots where they grew a bare subsistence crop of potatoes to feed their families. This precari-ous existence soon collapsed with the arrival of *phytothora infestans,* a fun-gus commonly known as the potato blight. Devastating Ireland's primary food crop repeatedly from 1845 to 1850, the blight led to starvation and dis-ease that left more than a million dead and drove some two million more to emigrate, mainly to the United States. The famine struck the south and west of Ireland particularly hard, and callous British attitudes toward its victims provided little relief. Destitute refugees from these areas would make up the majority of migrants heading for Boston and other North American cities.[3]

The Irish influx was quickly apparent in the Commonwealth. Out of a total population of 136,881 in Boston in 1850, roughly 35,000 were Irish-born; just five years later that number had risen to more than 50,000. Immigration dropped off as the Irish famine subsided, and the city's Irish population grew slowly for several decades. Further agricultural distress in Ireland fueled renewed emigration in the 1880s, bringing Boston's Irish population to its peak of more than 71,000—or one-quarter of the total population—by 1890. Thereafter, the number of Irish-born would gradually decline, although the ranks of the second and third generations would multiply along with Irish American visibility and influence. In fact, Irish population levels in the city were among the highest in the country—significantly higher than Irish population levels in New York, Chicago, Philadelphia, or San Francisco.[4] For good reason, then, Boston became known as "the capital of Irish America."

Beginning in the 1880s, however, the arrival of new groups of migrants from Italy, Russia, Poland, and other countries on Europe's southern and eastern rim posed a challenge to Irish dominance. Coming in tandem, the two largest groups were Russian Jews and Italians. Both communities numbered only a few thousand in Boston in 1880; by 1920, each encompassed roughly 40,000 foreign-born residents. As in Ireland, population growth, industrialization, and agricultural disruption had swept their homelands, prompting many to pull up stakes and venture abroad.

In the region south of Rome known as the Mezzogiorno, the Italian peasantry came under increasing pressure in the 1880s and 1890s. Like the Irish, southern Italians experienced steady population growth that led to continued subdivision of land. Meanwhile, the Italian government's heavy taxation of crops increased rural poverty, reducing many to tenantry. Drought, crop disease, and poor harvests further aggravated the plight of the poor. Those who hoped to earn extra income through home production found they could not compete with cheaper manufactured goods. By the 1890s, Italy's grain and citrus industries were undercut by American competition, while its prized wine industry fell victim to a tariff war between Italy and France. This agricultural crisis prompted a growing number of southern Italian men to venture abroad in search of temporary work to supplement family incomes.

After 1900, however, the region's economic woes were exacerbated by a series of environmental catastrophes including three severe earthquakes in 1905–1908 and the eruptions of Mt. Vesuvius (1906) and Mt. Etna (1910). More than 150,000 Italians perished in that catastrophic decade. Those who survived—including many families of earlier migrants—now looked abroad for new opportunities, giving rise to more permanent Italian communities in Boston, New York, Buenos Aires, and other migrant centers in the Americas. In Boston, the southern Italian presence grew accordingly, overwhelming the small population of Genoese who had come from northern Italy in earlier years. The new migrants came mainly from Sicily, Campania, Calabria, Abruzzi, and Molise, where agricultural and economic dislocations were most severe.[5]

In Russia, similar trends of population growth and capitalist expansion were also causing hardships. The plight of Jews, however, was compounded by anti-Semitic laws and violence. Following the Russian conquest of Poland in the eighteenth century, the czarist government had confined local Jews to the Pale of Settlement stretching from the Baltic to the Black Sea. Over the course of the nineteenth century, Jews were subjected to periodic expulsions from their villages, interference with religious education, and forced military conscription. In the 1880s, Russian repression intensified following the assassination of Czar Alexander II. Violent pogroms were directed against Jewish communities, while the government passed the May Laws prohibiting Jews from owning or renting land outside towns or cities and excluding them from higher education via harsh quota systems. Working as middlemen traders in the rural villages, Jews were now subject to mass expulsions. Forced to crowd into the larger towns and cities of the Pale, they took up trades in which they faced bitter competition and growing impoverishment. As Mary Antin, an immigrant to Boston in the 1890s, described her hometown of Polotzk, "There were ten times as many stores as there should have been, ten times as many tailors, cobblers, barbers, tinsmiths. A Gentile, if he failed in Polotzk, could go elsewhere, where there was less competition. A Jew could make a circle of the Pale, only to find the same conditions as at home."[6]

Seeking to escape these dire conditions, a growing number of displaced artisans and merchants headed west to Europe and the Americas. Their numbers multiplied in the early twentieth century when anti-Semitic violence flared again in 1903–1906, causing thousands of Jewish casualties. Like other East Coast cities, Boston's Jewish population rose sharply over the next two decades. The new wave of Russian Jews joined a much smaller population of German and Polish Jews who had come to Boston in the mid-nineteenth century. The sheer numbers of newcomers, as well as their greater poverty and more orthodox religious style, would make for complicated relations between the two groups.[7]

During these same years, a much smaller group of Portuguese immigrants also made their way to the Boston area. Like the Russian Jews, they joined an earlier group of their countrymen who had been visiting and settling in Massachusetts since the mid-nineteenth century. Coming from the Azores islands in the mid-Atlantic, the descendants of the Portuguese who first settled those islands had been recruited by American whaling companies to work on their ships in the years before the Civil War. Some settled in the whaling port of New Bedford in southeastern Massachusetts and nearby Cape Cod. A smaller number—a few hundred at most—went to Boston. Although the whaling industry declined after 1870, rising population, land pressures, and forced military service in the Azores prompted many young men to follow their countrymen to New England. While the vast majority settled in New Bedford and Fall River, some 1,500 were living in Boston by 1915, along with more than 2,200 in nearby Cambridge.[8]

In these areas, the Portuguese, Russian Jews, Italians, and Irish lived interspersed with an assortment of other groups who had fled similar conditions in their homelands: population growth, land shortages, the decline of artisan crafts, forced military conscription, and religious and ethnic persecution. Among these Boston newcomers in 1910 were more than 4,000 Poles, 3,000 Lithuanians, 3,000 French Canadians, and 1,500 Greeks. The same ethnic groups also populated the nearby mill towns of Lowell, Lawrence, Lynn, and Brockton. Although the vast majority of second-wave immigrants came from Canada and southern and eastern Europe, a smaller number hailed from other parts of the globe. Beginning in the 1890s, a stream of Syrian-Lebanese migrants arrived in Boston, Cambridge, and Lawrence. Soon afterward, Armenian immigrants moved into the same areas, a trickle that became a flood following the Turkish-led Armenian genocide in 1915–1917. By 1930 both groups would number several thousand in the greater Boston area, making it home to some of the largest Armenian and Syrian communities in the United States.[9]

The plight of the Armenians under the Turks and the Irish under the British were just two of the many territorial and colonial struggles occurring around the world in the nineteenth and early twentieth centuries. European powers siphoned precious natural resources away from their colonies, while heightening racial and religious tensions where they ruled. Indeed, the yoke of colonial oppression and exploitation was another common spur to emigration, forging human pathways across both the Atlantic and the Pacific. In Boston, small communities of Chinese, West Indian, and Cape Verdean immigrants emerged when sojourning laborers left their colonized homelands and put down roots in the Bay State.

In China, colonization by European powers had led to warfare and anti-Western rebellions in the nineteenth century that ravaged Guangdong and other southern provinces. These conflicts only aggravated a longer-term crisis of overpopulation, land shortages, and recurring famines. Chinese men thus sought work overseas, most notably in the California Gold Rush and as construction workers on the transcontinental railroad. When mining and railroad work ended in the late 1860s, some Chinese came east to take up factory and service jobs in New York and Massachusetts. By 1900, the US census recorded more than a thousand Chinese living in Boston, many of them from the Toishan region of Guangdong province. Soon Boston would have the third-largest Chinatown in the United States after San Francisco and New York.[10]

The historic role of Massachusetts in the Atlantic maritime trade also gave rise to human networks between Boston and colonies in the Caribbean and the Cape Verde archipelago. Located off the coast of West Africa, the Cape Verde Islands had been colonized by the Portuguese in the fifteenth century and later became a way station in the Atlantic slave trade. Although slaves had initially been brought to Cape Verde to work on sugar plantations, the arid climate and frequent droughts made cultivation difficult. After emancipation, the mixed-race descendants of the African slaves and Portuguese settlers struggled to survive as farmers and fishermen in a depressed colonial economy. In the late nineteenth century, when New England whaling ships came in search of low-paid labor, young men on the islands of Brava and Fogo signed on as crewmen. Like the Azoreans a few decades earlier, most of them ended up in New Bedford and other parts of southeastern Massachusetts, while a few hundred settled in the Boston area prior to World War I.[11]

Around the same time, an influx of migrants from the British West Indies was also beginning to diversify Boston's black population. Like the Cape Verdeans, West Indian migrants had looked abroad to survive ailing colonial economies that relied on sugar-based agriculture, a stunted manufacturing base, and high unemployment. Caribbean islanders had developed a migratory existence since the construction of the Panama Canal, to which many island workers were recruited in the early twentieth century. Others sought low-paid employment with the burgeoning fruit export business controlled by the Boston-based United Fruit Company. Coming mainly from Barbados and Jamaica, West Indians followed work opportunities to Massachusetts, with more than 2,800 living in Boston by 1920. Even after the passage of federal immigration restriction laws in the 1920s, West Indian migration (which was not covered under those laws) continued to flow. By 1952, at which time Caribbean migration was curtailed under the McCarran-Walter Act, there were more than 5,000 West Indians living in Boston, making up 12 percent of the city's black population.[12] Together with Cape Verdeans, West Indians and their children would make up a small but growing portion of the area's population of African descent.

Whether from the islands of the Caribbean, the Irish countryside, or the Jewish ghettoes of the Pale, immigrants found their way to Boston via family, friends, and neighbors. Among most groups, adult men or women came first, secured work, and sent money home to bring over other family members. This process of chain migration was fueled not just by cash remittances but also by migrants' positive reports of life in America in letters, postcards, and return visits. As one Italian immigrant to Boston recalled, his fascination with America was first sparked by the return visit of a neighbor to his hometown in Apulia: "When he finally came back for a visit, I was much impressed. I remember . . . his purple, showy necktie, and a stickpin with brilliants. What impressed me most of all was the white collar which he wore. These things were great luxuries in our town, worn only by the well-to-do, and not by 'la gente,' or common folks, to which he belonged." Family, friends, and neighbors thus demonstrated the promise of better earnings or higher social status, which inspired migrants from across Europe. Not surprisingly, then, migration streams often flowed from the same regions, towns, or villages, transplanting communities en masse to ethnic enclaves in Boston. The introduction of prepaid tickets for transatlantic voyages in the 1850s facilitated this chain migration, as migrants could send steamer tickets directly to family members back home.[13]

In some cases, it was employers who recruited workers or otherwise facilitated their migration. For much of the nineteenth century, the influx of poor Irish provided a steady supply of labor for Boston employers, so there was little need to recruit abroad. After 1890, however, the rapid expansion of local industries and mill towns created a pressing demand for labor, and mill owners encouraged their workers to bring over their family and friends from the old country. Employers also facilitated migration by providing transatlantic passage to maritime workers who later jumped ship. Many West Indians, for example, came to Boston as deck-hands on ships run by the United Fruit Company, while Azoreans and Cape Verdeans arrived as crew members on New England–based whaling boats. As the whaling industry declined and schooners were replaced by modern steamships, enterprising Cape Verdeans purchased the old "Gloucester fishermen" and converted them for hauling passengers and freight. Plying between the islands and the mainland, the so-called packet boats became the main vehicle of migration for New England–bound Cape Verdeans. Without a doubt, the growing accessibility of transportation made migration easier and more affordable.[14]

WHERE THEY LANDED

For most newcomers, the most compelling reason to move to Boston and other East Coast cities was the promise of economic advancement. The search for jobs, homes, and business opportunities profoundly shaped the paths these immigrants took and the places they settled. Given their typically long work hours and the high cost of transportation, they tended to settle close to their workplaces on the waterfront, in factories, or near downtown shops and services. A growing number would follow jobs to nearby mill towns and outlying industries geared to a growing urban market. Still, the residential options of migrants would be limited by the ethnic and racial biases of the native born—particularly in the case of blacks and Asians and those, such as the Italians and Jews, who, in the early twentieth century, were not always perceived as fully white.

Prior to the Civil War, most Irish immigrants arrived in Boston without money or skills and found only limited job opportunities. Men of the famine generation worked mainly as laborers, picking up loading work on the docks or pick-and-shovel labor where they could. Among women, the largest portion hired out as domestics. According to the census of 1850, nearly two-thirds of Irish workers in Boston were concentrated in those two occupations, with 48 percent engaged as day laborers and another 15 percent as domestics. Others found service work in low-paid positions such as stablemen, teamsters, boatmen, and waiters. When necessary, Irish men followed labor contractors to distant locations to build roads, canals, and railroads. Closer to home, Irish laborers built dams, filled wetlands, leveled hills, and helped transform the urban landscape by creating land for port facilities, railroad yards, industrial space, and fashionable new neighborhoods such as the South End and Back Bay.[15]

The vast majority of Irish during this period lived in the North End and in nearby Fort Hill (now the financial district). These were the oldest and poorest sections of the city, close to the docks and warehouses. Abandoned by wealthy Bostonians after the Revolution, the North End's large homes were broken into apartments and rented to immigrants, with whole families sometimes occupying a single room. As more immigrants arrived new tenements were built, and by 1850 more than half of the North End's 23,000 residents were Irish. Overcrowding and poor sanitation contributed to recurrent epidemics of smallpox, cholera, and tuberculosis, giving the North End and Fort Hill the highest death rates in the city. Understandably, over the next few decades those who could afford to move to less congested areas did so. These more established Irish workers followed other Bostonians to newer districts in the West End and South Cove, leaving the North End to newer arrivals.[16]

Irish workers also found new job opportunities in the region's burgeoning textile and shoe mills. The most famous of these were located in the outlying cities of Lowell and Lawrence, but many large mills sprang up just outside Boston in communities such as Lynn, Chelsea, Waltham, Malden, and Framingham. Founded by wealthy Boston merchant families, the cotton and woolen mills initially depended on the water power of local rivers and the labor power of young Yankee women and families drawn from the surrounding countryside. By the eve of the Civil War, however, textile employers had replaced their native-born female workers with unskilled Irish men, women, and children. Although Yankee mill workers had tried to organize, the poverty and desperation of the Irish immigrants enabled employers to lower wages and speed up the pace of work with mechanization. The Irish were merely the first of many new groups—including French Canadians, Jews, Italians, Syrians, Portuguese—that employers would exploit in an effort to boost profits and thwart union organizing.[17]

Such union-busting efforts, in fact, helped give rise to the founding of Boston's Chinese community in the mid-1870s. The origins of Chinese settlement in Massachusetts date back to 1870, when the shoe manufacturer Calvin Sampson broke a strike launched by Irish and Canadian workers in his North Adams factory. Inasmuch as the union had successfully warned off local replacement workers, Sampson imported seventy-five Chinese men from San Francisco, where many had become unemployed following completion of the transcontinental railroad. The first group of Chinese recruits, who earned less than half the pay of the striking workers, was soon joined by fifty more. But as anti-Chinese sentiment grew, some of the workers drifted away from North Adams, moving east to Worcester and Boston. Several dozen were hired to build the Pearl Street Telephone Exchange in the South Cove neighborhood in 1875, and a Chinese tent colony sprang up in what is now Ping On Alley near the Boston & Worcester train depot (now South Station). The surrounding streets—Oxford, Beach, Essex, and Harrison—occupied mostly by the Irish in the late nineteenth century, would soon become the ethnic enclave known as Chinatown.[18]

The official census (which no doubt undercounted the Chinese) listed 133 Chinese in Boston in 1880, 497 in 1890, and 1,065 by 1900. The vast majority were men and most lived in Chinatown, working in Chinese-owned hand laundries and restaurants. A few dozen were recorded in Cambridge, Lynn, and other nearby towns, where they likely operated laundries. Strong anti-Chinese sentiment among white workers and unions prevented Asian workers from gaining a foothold in the region's mills and industrial plants: the laundry business, and a growing Chinatown restaurant and tourist trade, developed as ethnic niche enterprises that employed the bulk of Chinese residents well into the twentieth century.[19]

In the late nineteenth century, the expansion of railroads and the introduction of steam power and mechanization accelerated industrial development in Massachusetts. The de-skilling of work through mechanization allowed for the introduction of women and unskilled immigrant workers, and the promise of such jobs attracted new migrants from Quebec and southern and eastern Europe. New and bigger textile plants sprang up in Lawrence, Lowell, and dozens of smaller mill towns, while leather tanneries and shoe factories proliferated in Lynn, Peabody, and other towns north and south of the city. In Boston—one of the busiest ports on the East Coast—some ninety piers and three major railroads provided thousands of jobs in construction, transportation, freight handling, and shipbuilding. Manufacturing grew as well. Iron foundries, metal and woodworking shops, chemical plants, confectioners and distilleries (a legacy of Boston's role in the Caribbean sugar trade), rubber works, and the garment trade all blossomed in Boston and its surrounding suburbs. Many of the second-wave migrants found work in this expanding metropolitan economy.[20]

On their arrival in Boston, most newcomers followed the well-trod path into the bustling working-class quarters of the North End. As the Irish population dwindled, Jews and Italians moved into North End tenements in growing numbers; by 1895 there were approximately 6,200 Jews and 7,700 Italians, along with smaller settlements of Portuguese and eastern Europeans. The Jews initially settled in the lower western section of the North End but soon followed the more established German and Polish Jews to new enclaves in the West and South Ends. After 1900, the North End became progressively more Italian, with the proportion of Italian-born residents and their children growing from 27 percent in 1895 to 90 percent in 1920. As more immigrants arrived, the neighborhood's population grew to 40,000 in 1920, making it one of the world's most densely populated urban districts.[21]

The new migrants moved into an expanding array of working-class occupations. Like the Irish before them, Italian newcomers were heavily concentrated in unskilled labor. They found low-paying jobs on the docks and railroads, and their labor helped build sewers, reservoirs, roads, bridges, and the network of tunnels that made up Boston's new subway system. A smaller number worked as peddlers, fruit vendors, and owners of small retail businesses. In the first decades of the twentieth century, young Italian American women moved into the garment and textile industries; Italian men came to dominate the shoemaking operations in Lynn and Chelsea. In these industries, they joined a diverse immigrant workforce composed of Russian Jews, Syrians, Portuguese, and others who joined unions and sometimes became militant activists.[22]

Jewish immigrants, in addition to their work in the textile and shoe factories, tended to work as peddlers, small shop owners, and skilled garment workers. Building on their urban backgrounds as traders and tailors in the Pale, Jews in the United States took up similar occupations, often working for more established German Jewish firms. Mary Antin's family was typical. Arriving in Boston in the 1890s, her father initially sold refreshments on the beach in Revere but later opened a small grocery in the South End. Her older sister was a seamstress in the nearby garment district that had grown up around Harrison Avenue, the center of Jewish life in the South End. The Antins were just one of thousands of Jewish families who moved to this neighborhood in the early twentieth century. Here they lived interspersed with migrants from Syria, Greece, Italy, and Armenia, as well as groups of

Irish and blacks who had arrived before them. The South End thus became one of the most diverse working-class neighborhoods in the city; its wealthier, native-born families retreated to the Back Bay and Roxbury.[23]

These same immigrant families, however, eventually trickled out of the older ethnic core neighborhoods into what the settlement worker Robert Woods referred to as "the zone of emergence"—the districts where an Americanized second generation first emerged from the older, congested immigrant quarters. Following the extension of ferry service and streetcar lines, middle-class Bostonians drifted away from the central city to new neighborhoods on the urban periphery. These included the formerly separate towns of Charlestown, South Boston, East Boston, Roxbury, and Dorchester—annexed by Boston in the 1860s and 1870s—as well as the emerging working-class districts of East Cambridge and Cambridgeport across the Charles River. The diffusion of population and industry to these areas offered the possibility of new jobs, better housing, and healthier living for the more skilled immigrants or the second-generation workers who could afford to move there.[24]

The new outlying neighborhoods were more expansive and heterogeneous than the city's older immigrant quarters. At the turn of the century, all five areas were inhabited by native-born, middle-class families, along with more prosperous Irish Americans, reflecting the latter's longer tenure and rising economic status. In Charlestown, South Boston, and East Boston, Irish workers had originally been recruited to fill swamps and build rail and port facilities. Once completed, those new docks and railroad yards offered ample employment to the next generation, particularly during the defense boom of World War I. During those years, the shipyards and naval facilities of Charlestown and South Boston (as well as nearby Quincy) all hummed with activity, employing a diverse ethnic workforce. Newer immigrant groups to the areas were moving into working-class cottages, as well as the increasingly popular triple-deckers: three-story apartment buildings with family-size units on each floor. For enterprising immigrants, a triple-decker was a sound investment that provided decent housing for the owner on one floor and modest rental income from the other two. Immigrant owners could thus pay their mortgage while also providing living space for their relatives or coethnics, thus facilitating chain migration and upward mobility. Between 1880 and 1930, some 16,000 triple-deckers were built in Boston alone.[25]

By the 1920s, each of these neighborhoods had a distinctive economic character and ethnic mix. South Boston, with its many dock and railroad workers, remained heavily Irish, though it also contained communities of Poles and Lithuanians near Columbia Point. Charlestown likewise remained largely Irish American but also hosted smaller communities of Italians and Jews. With its proximity to the North End, East Boston became increasingly Italian American, though the area north of Maverick Square contained a sizable Jewish population. Across the Charles, the growing manufacturing districts of Cambridgeport and East Cambridge attracted Jews from the West End, as well as other eastern Europeans, Portuguese, Armenians, and West Indians. By 1915, East Cambridge had become the largest Portuguese American community in the metropolitan area and was expanding into adjoining Somerville. A smaller community of Armenians also settled in East Cambridge, where many came to work at a local rubber plant.[26]

South of downtown Boston, Roxbury and Dorchester were evolving from bucolic middle-class suburbs into bustling working-class districts. Both areas had growing Irish American populations by the late nineteenth century but were also beginning to attract more prosperous Jewish families from the South End. During the first decades of the twentieth century, Jewish settlement would spread progressively south along Blue Hill Avenue from Roxbury to Mattapan, with native-born and immigrant blacks following in their wake. The number of Irish Americans and other Catholic ethnics would continue to grow in other parts of Dorchester, forming a broad swath along the waterfront from Columbia Point to the Boston-Quincy border.[27] Ultimately, this mosaic of ethnic working-class neighborhoods would make Roxbury-Dorchester the most diverse area of the city by midcentury, one that would become especially important for the immigrants who would arrive after 1965.

That these outlying ethnic districts constituted a so-called zone of emergence was an idea first popularized by sociologists at the University of Chicago who assumed that urban social development was a centrifugal process by which immigrants moved outward from the old city core while moving upward into the middle class. Newer immigrants, meanwhile, took their place in the old central districts and then followed in the outward trek. This repeating pattern of ethnic succession and assimilation ultimately ended in the more affluent outer suburbs. Without a doubt, many European immigrant groups did follow this pattern. In the years after World War II, Irish Americans could be found in suburbs throughout the metropolitan area, but especially along the South Shore. Jews trekked to the suburbs as well, concentrating in the towns of Brookline, Newton, Swampscott-Marblehead, and Sharon. The city's Italian Americans drifted north of the city to places like Chelsea, Winthrop, Revere, Medford, Everett, and Malden. Significant numbers of Portuguese Americans gravitated to Somerville, Cambridge, and Framingham, while the Armenian community flourished in Watertown.

As historians have shown, however, ethnic succession was not a uniform process that worked equally well for all ethnic groups. First, the timing of this dispersion process varied by group. With their faster rate of upward mobility and highly mobile religious life, Jews tended to move out more quickly; Catholic ethnics, who were firmly anchored in fixed residential parish communities, tended to remain in urban neighborhoods longer. West Indian, Cape Verdean, and Chinese Americans, who encountered persistent racial segregation and employment discrimination, found themselves limited to older urban neighborhoods and adjoining "spillover" areas. Despite massive suburbanization after World War II, black migrants and their descendants remained heavily concentrated in the cities of Boston, Cambridge, and parts of southeastern Massachusetts. Although many were able to buy homes in the South End, Roxbury, and Dorchester, racially exclusive lending and real estate practices confined them to existing black neighborhoods. Likewise, racial discrimination kept the majority of Chinese Americans living in Chinatown until after World War II. Chinese exclusion laws, in effect from 1882 to 1943, slowed the development of an American-born population; it was not until the 1960s that significant numbers of Chinese American families began moving to Boston's suburbs.[28]

Another problem with the idea of ethnic succession is its linear geographic approach. Even European immigrants and their children have not always moved outward from city to suburbs. As early as the 1840s, Irish immigrants found employment in the mills of Waltham, Lynn, and other industrial communities outside Boston, founding small-town ethnic communities. North of the city, Russian Jews settled near the tanneries of Peabody and the burgeoning industrial town of Chelsea. By 1910, Chelsea had more than 11,000 Jews, who made up about one-third of the city's population. During these same years, Jewish and Italian migrants settled near other growing suburban industries in towns like Somerville, Revere, Malden, and Watertown.

But factories were not the only spur to suburban settlement. Just as Boston investment fed industrial development in the surrounding region, the expansion of the city and its infrastructure required material resources from its hinterlands. The hard labor required to extract those resources and do the building often fell to immigrant workers. The use of Irish labor in the construction of railroads and canals is well known, but such projects usually relied on temporary labor. Quarries, on the other hand, were longer-lived ventures. New England's quarries provided vast quantities of stone and gravel that supplied landfills and building material for countless city developments. Perhaps the best-known local quarries were those in Quincy, which in the 1820s spawned its own "Granite Railroad" to supply stone for the Bunker Hill Monument. Afterward, a growing Irish workforce quarried stone for roads, piers, bridges, and some of Boston's finest buildings. Later, Italian immigrants—some of whom were skilled stonecutters—found work there as well. By the turn of the century, the foreign born—most of whom were employed in the quarries—made up a third of Quincy's population.

Similarly, Boston's municipal water supply depended heavily on Irish and Italian labor. The city had begun tapping water from Lake Cochituate (14 miles to the west) in 1848. In the 1870s, by which time the water supply had proved inadequate, the metropolitan water commission built a system of dams and reservoirs, recruiting hundreds of Irish and Italian laborers and stonecutters. Many of them settled in nearby Framingham, where they found further construction and manufacturing work after the water system was completed. By 1905, Framingham's foreign born made up 21 percent of the town's population. There, and in several other suburbs, ethnic succession began quite early, paralleling that of the city itself.[29]

DISCRIMINATION

From the 1830s through the 1920s, Irish, Jewish, Italian, and other immigrants to Massachusetts periodically faced resentment, hostility, and even violence from native-born residents. Indeed, Boston was often at the forefront of nativist political organizing, as well as being an intellectual center for those advocating immigration restriction. Because of its critical role in the industrial revolution, the state attracted more than its share

of job-seeking newcomers, stoking competition over employment, housing, and public services. Economic rivalries, however, were not the only
source of tension and were overlaid with cultural and political biases. Most
notably, powerful currents of anti-Catholicism, anti-Semitism, and antiradicalism intensified nativist feelings to a fever pitch. These beliefs were
intertwined with racialized views of immigrant groups that increasingly
relied on scientific theories and expertise. The legitimation of such racist
thinking resulted in a series of federal laws restricting immigration beginning in the 1880s and culminating in the 1920s, legislation that would vastly
reduce immigration and change the ethnic makeup of Boston and other US
cities by the mid-twentieth century.

The Irish were the first group to face fierce opposition. Although
unskilled Irish workers initially posed little economic competition to a
predominantly skilled Boston workforce, their Catholicism provoked
grave concern among Yankee residents. Anti-Catholicism had been a
potent force in New England since colonial times, but the arrival of growing numbers of Irish Catholics in the 1830s magnified fears of a Catholic
invasion that threatened to subvert American democracy in favor of
"popery" and "Romanism." The Irish affinity for the Democratic Party
and their opposition to Protestant reforms such as temperance, abolition,
and Protestant-influenced public education convinced many Yankees that
a papist conspiracy was afoot. While local Yankee preachers and editors
stoked the fires of anti-Catholicism from the press and the pulpit, working-class Protestants clashed with the Irish in the streets. Long-simmering
tensions exploded in 1834 when an angry crowd of Protestant workmen
surrounded the Ursuline Convent in Charlestown and burned it to the
ground. Three years later, a confrontation between a native-born volunteer
fire company and an Irish funeral procession in the North End escalated
into a major riot involving several thousand people. The militia was called
out to suppress the violence, but not before a number of Irish were beaten
and their homes looted and burned.[30]

The deluge of Irish Catholic immigration during the famine years
heightened nativist feeling and gave rise to an organized political movement. As thousands of desperate and emaciated immigrants flooded the
North End and Fort Hill, the growing poverty and disorder of these quarters prompted new concerns about Irish disease and immorality. Working
feverishly to control drinking, prostitution, and other vices, Yankee leaders

increasingly viewed the immigrants as a burden on the city's taxpayers and charitable organizations. Labor competition also became an issue. As some Irish residents began to move into factory jobs in the 1850s, native-born workers blamed them for undercutting wages and breaking strikes. The Irish were thus banned from many workingmen's organizations, and a number of explicitly nativist fraternal organizations emerged in the early 1850s. They soon joined forces in the Know Nothings, a secret society so named because its members promised to keep silent about its existence (if asked, they pledged to respond, "I know nothing"). In the early 1850s, the Know Nothings entered the political arena as the American Party.

First launched in New York, the party quickly spread to other eastern states, but nowhere was it more successful than in Massachusetts. In the elections of 1854, the Know Nothings won the governorship and all other state offices while taking almost total control of both houses of the state legislature. Although they failed to pass their most draconian anti-immigrant measures, the Know Nothings circumscribed the rights of Irish Catholics in numerous ways. Among other measures, they disbanded Irish militia units, deported Irish paupers and mental patients, required the King James version of the Bible to be read in public schools (which was offensive to Catholics), and carried out a highly controversial investigation of parochial schools and nunneries in 1855. Their dominance was short-lived, however, as the Know Nothing Party foundered in 1858. The Republicans who succeeded them, though, achieved a number of their nativist goals, including the establishment of a state literacy requirement and a two-year waiting period for voting by foreign-born citizens.[31]

Nativist fervor cooled somewhat during the 1860s as immigration leveled off and the sectional conflicts of the Civil War era overshadowed other social divisions. By the 1870s, however, economic malaise and a backlash against Chinese labor in the western states reignited nativist forces. Ironically, given their experience as targets of nativism, Irish immigrants were at the forefront of a violent anti-Chinese movement in California. Railing against unfair competition from Chinese "coolie" or contract labor, Dennis Kearney and other leaders relied on deeply racist depictions of Chinese workers who subsisted on "rice and rats." Likening their labor to slavery, the anti-Chinese movement blamed Asian workers for undercutting wages, degrading white workers, and undermining the American standard of living. Through such campaigns, Irish workers sought to deflect nativist hostilities toward other groups and reinforce their own identities as white American citizens.

Although the movement first arose in California, the arrival of Chinese workers in North Adams, Massachusetts, in the early 1870s raised the specter of Chinese strikebreaking across the country. Eastern and southern employers, in fact, soon rushed to hire Chinese laborers in an effort to cut costs and undermine organized labor. As the *Boston Advertiser* crowed, manufacturers throughout the country had "felt to some extent the influence of trade unions, for which the most powerful enemy has now been found." Such brazen appeals brought counter pressure from labor and its political allies that spawned a national movement to ban Chinese immigration. After intense lobbying, Congress passed the Chinese Exclusion Act in 1882, barring all immigration from China with the exception of merchants, students, teachers and travelers. In effect for ten years, the act was made permanent in 1902 and remained in force until World War II.[32]

The passage of Chinese exclusion, however, did not put an end to anti-Chinese sentiments. Asian workers remained confined to a small number of occupations and residential areas, while their more dispersed businesses were frequently subject to harassment and vandalism. Official concerns over immigrants who entered illegally or with falsified documents also resulted in ongoing harassment of Chinatown residents. The most egregious example was the 1903 raid on Boston's Chinatown, in which fifty federal and local officers cordoned off the neighborhood and rousted hundreds of Chinese from their homes and businesses without a warrant. In the end, 234 were arrested, of whom 50 were deported; most were released after presenting documentation of legal residency. The scope of the raid was unprecedented and drew official protests from the Chinese consul. Moreover, fears of arrest and deportation spurred an exodus from the city, reducing the city's Chinese population from 1,065 in 1900 to 815 in 1910. As Erika Lee has argued, Chinese exclusion and enforcement practices set a precedent for more general immigration restriction in the twentieth century.[33]

As a new wave of southern and eastern European immigration swelled the urban population after 1880, Boston nativists looked to restrictive legislation as a potential solution. Their objections to these newest immigrants were similar to earlier complaints about the Irish: their poverty, illiteracy, and degraded living conditions were a danger to the public and a burden on the community. But unlike many of the Irish, who at least spoke English, the new immigrants spoke a babel of foreign tongues and seemed to have little interest in staying in the United States permanently. The high percentage of return migrants among the Italians and other Mediterraneans, their tendency to send part of their income back home, and their low rates of naturalization suggested that they had little investment in American life. Moreover, economic competition grew despite an expanding economy and strong demand for labor. Skilled workers—many of them earlier migrants from Ireland and Canada—resented the new influx of unskilled migrants whose presence enabled employers to reduce wages, break strikes, and mechanize the workplace. On the neighborhood level, competition over housing, politics, and use of the streets also pitted the Irish against Italian and Jewish newcomers. Conflicts between the Irish and Italians in the North End were particularly bitter. In the early 1900s, Irish gangs controlled many of the street corners, harassing and assaulting Italians who dared pass through. When Sicilian immigrant fishermen returned home from sea after dark, they would sleep in their boats rather than run the gantlet through the Irish-occupied blocks that surrounded the waterfront. Jews and blacks in the South and West Ends were also targeted for abuse as a declining Irish population sought to maintain control of its shrinking turf.[34]

As street-level ethnic tensions engulfed the working class, Boston's Brahmin elite was devising an intellectual and scientific foundation for the anti-immigrant movement. In 1894, three Harvard graduates from old-line Yankee families—Prescott Hall, Charles Warren, and Robert Ward—founded the Immigration Restriction League, a national organization to defend Anglo-Saxon society from the immigrant hordes. Composed of 670 members, the league was a who's who of Boston Brahmins that included such notables as Harvard president A. Lawrence Lowell, MIT president Francis Walker, and Massachusetts senator Henry Cabot Lodge. Having already lost control of the city to Irish political bosses, league members were determined to control the rising threat of "inferior" southern and eastern Europeans. Building on popular theories of social Darwinism and eugenics, league member Madison Grant and other intellectuals argued that "mongrelized" immigrants from southern and eastern Europe threatened the survival of America's native stock of fair-skinned "Nordic" peoples. Low reproductive rates among the nation's Nordic stock were no match for the high birth rates of immigrants, they argued, and this imbalance portended "race suicide" for Anglo-Saxons. American democracy and political institutions, they believed, were similarly endangered by the corruption and ignorance of the newcomers.[35]

This new scientific ideology relied on an array of popular racist beliefs that saw new immigrants as "swarthy" peoples who were unassimilable and not fully white. Even some of the city's Progressive reformers shared these racial biases and popularized them in published surveys about immigrant life. In the case of Jewish immigrants, a long-standing Euro American tradition of anti-Semitism fed stereotypes of Jews as clever, money-hungry, quarrelsome, and dirty. As the settlement worker Robert Woods described it, the Jewish South End was a drab and squalid quarter occupied by those with "the shrewd but ingratiating look which so often means financial gain at any cost, even at the cost of self respect." Viewed as an insular and clannish "race," Jews who succeeded academically or professionally were still seen as unassimilable. In 1922 Harvard University announced that it would use quotas to limit Jewish admissions; it later retracted the policy, but other more subtle forms of discrimination persisted. By contrast, Italians were viewed as colorful and picturesque—but also backward, illiterate, and prone to crime and violence. Their reliance on labor contractors, or *padrones*, also engendered fears that Italians (like the Chinese) were a passive, servile labor force that employers could exploit at will and thus use to degrade American living standards. The alleged racial inferiority of Italians, Jews, and other new immigrants helped convince Congress to back legislation that the Immigration Restriction League had long championed. Under the leadership of Senator Lodge, Congress passed a bill in 1917 requiring that all immigrants pass a literacy test in order to enter the country. In addition, the law expanded exclusionary measures (heretofore limited to the Chinese) to cover virtually all of Asia.[36]

The restrictionist impulse was far from spent, however. The nationalist fervor of World War I served to heighten xenophobia, while the Bolshevik revolution in Russia led to a surge of antiradicalism. Antipathy toward communists, anarchists, and syndicalists had been growing since the late nineteenth century. In Massachusetts, the successful strike led by the Industrial Workers of the World in Lawrence in 1912 heightened those fears by showing that immigrant workers were capable of fighting back. For several years thereafter, Lynn, Massachusetts, was also home to a militant Italian anarchist movement led by Luigi Galleani that carried out a series of bombings directed at corporate leaders, public officials, and police. In 1917, the US government rounded up Galleani and several of his followers in the Boston area, and in 1919 a series of anarchist bombings led to a Justice Department campaign of raids and deportations that violated due process and terrorized the local Italian community. Most notable, however, was the 1920 arrest of two anarchist shoe workers, Nicola Sacco and Bartolomeo Vanzetti, who were accused of robbing and killing two company payroll guards in South Braintree. A long legal battle ensued that became an international cause célèbre but ended with the execution of Sacco and Vanzetti in 1927. Although anarchists made up only a small percentage of the migrant community, the relentless surveillance and raids directed at Italian institutions and neighborhoods, and the resulting stigma of violence and criminality, affected all Italians to some degree.[37]

The convergence of antiradicalism and scientific racism, combined with a sharp economic downturn in the 1920s, finally succeeded in rallying support for comprehensive immigration restriction. In 1924 Congress passed the National Origins Act, which limited the number of immigrants from any country to no more than 2 percent of those from that country who were living in the United States in 1890. This would reduce immigration to about 165,000 per year thereafter (compared with more than a million annually prior to 1914). By pegging the quotas to the census of 1890—before the greatest influx of southern and eastern Europeans—legislators purposely created larger quotas for older immigrant groups from northern and western Europe while more tightly restricting those they deemed undesirable. The annual cap on immigration was reduced to 153,000 a few years later, with quotas based on the 1920 census, but the restrictions continued to work disproportionately against southern and eastern Europeans. With minor modifications, the quota system endured until 1965.[38]

Immigration restriction had a profound impact on the population of Boston and other US cities. In 1910, the peak census year for immigrants, 36 percent of Boston's population was foreign born. Because of the literacy bill and the slowing of migration during the war years, the foreign born share of the city's population dropped to 32 percent by 1920. Once quota restrictions were in effect, the immigrant population dropped to 30 percent in 1930, and the port of Boston ceased to be an important immigrant gateway. Migration contracted further during the Great Depression, reducing the foreign-born population to 24 percent by 1940. Despite some loosening of restrictions to accommodate refugees and war brides after

World War II, the percentage of immigrants in the city continued to drop for several decades, reaching a low point of 13 percent in 1970.[39] While some of the children and grandchildren of immigrants continued to identify with their ethnic roots, the pressures of assimilation and suburbanization in the postwar period steadily eroded immigrant communities, leaving dwindling urban enclaves occupied mainly by the poor and the elderly.

RELIGION

Predominantly Catholic and Jewish, immigrants arriving in Boston in the mid-nineteenth century brought distinctive religious cultures to an overwhelmingly Protestant city. In transplanting their faiths to new soil, newcomers adapted their Old World religion, allowing some traditions to erode while cultivating new practices suited to the American cultural context. Although many of the new churches and synagogues prospered, the arrival of a second wave of migrants in the late nineteenth century posed serious challenges and tested their ability to absorb newcomers. In many cases, newly arrived Jews, Italians, and other groups organized their own congregations, both within and outside the existing religious framework. Catholics, for the most part, formed parishes that remained under the Roman Catholic hierarchy, while Jews tended to form independent congregations that were distinct from their predecessors. In both cases, however, Jewish and Catholic immigrants challenged the dominant religious leadership and pioneered new practices and organizations that would become part of Boston's larger faith community.

Envisioned by John Winthrop as the biblical "City on a Hill," colonial Boston was shaped by its Puritan founders, who were determined to keep out religious competitors. Although their descendants embraced a number of other denominations, the city remained a Yankee Protestant stronghold for several decades after the Revolution, with only small numbers of Sephardic Jews and French and German Catholics. It was not until the 1840s, with the arrival of large numbers Irish Catholics and central European Jews, that these two groups became significant forces in the religious life of the city.[40]

For Jews, this period marked the founding of the city's religious community. Unlike many eastern port cities, Boston had attracted few Sephardic Jews in the seventeenth or eighteenth centuries—never enough permanent residents to form a congregation. The central European Jews who arrived in the 1840s, by contrast, intended to stay and built the city's first synagogue, Ohabei Shalom, in the South End in 1852. A few years later, differences between German and Polish Jews prompted the former to break away and form a separate congregation, Adath Israel (later known as Temple Israel), a few blocks away. In 1856, another breakaway group from East Prussia formed a third congregation, Mishkan Israel (later to become Mishkan Tefila), also in the South End. While differing slightly in ritual style and liturgy, all three congregations initially practiced a traditional form of Judaism.[41]

Among Catholics, the mass infusion of Irish immigrants quickly overwhelmed the French and Germans who made up the early Boston church. In 1846, the first Irish bishop was appointed; he recruited a growing number of Irish clergy and before long, most of the diocesan hierarchy was Irish as well. From that point on, as the historian James O'Toole has noted, "Boston Catholicism meant Irish Catholicism." The number of parishes multiplied rapidly in the 1830s and 1840s, especially in Irish settlements near the Boston waterfront and in the region's burgeoning mill towns. By the end of the Civil War, there were well over a hundred parishes in the Boston diocese, the majority of them serving Irish immigrants and their children.[42]

During the latter half of the nineteenth century, both Catholic and Jewish religious practices underwent changes as leaders of both groups sought to adapt their faith to the modern world and retain the allegiance of their immigrant flocks. For both groups, these changes originated across the Atlantic but took firm root in Boston and other US cities. Acting on directives from Rome, Irish clergy in both Ireland and the United States launched the so-called devotional revolution of the mid-nineteenth century to strengthen religious observance and replace popular folk religion with more orthodox devotional practices prescribed by the church. The church thus mandated regular Mass attendance, confession, and celebration of the sacraments, as well as introducing a variety of devotional practices such as novenas, shrines, and the saying of the rosary. For the famine-era Irish, whose church attendance and devotional practices were often lax, the new regime was designed to turn nominal Catholics into practicing believers of a more orthodox and austere faith.[43]

By contrast, central European Jews and their children moved to liberalize their religious practices in the latter decades of the nineteenth century, laying the foundations of Reform Judaism. Like the devotional revolution, this current also originated abroad, in this case among university-trained rabbis in Germany who immigrated to the United States. In the 1870s, Adath Israel and Ohabei Shalom began moving toward Reform Judaism by shortening the service, introducing choirs, organs, and mixed seating in family pews, and moving Sabbath services from Saturday to Sunday. Such reforms were designed to update (or "protestantize") Judaism to make it more conducive to modern American life and to allow Jews to adhere to their faith without undue economic hardship (by allowing them to work on Saturdays). In adapting to American life, then, nineteenth-century Jews and Catholics took different paths: the former toward heterodoxy and liberalization, the latter toward a more orthodox, hierarchically defined Catholicism.[44]

Both groups, however, were unprepared for the deluge of new immigrants who began to arrive in the late 1800s. For the Catholic Church, the problem of incorporating new immigrants began in the 1860s as large numbers of French-speaking Canadians flocked to the region's mill towns. Feeling uncomfortable in the Irish-dominated churches, newcomers called on the bishop to provide priests who could preach sermons and hear confession in their own language and who were familiar with the migrants' ritual styles and devotions. In 1868 the bishop dispatched a French-speaking pastor and established St. Joseph's Church in Lowell.[45] A few years later, the diocese purchased a former Baptist church in the North End and established St. John the Baptist Church for joint use by newly arrived Portuguese and Italians. By recruiting foreign-born clergy or priests from religious orders that spoke the immigrants' own language, the church found a means of tending to an increasingly diverse immigrant flock. A loophole in canon law allowed for the creation of linguistically based churches that were superimposed over a network of geographically based (mainly Irish) parishes. In neighborhoods in which new immigrants were settling, existing churches often operated missions (in the basement or in nearby chapels) to which traveling priests of the new ethnic group came once a week to say Mass and hear confessions until the bishop determined there were enough followers to support a separate parish.[46]

Over the next fifty years, the archdiocese would create more than sixty ethnic churches, nearly a quarter of its total. French Canadians occupied the greatest number of parishes (twenty-one by the 1920s), while Italians and Poles each had more than a dozen. Portuguese, Syrian-Lebanese, and Lithuanians also claimed a handful of parishes. The new parishes diversified Boston Catholicism, bringing not only new language groups but new religious styles and devotional practices as well. Churches named after St. Stanislaus (Polish, Chelsea), St. Tarcisius (Italian, Framingham), and Our Lady of the Cedars of Lebanon (Maronite, South End) joined the older parishes named after St. Mary, St. Patrick, and the Sacred Heart.

Looking to save souls and expand the ranks of the church, the Catholic hierarchy accommodated the newcomers partly as a defensive action against the fervent efforts of Protestant evangelists. Baptist, Methodist, and Episcopalian missionaries scoured the East Boston docks in search of converts among the newly arrived migrants and opened storefront missions in the North End offering food, clothing, and other services along with religious indoctrination. In fact, between 1880 and 1930 there were at least 115 Protestant missions operating in the city. To counter these efforts, and to meet some of the critical needs of the immigrant poor within a familiar Catholic context, the church founded a spate of social welfare institutions. These included infant asylums, orphanages, homes for wayward boys and girls, industrial schools, medical dispensaries, and several Catholic hospitals. Many of these facilities were founded in the 1860s to serve Irish immigrants but were retooled and expanded to meet the growing needs of second-wave migrants. In 1903 the archbishop brought these agencies together under the umbrella of the newly established Catholic Charitable Bureau. The forerunner of today's Catholic Charities, the bureau created an Immigrant Welfare Department in 1921 that would meet newcomers as they debarked on the docks in East Boston. Although this service proved less necessary after the passage of immigration restriction a few years later, Catholic Charities would continue its work with the needy and provide critical services for new immigrants and refugees arriving after World War II and up to the present day.[47]

Although earlier Catholic efforts to counter the "leakage" of immigrant Catholics to Protestant faiths were largely successful, creating and managing a diverse immigrant church was not without difficulties. Recruiting qualified bilingual clergy was a challenge, and the fiscal demands of the new parishes sometimes resulted in mismanagement, debt, and scandal. Moreover, the Irish-dominated hierarchy was not always sympathetic to the divergent religious attitudes and practices of the newcomers, and the latter, in turn, challenged church policy on a number of occasions.[48]

The archdiocese was especially slow in responding to the needs of Italian Catholics, whose ranks had grown considerably in the late nineteenth century. The Irish hierarchy was generally suspicious of the new Italian migrants who practiced a boisterous and expressive form of folk Catholicism that included street processions and festivals honoring the patron saints of their home villages. Nor did they understand the widespread anticlericalism of many Italian men who were alienated from the church hierarchy, which in Italy had traditionally allied with the ruling classes (unlike Irish clergy, who generally supported popular resistance to British rule). In the North End, for example, a group of Genoese Catholics at St. Leonard's raised money for a new church in North Square in the 1880s but insisted on maintaining title to the property. The archbishop refused to authorize the church, and a five-year standoff ensued. Eventually a settlement was reached through the intercession of the Missionaries of St. Charles (Scalabrinians), an Italian religious order that agreed to operate the parish on behalf of the archdiocese. Similar conflicts erupted in Polish parishes, where disputes over church property, clerical leadership, and lack of Polish-speaking priests prompted several parishes to break away and join independent church federations. In the early twentieth century, Polish parishes in Cambridge and Lynn left the archdiocese to affiliate with the Polish National Catholic Church headquartered in Pennsylvania. The Catholic Church's fierce opposition to communists and anarchists also stirred tensions in Italian and Lithuanian churches during the 1910s and 1920s.[49]

In general, though, the ethnic parish system proved effective in binding immigrants to the church, cementing their loyalty with the brick and mortar of a growing number of Catholic churches and schools. For the second generation, the establishment of more than fifty native-language parochial schools between 1860 and 1920 provided a linguistically and religiously supportive alternative to the overcrowded public schools. For some, these schools became feeders into local Catholic universities, such as Boston College and College of the Holy Cross, which made possible upward social mobility. But as the younger generations learned English and immigration restriction reduced new membership, ethnic parishes became bilingual—with Masses in English for the young and foreign-language Masses mainly for older members. As later generations dispersed to the suburbs, many of these parishes shrank. Some of them would be among those shuttered during the parish closings of the late twentieth century; others would be retooled to serve new immigrant populations in surrounding neighborhoods.[50]

The unprecedented expansion of the immigrant church in the late nineteenth and early twentieth centuries was accompanied by an equally explosive growth in the ranks of Judaism. As growing numbers of eastern European Jews arrived in the city in the 1870s and 1880s, many of them found themselves unwelcome or uncomfortable in the reform synagogues of their predecessors. Unlike the more affluent and assimilated central European Jews, the new migrants were often impoverished and more orthodox in their religious practices. Holding fast to traditional liturgy and ritual, they found Reform Judaism to hold little appeal for them. Rather than joining the older established synagogues, newcomers bonded with fellow immigrants from their home village or region in a *chevra*, or mutual benefit society. Originating in the Pale as craft associations, the *chevrorth* in the United States provided sickness and death benefits, burial sites, and prayer groups. The prayer groups originally met in rented rooms along Hanover Street in the North End, and several of them later merged to form Shomre Beth Abraham in 1886. A few years later, the congregation moved into an old church on Baldwin Place, where it was joined by a Jewish religious school and became the center of Orthodox Judaism in the city for several decades. As Jews moved into the West End around the turn of the century, other congregations formed and took up residence in the African Meeting House and other churches sold by black residents then debarking for the South End. (Ironically, some of these black Bostonians would relocate their churches to old synagogue buildings in the South End that were being sold off by central European Jews who began moving to Roxbury around the same time.) By the turn of the century, there were more than fifty Jewish congregations in the North and West Ends, nearly all of them orthodox.[51]

While few immigrants joined the established reform synagogues, the central European Jewish community reached out to newcomers through a variety of philanthropic organizations. Like their Catholic counterparts, Jews sought to provide an alternative to Protestant-dominated charities, but they also drew on a long tradition of Jewish self-help that had developed in the Pale of Settlement. Beginning in the 1860s, members of Adath

Israel and Ohabei Shalom, mostly retailers and manufacturers who had prospered during the Civil War, formed the Hebrew Benevolent Society to aid new arrivals. Acting on their belief in helping others but also concerned that the problems of the new immigrants might aggravate anti-Semitism, Benevolent Society members and their wives (who founded the Ladies Aid Society in 1897) established a network of Jewish charity organizations. These included a home for orphans and the elderly, a shelter for impoverished immigrants, an employment bureau, industrial schools, and a burial service for the poor. In 1895 these organizations joined together as the Federated Jewish Charities of Boston. Over the years the federation would be expanded, reorganized, and renamed, but one of its descendant organizations, Jewish Family and Children's Service of Greater Boston, would help resettle thousands of Nazi refugees in the 1940s and Soviet Jewish refugees in the 1980s.[52]

As more affluent Jews established beachheads of settlement in Roxbury, they initiated a suburban exodus that would lure many of the city's eastern European Jews and their families outward to Roxbury, Dorchester, and beyond. New synagogues founded in this area beginning in the 1890s—Adath Jeshurun, Beth Hamidrash Hagadol, Beth El, and others—attracted a growing Jewish community that was increasingly working class by the 1920s. Around the same time, Mishkan Tefila, one of the city's original congregations that had moved to Roxbury from the South End in 1907, embraced the new Conservative movement, which staked out a moderate theological position between reform and orthodoxy. Composed of the more Americanized children of eastern European Jews, Mishkan Tefila members sought to conserve more traditional Jewish learning and ritual while accommodating these practices to modern American life. They thus maintained most features of the traditional Hebrew service but offered mixed family seating, Friday night services, and other "modern" practices. Other second-generation Jews embraced Modern Orthodoxy, a more traditional approach but one that also sought to synthesize traditional Judaism with the modern secular world. By the mid-twentieth century, the rigid distinctions between central and eastern European Jews had dissipated and their descendants would mix in a variety of suburban congregations that ranged from ultraorthodox to liberal reform. Overall, though, a distinct drift toward modernization was evident among later generations of eastern European Jews, however much their immigrant parents had once resisted it.[53]

Although both immigrant Jews and Catholics successfully transplanted their faith to the Boston area, the process presented challenges to the established Catholic Church and older Boston synagogues. Ultimately, the Catholic hierarchy ensured that most immigrant Catholics would remain within the fold of the archdiocese through the use of ethnic parishes as vehicles for incorporation. Lacking a centralized hierarchy, Jews established a bevy of new synagogues that ultimately produced different religious styles and practices. In both cases, newcomers initially worshipped in separate immigrant congregations, but their Americanized children brought these institutions into the mainstream or moved into mixed congregations in the suburbs. The absence of a strong central hierarchy in Judaism, however, meant that Jewish congregations were more autonomous and mobile than Catholic ones (especially the geographically based Irish parishes). As Gerald Gamm has argued, canon law rules governing parish formation and the church's investment in buildings, schools, rectories, and other facilities led to a rootedness in many Catholic parishes that was unknown among Jews or Protestants. Jewish congregations, by contrast, could move relatively easily if key members chose to. Many older congregations moved at least three times—from downtown, to Roxbury and Dorchester, and eventually to suburbs such as Brookline or Newton. Such mobility meant that Jewish neighborhoods were less rooted and more likely to experience rapid racial transition in the mid-twentieth century as African American migration pressed the boundaries of black settlement outward from the South End and Lower Roxbury. As Jews abandoned their old synagogues and neighborhoods and blacks moved in, remaining Irish Catholic neighborhoods in South Boston and Dorchester ferociously defended their parish-based turf. Blistering racial conflict accompanied this transition in the 1960s and 1970s, culminating in the busing crisis of 1974–1975.[54] It was into this bitter, racially charged climate that new migrants of color would arrive in the 1970s and afterward.

ETHNIC POLITICS

The Irish American dominance of Boston politics has become a truism that obscures a long and uneven history of immigrant political life in the city. Like recent migrants, Boston's older immigrant groups did not jump immediately into electoral politics but spent years preparing the groundwork

through the creation of ethnic networks, engagement with partisan political organizations and reform groups, and the rise of an American-born
generation that spoke English and could better navigate the political waters
of the city and state. Because of their early arrival, large numbers, and proficiency in English, the Irish came to dominate the city's political landscape for much of the twentieth century. Other groups, however, learned to
work with—or openly rebelled against—the Irish-dominated Democratic
machine and gradually established a political foothold.

Prior to the Civil War, Boston was ruled by a Yankee elite, descendants
of the Puritan families who had founded the city as well as the new mon-
ied interests of the textile industry. Known as the Brahmins, families such
as the Lowells, Cabots, Quincys, Lawrences, and Appletons ruled the city
with little interference from below. But party realignments in the mid-nineteenth century prompted some of the Brahmins (many of them former
Whigs) to join the Democrats, and after the war they began rebuilding the
party through alliances with conservative Irish immigrant leaders such as
Patrick Collins and Patrick Maguire.[55]

As Irish population and voting power in the city grew, Irish leaders
encouraged their countrymen to run for the board of aldermen and common council while supporting Brahmin Democrats for mayor. By 1884,
with the strong support of political boss Patrick Maguire as well as Brahmin
Democrats, businessman Hugh O'Brien became Boston's first Irish Catholic
mayor. O'Brien's successful four-year stint was later followed by that of
Patrick Collins, a local Irish Democratic leader who served three terms in
Congress before winning the mayoralty in 1901. Both Collins and O'Brien
were fiscally conservative businessmen who were acceptable to Brahmin
Democrats, exemplars of the "better sort" of self-made Irishmen who were
well dressed, well spoken, and cordial with their Brahmin associates.[56]

The growing Irish voting power that made O'Brien's and Collins's elections possible also propelled the careers of local Irish leaders in the city's
working-class immigrant wards. The late nineteenth century saw the rise
of colorful ward bosses such as Martin Lomasney (West End), John "Honey
Fitz" Fitzgerald (North End), Patrick J. Kennedy (East Boston), and
"Smiling Jim" Donovan (South End). Some of the bosses went on to hold
powerful offices—such as Fitzgerald, who was mayor for six years, and
Kennedy, who served eight terms in the state senate (both were grandfa-
thers of President John F. Kennedy). But the bosses' real power rested in

their ward headquarters, local political clubs in which members socialized, exchanged information, organized election efforts, and, most important of all, provided patronage jobs for their loyal supporters. While the Irish made up the heart of the local machines, they expanded their reach by occasionally nominating candidates from among the Jews, Italians, and other newly arrived groups in their districts.[57]

The proliferation of Irish bosses and ward organizations across the city alarmed many native-born Bostonians. Tensions between Protestant elites and Irish immigrants were deeply rooted, but the need for political cooperation among Democrats had fostered a degree of cooperation. As the Irish came to dominate many ward-based organizations by the turn of the century, however, hostility and suspicion toward Irish influence resurfaced. When in 1905 Irish votes catapulted boss Fitzgerald of the North End into the mayor's office, beating out his Brahmin Republican challenger, the Yankee elite was appalled. They feared, as many Progressive reformers did at the time, that corrupt "boss rule" would result in stolen elections, unqualified men on the city payroll, and the plundering of the treasury. Instead, Progressives called for enlightened public service, scientific expertise, and managerial efficiency.[58]

To this end, Boston reformers established the Good Government Association in 1903, which began work on a major charter reform. Passed by the state legislature and approved by Boston voters in 1909, the new charter abolished the old board of aldermen and replaced the seventy-five-member common council (representing all twenty-five wards in the city) with a new nine-member city council elected at large. The mayor's office was made more powerful, with an expanded four-year term and veto power over decisions of the city council, but with less patronage power. Perhaps most important, all city elections would henceforth be conducted on a nonpartisan basis, thus reducing the influence of party bosses and ward-based organizations. The new charter was thus designed to expand executive power—presumably wielded by trusted and competent Yankee mayors—while reducing the influence of the Democratic bosses and their lackeys in the common council.[59]

The Progressive revolt against bossism, however, was not limited to Yankee business elites and reformers. As the historian James Connolly has argued, some Jews and Italians (and even a number of Irish Americans) embraced the language of Progressive reform to challenge the dominant

Irish political machines. Living as they did in the shadow of such machines, few non-Irish ethnics had managed to establish successful political careers prior to World War I. One exception was Leonard Morse, a wealthy German-Jewish clothier who served five terms in Congress between 1877 and 1889 with the support of influential Brahmins. Another was George Scigliano, an Italian American lawyer and reformer from the North End who won a seat on the common council in 1900 but died a few years later. For the most part, however, Jewish and Italian neighborhoods in the North, West, and South Ends remained firmly in Irish control.[60]

The Progressive campaign against bossism, however, provided ammunition for ethnic leaders who sought to buck the machines. In 1905, a scandal involving misappropriation of school funds in the West End led to a Jewish revolt against Martin Lomasney and his sister, who served on the Boston School Committee. Jewish Progressives, who included renowned legal reformer Louis Brandeis, Harvard professor Horace Kallen, and Jacob de Haas, editor of the Jewish *Boston Advocate*, took up the cause by running an independent slate of candidates for the school committee. Over the next few years they directly challenged Lomasney, whom they dubbed "the czar of the West End," by supporting Jewish candidates to run against him and his allies. Although the reform candidates mostly lost, the campaign helped introduce a distinctively Jewish presence into West End politics that reformers would build on in the future. Periodic efforts to counter anti-Semitism, and growing support for Zionism and a Jewish homeland, would further reinforce this emerging Jewish political identity.[61]

A similar revolt against bossism developed in the Italian North End. Despite the neighborhood's growing Italian majority in the early twentieth century, the North End remained firmly in the control of boss Fitzgerald. Provincial rivalries, lack of English proficiency, and high rates of return migration led to low levels of political participation among Italian immigrants that allowed Fitzgerald's forces to stay in control. Eager to build Italian political power, influential community leaders such as James Donnaruma, editor of the Italian-language newspaper *La Gazzetta*, and Dominic D'Alessandro, head of the Italian Laborers Union, soon embraced the Progressive formula of anti-bossism. During Fitzgerald's first mayoral term, when his administration was rocked by a series of fiscal scandals, Donnaruma, D'Alessandro, and other Italian leaders joined the reform effort against his re-election in 1905. They then formed a separate Partido

Italiano Independente and ran two Italian American lawyers for common council in the hope of challenging Fitzgerald's machine. While the Partido's electoral strategy generally failed, its reform agenda helped legitimize an Italian American political identity that would become more common in the future.[62]

Ultimately, Progressive hopes of vanquishing Irish dominance in city politics came to naught. Although Mayor Fitzgerald faced a temporary setback by losing his 1907 re-election bid, he rebounded in 1909 to win a now longer four-year term. Fitzgerald was then succeeded by another Irish American mayor, who would prove to be the Progressives' worst nightmare—the pugnacious and irrepressible James Michael Curley. Born to a working-class Irish immigrant family in Roxbury, Curley had a driving ambition that led him to take on Irish bosses and good government reformers alike. After serving in the state legislature, the city council, and the US Congress, Curley won the first of four terms as mayor in 1914, rotating in and out of City Hall for the next thirty-five years. Through it all, including two jail terms for fraud and misuse of city funds, he built his power not through old-style machine politics but via a personal empire built on the vilification of the Yankee elite and appeals to an aggrieved Irish and immigrant working class. Patronage and graft were certainly part of Curley's success, but they were administered by him personally rather than by ward-based party machines. Ironically, then, Progressive charter reforms that made city elections nonpartisan helped bring about a new politics of personality and centralization that Curley effectively used to maintain power.[63]

Curley's lengthy regime and the benefits that flowed from Franklin Roosevelt's New Deal in the 1930s helped to lay the groundwork for Irish Democratic dominance of City Hall for much of the twentieth century. Indeed, no Republican would be elected mayor after 1930, and all mayors thereafter until 1993 would be Irish American. Although the dominance of earlier Irish machines was possible because of the low voting rates of new immigrants, Curley's strength came partly from his wooing of Jewish, Italian, and other ethnic leaders and his extensive social welfare and public works projects targeted at working-class neighborhoods. Second-generation ethnic Jews and Italians were also more likely to vote, and Curley often appealed to their ethnic identity to garner support.[64]

Nevertheless, Jewish, Italian, and other non-Irish Bostonians remained largely shut out of the city's elective offices until 1923. In that year, working-class ethnic voters ensured the victory of a ballot initiative that revived ward-based elections and expanded the city council to twenty-two members. Over the next twenty-six years, twelve Jewish and four Italian American city councillors were elected. Although another round of charter reform in 1949 returned the city to costly at-large elections, Jewish and Italian candidates were sometimes able to finance successful citywide and even statewide elections by the 1950s. It was not until 1993, however, that the city would elect its first Italian American mayor, Thomas Menino, and it would be another decade before Italian Americans would ascend to the speakership of the state legislature. Jews also made great strides in postwar politics, but their success in Boston was undercut by their earlier dispersion to Brookline, Newton, and other suburbs.[65]

The struggle for immigrant political incorporation has been a protracted one that depended not only on sheer numbers but also on cultural factors and changing political practices and opportunities. Even the Irish—who had the benefit of a large and steadily growing population, English proficiency, and a penchant for politics at a time when the Democratic Party desperately needed their support—had been settling in Boston for more than forty years, following the famine, before winning the mayoralty. Jews, Italians, and other groups trod an even longer path as they struggled to learn English, battled entrenched Irish bosses and Protestant nativism, and found themselves effectively locked out of politics through at-large elections. Charter reform in the 1920s, combined with the galvanizing power of the New Deal, finally allowed these groups to win a modest level of participation and incorporation. It was not, however, until after World War II that the number of second- and third-generation ethnic elected officials began to reflect their proportions in the population and that members of these immigrant groups would achieve top leadership positions in the city and state.

In focusing on electoral politics, however, we tend to miss other more quotidian forms of political action among immigrants. Much of the initial political life of Boston's newcomers was in fact centered around building the immigrant community through charitable institutions organized by the Catholic Church and Jewish synagogues—efforts that were essential to community survival before the rise of the welfare state. The Irish, Jews, and Italians also founded hundreds of mutual aid associations and were the prime movers in union struggles for shorter hours, better pay, and safer working conditions. The Irish were the dominant force in the city's trade unions, but Jews founded several local unions in the needle trades and in 1904 Italians started their own laborers' union. Jewish immigrants were a major force in Boston's Socialist Labor Party in the early twentieth century, while some local Italians were part of the international anarchist movement. Both ethnic groups supplied support for the massive Lawrence textile strike of 1912, and some North End Italians helped organize an international defense effort for Sacco and Vanzetti. Immigrants were also involved in international causes, most notably the Irish who supported the republican cause through the Fenian Brotherhood in the nineteenth century and Jews who promoted Zionism in the twentieth. Such activities often influenced electoral politics in the city and beyond.[66]

Immigrants' engagement with international concerns and the effect of global affairs on their lives is clearly nothing new, though it has intensified. As we will see, Boston's old and new immigrants had a great deal in common, but there is also much that has changed. We begin by exploring the origins of more recent immigration to see what connections exist to earlier experiences, as well as some of the forces that have been transforming life in the region since the 1960s.

CHAPTER 2

Roots and Routes

In the early twentieth century, newcomers debarking from ships at the East Boston immigration station were a hardened bunch. Their simple clothing and bundles betrayed their peasant and working-class backgrounds, while their grim expressions reflected the harsh and overcrowded conditions of the transatlantic voyage. Immigrants arriving in East Boston a hundred years later, however, are much more difficult to describe. Arriving on jets at Logan Airport, they have included impoverished farmers and urban workers, but also world-class physicists, doctors, and computer software engineers. They have arrived not only from Ireland, Italy, and eastern Europe—as did many earlier migrants—but also from places like Haiti, Brazil, India, Vietnam, and Nigeria. As late as 1970, most of Boston's foreign born came from Europe and Canada; since 1980, however, the majority have come from the Caribbean, Latin America, and Asia. By 2010, these three regions accounted for more than 80 percent of the city's immigrant population and 75 percent of the metro area's. The sheer diversity of the newcomers is perhaps the hallmark of the new immigration.[1]

The more recent migration experience differs in other ways as well. First, while older immigrants were certainly influenced by the transnational currents of economic and cultural change, recent immigrants have felt these global influences with far greater intensity. New transnational economic forces and media have spurred migration, and new forms of transportation and communication have facilitated it, while also enabling migrants to maintain stronger ties with their homeland. Second, the state—and particularly the federal government—has become a more critical agent in both facilitating and restricting the flow of migration in ways that had few parallels in the nineteenth and early twentieth centuries.

Historians have long emphasized the role of the state in fostering the new immigration, mainly through the passage of the 1965 Immigration and Nationality Act. That legislation was indeed a critical factor: it ended many of the discriminatory national and racial quotas established under the earlier national origins system, allowing more diverse migration streams from across the globe. At the same time, however, it also put new restrictions on migration from the Western Hemisphere, laying the groundwork for vexing problems of unauthorized immigration in the future. Equally important was the act's expansion of preferential treatment for the highly skilled and for the family members of American citizens. Building on the skill- and family-based preferences of earlier legislation, the 1965 act gave an even higher priority to family reunification, allowing the spouses, unmarried children, and parents of American citizens to enter *outside of* the quotas. This measure thus initiated a parallel stream of non-quota immigrants above and beyond the original 290,000 allowed under the 1965 quota system. It also expanded the criteria for skilled labor, including new preferences for professionals, scientists, and artists "of exceptional ability." After the Immigration Act went into effect in 1968, the flow of professional and skilled migrants from across the globe accelerated, and newcomers used family exemptions to build fast-growing migration networks across Asia, Latin America, and the Caribbean.[2]

But the 1965 act was not the only force driving the surge of new immigration. In fact, one might better understand it as a kind of general framework rather than a determining factor as to who would come. As figure 4 suggests, there was no sudden explosion of immigration in 1968 (the year the new regulations were implemented); rather, the increased flow of immigrants to Boston began in the mid-1960s and increased sporadically thereafter, reflecting a host of changing global conditions and the dictates of US foreign policy.

Immigrants to Massachusetts, 1954–2013

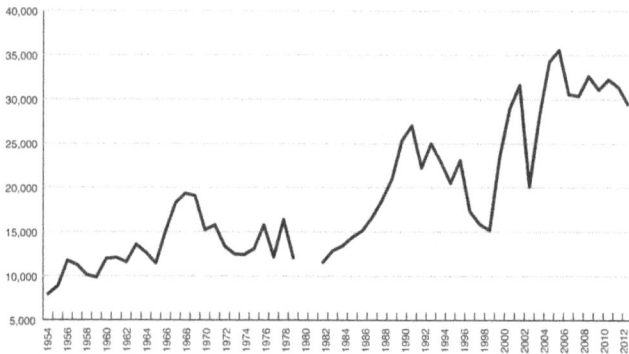

FIGURE 4. Immigrants headed to Massachusetts, 1954–2013. Source:
US Immigration and Naturalization Service (INS), *Annual Report of
the Immigration and Naturalization Service*, 1959, 1969; INS, *Statistical
Yearbook of the Immigration and Naturalization Service*, 1978–2000;
Department of Homeland Security, *Yearbook of Immigration Statistics*,
2012. Figures for 1951–2003 are for "immigrants admitted by state of
intended residence"; those since 2004 are for "persons obtaining Legal
Permanent Resident status."

Among the most important factors were the Cold War and the international refugee crises that accompanied it. Following World War II, the
United States passed a series of laws authorizing refugee admissions, initially
from Eastern Europe and later from other parts of Europe, Asia, and Latin
America. The US commitment to fighting communism underlay its evolving
refugee policy, and those fleeing from Soviet-sphere countries were readily
admitted. Moreover, US foreign policy during the Cold War helped spur
migration from Asia, the Caribbean, and Latin America as American intervention in those areas contributed to political instability, repression, and
economic chaos. The Vietnam War and its aftermath spurred the largest refugee migrations of the 1970s and 1980s, but Cold War policies also brought
new flows of Cuban exiles, Soviet dissidents, and Central Americans fleeing
the civil wars of the 1980s. Responding to some of these new challenges,
Congress passed the Refugee Act of 1980, which redefined refugees more
broadly, created a right to asylum, and established a federal program to facilitate refugee resettlement in Boston and other US cities. With the waning of
the Cold War in the late 1980s, new federal initiatives and legislation ushered
in an even more diverse flow of migrants and refugees, including many from
Africa, the Middle East, and south Asia.[3]

Some of these newcomers landed in the Boston area, laying the foundations for some of the new immigrant communities that would blossom in the 1980s and beyond. This chapter explores the roots of the area's new populations, why they came, the routes they took, and what influenced them to settle in the Boston area. Although many migrant groups retained distinct national identities and resisted inclusion within existing racial/ethnic categories, many formed at least tentative connections with other groups with whom they shared a common language, ancestry, or region of origin. As such, they developed broad panethnic identities as Latinos or Asians, problematic identities that were not always accepted by the immigrants themselves but that came to define how we think about the new immigration and, increasingly, how the second generation came to think about themselves. The evolution of these broad groupings, however, has a long history shaped by the ebbs and flows of migration as well as by the changing urban economy and political scene, subjects that will be explored in later chapters.

LATIN AMERICANS

As in other East Coast cities, the foundations of Boston's Latino communities date back to the 1950s, when the first wave of Puerto Rican migrants settled in the Commonwealth. Although small numbers of Puerto Ricans, Cubans, and other Latin Americans had come to Boston in the early twentieth century, settling alongside other immigrants in the South End, it was not until after World War II that large-scale migration of Puerto Rican workers gave rise to sizable Spanish-speaking communities. This labor migration first began during World War II when New England farm owners encountered critical labor shortages and received government encouragement to recruit seasonal workers from Puerto Rico. Farm labor shortages continued after the war, and growers signed contracts with government agencies to bring in additional workers from the island. The earliest groups came to pick shade tobacco in the Connecticut River valley between Hartford and Springfield, but migrants soon moved north and east, finding work in the vegetable farms, cranberry bogs, and nurseries of Massachusetts.[4]

Like Mexican farm workers in the West who gravitated to Sunbelt cities, Puerto Ricans in the Northeast soon found their way into industrial and service jobs in nearby towns and cities. Eager for a steady labor supply, employers tapped Puerto Rican family networks to recruit new workers from employees' hometowns and villages. Israel Maldonado, a Puerto

Rican migrant who arrived in Cambridge in the 1960s, went to work at the Fannie Farmer plant and soon brought his brother to work there as well. "When I worked in the candy factory, they asked me if I could bring people to work—they pay me $10 for each. I brought my brother and they gave me $20 because he did a good job." The NECCO plant and other local factories, he said, did the same. Many workers continued to practice seasonal or circular migration, but a growing number found steady employment and settled with their families in the Boston area. Although the island exodus slowed during periods of US economic recession, high unemployment and low wages on the island ensured a steady supply of migrants to the Bay State for decades.[5]

While Puerto Ricans came mainly for economic reasons, Cuban migrants to Boston arrived as political exiles fleeing the regime of Fidel Castro, who came to power in 1959. Under a program established in 1961, the United States welcomed thousands of anticommunist refugees from Cuba in the early 1960s, providing funds for the initial resettlement of mainly professional and technical groups with ties to US interests. A second wave of refugees, mainly working class and middle class, arrived on US-organized "Freedom Flights" from the island between 1963 and 1968. At that time, Boston was designated as one of several resettlement sites, so it was primarily from this group that Boston's Cuban American community originated. Unlike most other Latino migrants, Cubans benefited from federal refugee assistance programs that provided funds to ease their transition into American life. The middle-class background and occupational skills of many of these migrants, combined with substantial refugee assistance, likely explain the greater educational and occupational advancement of Cubans relative to other Latinos. By the early 1970s, Cubans made up about a quarter of the city's Latino population; a subsequent group of about fifteen hundred refugees would come via the Mariel boatlift in 1980. Over the next several decades, however, Boston's Cuban population declined as it fanned out to northern suburbs or moved to the booming Cuban metropolis in south Florida. Nevertheless, Cubans played a key role in founding a number of the area's Spanish-speaking businesses and communities (fig. 5).[6]

Arriving around the same time as the Cubans were migrants from the neighboring Dominican Republic. Like Puerto Rico and Cuba, the Dominican Republic had witnessed much US involvement, with the marines

FIGURE 5. Cuban refugees arrive at Logan Airport in 1962, some of the thousands who fled Cuba following the 1959 revolution led by Fidel Castro. Photo courtesy of *Boston Globe*.

occupying the country from 1916 to 1924 and invading again in 1965 after the assassination of Rafael Trujillo, a military-backed dictator who had ruled the country through corruption and torture for more than 30 years. Continuing political instability, falling wages, and high unemployment sent thousands of Dominicans to the Bay State, many of them coming initially from the northern Cibao region. While the migration stream of the 1960s and 1970s had been made up of more urban, educated, middle-class families, those arriving in the 1980s and 1990s tended to be working class.[7]

Thus, by the early 1980s, Boston's Latino community was overwhelmingly from the Caribbean islands of Puerto Rico, Cuba, and the Dominican Republic. This island-based population, however, would noticeably shift during the 1980s and 1990s with the influx of thousands of migrants from Central America. The rise of violent military-led governments in that region had sparked widespread popular resistance, and after the Sandinista takeover of Nicaragua in 1979 violence in the rest of Central America only grew. With the United States supporting anticommunist dictatorships in the region, civil war broke out in both El Salvador and Guatemala, ravaging the countryside and leaving civilians to face death squads that carried out mass killings and other human rights abuses. The ongoing war and repression produced a flood of refugees, many of whom headed to the United States. Because of its ties to ruling regimes in the region, however, the United States did not grant refugee status to Salvadorans or Guatemalans. Most entered the country illegally and headed to border states or other areas where local churches offered sanctuary to asylum-seekers.[8]

Roberto and Rosa Flores were among those who fled the growing wave of violence in the early 1980s. Employed as a foreman at a factory in eastern El Salvador, twenty-five-year-old Roberto joined with fellow workers in a union that opposed the Salvadoran government. Following several strikes and protests, the company suspended their wages, and the union launched a petition drive against government policies and repression. Death squads targeted those who had signed the petition, and eight of Roberto's coworkers were brutally killed. One night in 1981, men with guns came to the Floreses's house several times after midnight as Roberto, his wife, Rosa, and their two-year-old son hid inside. Hearing of other arrests that night, Roberto and his family fled out the back window and headed to the nearby city of San Miguel. In the early morning hours a bomb went off, destroying their home.

Fearing that the government would find him, Roberto set off across the border in 1983, made his way through Guatemala and Mexico, and then worked picking tomatoes in Matamoros to pay for passage across the US border. After he had worked for two months in Houston, his brother in Boston sent him a plane ticket to come north. Roberto soon found work in a restaurant at Government Center and after two years had saved enough to hire a coyote, or human smuggler, to bring his wife and two sons across the border. They later got political asylum and helped bring several siblings to the United States as well.[9]

Roberto arrived in Boston the same year that religious and human rights workers in Cambridge were organizing a sanctuary movement to help the flood of Central American refugees arriving in the region. Salvadorans made up the largest percentage of these migrants, followed by Guatemalans and Hondurans. The majority were workers and peasants, including indigenous Maya displaced from rural regions of Guatemala. Although the civil wars had ended in the early 1990s, economic upheaval, free trade policies, and gang violence in the postwar period continued to fuel outmigration that brought a steady stream of Central Americans to the region.[10]

During these years, Central Americans were joined by a growing Mexican population, as well as a surge of newcomers from Colombia and Brazil. In the late 1980s, Mexican migrants began moving beyond traditional areas of settlement in the West and Midwest, where labor markets had become saturated. The 1986 Immigration Reform and Control Act, which stipulated penalties for employers hiring undocumented immigrants, led to a tightening of the job market in traditional areas of settlement in the Southwest, pushing undocumented Mexicans to other areas of the country. For authorized Mexican immigrants who moved from California to Massachusetts during this period, drug- and gang-related violence in Los Angeles may have been another motivation. An influx of Colombian migrants further diversified the Latino community in the 1980s as the drug wars in that country terrorized citizens and crippled the government. A small number of skilled textile workers from Medellín had moved to Massachusetts in the 1960s; later, a much larger stream of migrants came from across the socioeconomic spectrum. Colombian professionals, technicians, and university students were among a small but growing stream of more affluent, educated migrants who came from South America during these years.[11]

Over the latter half of the twentieth century, the procession of new migrant groups from Latin America and the Caribbean transformed the Latino communities of the Boston area. While census figures are not an accurate reflection of this population (especially of the undocumented), they nevertheless suggest a phenomenal growth rate within the city of Boston, from fewer than 18,000 in 1970 to more than 107,000 in 2010. Although still heavily Puerto Rican in origin, these communities came to have sizable minorities of Cubans, Dominicans, and Central Americans. This diversification continued in the 1990s and 2000s as Mexicans, Colombians, and other South Americans settled in the area, some of them quite skilled and well educated (fig. 6). The majority of Latino migrants,

Makeup of City of Boston's Latino Population, 1980

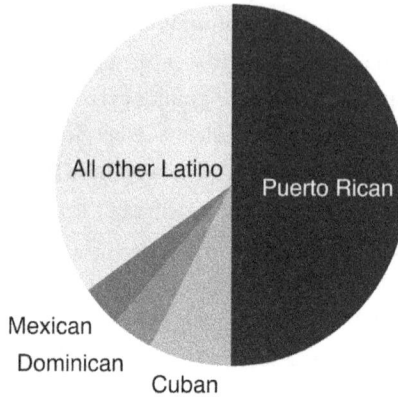

Makeup of City of Boston's Latino Population, 2010

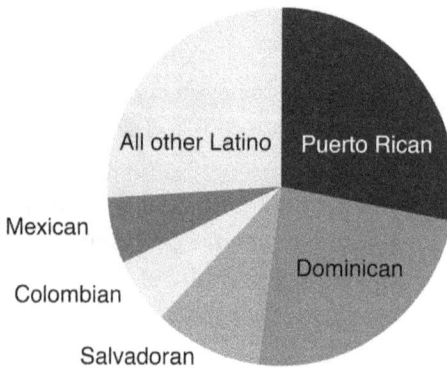

FIGURE 6. Origins of Latino population in City of Boston, 1980 and 2010. Source: US Census Bureau, *Census of Population and Housing*, 1980, Persons of Spanish Origin; *Census of Population and Housing*, 2010, Hispanic or Latino by Type.

however, arrived with relatively low levels of education and skill, giving them limited options in the local economy.[12]

The other notable category of Latin Americans who came during these years were the Brazilians. As Portuguese speakers, however, they do not fit comfortably into the Latino category; indeed, most Brazilians eschew the label, and very few identify themselves as such in the census. Coming initially from the city of Governador Valadares and the southeastern state of Minas Gerais, Brazilians first entered in significant numbers in the mid-1980s. The origin of this migration dates back to World War II, when Boston area engineers and technicians were posted to Minas Gerais to work on the mining and processing of sheet mica—a material used to insulate radio tubes and detonators. Ongoing contact between these Bostonians and the local residents of Minas Gerais laid the groundwork for later migration to New England. When the mining industry there went into decline in the 1960s, small numbers of Brazilians moved to Boston to attend schools and universities or to work seasonal jobs in Cape Cod. During Brazil's economic crisis of the 1980s, migration to the Boston area accelerated, drawing emigrants from Espírito Santo, São Paulo, and other parts of southern and southeastern Brazil. The newcomers included many well-educated, middle- and working-class Brazilians who had been battered by skyrocketing inflation and a failing currency. By 2005 their rapidly growing numbers made the Boston area the top destination for Brazilian immigrants to the United States. After that peak, however, the revival of the Brazilian economy and the impact of the Great Recession led to a drop-off in new arrivals and a significant return migration. Nevertheless, Brazilians continue to make up a substantial portion of Latin American migrants in greater Boston.[13]

ASIANS

Newcomers from Asia made up another major portion of the area's new immigrants, and, like Latinos, these immigrants became more ethnically and economically diverse over time. On the eve of World War II, Boston's Asian population was almost entirely Chinese, heavily male, and dwindling in number—there were fewer than 1,400 in 1940. Chinese exclusion had been in effect since 1882, and the immigration restriction laws of the 1920s confirmed that Asians, who were "ineligible for citizenship," would be barred from the United States. World War II and the early Cold War, however, reoriented US foreign policy toward China and gradually reversed these exclusionary measures. First, China's alliance with the United States during World War II prompted the US to repeal Chinese exclusion in 1943 and establish a small quota for Chinese immigrants. Then in 1945 the War Brides Act admitted the wives and children of US servicemen outside the quotas, a measure that allowed Chinese American servicemen to bring home their wives and families, and thus equalized the sex ratio among the younger generation. Moreover, in an effort to help rebuild China after the war, the US and Chinese governments cooperated in recruiting Chinese students and professionals for advanced training in engineering and other technical fields at American universities. Harvard and MIT were among those Massachusetts schools that enrolled a total of 140 Chinese students in 1952. After the Chinese Revolution, these so-called stranded students were offered refugee status, another indication of how Cold War politics shaped US immigration policy. Many of those in Boston opted to stay and went on to careers in science, engineering, and academia.[14]

After the People's Republic of China (PRC) curtailed emigration in the early 1950s, Chinese immigrants to Boston came exclusively via the Republic of China in Taiwan or the British colony of Hong Kong. Taiwanese immigrants, who included natives of the island as well as exiled republican elites from the mainland, were mostly university students and professionals who entered under special visas or skill preferences. Immigrants from Hong Kong, some of whom had slipped across the border from the PRC, also tended to have high levels of education and included many business owners. After the 1965 Immigration Act expanded visa allocations for Taiwan and Hong Kong, Chinese immigration increased, particularly among those seeking graduate and postgraduate education. Higher education in Taiwan and Hong Kong was extremely competitive, with very limited enrollment at the more prestigious schools. Foreign education thus became an attractive alternative, and some of these highly skilled students remained in the United States by finding jobs with American employers willing to sponsor them. Moreover, many Hong Kong residents immigrated to the US—including Boston—prior to the end of British rule in 1997 and the incorporation of the region into the PRC.[15]

Chinese migration shifted significantly in the last two decades of the twentieth century. The normalization of relations between the United States and the PRC resulted in the lifting of travel restrictions for mainland

Chinese and the creation of a separate visa allocation for the PRC in 1979. Immigration from the mainland grew rapidly and soon surpassed that of Taiwan and Hong Kong. Unlike the first wave of Chinese immigrants, who had come mainly from Guangdong Province, these newcomers hailed from all parts of the country, speaking different dialects but relying on Mandarin as a lingua franca. Their class and educational backgrounds varied as well. Many educated Chinese came with student or H-1 visas, and by the 1990s the PRC was one of the leading nations of origin for students at many Boston-area universities. There were also, however, large numbers of new working-class Chinese migrants who arrived with few skills and little English. The Chinese immigrant community thus developed a two-tiered social structure that included "uptown" Chinese professionals and business owners on the one hand and "downtown" low-income workers on the other.[16]

Although the Chinese made up the largest portion of newcomers from Asia, refugees from Vietnam and Cambodia also fueled the growth of Boston-area Asian American communities after 1975. Arriving between 1975 and 1992, Southeast Asians moved to the region in the wake of the Vietnam War, a thirty-year-long conflict that left millions dead and devastated the Vietnamese economy and countryside. Given America's central role in the war, and its unsatisfactory conclusion, the United States joined in taking responsibility for the postwar refugee crisis, ultimately resettling about a million Southeast Asians. Massachusetts was one of the top ten resettlement sites, with Boston and Lowell hosting the largest refugee concentrations. Nearly 20,000 Southeast Asian refugees arrived in the state between 1983 and 1995, making them the single largest refugee population to come in the twentieth century and one that would attract additional Vietnamese and Cambodian migrants in the years to come.[17]

The refugees came in three main waves over a twenty-year period. The first arrived shortly after the end of the war in 1975. Composed mainly of elite Vietnamese, many of these early arrivals had ties to the South Vietnamese government or the US military. Largely Catholic, this group included teachers, journalists, business owners, and landlords.[18] A much larger wave of refugees arrived in the early 1980s, following Vietnam's invasion of Cambodia in 1979 and the Chinese-Vietnamese border war that followed. The latter conflict accelerated the expulsion from Vietnam of ethnic Chinese, an entrepreneurial minority who had long been a target of resentment. Thousands fled the country in small, leaky boats, and many drowned or were attacked by pirates. At the same time, Vietnam's toppling of the Khmer Rouge regime in Cambodia led to a mass exodus of Cambodians who headed by land for the Thai border. In both cases, refugee camps were established in neighboring countries that struggled with the deluge of refugees. Responding to the crisis, the United States accepted refugees under the UN's Orderly Departure Program and with federal support provided under the Refugee Act of 1980.

The story of the Tran family provides a graphic example of the hardships faced by Vietnamese refugees during these years. In 1980, nineteen-year-old Tuan Tran and his brother Dung fled Saigon as war-induced chaos engulfed the city. Their father, a former South Vietnamese military intelligence officer, had been airlifted out by US forces in 1975 and was then living in Braintree, Massachusetts. Hoping to reunite with him, the two brothers headed for the coast, using gold coins to bribe their way across the county and paying $5,000 to get passage on a boat to Thailand. What should have been a one-day boat ride, however, turned into a month-long nightmare for the brothers and some forty other refugees packed onto a small fishing boat. The low point came when pirates attacked them, raping the women and robbing and terrorizing everyone on board. Later the engine failed, and the overcrowded boat began taking on water. Hoisting a blanket for a sail and bailing furiously, they made it to an island where they took refuge in caves. Eventually they were rescued and transported to Bangkok, where the brothers were detained in the Songkha refugee camp outside the city. After four months, their paperwork was approved and they departed for Boston to be reunited with their father. They later brought their mother to the United States, and the family settled in Quincy.[19]

Although the Tran family was part of a more elite group of Vietnamese émigrés, the second wave of refugees tended to be poorer, more ethnically diverse, and often severely traumatized. Those coming to Massachusetts included rural Vietnamese, ethnic Chinese from the cities, survivors of the Cambodian "killing fields," and small groups of Laotians and Hmong. The Cambodian influx was particularly great during these years, giving Massachusetts the second largest Cambodian population in the country after California. Moreover, the successful resettlement of these refugees provided crucibles for future immigrant communities in greater Boston that developed as the refugees brought family members to join them from their homelands and from other resettlement sites.[20]

A final surge of Vietnamese refugees arrived in the area in 1990–1992. This last group was made up of political detainees who had been released from Vietnamese prison camps and Amerasian children and their families. Both came under special refugee programs established in the late 1980s— the Humanitarian Operation and the Amerasian Homecoming Act. The latter was a humanitarian effort to resettle the children of Vietnamese women and American GIs; these children had been subject to much abuse and discrimination in Vietnam (particularly those of African ancestry). Once granted refugee status, however, they became "golden children" who might be adopted by other family members or even strangers eager to secure exit visas. The Amerasian influx had dropped off by the mid-1990s, as did the flow of Southeast Asian refugees more generally.[21]

While Southeast Asians and Chinese made up the bulk of the migration from Asia, smaller streams—of Indians and Koreans—also arrived in greater Boston. Both groups came with higher levels of education and technical skills, generally looking to pursue educational or professional opportunities. Indians, who had been excluded from the United States until 1946, started arriving in significant numbers after 1965, and particularly after 1990. Many came to work in the medical and computer industries via employer-sponsored H-1B visas. Established in 1990, the H-1B program allowed employers to hire highly skilled migrants in certain industries as temporary workers who could potentially later apply for permanent residency. In Massachusetts, the H-1B program was widely used in the technology sector and helps explain the rapid rise of the Indian population in the 1990s, at which time Indians became the fastest-growing foreign-born group in New England. The Korean community also showed marked growth during these years. The area's universities were a major draw for them, with fully a third enrolling in college or graduate school in 2000. For both Indians and Koreans, the expansion of high-level jobs, laboratories, and technical facilities at home had not kept pace with rising educational levels and expectations, thus prompting some to look abroad.[22]

Like Latinos, Asians settling in greater Boston in the last quarter of the twentieth century markedly increased their share of the immigrant population while becoming far more diverse in their origins. Asians made up only 8 percent of Boston's foreign-born population in 1970 but accounted for 26 percent by 2010, and they made up nearly a third of the metro area's foreign born. While the Chinese continued to be the largest Asian group, by 2010, immigrants from Vietnam, India, and Korea had made up sizable numbers of the region's Asian newcomers (fig. 7). The social and economic profile of Asian immigrants also varied, clustering at both the bottom and top ends of the education and skill spectrum.[23]

OTHER NEWCOMERS

In addition to Asia and Latin America, the Caribbean has sent a vast number of migrants to the Boston area. As noted above, many of these newcomers were from the Spanish Caribbean, but a significant portion came from islands formerly ruled by the French or British. Boston's long-standing commercial ties to the region had facilitated earlier migration from the British West Indies, a phenomenon that resumed after 1965, particularly from Jamaica, Trinidad, and Barbados. Even more numerically significant, however, was the growing infusion of Haitian immigrants to the city. Mainly professionals, artists, and intellectuals from the island's Catholic, French-speaking elite, Haitians began moving to Boston in the 1950s and 1960s for educational opportunities and to escape the repressive Duvalier regime. This first generation established a beachhead for middle-class and working-class Haitians arriving in the 1970s and 1980s, while even poorer, less educated migrants followed in the 1990s as political violence and instability continued to fuel the Haitian diaspora. Although many were able to enter the country through family reunification preferences, a growing proportion of those who fled Haiti's political violence in the 1980s and 1990s came as unauthorized migrants. Some were later granted asylum or temporary visas, including many who came to Boston following the devastating earthquake of 2010. Since the 1980s, new arrivals have come from both rural and urban parts of the island, include more Kreyol speakers, and are more religiously diverse. Arriving over a period of more than fifty years, Haitians have become one the largest foreign-born groups in the city, and greater Boston has become one of the top three destinations for Haitian immigrants to the United States.[24]

Black immigrants from the Caribbean settled alongside burgeoning communities of Cape Verdean immigrants whose home islands had won independence from Portugal in 1975. The Republic of Cape Verde thus gained its own national quota and sent a steady stream of displaced farmers and workers to Boston, Brockton, and southeastern Massachusetts. In the late

Makeup of Asian Foreign Born in City of Boston, 1980

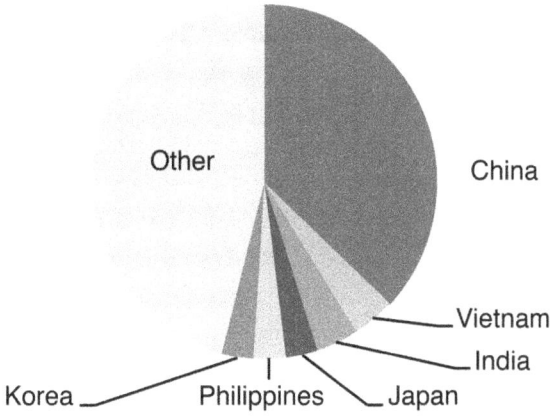

Makeup of Asian Foreign Born in City of Boston, 2010

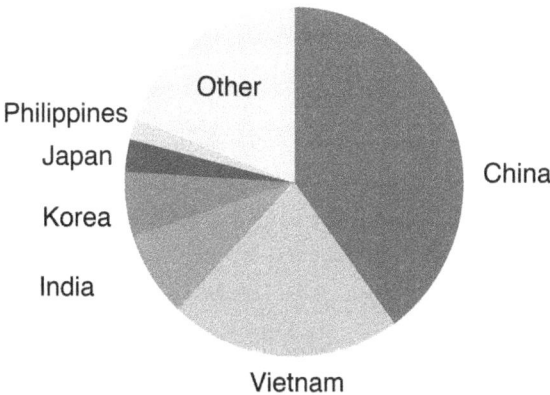

FIGURE 7. Origins of Asian foreign-born in City of Boston, 1980 and 2010. Source: US Census Bureau, *Census of Population and Housing,* 1980, Country of Birth of the Foreign Born; US Census Bureau, American FactFinder, 2008–2012 American Community Survey 5-year estimates: Place of Birth for the Foreign-Born Population.

1980s and 1990s, new African refugee groups began arriving from Ethiopia, Liberia, Somalia, and Sudan. They included many urban professionals and elites but also poor and traumatized rural populations (including former child soldiers). Moreover, under the 1990 Immigration Act, the US government established a new diversity lottery for visas that allowed underrepresented national groups—including Nigerians, Moroccans, and other Africans—to come to Massachusetts in greater numbers. In 2010, African immigrants and refugees made up 10 percent of Boston's foreign-born population and 8 percent of the foreign-born population of the metro area. These newcomers, together with black immigrants from the Caribbean, have profoundly affected the composition of Boston's black community. In 1970, immigrants accounted for only 6 percent of Boston's black population; by 2010, the foreign born made up more than 30 percent of the city's black population and more than a third of blacks in the metro area.[25]

Although African, Asian, and Caribbean/Latino migration made up the majority of the newcomer population, select groups of European immigrants continued to arrive in Boston after 1960, mainly from Portugal, Ireland, and the former Soviet Union. Building on the large Portuguese American communities founded earlier in the century, several thousand Azoreans moved to the area after 1957, when a massive earthquake struck the islands. Soon afterward, Congress approved the Azorean Refugee Act, authorizing visas for thousands of refugees, many of whom moved near to family members in New England. After 1965, Azoreans and mainland Portuguese took advantage of additional quota slots under the Immigration and Nationality Act to continue the exodus to Massachusetts. Another older immigrant group that saw a post-1965 resurgence was the Irish, who came in a brief but much-discussed influx during the 1980s, when skyrocketing unemployment sent young Irish job seekers abroad. After 1990 they also benefited from the diversity lottery that provided visas to "underrepresented" groups—quite an irony given Boston's history.[26]

By far the largest group of white Europeans coming to the area after 1965 were refugees from the former Soviet Union. Fleeing anti-Semitism, limited career and educational opportunities, and government harassment and censorship, Jews in the Soviet Union pressed for the right to emigrate beginning in the 1960s. The Soviet government, however, limited emigration to a trickle, and only a small number arrived in Massachusetts in the 1970s. But under sustained political pressure from the West, Soviet premier

Mikhail Gorbachev lifted travel restrictions in 1987 and a surge of emigration followed. From 1987 to 1992, between 1,000 and 2,500 Soviet refugees settled in Massachusetts annually, mainly in the Boston area. Many of these migrants came with high levels of education and skills in fields such as computer technology, medicine, and engineering, and they proved to be some of the region's most economically successful newcomers.[27]

FROM WHENCE THEY CAME

Like earlier immigrants to Boston, more recent migrants have faced demographic and economic changes in their homelands that propelled them to seek new opportunities abroad. Post–World War II developments in the Caribbean, for instance, echoed earlier transformations in Ireland and Italy, where population growth and agricultural decline left many residents mired in poverty. Such was the case in Puerto Rico, where the US government's postwar industrial development program, Operation Bootstrap, undermined the agricultural economy while failing to create sufficient industrial jobs for a growing population. Puerto Ricans looking to support their families left the island in search of better-paying jobs, which were simply not available at home. Similar patterns of population growth, agricultural decline, and industrial underdevelopment fueled out-migration in the Dominican Republic, the Cape Verde Islands, and other former colonial outposts.[28]

These well-known effects of modernization have been compounded in recent years by globalization of the economy and culture. While earlier immigrants learned of American living standards through migrants' letters and visits, images of American consumer culture since the 1960s have been broadcast across the globe through television, movies, radio, and the Internet. Rising expectations for modern amenities and consumer goods have thus run headlong into stagnant local economies that failed to provide jobs to meet peoples' needs and aspirations. While earlier immigrants used their US earnings to buy land or support family members at home, more recent migrants have also felt pressure to deliver TVs, refrigerators, brand-name clothing, and a wide range of other consumer goods to their families both here and abroad.[29]

Moreover, new global economic forces such as the World Bank, the International Monetary Fund (IMF), and free trade agreements have deepened the economic woes of many developing nations. In Colombia in the early 1990s, for example, an economic restructuring plan devised by the IMF to globalize the Colombian economy resulted in business closings, skyrocketing unemployment, and rising poverty rates that drove many abroad. In Brazil, rising international interest rates on the foreign debt and an IMF austerity program in the 1980s resulted in massive inflation that fueled emigration. More recently, the North American and Central American Free Trade Agreements, while creating jobs in some sectors, eliminated trade barriers, thus allowing the United States to flood Mexico and Central America with cheaper food products that put many local farmers out of business. Throughout the region, displaced agricultural workers as well as low-paid workers in foreign-owned industries often opted to go north for better-paying employment.[30]

Economic conditions were not, however, the only factor: war and political repression also fueled the new migration. This is, of course, a familiar story in immigration history. The plight of the Irish under British rule, anti-Semitism in Russia and eastern Europe, and the Armenian genocide were some of the major causes of earlier migration to the Bay State. With the rise of US power around the globe, however, the treatment of immigrants and refugees became more closely tied with American strategic and diplomatic interests. From the 1950s through the 1980s, the larger geopolitical context of the Cold War was particularly influential in shaping migration patterns. US efforts to contain the Soviet threat led to wars and diplomatic efforts designed to thwart the spread of communism and bolster America's noncommunist allies. The refugee streams from Southeast Asia, Cuba, and the Soviet Union were the most obvious examples of immigration growing out of Cold War policies—namely, the Vietnam War, the stand-off with Fidel Castro's regime in Cuba, and US advocacy of Jewish emigration from the Soviet Union.[31]

Less obvious, but no less important, was the US history of intervention and support for repressive anticommunist regimes in the Caribbean and Latin America. Fearful of the rise of "another Cuba" in the Western Hemisphere, the United States invaded the Dominican Republic in 1965 following the assassination of dictator Rafael Trujillo and subsequently supported emigration as a means of stabilizing the island's economy and government.[32] In neighboring Haiti, the US reluctantly backed the brutally repressive regimes of François and Jean-Claude Duvalier as a bulwark against communism in the region, but wholesale human rights abuses there sent thousands into exile. Later in the 1980s, the United States aided military-backed regimes in Guatemala and El Salvador in their wars against left-wing guerrillas. Fleeing violence and repression in these countries, Central Americans and Haitians found the US government notably unreceptive to their petitions for asylum. Their treatment stood in stark contrast to the generous government assistance offered to Cuban, Southeast Asian, and Soviet refugees.[33] Although the groups were received quite differently, all of them came from countries that had been affected by the vicissitudes of the Cold War and the strategic aims of US policymakers.

Migration patterns were also shaped by Cold War initiatives designed to strengthen the scientific and technical expertise of the United States and its allies. The emphasis on education and skill preferences in postwar immigration law led to a worldwide recruitment, or "brain drain," of technical talent. While such efforts were seen as vital to winning the arms and space races of the early Cold War, granting foreign nationals access to American higher education also served as a means of cultivating good relations with US allies and nonaligned nations (and challenging Soviet allegations of US racism during the civil rights unrest of the 1950s and 1960s). The recruitment of foreign talent continued, however, even after the Cold War ended. American businesses successfully argued that the recruitment of high-tech foreign expertise was essential to the country's leadership in fields such as computer science, medicine, and biotechnology. The number of visa slots reserved for such individuals was expanded under the H-1B program of the 1990 Immigration Act. That provision has been particularly important in the Boston area, with its concentration of universities, medical centers, and high-tech industries. According to the Massachusetts Technology Collaborative, one-third of immigrants arriving in the state from 1990 to 1996 were employed in highly skilled occupations, compared with only 25 percent nationally.[34] This educated and highly skilled segment of the migrant population had no real counterpart in the city's earlier immigration waves, which were dominated by the poor and unskilled.

In some cases, elite Cold War migrants constituted the leading edge of a much larger, more heterogeneous flow of migrants from the same country or region. Haitian and Chinese immigrants of the 1950s and 1960s, for example, were pioneers in what would become a more diverse stream that also included poor and working-class migrants in the 1980s and 1990s. Refugee groups followed this pattern as well, with the elite allies of anticommunist governments in Cuba and Vietnam paving the way for poorer refugees who later joined them in Boston. In such cases, family and community networks were critical in facilitating migration. Historians have documented the importance of such chain migration among earlier immigrants, but since 1965, the US government has reinforced these networks through family reunification policies that enabled permanent residents and naturalized citizens to sponsor their family members. The results of such chain migration have been evident in the distinct clusters of migrants in greater Boston who hail from the same town or region: Miraflores in the Dominican Republic, Minas Gerais in Brazil, and Yucuaiquín in El Salvador, to name just a few.[35]

Such strong connections to particular towns or regions meant that some immigrants retained hopes of returning or retiring to their homelands after years of living and working in Massachusetts. Like earlier European migrants, who returned to Italy or Portugal, more recent immigrants from places like Brazil and Ireland moved back as the political or economic climate of their home countries improved. Others, like those from Haiti or El Salvador, often expressed a strong desire to return but were deterred by ongoing political strife or economic crises back home. For them, the desire to go back became "the myth of return," especially after extended periods in the United States. One longtime Haitian immigrant explained the dilemma this way: "I would love to return . . . but I think I have work to do in Boston. Once you have children, once you get married, once you own property, it's hard to go back." But staying in Boston, he continued, "did not mean that we don't support Haiti. We support Haiti 100 percent, just like the Jews support Israel." For him and many other immigrants, contributing financial, technical, and professional support to their communities back home became a way of staying involved with their homeland while settling permanently in Massachusetts. As a Latina immigrant explained in the 1990s, "Maybe we're realizing the dream of going home was a dream and this is the reality."[36]

THE JOURNEY TO BOSTON

While family and community networks have remained central to the migration experience, the ordeal of long-distance travel and resettlement has changed dramatically. For many newcomers, lengthy ship voyages in steerage have been replaced by relatively short plane flights that can reunite family members within hours. The convenience of air travel also makes return visits or circular migration more feasible, allowing migrants to stay in closer touch with family and friends back home. The exceptions have been those who have come without documents or as refugees. For many of them, the trip to Boston was a one-way affair; returning home was too dangerous, or undesirable, or simply impossible.

The refugee experience has been distinctive in many ways. As in the past, refugees from war, famine, or natural disasters have often faced horrifying ordeals in their homelands or while leaving the country. Exiles from Southeast Asia, Central America, Africa, and other regions have witnessed warfare and bloodshed on a mass scale, many of them losing close family members.[37] Although the perils and trauma of their experiences were similar to those of earlier refugees, the rise of international human rights law and organizations since World War II has helped facilitate refugee evacuation and resettlement. Working with the UN high commissioner for refugees, the United States resettled several million refugees in the late twentieth century, including tens of thousands in greater Boston. In the 1970s and 1980s especially, the federal government together with religious and voluntary agencies resettled large numbers, linking them with local sponsors and helping them access federal and state aid programs for housing, English classes, employment, and medical benefits. Under the Refugee Act of 1980, passed in response to the Southeast Asian "boat people" crisis of the late 1970s, the federal government provided three years of cash and medical assistance for refugees, although the eligibility period for such benefits was soon reduced, dropping to 18 months in 1982, 12 months in 1988, and 8 months by 1991. Many of the local communities that hosted the largest concentrations of refugees found their resources hard pressed. In response, the Massachusetts legislature created the Gateway Cities Program in 1986 to subsidize English-language classes, translators, and other services to help transition immigrants and refugees in local towns and cities with large foreign-born populations.[38]

Partially as a result of these immigrant-friendly programs, Boston-area refugee communities grew rapidly, attracting migrants from other resettlement sites around the country. This pattern of "secondary migration" was especially common among refugees of the 1970s, whom the government had deliberately dispersed around the country. Those placed in rural areas or in areas with few other migrants faced a difficult adjustment. One Cambridge historian described the plight of a Vietnamese refugee she interviewed in

1975, Nguyen Thi Anh, who had been resettled in a small Vermont town. Later the woman arrived at her doorstep, suitcase in hand: "She, her husband and her children had come to Boston. . . . She said that she had had 'no problem' with the sponsors, but that she and her husband were very lonely in Vermont. They had no neighbors, and the nearest village had a population of a few hundred in the winter months." Anh and her family initially stayed with other Vietnamese in the area but soon found an apartment. Such stories were typical of refugee communities in the 1970s and 1980s, when Southeast Asian refugees from California, New York, Georgia, Michigan, and Minnesota relocated to Massachusetts in large numbers.[39]

This pattern of secondary migration, however, was not limited to refugees. Large numbers of Haitians, Dominicans, and Colombians came to the Boston area after initially settling in New York or Miami, the major immigrant gateways on the East Coast. Some were put off by the poverty and crime of New York's low-income neighborhoods; others were attracted by Boston's colleges and universities, hoping that the city's reputation for higher education would bode well for their children. Most commonly, though, immigrants came to the area to unite with family members. Finding inexpensive flights to Florida, or initial work offers in New York, became the first step in rejoining spouses, parents, children, or siblings in Boston.[40]

For those who could not enter under programs aiming at family reunification or skill preferences, or who were not recognized as refugees by the US government, gaining entry to the United States could take many years. A growing number of immigrants thus came without authorization, especially after the mid-1980s. The Immigration and Naturalization Service estimated that there were 53,000 undocumented immigrants in Massachusetts in 1990, rising to 87,000 in the year 2000. One reason for this growth was the new flow of unauthorized refugees from Haiti and Central America, many of whom were fleeing violence, war, and political persecution. But because the Reagan administration largely rejected their claims for asylum, many Salvadorans and Guatemalans stayed without authorization, as did many Haitians. Economic factors were key for other undocumented groups, such as the Irish and Chinese, who came seeking jobs during the economic upswing of the mid-1980s—the so-called Massachusetts Miracle. The amnesty provision of the 1986 Immigration Reform and Control Act helped some of these migrants adjust their status—at least those who could prove that they had lived in the United States continuously since 1982.[41]

For groups that had arrived in large numbers in earlier years, then, the steady increase of naturalized citizens and the surge of the newly authorized population under the 1986 amnesty provided a foundation for future chain migration. Because citizens could bring over their immediate family members and parents, outside of the national quotas, the volume of authorized migration for these groups grew. By contrast, Brazilians and others who arrived mainly after 1982 were at a distinct disadvantage. One study of Brazilians in greater Boston indicated that approximately 70 percent of adult migrants were undocumented in 2007, and that the vast majority had arrived after 1986. A parallel study of Dominicans in the area found that only 8 percent were undocumented. The longer history of Dominican migration to the region—dating back to the late 1950s—coupled with the sharp spike of newly authorized immigrants in the post-amnesty years, likely explains this dramatic difference in legal status.[42]

For migrants coming to the United States illegally, the trip here has become increasingly costly, difficult, and dangerous. In the early years, the most common path to the United States was via airplane with a valid tourist or temporary work visa. Known as "visa overstayers," such newcomers arrived legally but then remained in the country after their visas had expired. This mode of entry was common among Irish immigrants in the 1980s—for example, many came as tourists or on temporary work permits for seasonal jobs on Cape Cod. Some Chinese immigrants also overstayed tourist visas, but some of the poorest came on ships run by human traffickers. In the 1990s the apprehension of several boatloads of Fujianese migrants destined for Massachusetts, and the kidnapping of two Chinatown workers, led to extensive publicity about these smuggling operations. In these cases, migrants testified to paying as much as $28,000 for their passage and being confined in the dark holds of ships for two months with minimal food and water. Chinatown residents reported that undocumented men were forced to work off their debts through long shifts at below-minimum-wage jobs and faced robbery or kidnapping if they did not meet their payments. A 1996 sting operation put some of these traffickers out of business, and, more important, increased coastal security following 9/11 made water-based landings more difficult. Increased government scrutiny has also made it harder to secure tourist and work visas, making overstayers less common than they once had been.[43]

Heightened security measures have forced many unauthorized

immigrants to attempt dangerous border crossings via Mexico. This has long been the main path of entry for Central Americans and Brazilians coming to Boston, but since 9/11 it has become more common for other groups as well. At the same time, the militarization of the border since 2001 has made the journey more difficult and dangerous. Sociologist Blanca Alvarado, who interviewed thirty-eight undocumented Central American women in Chelsea, offered some of the most detailed accounts of their crossings. The women she interviewed in 2005–2006 had crossed the border as young adults or children, nearly all with coyotes. Paying an average of $5,400, many ended up making two or three attempts before crossing successfully. The women suffered the usual hardships of hunger, thirst, and exposure, but several of them were also raped or robbed by the coyotes, who threatened to abandon them in the desert, turn them over to the US Border Patrol, or have their undocumented families in the United States deported. Often deeply traumatized by the border crossing experience, the women still had to pay back the large sums they had borrowed from family members, taking up to three years to settle their debts.[44]

Border crossers were also targeted by kidnappers in Mexico who demanded large ransoms from their families in the United States. In the case of Central Americans and Brazilians, who had to cross more than one border, the potential hazards were multiplied. And smugglers went after family members when a migrant's debts could not be paid. In 2004, Brazilian migrant Josias Peres was killed in an auto shop accident in Marlborough shortly after arriving illegally in the United States. Back in Valadares, Brazil, Peres's sister and eighty-four-year-old mother faced the loss of their home when smugglers claimed it as collateral for Josias's unpaid debt.[45]

The dangers and hardships endured by undocumented immigrants and their families have rivaled those of earlier immigrants, who faced horrendous ordeals escaping their homelands and crossing the ocean. But except for the Chinese, none of those earlier immigrants had been systematically barred from entering the United States prior to World War I, and their hardships were later celebrated in populist folklore. By contrast, unauthorized immigrants of recent years remain pariahs in mainstream American culture and have often been blamed for a variety of the country's ills. Such unwelcoming attitudes were also a problem for certain refugee groups, particularly those from Southeast Asia and other areas where there was extensive US military involvement. Ironically, as we will see, those new-comers who faced some of the hardest pre-migration and migration experiences—from which they suffered prolonged emotional and psychological distress—sometimes received the worst receptions.

Fortunately, the majority of Boston-area immigrants did not arrive under such difficult circumstances. Some have come bringing skills and education, easing their transition into mainstream society. Others have had a more challenging struggle and have depended heavily on their families and friends and the emerging ethnic communities of greater Boston. The diversity of these growing settlements is as varied as the immigrants themselves and is the subject to which we now turn.

CHAPTER 3

The Metropolitan Diaspora

Reinaldo Restrepo arrived from Colombia in the mid-1980s and soon found work in a Boston restaurant. A few years later, Restrepo and his family moved to East Boston, where Latino immigrants had begun to settle. A decade later, they had saved enough money for a down payment on a three-decker on Marion Street. Living downstairs, the Restrepos rented the third floor to newly arrived cousins from Medellín. Their pooled resources paid the mortgage while providing a comfortable home in a growing Latino community. Over the next two decades, the Restrepos' neighborhood—once plagued by boarded-up storefronts—would fill up with new immigrant residents and Latino-owned shops and small businesses.[1]

The Restrepos' experience in East Boston was typical of thousands of immigrant families that were settling in the city's older ethnic neighborhoods. Their collective strategies for home buying would have seemed quite familiar to the Irish and Italian immigrants who had settled in East Boston a hundred years before. Bostonians today often remark that new immigrants are following in the footsteps of the old, inheriting the triple-deckers and neighborhoods that once housed European newcomers. In reality, though, the settlement story has been more complicated, and it has changed markedly over the last half century. While newcomers have moved into many of the region's old ethnic neighborhoods and industrial communities, they have also gravitated to surrounding suburbs, including some of the more affluent outlying areas. Ultimately, new immigrants have displayed a wider range of settlement patterns than earlier groups, but the ability to pursue these options has varied widely by class, race, and ethnicity.

Even when newcomers settled in the old immigrant quarters of Boston, Cambridge, or Chelsea, they did not always do so for the same reasons as their predecessors. Although family, ethnic, and religious ties were important for both groups, the settlement patterns of new immigrants have been shaped by a very different economic and political context. Proximity to work has been less important than it was for old immigrants, while housing markets and government-sponsored refugee programs (often in association with local religious groups) have been more critical. Nor have most migrants been able to stay where immigrants settled prior to the 1980s, as redevelopment and gentrification have steadily pushed newcomers out of the core neighborhoods of Boston and Cambridge. Indeed, the most striking historical trend in immigrant settlement in the last thirty years has been the rapid diffusion of newcomers to the region's suburban towns and cities.

Moreover, suburban settlement among new immigrants has not always resulted in assimilation and upward mobility. Within the metro area, immigrants have moved into an array of outlying communities, from impoverished old mill towns to some of the region's most affluent suburbs. For those who moved to the latter areas, access to the suburban dream has been realized with unprecedented speed; for others, it remains less accessible. Still others have carved out a path in between, seeking homes in the older industrial towns and cities that surround Boston and helping to revitalize and reinvent those economies. There—as well as in many outlying city neighborhoods—new immigrants have been critical in replenishing population, revitalizing declining areas, and reversing some of the downward trends that have plagued greater Boston since World War II.

POINTS OF ENTRY: THE EARLY YEARS

The new migrant settlements of greater Boston first began to take shape in the 1960s as streams of Puerto Rican, Portuguese, Chinese, and other newcomers began to flow into the area. Unlike earlier waves of immigrants, few of these later arrivals settled in Boston's quintessential old ethnic neighborhoods—the North and West Ends. Although a small stream of Italian immigrants did continue to arrive in the North End, that picturesque ethnic quarter was evolving into a tourist mecca of restaurants and cafes where renovated apartments and waterfront condominiums were more likely to attract investment bankers than unskilled immigrants. Likewise, the old Jewish/Italian quarter of the West End was long gone, razed by the city in a 1950s urban renewal project that gave rise to luxury apartment towers, municipal offices, and parking lots. Other old core neighborhoods, such as Chinatown and the South End, continued to act as portals for new immigrants, but the redevelopment of the West End and the gentrification of the North End were precursors of a larger urban transformation that would affect numerous parts of Boston and Cambridge in the late twentieth century.

When possible, new immigrants tended to move near existing ethnic enclaves, where they shared common language and cultural traditions. Many of the region's new Latino communities, for example, were founded by Puerto Ricans who had left agricultural work to find manufacturing jobs in Boston and surrounding cities. For the most part they settled with longtime Spanish-speaking residents who lived around West Newton Street in Boston's South End, a small Spanish Caribbean community that dated back to the 1890s. Others moved to Jamaica Plain or across the Charles River to Cambridgeport, areas that had been home to a small number of Puerto Rican domestic workers in the 1950s. Settlements also sprang up in declining industrial towns such as Lynn and Chelsea, where factory owners recruited Puerto Rican workers in the 1960s. During these years, Catholic Charities established refugee centers for newly arriving Cuban refugees in several of these Spanish-speaking settlements. In all of these areas relatively inexpensive housing became available as the younger generation of white ethnics left for the suburbs in the 1960s and 1970s.[2]

As native-born whites moved out, the Puerto Rican population grew and was diversified by a growing stream of Cuban refugees and Dominican migrants. In the mid-1980s, Salvadorans and Guatemalans arrived in growing numbers, particularly to Cambridge, where in 1984 the Old Cambridge Baptist Church declared itself a sanctuary for those seeking asylum. Harboring a young Salvadoran woman who had fled multiple rounds of torture by state authorities, church members held a two-week

FIGURE 8. Fleeing civil war and violent repression in their homeland, an indigenous Guatemalan couple and their five children (hiding their identity to avoid retribution against their families back home) take refuge in the Old Cambridge Baptist Church in 1984. The church was a focal point of the local asylum movement, and many Central Americans subsequently settled in Cambridge and Somerville. Photo courtesy of *Boston Globe.*

vigil with her and sponsored dozens of public forums in which she and others gave testimony of their ordeal (fig. 8). The following year, the city council voted to make Cambridge a sanctuary city, meaning that it would not cooperate with federal agents seeking to deport unauthorized migrants. St. Mary's Catholic Church in Central Square, which served the nearby Puerto Rican / Dominican community, was also instrumental in providing aid, housing, and services for new Central American arrivals (see chapter 7). Although there would be tensions between Latino groups over the years, their common language, religion, and, in some cases, Caribbean origins made initially for cordial relations. As a result, the early Puerto Rican settlements provided a vital foundation for the region's emerging panethnic Latino communities.[3]

A similar evolution characterized the area's Portuguese-speaking communities. After the 1958 earthquake in the Azores, a new wave of Azorean migrants settled in the older Portuguese American communities of East Cambridge and Somerville. In addition, many from the island of Santa

Maria moved to Hudson, a town 30 miles west of Boston, to which the Portuguese American–owned Hudson Shoe Factory had drawn several thousand Azorean migrants over the years. Beginning in the 1960s, these same communities began to attract a few Brazilian migrants who trickled into the Boston area. Most settled in the Portuguese sections of Cambridge and Somerville, where a common language and access to Portuguese-speaking churches, community organizations, and bilingual services facilitated their adjustment. Carlos Ferreira, pastor of the Assemblies of God Alliance, a Brazilian church in Somerville, explained that Brazilian migrants "started coming here because they found some people speaking Portuguese . . . . There was a lot of *amizade* [friendship] in the beginning." Other areas of older Portuguese settlement, such as in Allston and Framingham, would see Brazilian communities take hold there in later years.[4]

While linguistic ties facilitated the settlement of Spanish- and Portuguese-speaking migrants, religious affiliation proved more important for early Haitian settlers. Coming mainly from middle-class and professional backgrounds, Haitians arriving in the 1950s and 1960s settled mainly in south Dorchester, which was then predominantly white. As Regine Jackson has shown, these migrants did not settle with African Americans in Roxbury, perhaps in an attempt at self-distancing based on class and ethnicity. More important, she found that Catholic churches became magnets for Haitian settlement and community building. As one migrant explained, "It wasn't like New York where there were so many Haitians; and we didn't want to live in the projects with the blacks. The Church was one of the only things here that was part of our culture too." Despite initial hostility toward them from white parishioners, Haitian immigrants clustered around St. Leo's and St. Matthew's Churches in Dorchester and, later, St. Angela's in Mattapan. Like the Irish and Italian immigrants who had occupied these parishes before them, Haitians developed a sense of place around a faith-based community that was territorially rooted.[5]

For most Chinese immigrants arriving in the postwar period, the benefits of possessing higher education and occupational skills—combined with waning anti-Asian sentiment in some quarters—allowed a small number of newcomers to move directly into the suburbs. As noted in chapter 2, many Chinese arriving prior to 1979 were either skilled professionals or came to attend local universities. Mainly from Taiwan and Hong Kong, they did not speak the Toishanese dialect of most Chinatown residents, and they tended to live on college campuses or in student neighborhoods. Some Chinese graduates of Harvard and MIT went on to become permanent residents after finding employment with local companies. Earning good salaries, Chinese technical and professional workers tended to settle in Allston-Brighton, Cambridge, or in nearby suburbs such as Lexington, Newton, and Brookline. There they were joined by a growing number of second-generation Chinese Americans whose professional achievements or business success had enabled them to move to more prosperous suburbs. Both groups, however, regularly visited and retained strong connections to Chinatown, which continued to serve as the region's Asian cultural center. Beginning in the late 1960s, less skilled immigrants from Hong Kong and, later, ethnic Chinese newcomers from Vietnam began settling in Chinatown. For the latter, anti-Chinese resentment among the Vietnamese and long-standing cultural and linguistic ties to Guangdong Province (also the home region of Chinatown's old settlers) made the downtown neighborhood a logical destination.[6]

For most Southeast Asian arrivals, however, federally sponsored refugee programs proved more important in shaping initial settlement patterns. In response to the flood of refugees in the late 1970s, resettlement programs were established under the Indochinese Refugee Acts of 1975–1977 and later under the Refugee Act of 1980. Federal funds for refugee resettlement were channeled through government-approved voluntary agencies (known as VOLAGS), mainly religious and refugee organizations that worked with local churches and individuals to find housing and sponsors for refugee families. In metro Boston, some of the key agencies were the International Rescue Committee, the International Institute, the Lutheran Immigration and Refugee Service, and Catholic Charities. With the aid of the Lutheran and Catholic agencies, Southeast Asian refugees were sometimes resettled around sponsoring churches, such as Our Savior's Lutheran Church in East Boston and St. Peter's Parish in Dorchester, which subsequently developed refugee and immigrant assistance programs.[7]

In many other instances, though, refugees were dispersed in and around the city, wherever low-cost housing and public transportation were available. Southeast Asian refugees were thus resettled in Chinatown, Allston-Brighton, South Boston, East Boston, Dorchester, and Charlestown, as well as in older inner-ring suburbs such as Chelsea, Revere, Lynn, and Quincy. As the local Vietnamese population grew, however, refugees soon left some neighborhoods and clustered in others. Moreover, new migrants arriving in the 1980s were permitted to settle with family members already in the area who served as sponsors. By the mid-1980s, Allston-Brighton and the Fields Corner area of Dorchester had emerged as significant centers of Vietnamese settlement, while East Boston, Chelsea, Lynn, and Revere became home to newly arrived Cambodians.[8]

Why this happened is not entirely clear, but it seems likely that the presence of government-subsidized mutual assistance associations (MAAs) was an important factor. The formation of these ethnically based associations was reminiscent of the earlier mutual aid societies founded by European and Chinese immigrants in the nineteenth and early twentieth centuries. But the more recent organizations were created with the explicit support of federal and state governments to aid new refugee populations that had few ethnic or family ties to US residents.

The promotion of mutual assistance first began in 1976 under a federal task force charged with overseeing Indochinese refugees; a few years later, the Refugee Act of 1980 established a permanent federal agency, the Office of Refugee Resettlement, that made mutual assistance a key component of resettlement policy. The Office of Refugee Resettlement called for the creation of state-level refugee agencies, leading to the creation of the Massachusetts Governor's Council on Refugees in 1983 and the Massachusetts Office of Refugees and Immigrants (MORI) in 1985. Charged with coordinating resettlement efforts in the state, MORI actively encouraged the formation of grassroots mutual assistance organizations to provide services in a culturally and linguistically sensitive manner. This approach reflected the political legacy of the antipoverty programs of the 1960s and 1970s, adapting some of the identity-based and multiservice organizing strategies of black, Latino, and Asian American communities and applying them to new refugee populations. Between 1982 and 1994, Massachusetts would receive $1.2 million in federal funding to promote the growth of MAAs and other community-based refugee services.[9]

These mutual assistance groups became important anchors for new Southeast Asian refugee communities in Boston and adjoining cities. In Boston, the rise of MAAs such as the Indochinese Refugee Assistance Program in Brighton and the Vietnamese American Civic Association in Fields Corner provided a service nexus around which sizable Vietnamese communities developed. Similarly, the Cambodian Association of Massachusetts provided services for growing refugee communities in East Boston and Chelsea. In Revere and Lynn, Cambodian settlements took root around Khmer Buddhist temples that had been founded by refugees in the early 1980s.[10]

Connections between religious institutions, federal agencies, and refugee settlement were even more evident in the case of Jews from the Soviet Union. With the onset of Jewish emigration in the late 1970s, the federal Office of Refugee Resettlement partnered with Jewish Family and Children's Service (JFCS), a descendant of the Ladies Aid Society founded to help earlier Jewish immigrants (see chapter 1). JFCS worked with area synagogues to organize resettlement committees and find sponsors for refugee families. In fact, some of the volunteers were themselves post–World War II refugees who had been helped by JFCS in the 1940s and 1950s. Refugees were settled primarily in Allston-Brighton, Framingham, and Lynn. On the North Shore, JFCS secured a cluster of apartments near downtown Lynn, a city that had housed earlier generations of Jewish shoe workers. One particular apartment building on Newhall Street (where some of the sponsors themselves had first settled years before) contained so many Soviet émigrés that it was dubbed "the Russian Hilton."[11]

An extensive array of ESL, job training, and other services offered through Jewish agencies, together with the personal attention and contacts available through sponsors and synagogues, helped Soviet refugees move into the mainstream relatively quickly. Equipped with higher education and job skills, many soon dispersed from these settlements to suburbs such as Brookline, Newton, Swampscott, and Marblehead, where there were substantial Jewish populations. In the case of the Soviet refugees, then, settlement patterns were shaped by a long-standing tradition of Jewish mutual assistance, but one that was aided by federal programs and funding.[12]

The settlement of Caribbean and African immigrants in Boston was also shaped by government-backed programs. Because most migrants from the Caribbean and Cape Verde Islands did not qualify under federal refugee programs, they tended to settle in whatever neighborhoods were available to black renters and home buyers in a racially segregated market. In the 1950s and early 1960s, when migrants from Haiti, the West Indies, and Cape Verde began to arrive, those areas were primarily in the South End, Roxbury, and in small pockets of Dorchester. Beginning in 1968, however, the area of black settlement expanded significantly under a federally backed home loan program administered by a group of local banks known as the Boston Banks Urban Renewal Group (BBURG). Responding to growing black and Latino protests against urban renewal and displacement in the South End, the city worked with BBURG to make home loans available to black buyers who had little access to conventional financing because of discrimination and redlining (that is, denying loans in minority or racially mixed areas).

In an effort to reverse redlining, BBURG made low-interest loans only to black homeowners in an area that included parts of the South End, Jamaica Plain, Roxbury, Dorchester, and Mattapan. The program, however, unleashed a wave of block-busting, as real estate agents reaped steep profits by encouraging panic selling by white homeowners who feared racial transition. Such practices heightened tensions and accelerated the process of racial transition—particularly in the old Jewish neighborhoods of Dorchester and Mattapan. Among the new home buyers who took advantage of the BBURG loans were Haitian and West Indian migrants who purchased single-family homes and triple-deckers near Franklin Field, Codman Square, and in the Wellington Hill section of Mattapan. To the north, a growing number of Cape Verdean immigrants settled in Grove Hall and later in Uphams Corner as racial barriers fell in the wake of BBURG. While black immigrants and African Americans found much-needed housing in these neighborhoods, their settlement choices were constrained by biased real estate and lending practices, and their communities, if not already black, quickly resegregated. Mattapan, for example, which soon became the center of Boston's Haitian community, went from 99 percent white in 1960 to 85 percent black by 1975.[13] These early settlements in Roxbury, Dorchester, and Mattapan thus became the crucibles for distinctive Afro-Caribbean and Cape Verdean communities and businesses. Their initial location and subsequent development, however, were shaped by a racialized housing and lending market that would leave black immigrants significantly more concentrated and segregated than other newcomer groups.

THE TRANSFORMATION OF IMMIGRANT BOSTON

While some newcomers to the Boston area arrived during the city's economic nadir in the 1960s and 1970s, an even larger influx came in the 1980s and afterward. These later arrivals found a city that was rapidly changing because of an emerging knowledge and high-tech economy and a revitalized urban landscape that favored those with skills and higher income. Some of the most dramatic transformations occurred in Chinatown and the South End, while others took place in areas adjoining fast-growing universities and medical centers. In both cases, ethnic residents organized to protect their neighborhoods, but overcrowding and rising housing costs ultimately forced new arrivals to move to more affordable areas. Financial pressures also encouraged those who had arrived earlier to relocate out of the core neighborhoods, particularly when purchasing homes. As the foreign born dispersed from their original settlements, a new immigrant geography emerged beginning in the 1980s, creating additional ethnic enclaves and polyethnic communities throughout the city (fig. 9).

Chinatown was one of the first communities to feel the effects. From the 1950s to the 1970s, Chinatown faced a host of development pressures that eroded the supply of affordable housing. First, the construction of the Southeast Expressway and the Massachusetts Turnpike Extension displaced more than three hundred families from the Chinatown / South Cove area in the 1950s and 1960s. Soon after that, the South Cove Urban Renewal Project displaced hundreds more families from the same area, while the development of the Tufts New England Medical Center claimed several additional blocks. Meanwhile, an adult entertainment district known as the Combat Zone emerged on Chinatown's western flank after the city razed the old Scollay Square red light district to build Government Center. The rapid proliferation of strip clubs, sex shops, and porn theaters upset many Chinatown residents, who said that such enterprises attracted prostitution and other criminal activity into a densely packed family neighborhood.[14]

Nevertheless, the population of Chinatown grew rapidly as new migrants arrived from Hong Kong and Southeast Asia. The neighborhood's growing population thus occupied a shrinking land base: between 1960 and 1970, Chinatown's population grew by more than 25 percent while its land area was reduced by half. During the 1970s its population more than doubled, with the foreign born making up roughly 60 percent of its residents by 1980. Chinatown activists challenged new development projects and pressed the city to build more affordable housing, but it was an uphill battle. As vacancy rates dropped and waiting lists for the area's low-income housing projects grew to more than seven years by the mid-1980s, new immigrants

Boston neighborhoods

1970

Charlestown

East Boston

Foreign-born population

Back Bay/
Beacon Hill

less than 10%

Central

10-20%

Allston/Brighton

Fenway/Kenmore

20-30%

South End

South Boston

30-40%

40-50%

Roxbury

more than 50%

Jamaica
Plain

Dorchester

West Roxbury

Roslindale

Mattapan

2010

Charlestown

East Boston

Back Bay/
Beacon Hill

Central

Allston/Brighton

Fenway/Kenmore

South End

South Boston

Roxbury

Jamaica
Plain

Dorchester

West Roxbury

Roslindale

Mattapan

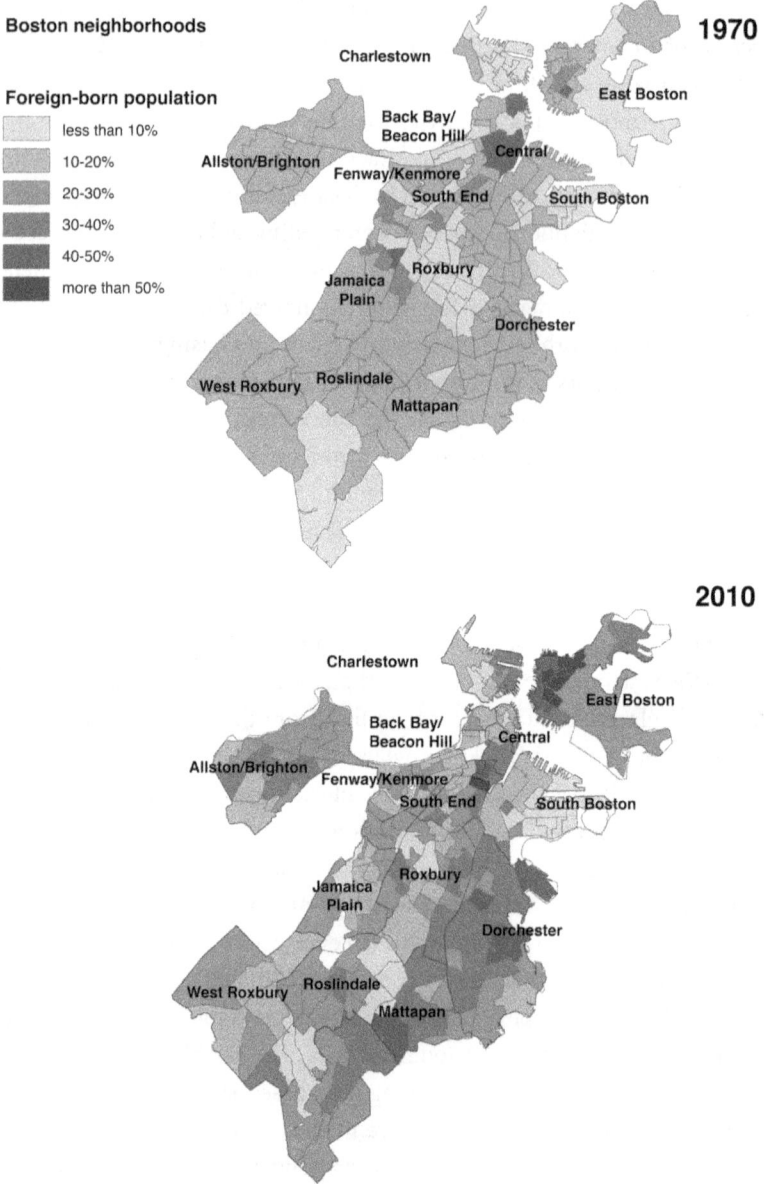

FIGURE 9. Maps of foreign-born population in City of Boston, 1970 and 2010. Source: US Census Bureau, *Census of Population and Housing*, 1970 and 2010.

began to disperse. They initially moved to the nearby South End, but also to the Fenway, Mission Hill, and Allston-Brighton. The latter was particularly important; by 1985, 30 percent of the city's Asian population lived in Allston-Brighton, constituting 12 percent of the area's residents. By 2000, a third of Allston-Brighton's population was foreign born, with the Chinese making up the largest immigrant group. New ethnic businesses helped revitalize the neighborhood in the 1970s and 1980s, making Allston "the mecca of ethnic food establishments."[15]

As in Chinatown, the pressures of redevelopment in the 1960s and 1970s threatened to displace the Puerto Rican community of the South End. Since the end of World War II, the loss of jobs, the deterioration of housing stock, and the emergence of a skid row district in the South End had prompted the city to target the neighborhood for urban renewal. After hundreds of housing units were razed for the Central Artery and other projects in the 1950s and early 1960s, neighborhood resistance grew. As will be shown in chapter 7, community mobilization succeeded in getting the city to build Villa Victoria, a subsidized housing complex that became the new center of the Latino community. The project provided an affordable housing alternative for hundreds of poor and working-class families that proved essential as the forces of gentrification enveloped the South End. Over the next two decades, the neighborhood's proximity to downtown and its stately nineteenth-century brownstones attracted affluent white professionals and a thriving gay community. Meanwhile, many of the neighborhood's black and Latino residents were forced out, leaving Villa Victoria and one other nearby housing project as ethnic enclaves that housed the vast majority of the South End's Latino population. As migration accelerated, pressures for affordable housing grew and long waiting lists ensured that new Latino immigrants would have to look elsewhere.[16]

A similar housing crunch confronted Latino residents across the river in Cambridge. During the 1960s and 1970s, Puerto Rican and Dominican migration had been expanding Latino settlement from Cambridgeport into the area northeast of Central Square (known as Area 4, or "the Port"). Columbia Street and the Columbia Terrace housing development gradually became the center of Cambridge's Latino community. At the same time, many of the area's old manufacturing industries were closing down while a burgeoning computer and high-tech sector was expanding around MIT—just a few blocks to the east. The development of Technology Square, a high-tech office complex that would house Polaroid, IBM, and countless MIT programmers and engineers, was one of several redevelopment projects that reduced the supply of affordable housing while attracting a growing corps of well-paid researchers and professionals. Their arrival sparked a wave of condo conversions and rising rents that priced many Latinos out of the market, especially after rent control was discontinued in 1994. As the Salvadoran community worker Nelson Salazar explained, "you're being gentrified every time you try and settle in, rents go up, and you have to keep going."[17]

A similar pattern of redevelopment and gentrification affected other Boston neighborhoods with expanding universities, medical centers, and research facilities. The Fenway, Mission Hill, and Allston-Brighton neighborhoods all lost affordable housing stock as nearby universities and medical centers expanded along with their enrollments and workforce. Allston-Brighton, for example, saw a steady influx of student renters from Boston University, Harvard, and Boston College, many of whom shared apartments and could afford higher rents, thus driving out working-class families. By the early twenty-first century, a staggering two-thirds of Allston residents were between the ages of eighteen and thirty-five. Although foreign students made up a growing percentage of this population, working-class immigrant families were less likely to settle there than in earlier years.[18]

So where did most new immigrants go after 1980? In many cases they moved to outlying neighborhoods where white flight was still occurring and property values remained lower. For the most part, these areas were in the old zone of emergence where rising Irish, Italian, and Jewish families had settled earlier in the century. In the case of Latinos, they were likely to move to Jamaica Plain, a predominantly Irish American neighborhood that soon became the "Latino crossroads of the city." By the early 1980s, Jamaica Plain had the highest concentration of Latinos in Boston and the most diverse mix of Latino groups: Cubans lived along Centre Street near Hyde Square; Dominicans settled nearby on Mozart Street and surrounding blocks; Puerto Ricans moved in along Washington Street around Egleston Square. Some of the pioneer Latino settlers in the South End and Cambridge later purchased homes or triple-deckers in Jamaica Plain. Entrepreneurs like Ramon Acevedo and Rafael Benzan, two Dominicans from the Port, began buying apartment buildings in Jamaica Plain in the 1970s and renting them to other Dominicans, facilitating the shift of Latino settlement to the area. By the 1990s, however, the Latino population of Jamaica Plain peaked as gentrification began to push rents upward. Thereafter, Latino settlement would shift to the adjoining area around Egleston Square in Roxbury.[19]

Newcomers from Central America, on the other hand, were more likely to go to East Boston, where a small Puerto Rican community had sprung up around Maverick Square in the 1970s. Still predominantly Italian American, the area had deteriorated as many longtime residents left for the suburbs, leaving boarded up storefronts along Maverick Square. With the arrival of more than fourteen thousand immigrants from El Salvador, Colombia, and other parts of Latin America, East Boston went from being 96 percent white in 1980 to nearly 40 percent Latino by 2000, with migrants spreading from Maverick Square in the south to Day Square in the north. Some of the new Salvadoran residents had relocated from Cambridge, but others came directly from Central America. After 1990, they were joined by a growing number of Brazilians and Mexicans as well.[20]

Along with East Boston, Dorchester experienced a dramatic immigrant influx after 1980, bringing greater diversity to what had been a mostly native born white population. With the departure of many Jewish residents in the 1950s and 1960s, the area had become largely black and Irish American in the 1970s. While many Haitians, West Indians, and Cape Verdeans had moved into Dorchester after BBURG, a growing number of Latino and Asian migrants also arrived after 1980, along with a new wave of Irish immigrants. Accordingly, the foreign-born population of the area grew to nearly a third of the population in 2000, with blacks, Latinos, and Asians making up more than two-thirds of the total. Taking advantage of lower housing costs and easy access to downtown via the Red Line, a remarkable array of groups settled in the area, making the five-mile stretch of Dorchester Avenue a diverse cross-section of the city's global population.[21]

Perhaps the most visible development in Dorchester in the 1980s was the emergence of a large Vietnamese community in Fields Corner. While by the 1990s rising housing prices discouraged new Vietnamese settlement in Allston-Brighton, Fields Corner continued to suffer from the economic effects of white flight and urban disinvestment. Dilapidated storefronts and abandoned triple-deckers were soon bought up by Vietnamese owners and entrepreneurs who began renting them to coethnics, a growing stream of whom were arriving under family reunification provisions. Fields Corner and neighboring Savin Hill also attracted Vietnamese migrants from Chinatown who relocated or expanded their businesses into Dorchester. From roughly two thousand in 1980, the Vietnamese population of Dorchester grew threefold by the end of the decade, accounting for roughly two-thirds of the city's Vietnamese residents. Homeowners made up a significant proportion of the newcomers; by 2000, an estimated four to five hundred Vietnamese families had purchased homes in the area.[22]

During these same years, immigrants were buying homes in other Boston neighborhoods as well. Some of the city's southernmost areas—especially Hyde Park and Roslindale—saw marked increases in the number of foreign-born residents who left Roxbury, Dorchester, and Mattapan to purchase homes in these more suburban-like areas. Haitians accounted for the largest percentage of new residents in both Hyde Park and Roslindale, although other Afro-Caribbean migrants—from Jamaica, the Dominican Republic, and Trinidad—also registered significant gains. Here they joined older white settlers whose families had come from Greece, Ireland, Italy, and Lebanon. By century's end, these formerly white, middle-class neighborhoods had become strikingly diverse places, bringing immigrant life to the farthest reaches of the city.[23]

The demographic changes were confirmed by the census of 2000, which showed that Boston had become a "minority-majority" city for the first time, with nonwhites making up 51 percent of the population. Most critical in this shift was the loss of white population, which fell from 68 percent in 1980 to 49 percent in 2000, and to 47 percent in 2010. Making up for these losses were growing numbers of Asian, Latino, Caribbean, and African immigrants. This dramatic transformation of the city's social landscape, however, did not mean that ethno-racial integration would necessarily follow. On the one hand, the number of Boston census tracts that had become multiracial (which demographers define as having three or more racial groups making up at least 10 percent of the population) grew from thirty to forty-eight between 1990 and 2000. While some of the change was due to nonwhite migrants moving into formerly white neighborhoods, the continuing exodus of white residents from those same areas suggests that they were resegregating, just as had happened earlier in Mattapan. Moreover, some of the reduction in segregation rates was the result of higher-income whites moving into gentrified areas such as the lower South End and

Jamaica Plain, places where immigrants and low-income residents were being forced out by rising rents. If the earlier trends in the upper South End and the Port are any indication, the recent increases in white population in some areas may be harbingers of gentrification and displacement, rather than the development of stable, racially integrated communities.[24]

THE SUBURBAN SHIFT

Just as many new immigrants dispersed from the old city core to outlying neighborhoods after 1980, a parallel shift occurred from the city of Boston to its surrounding communities (fig. 10). By 2010, twenty-nine towns and small cities in the metro Boston area had foreign-born populations that were larger than the statewide average (table 1). Popular accounts identify these areas as "suburbs," but in reality the greater Boston area includes a confounding array of towns and cities that do not easily fit into popular notions of middle-class suburbanization and upward mobility. Many of these communities have long histories dating back to the colonial era. Some emerged as outlying mill towns in the nineteenth century, others as nearby industrial communities with easy rail, water, or highway access to Boston. After World War II, another surge of suburban development took place to the west of the city following the building of Route 128 (I-95) and other highways. In recent years, both academics and the press have heralded the rise of immigrant suburbanization, noting that some recent arrivals have been moving directly to the suburbs, bypassing the traditional urban immigrant enclaves. Although that has certainly been true in the Boston area, exactly why this movement has occurred and what it means is a more complicated story.

First, a significant proportion of new immigrants moving outside Boston have gravitated toward the Commonwealth's older industrial cities—places like Chelsea and Lynn. Built around burgeoning shoe factories and other industries in the nineteenth century, those cities saw their industrial production and population peak in the 1920s, followed by protracted decline. The downturn in manufacturing in the decades following World War II was particularly devastating, bringing between 1940 and 1980 staggering population losses (primarily of white ethnics): 38 percent in Chelsea and 20 percent in Lynn. Few would consider these old industrial cities to be "suburbs," but the loss of employment and increased commuting meant

1970

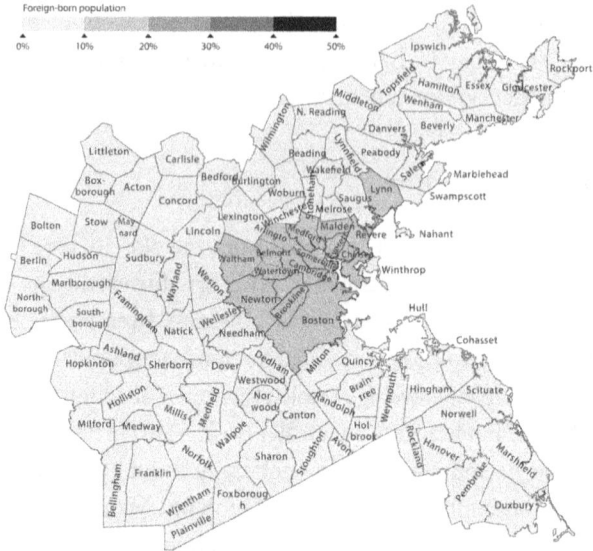

2010

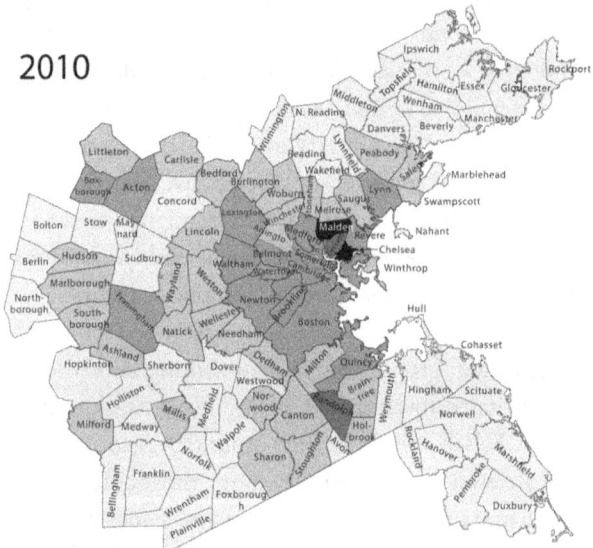

FIGURE 10. Maps of foreign-born population in metro Boston, 1970 and 2010. Source: US Census Bureau, *Census of Population and Housing*, 1970 and 2010.

that many of their residents had joined a mobile metropolitan workforce. Despite the loss in employment, however, these communities showed significant population growth after 1980, largely the result of immigration. During these years, thousands of foreign-born newcomers took up residence in areas like West Lynn and Chelsea's Downtown district. By 2010, the foreign-born population of Chelsea had reached 45 percent—the highest in the state—while Lynn's immigrant population had reached 30 percent. These figures equaled or exceeded those cities' immigrant population rates in 1910, showing that new immigrants were settling in many of the same places their predecessors had a hundred years earlier.[25]

Unlike European immigrants who flocked to the mills, however, jobs were not the decisive factor for those choosing these smaller cities. While struggling local industries sometimes recruited immigrant workers in the 1960s and 1970s, those arriving after 1980 were more likely to commute to Boston or the surrounding suburbs to find work. Their own cities, meanwhile, continued to suffer from job loss and unemployment and poverty rates well above the state average. Moreover, the high crime rates, failing schools, and ongoing fiscal crises that plagued these communities did not make them an obvious choice for settlement. As noted earlier, federal programs resettled refugee families in these cities, planting the seeds of growing Southeast Asian (particularly Cambodian), Russian, and African communities. But refugees accounted for only a portion of the migrant influx. To understand why thousands of other migrants moved there, we need to look at the larger metropolitan housing market and how it influenced newcomers' residential options.

More than any other group, Latinos proved to be the most likely to move to the older industrial cities such as Chelsea and Lynn. Puerto Ricans began settling in both communities in the 1960s and 1970s, but Dominicans, Central Americans, and other Latinos arrived in growing numbers thereafter. In 1980, Latinos constituted 14 percent of Chelsea's population and less than 3 percent of Lynn's. By 2010, Chelsea was a majority Latino city, the result of a wave of Salvadoran and other Central American migrants. In Lynn, Latinos made up a third of the city's population by 2010, reflecting the growing influx of Dominicans and Guatemalans. Some of these cities' Latino newcomers had been displaced from or priced out of the South End and Cambridge; others were new arrivals coming directly from the Caribbean and Central America. A growing number were also secondary migrants from New York who chose to leave crowded and increasingly drug- and violence-ridden neighborhoods. A 1990 study of Chelsea highlighted that city's appeal for Latino families, noting that 87 percent of Chelsea's Latino households had children under eighteen, compared with only 73 percent of such households in Boston. The supply of relatively affordable housing in these older industrial communities—including thousands of aging triple-deckers—provided a strong incentive for working-class Latino families, many of whom preferred the quieter setting of smaller cities.[26]

These Massachusetts communities are part of a larger group of second-tier industrial cities in the Northeast that have become increasingly important centers for poor and working-class immigrants. Although some observers have claimed that the new migrants are simply following in the footsteps of the old, the larger restructuring of the metropolitan economy means that the new arrivals have few job prospects near their homes and live in depressed communities where economic disinvestment has led to substandard housing, troubled schools, and inadequate services. The situation for Latinos has been particularly dire. Since the 1980s, heavily Latino communities such as Lynn and Chelsea have had some of the lowest median incomes and highest poverty rates in the Commonwealth. They have become what one scholar calls "the tenements of the state"—reservoirs of lower-cost housing where migrants have struggled to build communities. As Miren Uriarte and Ramón Borges-Méndez explain, the diffusion of Latinos from Boston to these outlying communities does not resemble the classic pattern of suburbanization and ethnic integration so common among white ethnics in the post–World World War II era. Nor have the restructured economies that greeted Latinos in these cities facilitated the assimilation and upward mobility enjoyed by the earlier European immigrants.[27] On the other hand, new immigrants have helped replenish the population of these once declining cities and have launched small businesses that have helped revitalize their downtown districts. Moreover, the rapid population turnover among Latinos and Asians in both Chelsea and Lynn suggests that those cities function as gateways for new arrivals, at least some of whom manage to move on to communities with better housing, schools, and services.

While many poorer migrants and refugees were relegated to the old industrial cities, educated and highly skilled newcomers found homes in

TABLE 1: PERCENTAGE FOREIGN-BORN IN SELECTED BOSTON SUBURBS
(those with higher % of foreign born than statewide average in 2010)

TOWN/CITY	1910	1970	1980	1990	2000	2010	TOP GROUPS IN 2010
State	31	9	9	10	12	14	China, Dom. Rep., Brazil, Portugal, India, Haiti
Boston	36	10	16	20	25	26	Haiti, China, Dom. Rep., Vietnam, El Salvador
Acton	--	(4)	(8)	10	14	22	China, India, UK, Brazil
Arlington	(25)	11*	11	12	14	16	China, Canada, Greece, Portugal
Belmont	(28)	14*	12	12	15	22	China, Greece, Canada
Boxborough	--	--	--	(8)	13	20	India, China, UK
Brookline	(30)	16*	17*	21*	27*	25	China, Russia, Japan
Burlington	--	(6)	(7)	(9)	15	20	India, China, Italy
Cambridge	33	15*	18*	22*	26*	27*	China, Haiti, India, Canada
Chelsea	42	14*	13	22*	36*	45*	Central America, Columbia
Everett	(29)	13*	11	11	22	39*	Brazil, El Salvador, Haiti, Italy
Framingham	(24)	(7)	(8)	12	21	26*	Brazil, India, China
Hudson	(27)	9	16	14	16	17	Portugal, Brazil
Lexington	(23)	(7)	10	13	17	23	China, India
Lynn	31	10	9	14	23	30*	Dominican Rep., Cambodia, Guatemala, Russia
Malden	(30)	10	9	14	26*	41*	China, Vietnam, Brazil, Haiti,
Marlborough	(23)	(6)	(6)	(9)	16	19	Brazil, India, Guatemala
Medford	(22)	10	11	12	16	21	Italy, Haiti, Brazil, China
Milford	33	10	9	10	12	19	Portugal, Brazil
Newton	(28)	11*	12	13	18	21	China, Russia, Italy
Norwood	32	(8)	(8)	(9)	12	15	India, China, Ireland, Italy
Quincy	33	9	(8)	11	20	28*	China, Vietnam, Ireland
Randolph	(16)	(5)	(8)	12	22	30*	Haiti, China, Vietnam
Revere	(29)	10	9	13	21	32*	Italy, Cambodia, Columbia, Brazil, El Salvador
Salem	(30)	(8)	(8)	(9)	12	17	Dominican Rep.
Sharon	--	(6)	(7)	(9)	12	17	Russia, China, UK, India
Somerville	(27)	15*	17*	22*	29*	26*	Brazil, Portugal, El Salvador, China, Haiti
Stoughton	(23)	9	12	11	14	16	Portugal, Haiti, Poland, Brazil
Waltham	(27)	15*	12	15	20	28*	India, Guatemala, China, Haiti, Italy
Watertown	32	17*	18*	17	20	24	Greece, Italy, Ireland, Russia, Iran, Lebanon, Syria, Turkey, Armenia
Woburn	(26)	(6)	(5)	(6)	(10)	16	Portugal, Brazil, Haiti

( ) Connotes less than statewide average
*Indicates higher percentage of foreign-born than the City of Boston
Source: *US Census of Population*, 1910, 1970, 1980, 1990, 2000; 2010 data is based on American FactFinder,
    Five-year Sample Census, 2008-2012.

some of the region's most affluent suburbs. Attracted by Boston's burgeon-ing universities, medical centers, and high-tech industries, foreign-born professionals and technical workers began settling in Cambridge and Brookline during the Cold War era, when the US government was actively recruiting foreign scientists, engineers, and other researchers. Well served by public transportation, those communities offered easy access to Harvard, MIT, and Boston University, and since the 1960s they have both hosted a higher proportion of foreign-born residents than the city of Boston itself (see table 1).

While these skilled migrants initially settled near centrally located uni-versities and research facilities, some began moving to affluent western suburbs. Propelling this centrifugal movement was the growth of the high-tech sector around Route 128. Opened in 1952, the nation's first circum-ferential highway ran through a string of towns 12 miles west of the city, fueling the development of commercial properties for office and indus-trial parks. Within five years, a hundred companies had located along the Route 128 corridor; by 1973 there were more than twelve hundred. Over the next two decades, the high-tech sector expanded out to Interstate 495 and included major employers such as Polaroid, Digital Equipment, Data General, Raytheon, and Honeywell.[28] In the meantime, suburbs like Waltham, Lexington, and Newton became home to a growing cadre of high-tech workers from China, the Soviet Union, and western Europe.

Asian immigrants were especially visible in this movement, relocating to affluent suburbs where good public schools were the principal draw. As Sophia Ho, a longtime Lexington resident explained, most of her Chinese neighbors were successful professionals and businesspeople who "want to raise their children in a town where education is very important." Between 1980 and 2010, Lexington's Asian American population grew from less than 3 percent to more than 20 percent, with those of Chinese descent predominating. Joining the original Chinese and Chinese American sub-urbanites were growing streams of Indians and Koreans. During the 1990s, Indian programmers and engineers recruited by computer firms under the H-1B program joined the suburban rush, becoming the top foreign-born group in the high-tech towns of Burlington and Waltham. Indians and other Asian immigrants sometimes clustered in suburban apartment com-plexes in towns like Burlington and Quincy, but most eventually dispersed more widely into suburbs across the region. Their high levels of education,

English proficiency, and professional ties through local employers facilitated this integration. By the end of the decade, the founder of a regional
group of Indian technology entrepreneurs noted that "Indians are every-
where, and they are moving to suburbs because that is where the jobs are."[29]

For these highly skilled migrants, then, employment and education
played an important role in where they settled, but that was not typically the
case for less prosperous immigrants. Although the tech sector created both
high- and low-skill jobs throughout the region, very few unskilled immigrants were able to settle in the pricier western suburbs. Fearing overdevel-
opment and changes in the social fabric of their communities, many of the
towns along Route 128 had enacted large-lot, or "snob," zoning restrictions
that precluded the building of affordable smaller homes or multifamily
dwellings. Nor did they build much subsidized housing, except for projects
designed for the elderly. As a result, very few unskilled immigrants—other
than those employed as live-in domestics—settled in these areas. Soaring
housing costs and restrictive housing policies, combined with discriminatory real estate and lending practices, meant that these suburbs would
remain heavily white and (to a lesser degree) Asian. Ultimately, the concentration of the area's foreign born in Cambridge, Brookline, and the western
suburbs on the one hand, and old industrial cities like Lynn and Chelsea
on the other, reflected the class and racial divide of the dual knowledge/
services economy that has developed since the 1960s.[30]

Although new immigrants have been concentrated at these two ends of
the metropolitan economic spectrum, a growing number have also been
moving into the region's more conventional working-class and middle-class
suburbs. Asian American scholars have characterized these communities
as "one-step-up suburbs," signifying their importance as centers of upward
mobility for immigrants, just as many post–World War II suburbs were for
earlier European ethnic groups.[31] The most popular destinations have been
older industrial communities just north of the city, but a few of the more
heterogeneous South Shore and western suburbs also fit this description.
In both cases, these communities had a long history of industrial development that attracted earlier waves of immigrants who built thriving ethnic
communities. Since the 1980s those communities have been claimed by
newer immigrants, who by 2010 made up as much as 40 percent of the
local population. In the process, they have revitalized and transformed
these aging suburbs as they helped reinvent their economies.

To understand this process better, we will look more closely at three Boston suburbs with large immigrant populations: Quincy, Framingham, and Malden. I have chosen these communities because of their varied geographic locations—south, west, and north of the city, respectively—and because of the variety of ethnic groups who have settled in them. Moreover, the three communities felt the initial impact of the new immigration at different times: Quincy in the 1980s, Framingham in the 1990s, and Malden most notably after 2000. In all three, the new immigrants took up residence in older neighborhoods as white ethnics departed. But while the newcomers shared their predecessors' aspirations for middle-class suburban lifestyles, their movement into these communities has been shaped by different forces and has led to a rather different configuration of work and community life.

One of the earliest examples of immigrant suburbanization occurred in Quincy, just south of Boston along the South Shore and adjacent to the city's Dorchester district. Originally part of Old Braintree, Quincy became a separate town in 1792 and became well known as the birthplace of presidents John Adams and John Quincy Adams. As noted in chapter 1, the community had a long history of industrial development and immigrant settlement. Quincy's rural beginnings were first transformed in the nineteenth century by a booming granite industry that attracted thousands of skilled European quarrymen and stonecutters. At the same time, Quincy also developed an important shipbuilding industry that built sloops and schooners for the granite trade. In 1900, local shipbuilders founded the Fore River shipyards in Quincy Point to produce steel ships for the navy. Bethlehem Steel purchased the yards in 1913, and Fore River became one of nation's busiest shipbuilding centers during World War I. An even bigger boom accompanied World War II, when Bethlehem employed roughly forty thousand workers to build destroyers, cruisers, and aircraft carriers. The yards attracted thousands of new workers to Quincy, including many women and immigrants. Older communities of Irish, Finnish, and Italian workers were now joined by new groups of Greeks, Lebanese, Syrians, and others. Many lived in Quincy Point, a working-class neighborhood just west of the Fore River yards.[32]

Despite its industrial character, Quincy was also developing as a commuter suburb for middle-class Boston workers served by the Old Colony Railroad. Open farmland on the north side of town had been subdivided by real estate developers in the 1870s, launching a residential building boom in

Wollaston and North Quincy. For much of the twentieth century, the city's middle-class north side coexisted with its working-class settlements to the south and west. Gradually, however, Quincy's blue-collar workers saw their employment base contract. Competing with concrete and steel, the granite industry shrank dramatically during the Depression and World War II, with the last quarry closing in the 1960s. Shipbuilding, by contrast, continued at reduced levels during the postwar era. General Dynamics took over the Fore River shipyards in 1964, repairing naval vessels and building liquefied natural gas carriers until foreign competition resulted in its closing in 1986. The city lost population for the first time in its history after 1975.[33]

Quincy's downturn occurred just when it should have been thriving. In 1971 the Massachusetts Bay Transit Authority had expanded Red Line service into Quincy, with stops in Wollaston, North Quincy, and Quincy Center. City planners hoped the quick subway commute to downtown and the city's scenic location along the bay would attract a new generation of middle-class Bostonians. In fact, the city had issued building permits for thousands of new homes and apartments, expanding the housing stock by more than seven thousand units between 1960 and 1980. Quincy did become a popular destination for many Irish American working-class families from Dorchester, where racial transition, block-busting, and violence caused many to flee. But these new arrivals did not offset the continued loss of the city's older residents, causing Quincy's population to fall from a peak of 91,487 in 1975 to 84,944 in 1980.[34]

Over the next few years, however, the population would begin to grow again as Asian immigrants discovered the city. By this time, the pressures of urban redevelopment in Chinatown had become critical and many of the neighborhood's foreign-born residents had begun to move out. In a survey conducted in 1988, the *Patriot Ledger* found that many Asian newcomers to Quincy were Chinese from Hong Kong, Taiwan, and Canton who had initially settled in Chinatown. Quincy's abundant stock of rental properties attracted a small stream of these migrants in the late 1970s, many of whom later purchased homes in North Quincy and Wollaston. They did so by pooling assets and sharing homes with extended family members, typically with multiple wage earners per household. Some were restaurant or garment workers who were buying homes for the first time. Eighty percent of those interviewed cited the presence of the Red Line as a key factor in choosing Quincy. For those who worked or shopped in Chinatown, mass transit to downtown was critical. As Millie Chan, who moved to Quincy with her family in the 1970s, explained, "The community was affordable and the transportation was convenient."[35]

Quincy also attracted a growing number of Vietnamese families, many of whom were sponsored or assisted by the Wollaston Lutheran Church, which began outreach to the local Asian community in the mid-1980s. The church hired a Chinese- and Vietnamese-speaking pastor in 1988, and it provided ESL classes, job placement, and other services for refugees and immigrants. Soon such families were sponsoring relatives who came directly from China and Southeast Asia. Quincy's newcomers thus included a range of poorer refugees, working-class families, and middle-class business owners and white-collar workers. Economically and educationally, they fell somewhere between the low-income workers of Chinatown and the high-earning professional and technical workers of the western suburbs.[36]

Affordable housing, accessible transportation, and basic immigrant services helped push Quincy's Asian American population from 330 in 1980, to 5,577 in 1990, to 17,628 (or 19 percent of the city's population) in 2010. Along with other newcomers, they pushed the city's aggregate population upward once again. Chinese and Vietnamese immigrants were not, however, the only newcomers in Quincy. Irish immigrants flocked there in the 1980s, Indians arrived in the 1990s, and a growing Arab and Muslim community coalesced around the Islamic Center in Quincy Point, a mosque founded by an earlier generation of Syrian and Lebanese immigrants (see chapter 6). But the sheer dominance of Chinese and Vietnamese immigrants—who constituted more than 50 percent of the foreign-born population in 2000—gave the city a distinctive Asian identity.[37]

This burgeoning community supported a growing number of Asian-owned restaurants, stores, and services that sprang up along Hancock Street in North Quincy and Wollaston. Asian cultural and social service programs were also established, some of them satellite offices of Chinatown organizations. In 2003 the city's first Asian American shopping center opened in Quincy Point, anchored by a large Chinese-owned supermarket. The opening of the mall sparked considerable attention and speculation that Quincy was becoming "Chinatown South" or "the new Flushing"—a reference to the Queens, New York, neighborhood in which upwardly mobile Asian immigrants had settled. By 2000, in fact, Quincy's Asian American population was more than three times larger than the Asian American population of Boston's Chinatown.[38]

Although the local press hyped Quincy as a "new Chinatown," the moniker is misleading. As the geographer Wei Li has argued, suburban "ethnoburbs"—as she calls them—are new types of communities that are different from both traditional urban enclaves and the post–World War II suburbs where European ethnics moved into the middle class. Unlike the latter, they have not been sites of assimilation but rather places where immigrants have retained strong ethnic identities and communities. But they are also different from traditional urban Chinatowns in that they have been profoundly shaped by global investment and trade, house a wider array of Asian ethnic groups and social classes, and are less politically and socially insular.

While Quincy has much in common with the ethnoburbs that Wei studied, there are also important differences. For one, Asian Americans in Quincy do not make up a majority, or even a plurality, of the population, as they do in the California ethnoburbs. Moreover, Quincy's Asian community has been built on a different and much older foundation as an industrial suburb whose previous ethnic neighborhoods, working-class housing, and accessible rail connections to downtown served as a powerful magnet for newer Asian immigrants. While the latter have inherited the homes and neighborhoods of earlier ethnic groups, they did not come to Quincy to work in local manufacturing industries, and many pursue work lives that take them away from home for many hours a day. According to a survey conducted in 1989, 76 percent of Asians in Quincy traveled to Boston's Chinatown at least once a week, while 40 percent commuted daily or several times a week. Many told survey takers that they worked long hours and thus did not have time for community activities or for meeting their non-Asian neighbors. As Tuan Tran, a Vietnamese refugee living in Quincy, noted, "In this country, go to work, watch TV, read and eat. . . . I don't know anything about next door." Although the emergence of an Asian enclave economy in the 1990s no doubt enriched local community life, long hours of work and commuting left new immigrants less connected to the Quincy community than earlier immigrants who had worked in nearby quarries and shipyards.[39]

Like Quincy, Framingham also has a long history of industrial development and immigrant settlement. Located 12 miles west of Boston, the town grew rapidly with the construction of the Boston & Worcester Railroad in

the 1830s. Several large carpet and woolen mills were established around
the Saxonville falls on the Sudbury River in the 1840s, and after World
War I the mammoth Roxbury Carpet Company relocated to the same site.
Like other New England textile operations, the Saxonville mills began
employing large numbers of Irish, Canadian, and other immigrant workers after the Civil War. European immigrants also found work building the
reservoir system and working for new employers such as the Dennison
Company, a paper and box manufacturer that relocated from Roxbury to
downtown Framingham in 1897. During these years, distinct communities
of Irish and Canadians formed around Catholic parishes in Saxonville and
Framingham Center, while Italians and Portuguese settled near the downtown. Even after World War II Framingham's manufacturing base continued to grow as more Boston firms moved to the suburbs and, most notably,
when General Motors opened an assembly plant there in 1948, employing
thirty-five hundred workers at its peak. These industries provided ample
employment for many second-generation ethnic residents, as well as for
later Puerto Rican and Portuguese migrants.[40]

At the same time, Framingham benefited from the new service/retail
economy blossoming around Route 128 and the Massachusetts Turnpike
(first opening in 1957 and connecting to downtown Boston in 1965). Even
before it was completed, the turnpike exit became a magnet for retail and
commercial development. In 1951, Shoppers World, one of the country's
first shopping malls, opened on Route 9. By the time the turnpike was
completed, dozens of other retailers, including an even larger mall in
adjoining Natick, made up the "Golden Triangle"—New England's largest
suburban shopping district. After 1980, new high-tech companies such as
Bose and Genzyme would also move into the area.[41]

A residential building boom accompanied the new commercial development as thousands of new homes were constructed under federal loan
programs for veterans. Unlike most other towns near the Route 128 corridor, however, Framingham also constructed dozens of new apartment
complexes to house its large young and blue-collar workforce. During these
years, in fact, residents repeatedly rejected attempts to implement restrictive zoning that would have required minimum lot sizes or barred multifamily housing. During the 1960s, thousands of rental units were added
to the town's housing stock, including a string of high rises along Route
9. Growing local opposition to this type of development resulted in an

amendment to the zoning laws in 1972, banning most apartment construction—but not before contractors secured permits for an additional three thousand units in 1971–1972. The bonanza of new homes and apartments allowed Framingham's population to swell from 28,086 in 1950 to 65,113 in 1980, transforming it into an "edge city"—a concentrated center of business, shopping, and entertainment serving outlying suburban areas.[42]

As what came to be called the "Metrowest" region was shifting to a retail and service economy, Sunbelt and global competition was simultaneously undermining its manufacturing sector. A clear sign of trouble came when one of the town's oldest employers, Roxbury Carpet, shut down in 1973. A growing exodus of companies followed, including cap and gown maker Bancroft Cap in 1983, General Motors in 1984, and Dennison in 1990. Framingham thus saw a major erosion of its manufacturing base in the 1980s and 1990s as it lost more than twelve thousand jobs. As older white ethnic employees retired or followed jobs to the Sunbelt, the town's working-class south side lost population. In particular, the downtown area deteriorated, a process that had begun in the 1960s as many stores struggled to compete with the Golden Triangle malls.[43]

As the local population abandoned the downtown, migrant newcomers gradually moved in. Puerto Ricans, who were hired at local farms and garden centers, first settled around downtown in the late 1950s and 1960s. Over the next two decades, they were joined by a growing number of newcomers from the Caribbean and Central and South America. Framingham's Latino population grew by 142 percent in the 1980s, making it one of the largest in the metro area. During these same years, local synagogues helped resettle dozens of Soviet Jewish refugees, while high-tech firms began recruiting Chinese, Indian, and other highly skilled immigrant workers. Framingham's foreign-born population thus expanded from less than 7 percent in 1970 to more than a quarter of the population in 2010.[44]

Among this new wave of immigrants, Brazilians made up the largest group by far. Beginning in the late 1980s, a steady stream of Brazilian migrants moved to the downtown area, where they found affordable apartments and a Portuguese-speaking community around St. Tarcisius, a Catholic parish that had served Italian and later Portuguese immigrants. Framingham was also one of the few Boston suburbs that offered bilingual education in Portuguese, an attractive alternative for those with children. Compared with the two other top destinations for Brazilians, Boston and Somerville,

Framingham attracted many more migrant families with children—14 percent of the town's Brazilian population in 1999–2001, compared with less than 9 percent in Boston and Somerville.[45] Moreover, rising rents in Allston (the center of Boston's Brazilian community) likely encouraged families to seek housing elsewhere. In Framingham, the typical suburban attractions of safety, amenities, and services—financed by a healthy tax base of retail business and commercial services—were enhanced by a linguistically friendly community and relatively affordable multifamily housing.

The town's Brazilian population thus grew rapidly in the 1990s, accounting for roughly 7 percent of the population by 2000 (the actual numbers were no doubt much higher, as many new Brazilian arrivals were undocumented). By 2003, Framingham had the highest percentage of Brazilian-born residents in the state, and likely the country. The newcomers were credited with revitalizing the old downtown area and founding more than forty new businesses by 1999, many of them occupying once vacant storefronts. Many also bought homes in the area, renovating deteriorating properties. Police Lieutenant Steve Carl, who was in charge of the downtown substation in the mid-1990s, commented: "If it wasn't for them [Brazilians], this town would be a ghost town." In 2004 Framingham became a sister city of Governador Valadares in Minas Gerais, the home region of many of the town's Brazilians; migrants built on this relationship to develop numerous transnational organizations and businesses connecting the two cities. It was thus not surprising when, in 2005, *O Estado de Sao Paulo,* a leading Brazilian newspaper, dubbed Framingham "the capital of Brazuca," the Brazilian diaspora. Like Asians in Quincy, Brazilians created a thriving ethnoburb in Framingham on the remains of an older working-class community. After 2008, the recession helped fuel a substantial return migration to Brazil and a surge of downtown business closures and short sales. Nevertheless, the town continues to be the most visible and concentrated settlement of Brazilians in greater Boston.[46]

Meanwhile, to the north of Boston, a similar type of ethnoburb seemed to be emerging in Malden; over time, however, it would evolve into something different. Like both Quincy and Framingham, Malden had been a rural agricultural area, until the Boston & Maine Railroad arrived in 1845, giving rise to a bevy of local industries including shoes, tanneries, paints, chemicals, and soap. The town's largest employer, the Boston Rubber Shoe Company, was taken over by Marquis Converse in 1908 and reorganized as the Converse Rubber Shoe Company, which developed the popular All-Star basketball shoe in 1917. Converse and other industries were concentrated in the Edgeworth district along the tracks west of downtown, as were many of the plants' immigrant workers—mainly Irish until World War I but thereafter increasingly Italian. Jewish immigrants, who moved to Malden in large numbers after a major fire in Chelsea in 1908, made up the second largest group after the Irish, settling east of downtown in the old Suffolk Square neighborhood. By 1910 the foreign born made up 30 percent of Malden's population, many of them owning modest homes or living in the triple-deckers that proliferated after building regulations were changed to allow apartment construction. A few hundred African American families also lived on the edge of the Jewish district.[47]

With its expanding workforce, Malden's population grew steadily until the Great Depression, at which time it leveled off. A number of the city's older mills and tanneries had closed down during the 1920s and 1930s, but a new crop of knitting mills—including the well-known Malden Mills—opened in the early twentieth century and profited from government contracts during the two world wars. After 1945, however, the city began to lose key industries. Malden Mills relocated to Lawrence in 1956, while Converse, Lewis Candy Company, and other older industries shut down operations in the late 1970s and 1980s.[48]

With the city hemorrhaging jobs and losing younger residents to outlying suburbs, the League of Women Voters and other civic groups called for urban renewal. Mayor Walter Kelliher initiated one of the state's largest redevelopment campaigns in 1956, bringing in $39 million in federal funds over the following fifteen years through the newly created Malden Redevelopment Authority. Targeting five different sites, the Redevelopment Authority essentially razed and rebuilt the city's industrial and commercial base and produced more than fifteen hundred low- and moderate-income apartments in Suffolk Square, Edgeworth, and other old neighborhoods. As in Quincy, much of the new residential construction was concentrated around the planned Orange Line train, which began service to Malden in 1977. Despite all the new housing and industrial space, however, the city continued to lose population until the mid-1980s. Nor did redevelopment help stem the loss of manufacturing jobs, as Converse shut down in 1978 and the percentage of manufacturing jobs in the city fell from 22 in 1950 to 16 percent in 1980.[49]

As had happened in Quincy, the availability of affordable housing and accessible mass transit in Malden began attracting Chinese and Vietnamese immigrants in the 1980s. The newcomers settled in the redeveloped areas west of downtown around the Malden Center and Oak Grove stops on the Orange Line. Many of them purchased homes, the medium values of which were significantly lower than in Boston and slightly lower than the state average. Like Quincy's newcomers, Asian immigrants in Malden had higher incomes and educational levels than those in Chinatown but lower than Asians statewide. The Asian American population of Malden mushroomed from less than 1 percent in 1980 to 18 percent by 2010.[50]

Although it the grew rapidly in the 1990s, the Asian community was not as dominant in Malden as in Quincy. Malden's Asian-owned businesses and services were relatively slow to develop, and its newcomers remained more dependent on Chinatown for shopping and socializing. After 2000, Malden's foreign-born population became more diverse, attracting growing numbers of Haitians, Brazilians, North Africans, and others. The percentage of immigrants from Asia meanwhile dropped slightly between 2000 and 2010, while those from Africa, Latin America, and the Caribbean increased their share of the foreign-born population from 35 to 47 percent.[51]

Such trends suggest that Malden is evolving into a polyethnic, multiracial suburb, much like its neighbors Somerville, Everett, and Revere. Indeed, one Brazilian entrepreneur described the entire area as "Greater Somerville," noting how Brazilians and other immigrants have spread out from that city to Malden and Everett. The recent growth and diversification of Malden's immigrant community may be due in part to sharply rising home prices in Somerville (which borders upscale Cambridge). Median home values in Somerville increased by more than 50 percent from 2000 to 2008, while the foreign-born population dropped 4 percent. Home values in Malden, while showing a similar increase, remained on average more than $100,000 below those in Somerville. Malden's more affordable housing stock and its well-regarded schools helped boost its foreign-born population to 45 percent by 2012, giving it the second highest percentage of immigrants in the metro area—higher than the city of Boston and second only to Chelsea.[52]

So what do these one-step-up suburbs of Malden, Framingham, and Quincy have in common? As older industrial communities, they all had aging infrastructures and a native-born, working-class population that was leaving as jobs moved to outer ring suburbs, the Sunbelt, or abroad.

Facing such decline, all three cities moved aggressively to reinvent themselves, either as edge cities or inner-ring commuter suburbs with ample multifamily rental housing. Immigrants proved to be vital to this process as the native-born continued to abandon these cities in the 1960s and 1970s. Ironically, it was this depopulation and deindustrialization that made the immigrant influx possible as housing stock and commercial properties became more available and affordable. Mass transit, as well as better quality and linguistically friendly schools, also played a role. Ultimately, such suburbs have constituted the new immigrant zone of emergence, where the desires of striving newcomers have meshed well with the revitalization needs of local communities. But popular enthusiasm for immigrant-led suburban revitalization must be tempered with the knowledge that the newcomers' success is likely to result in an escalation of property values and rents in the future that may well price newer immigrants out of the market, a process already well under way in Cambridge and Somerville.

The reinvention of urban life has not been limited to these suburbs but has affected the entire metropolitan area as global competition and economic restructuring have transformed the landscape since the 1960s. Arriving in the final stages of the city's manufacturing era, migrants in the 1960s and 1970s went mainly to Boston and Cambridge. But it was not long before the forces of redevelopment and gentrification pushed them out of the old urban core into outlying districts such as Allston-Brighton, Dorchester, and East Boston. Meanwhile, poorer groups of Latinos and Southeast Asians also moved into hard-pressed industrial suburbs such as Lynn and Chelsea. In both areas, newcomers repopulated and revitalized once ailing neighborhoods, bringing new life to declining commercial districts and institutions. But life in such communities also came with significant hardship: lack of jobs, long commutes, high poverty rates, failing schools, and widespread crime and drug use that made social integration and upward mobility unattainable for many migrant families. At the other end of the spectrum, immigrants with advanced training and professional skills found rapid acceptance in upscale neighborhoods of Boston and Cambridge, as well as in some of the region's most affluent western suburbs—an unprecedented development. This new global economy not only influenced metropolitan settlement but, as we shall see in the next chapter, was also critical in shaping the work opportunities of new immigrants and their prospects for economic advancement.

CHAPTER 4

Immigrants and Work in the New Economy

O riginally built in the 1840s, the Assabet Mill in Maynard, Massachusetts, began as a carpet factory powered by the Assabet River. Located some 20 miles west of Boston, the Assabet Mill became the world's largest woolen mill in the early twentieth century, employing thousands of textile workers. Mostly immigrants from Ireland, Finland, Poland, Russia, and Italy, many of them attempted to organize, founding a local of the CIO Textile Workers Union in the late 1930s. After a fitful thirty-year decline, the American Woolen Company shut down the Assabet Mill permanently in 1950, laying off its twelve hundred workers. Seven years later, the new computer maker Digital Equipment Corporation took up residence in one of the renovated buildings and later purchased the entire mill complex, leasing it to more than thirty mostly high-tech companies.[1]

Like other recycled factories in Boston, Cambridge, and Waltham, the Assabet Mill is a living testament to the global economic forces that affected greater Boston in the late twentieth century. As the region shifted away from manufacturing and toward knowledge-based industries, its infrastructure and workforce changed along with it. Immigrants have played a key role in this transformation, providing labor for both the lower and upper rungs of the new service-based economy. Indeed, most of the growth in the state's and metro region's labor force between 1980 and 2010 occurred as a result of the immigrant influx. But the economic transformation of the past fifty years has not been as smooth as the story of the Assabet Mill might suggest. Immigrants arrived in the midst of wrenching economic changes, uneven development, and often exploitative practices as the older industries gave way to the new. Since the 1980s, moreover, a new bimodal pattern of labor has emerged, one that has presented both problems and opportunities for the foreign born. These developments, along with new issues around documentation and deportation, have led to a distinctly different economic scenario than that faced by earlier European immigrants. Although newcomers have undoubtedly helped to rebuild and revitalize the economy of greater Boston since the 1980s, the prosperity created by the new economy has not been equally shared.

ECONOMIC RESTRUCTURING: FROM MILL-BASED TO MIND-BASED

The transformation of Massachusetts's industrial economy had been under way for much of the twentieth century. Prior to World War I the state was among the most highly industrialized in the nation, with hundreds of textile and shoe mills employing the bulk of its workers. But other industries were also important: Cambridge was the candy-making capital of New England; rubber goods were king in places like Watertown, Chelsea, and Woburn; Lynn and Salem churned out electrical products; and cities and towns throughout greater Boston produced chemicals, foods, paper goods, soap, machinery, and other products. In the 1920s, however, the textile and shoe industries began shifting their operations to the South in search of cheaper, nonunionized labor, while the Great Depression resulted in scores of local factory closures. Although many New England industries revived with government contracts during World War II, the downward spiral continued in the postwar period as many companies relocated to the suburbs, to the South, or abroad. Along with the loss of jobs and industry, the population of Boston declined by a staggering 30 percent, from a high of 801,444 in 1950 to 562,994 in 1980.

By the 1980s, however, the foundations of the region's new knowledge-based economy were already in place. During the postwar era, Boston's universities, medical centers, and defense-related industries benefited from massive federal funding for education, healthcare, scientific research, and military contracting. Moreover, a burgeoning electronics industry led by MIT-trained engineers gave rise to a spate of new computer and high-tech firms that would enjoy record profits in the mid-1980s (the so-called Massachusetts Miracle) and the dot-com boom of the late 1990s. Financing for these industries came from earlier fortunes earned in textiles and shoes that were rechanneled as venture capital, making the financial industry a major player in the new economy as well. Boston's highly regarded medical schools, laboratories, and teaching hospitals also became centers for research that yielded new ventures in pharmaceuticals, medical instruments, and, later, biotechnology.[2] Immigrant workers have been essential to this new service-based economy, from sweeping the floors to starting the companies.

Although mill-based industries in Massachusetts experienced a steady decline in the late twentieth century, they were still an important part of the area's economy during the early years of the new immigration. In fact, in the 1960s and 1970s, local manufacturers recruited Asian and Latino migrants as low-paid, nonunionized labor that helped sustain declining industries such as textiles, shoes, and garments. In the process, these new workers established beachheads of settlement in older urban neighborhoods and industrial communities that would continue to grow even after those jobs disappeared. In the short term, their labor power helped local employers "ride the decline" and extend the life of struggling manufacturing operations facing national and global competition.[3]

Puerto Ricans and other early Latino migrants occupied this role in many of the state's waning industries. In the 1960s, some of the remaining textile mills began recruiting Puerto Rican workers who labored seasonally in local agriculture or had been laid off from textile plants that had closed in other parts of the Northeast. Local employers also recruited skilled textile workers from Colombia who could repair old-style, Massachusetts-made looms that had been exported to Latin America as New England mills closed down. Shoe manufacturers in Lynn and clothing manufacturers in Boston also recruited Puerto Rican and Dominican workers in the 1960s, relying on chain migration among their Latino employees and sometimes offering referral fees to those who could bring in new workers. Doña Suncha, a Puerto Rican woman from Orocovis who was one of the first Latinos to settle in Waltham in the late 1950s, explained how her family aided this migration: "My husband's cousin who worked on a tomato farm in Lexington got a job for my husband in the same place. . . . Later my husband, searching for something better, began working in a metal factory." Soon she was hosting dozens of young friends and neighbors arriving from Orocovis in search of work in Waltham factories. Jaime Cárdenas and his family played a similar role for Dominicans settling in Jamaica Plain around the same time, providing temporary housing and helping them find jobs at a local shoe factory.[4]

In Boston, Chinese women played an integral role in the declining garment industry. Jewish and Italian women had dominated this work in the early twentieth century, with many of them joining the International Ladies' Garment Workers' Union in the 1930s. In the 1960s, Puerto Rican and Chinese women were recruited by a burgeoning network of sweatshops in Chinatown and East Boston seeking low-cost labor to compete with the emerging garment centers in Asia. With the expansion of Chinese immigration after 1965, new migrants from Guangdong streamed into Chinatown factories. Most found their jobs through personal contacts and referrals from friends, neighbors, and churches. English was not required; many shops were run by Cantonese-speaking supervisors who—like earlier Jewish and Italian employers—sometimes allowed women to bring their children to work, return home to cook meals, or take work home in the evening (though that latter practice was illegal). Most of the jobs were low paying; working conditions were poor, and many of the shops were nonunionized. But for those who did secure jobs at union shops, the ILGWU provided health insurance for members and their families (a valuable benefit, since many of their husbands worked in nonunionized Chinatown restaurants). Such benefits, as well as the chance to work close to home among a community of coethnic women, were appealing to many new immigrants. By 1978, more than 70 percent of the city's Chinese women workers were employed in the apparel industry.[5]

By this time, however, the industry was already in decline. Between 1970 and 1985, the number of Boston firms dropped from 383 to 146, reducing the workforce from roughly eleven thousand to five thousand. By the late 1980s, hundreds of Chinese women were unemployed and trying to retrain for other occupations. Hing Seto, a Chinese immigrant who worked as a stitcher for the P & L Sportswear Company, described how difficult it was for her and other immigrant women who were laid off in

Occupations of the Foreign Born in
Boston, 1980–2010

FIGURE 11. Occupations of foreign born and native born in Boston, 1980–2010.
Source: Steven Ruggles, J. Trent Alexander, Katie Genadek, Ronald Goeken, Matthew
B. Schroeder, and Matthew Sobek, *Integrated Public Use Microdata Series: Version 5.0*
(Minneapolis: University of Minnesota, 2010).

1985: "We knew how to work, but we didn't know how to speak [English],"
Seto explained. "Many, many factories were closing. There was nowhere
to go. I felt like nothing because I couldn't find a job." With the help of
the Chinese Progressive Association, hundreds of laid-off Asian garment
workers rallied at the statehouse in the spring of 1986, calling for access to
retraining programs, English classes, and unemployment benefits. In this
case the legislature responded, setting up programs that allowed Seto and
her coworkers to train for new jobs in the transitioning economy.

A study of laid-off Chinese garment workers in Boston in the early
1990s found that the majority shifted to service occupations. Expanding
service industries, such as the new Tufts New England Medical Center, had
contributed to raising Chinatown's real estate prices, which helped drive
many small garment shops out of business. Many of the former garment
workers later found work as housekeepers and food service workers in the
new hotel complex at Copley Square. Others secured jobs in childcare,

domestic service, and assembly work in electronics and pharmaceutical plants. A small number, like Seto, got computer training and moved into clerical work.[6] In this way there occurred a wholesale shift of immigrant workers from the city's declining manufacturing industries to the bottom rungs of the rising service and high-tech/medical sector of the 1980s. As figure 11 shows, the share of immigrant workers engaged as operatives and laborers fell precipitously during the 1980s, from 23 to 14 percent, while those employed in the services increased their share from 23 to 31 percent.

Latino workers in the region tended to stay concentrated in manufacturing jobs longer than any other group, possibly because of lower levels of education and English proficiency and lack of access to other industries. Unlike Chinese and Southeast Asian migrants, though, Latinos did not find much work in the assembly plants of the 1980s tech boom. Indeed, some computer and electronics employers actively sought out Asian assembly workers, for whom they provided job training, transportation, and English classes. Such employers took advantage of job placement programs for refugees and may have had preferences for groups they saw as hardworking, model minorities. The fact that professional Asian immigrants and their children occupied prominent positions in some of these companies (or even owned them) may also have influenced recruitment. In any case, the exclusion of Latino workers from the wage benefits of the Massachusetts Miracle and their concentration in the most unstable and declining industries led to some of the highest rates of Latino poverty in the country in the 1980s. Although they would continue to dominate the region's ailing manufacturing sector into the twenty-first century, Latinos also joined the shift to low-skilled service work during the 1990s.[7]

A closer look at the labor force in Boston between 1980 and 2010 shows just how important immigrants have been to the growth of the city's economy, particularly in the rising service sector. As figure 12 shows, the city's labor force grew from 275,571 in 1980 to 362,846 in 2010, increasing by roughly a third over this thirty-year period. Immigrant workers have made up a growing proportion of this workforce, from 14 percent in 1980 to 32 percent in 2010.

In fact, over this thirty-year period, immigrants made up 89 percent of the overall growth in the city's labor force, while native-born workers accounted for only 11 percent. Moreover, a significant percentage of the new native-born workers have been young second-generation ethnics who began to enter the labor force as they reached adulthood. Indeed, without immigrants and their children, the city's labor force would have grown little if at all over those decades. And Boston's experience is indicative of a broader trend across much of the Northeast; a growing dependence on immigrant labor has in fact characterized the workforce across Massachusetts as well as in New York, New Jersey, Connecticut, and Rhode Island.[8] In Boston and other northeastern cities, the infusion of new immigrant workers has been increasingly concentrated in the service industries—both in skilled professional and managerial occupations and in the lower-skilled and lower-paid service jobs that have proliferated since the 1980s (see fig. 11).

As in many US cities, jobs in cleaning, grounds keeping, food service, childcare, elder care, and other services became the lifeblood of many of the area's less-skilled foreign workers. Their labor was critical to the emerging knowledge economy and to maintaining the lifestyles of the affluent and often stressed two-income families employed in the upper ranks of this new economy. But service jobs were not only the result of economic restructuring; they were also created in response to new career opportunities for middle-class women. Between 1970 and 2010, the number of Boston women employed in professional and managerial ranks increased from 42 to 54 percent of the city's workforce. As Barbara Ehrenreich and Arlie Hochschild observe, such new employment gave rise to "a growing 'care industry' [that] has stepped into the traditional wife's role, creating a very real demand for migrant women." Likewise, high-pressure careers for middle-class men left less time for tending the yard, making home repairs, or sharing domestic work and childrearing. In a state with an aging native-born population, longer life expectancies led to an expansion of hospitals, nursing homes, and assisted living facilities, which in turn required a vast army of orderlies, nursing aides, and other care givers. The arrival of growing numbers of immigrants coincided with these changes in the social landscape, while growing global inequalities limited wage-earning opportunities for migrants in their home countries. While Boston-area service jobs provided much-needed employment for newcomers, low pay, poor working conditions, and inadequate benefits often left them struggling to survive, much like earlier immigrants who labored in the region's kitchens and mills prior to unionization.[9]

New immigrants also resembled the old in their tendency to move into certain industries and employment niches. Although a wide assortment of

Foreign- and Native-Born Labor Force in the City of Boston, 1980–2010

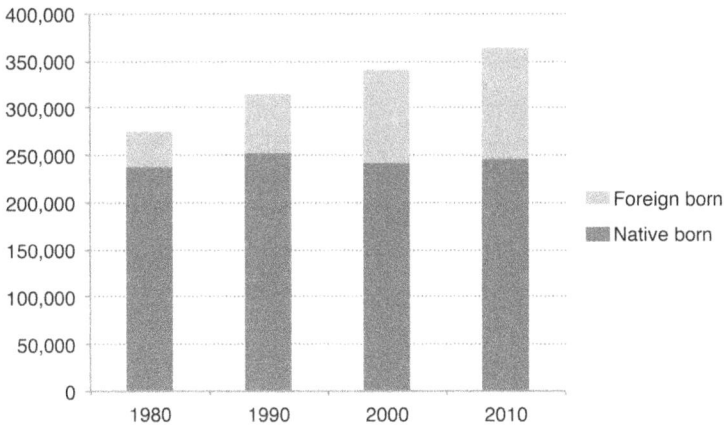

FIGURE 12. Foreign-born and native-born labor force in Boston, 1980–2010.
Source: Steven Ruggles, J. Trent Alexander, Katie Genadek, Ronald Goeken, Matthew B. Schroeder, and Matthew Sobek, *Integrated Public Use Microdata Series: Version 5.0* (Minneapolis: University of Minnesota, 2010).

ethnic groups found jobs in fields such as construction and food services, certain groups have clustered in particular jobs or industries. Latinos, for example—particularly women from Central America and the Dominican Republic—increasingly found work as office cleaners. Their entry occurred in the 1980s and 1990s as building services shifted to nonunionized labor, replacing older white and black male janitors who had earned union-scale wages and health benefits. The move to nonunionized immigrant labor accompanied the real estate boom of the 1980s and the rise of building service contractors like Unnico, which cut labor costs by hiring part-time workers and not providing health benefits. Latino men were hired first, but increasing numbers of Latinas were then recruited through family and ethnic networks. By 2002 Latinos made up roughly 70 percent of the city's janitors. Cape Verdeans and Brazilians also developed niches in janitorial work, though many of the latter subsequently shifted into residential house cleaning.[10]

Among Haitian (and later African) men, cab driving became a common occupation. Dominated by immigrants since the early twentieth century, taxi driving once offered a mobile, relatively independent work setting (often with healthcare and other benefits) and the possibility of owning a small business for those who could purchase taxi medallions and vehicles. Haitians who entered the industry in the 1960s and 1970s later bought medallions and began leasing their cabs to fellow Haitians, creating a niche in the industry. As in building services, though, the influx of immigrant workers coincided with the rise of large-scale subcontracting in which taxi corporations bought up hundreds of high-priced medallions and leased their cabs to drivers who were reclassified as independent contractors. Cabbies typically worked twelve- or twenty-four-hour shifts, putting in a minimum of seventy-two hours per week with no overtime or health benefits. They also had to pay for gas, taxes, tolls, and hefty leasing fees, and in some cases, daily bribes to taxi company dispatchers. During the 2008 recession, Haitian driver Chando Souffant told of working sixteen-hour shifts, seven days a week: "That's the only way you can survive," he explained. "They call us ambassadors of the city, but they treat us like slaves." During big conventions and other busy times, cabbies could make a living, but during recessions, dozens of drivers were left homeless and forced to sleep in their cars. Critics of the city's taxi system called it "sharecropping on wheels."[11]

While Haitian men were driving taxis, Haitian women flocked in large numbers into nursing jobs. The region's burgeoning healthcare complex and the opening of new nursing and assisted living centers created a swift demand for certified nursing assistants. Haitian women gravitated to these jobs, positions that required only eighty hours of classroom training. In 2003, roughly half of all Haitian women workers in the Boston area were employed in this field, and an astounding 80 percent of the region's nursing aides were of Haitian descent. Although many complained of oppressive workloads and racial bias, the niche grew because of the steady work available and pay rates that were above minimum wage. Some nursing aides were able to continue their schooling and earn certifications as licensed practical nurses or registered nurses, higher-paid occupations for which there was even stronger demand. But like the janitors and cab drivers, a growing number of nursing aides were hired through contracting firms that offered part-time work with few benefits or opportunities for advancement.[12]

Haitians and other immigrant groups that began arriving several decades ago developed expansive employment niches over time, but even newer and smaller groups have developed distinct occupational clusters. Many Ethiopians, for example, found work as parking garage attendants in Boston and other US cities beginning in the 1980s, when the first wave of refugees arrived. Using ethnic connections to secure jobs and developing a good reputation with employers, some Ethiopians used these low-wage jobs as stepping stones to managerial positions in the parking companies. Younger Ethiopians, by contrast, sought out quieter evening shifts that allowed them to combine work and studies while attending college during the day. Dejene Ahmed, a refugee who arrived from Ethiopia in the 1980s, found an evening job at a downtown garage that helped subsidize his education at Wentworth Institute. He went on to a position at a local high-tech firm and, with his wife (who also worked in a parking garage while attending college), bought a home in suburban Randolph. For refugees like Ahmed, who had a foundation of education in their homeland and some initial resettlement assistance from the government, such informal "work-study" jobs helped support their college education and upward mobility.[13]

Since the mid-1980s, certain sectors of the economy have also become niches for unauthorized immigrants. Prior to that time, lax enforcement measures meant that undocumented workers could move more freely throughout the workforce. But in the wake of the 1986 Immigration Reform and Control Act—which required employers to verify their workers' legal status—federal enforcement efforts were stepped up, making some employers leery of hiring the undocumented. Nevertheless, many companies and individuals—particularly smaller-scale and cash-based businesses such as restaurants, residential construction, landscaping, and domestic work—continued to hire these workers. As a booming trade in false Social Security cards emerged in the 1990s, even some large manufacturers and construction firms did not hesitate to hire the undocumented. The proliferation of temporary labor agencies and contracting firms also helped to insulate employers from prosecution by shifting the compliance responsibility to the contractors. Such operations, which provided transportation from poorer Latino and Southeast Asian communities to job sites throughout the metro area, often skimmed off as much as 40 to 50 percent of workers' wages. As one Colombian community activist explained, "The temporary employment agencies that pick [Latino workers] up on a corner and bring them every day to a different place to work, pay them minimum wage and then take out a fee for shoes, food, etc. So the person ends up with almost nothing in their pay check." Labor activists charged that these contractors fostered a "shadow labor force" that was ill paid and ill treated.[14]

Such attempts to secure cheap immigrant labor were hardly new. Contractors who built the railroads recruited Irish laborers from Boston in the nineteenth century, while in the early 1900s Italian *padrones* combed the docks in East Boston for newcomers to work in lumber mills and construction sites across New England. In recent years, however, the use of contingent immigrant labor has become a tool for deunionizing the workforce and a means of circumventing federal and state labor regulations. The issue of documentation has also created a potentially more coercive and exploitive work climate. Periodic immigration raids—such as the arrest of 83 workers at Suffolk Downs racetrack in 1988 and 360 workers at the Michael Bianco leather factory in New Bedford in 2007—showed how employers blatantly disregarded federal immigration law.[15] These raids and hundreds of smaller ones instilled fear in undocumented workers that made them vulnerable to exploitation. Labor advocates noted that some employers threatened to call immigration authorities if workers complained about pay or working conditions, or expressed interest in joining a union. Reports of unsafe conditions, withheld wages, or failure to pay overtime were widespread. Women workers also faced routine sexual harassment and even rape by employers or supervisors. Ann Philbin, director of an immigrant workers' center in Boston in 1992, noted that sexual harassment was "a constant in nearly every immigrant woman we see." Beginning in the 1990s, a few Salvadoran women broke the silence and filed claims against their employers, but most quietly endured for fear of being fired or deported.[16] As we will see in chapter 7, such abuse gave rise to workers' centers and other labor and community groups that would become an important front in the emerging immigrant rights movement.

ETHNIC ENTREPRENEURS

For both documented and undocumented immigrants, one way to minimize exposure to workplace abuse was through self-employment. For the undocumented, starting a small cash-based business could reduce problems of documentation and the likelihood of detection; for documented migrants, entrepreneurship enabled them to work for themselves and avoid exploitation by employers or labor contractors. Like Jewish, Italian, Greek, and other earlier immigrants who had founded corner groceries, dry goods stores, and restaurants, recent immigrants have launched thousands of small businesses, including more than 8,800 in the city of Boston alone in 2007. While not all migrant groups have been as able or inclined to take up self-employment, migrants from Brazil, China, and Vietnam, among others, have had a significant impact on economic life in the region. Their efforts have driven a resurgence in entrepreneurship that has characterized greater Boston and other metropolitan areas since the 1980s.[17]

A large portion of the growth in small business has been among Asians and Asian Americans, among whom the number of small businesses grew by 158 percent between 1992 and 2002. Among the Chinese, restaurants have been the foundation of the ethnic economy since the early twentieth century, when Chinatown eateries sprang up to serve inexpensive meals to male sojourners and later offered more Americanized fare to Chinatown diners and tourists. Since the 1960s, however, growing American demand for more authentic Asian cuisine and the arrival of new immigrants from Hong Kong, Thailand, and Vietnam have resulted in an explosion of new restaurants throughout the metro area. As more restaurants opened in the suburbs, a growing fleet of vans converged on Chinatown each day to ferry immigrant workers to kitchens in Brockton, Tewksbury, Saugus, and even southern New Hampshire. Offering only low wages, long hours, and few benefits, these restaurants employed thousands of less skilled immigrants who struggled to make ends meet, but they also enriched a smaller number of owners and chefs who managed to succeed in a highly competitive industry.[18]

Other Asian groups also opened ethnic restaurants and niche businesses. Vietnamese, for example, opened restaurants serving pho (a hearty noodle soup) and other Southeast Asian specialties, as well as establishing a growing number of nail salons and floor sanding businesses. By the early 2000s, the Vietnamese owned roughly half of all nail salons in Boston, where owners leased chairs to coethnic "independent contractors" who had completed certification courses for around $750. As in the restaurant business, the oversaturation of the nail industry led to cutthroat pricing and falling wages for workers, but owners whose businesses survived made a reasonable living. Among Koreans, dry cleaning businesses became the most common form of entrepreneurship. By the late 1990s there were more than 250 Korean-owned dry cleaning establishments in New England, a large percentage of them in the greater Boston area.[19]

Some of the most dynamic ethnic entrepreneurship occurred among Brazilian immigrants, who developed substantial niches in construction, landscaping, and house cleaning in the 1990s. In fact, 15 percent of Brazilian immigrants in metro Boston were self-employed in 2000, a rate nearly four times that of the total foreign-born population. This impressive showing was based on Brazilians' relatively high levels of education and financial capital and a strong and valued culture of entrepreneurship in their home country. Many migrants, especially those who arrived in the 1980s and 1990s, had graduated from high school or college in Brazil and had work experience in sales, teaching, banking, and other middle-class occupations. Before learning English, many took low-paying jobs in Boston area manufacturing or service industries.[20]

Some, like Maria da Graca de Sales, a former school teacher from Governador Valadares who found work as a housekeeper for a Boston hotel in the mid-1980s, saw that she could earn more by starting her own cleaning business. "Hotels paid $5 an hour, but people who wanted homes cleaned were paying $8," explained de Sales's daughter, Rosangela. Targeting prosperous suburbs with busy two-earner households, house cleaners charged competitive rates and built up routes of twenty or more homes per week. By 2006, de Sales had acquired seventy clients that brought in more than $100,000 per year. Successful businesses like hers hired more workers (typically new arrivals), spun off new routes to family members, or sold client referrals to other immigrants via the Brazilian American press. Through such practices, the niche expanded and house cleaning became the single largest occupation among Boston area Brazilians.[21]

The success of Brazilian house cleaning, though, prompted criticism in some quarters. As in the nail salons and taxi business, house cleaners often hired coethnic helpers as "independent contractors," who were paid in cash, had no taxes withheld, and received no benefits. Like the nail business, house cleaning involved steady contact with dangerous chemicals that led to respiratory and skin problems. Moreover, some cleaners who had small family operations relied on their teenage children to work long hours that interfered with their education and, in some cases, led them to drop out of school entirely. And, like a number of other immigrant businesses, house cleaning employed a large number of unauthorized migrants who could be paid in cash and remain relatively invisible to immigration authorities. This left the undocumented employees vulnerable to exploitation and abuse, as family and ethnic ties did not always guarantee humane treatment. For those who became owners, however, a successful cleaning business helped them support family back in Brazil, buy homes, educate their children, and enjoy a degree of social mobility.[22]

Brazilian cleaning companies and other small businesses also provided capital for development efforts, both in Brazil and in Massachusetts. Cleaners interviewed by journalists and scholars described how they used cleaning profits to build houses and businesses in Minas Gerais or to buy and renovate properties in Massachusetts. The Quintelas family—six brothers who founded a house cleaning business in the 1990s—later used their earnings to buy and renovate three rundown duplexes in downtown Framingham. Other Brazilian entrepreneurs opened stores in old, boarded-up storefronts in the same area, sparking the downtown revival described in chapter 3. A similar process took place in Everett in the early 2000s as Brazilian immigrants bought and fixed up old downtown storefronts.[23]

Brazilians were not the only group leading such neighborhood revivals. In fact, immigrant-led urban revitalization in the region dates back to the 1970s, when large numbers of Cuban, Dominican, and Vietnamese immigrants began settling in old working-class neighborhoods. The first area to experience a turnaround was Hyde Square in Jamaica Plain, where Cuban and Dominican merchants began renovating older buildings for new businesses to serve the neighborhood's growing Latino population. Meeting weekly at Blessed Sacrament Catholic Church, the merchants devised plans for attracting new businesses and reducing crime and vandalism. Their efforts succeeded, and Centre Street developed into the city's largest Latino commercial district by the 1980s. A decade later, in East Boston, Colombian and Salvadoran businesses helped revitalize old shopping districts in Maverick and Central squares, while Vietnamese restaurants and retail businesses injected new life into a declining Fields Corner neighborhood.[24]

But perhaps the most remarkable example of revitalization occurred adjacent to Chinatown. There, Vietnamese and ethnic Chinese refugees opened restaurants, video stores, and gift shops in the city's notorious adult entertainment district, known as the Combat Zone. With little available credit and few contacts in the older Chinatown community, aspiring Southeast Asian entrepreneurs were relegated to storefronts on Washington Street, a seedy district of adult bookstores, strip clubs, and a thriving prostitution trade. Many of the newcomers had been merchants in Vietnam, and some spoke both Cantonese and Vietnamese. By the late 1990s, an estimated 30 percent of all Chinatown businesses were owned by Vietnamese immigrants who, along with the ethnic Chinese, were credited with reclaiming Washington Street and helping drive the Combat Zone out of business. Entrepreneurial success, however, proved to be a double-edged sword. As revitalization took hold in both Chinatown and Jamaica Plain, gentrification increased rents and property values, driving away coethnic customers and some of the small ethnic businesses they patronized.[25]

THE KNOWLEDGE SECTOR

One of the most distinctive characteristics of the new immigration has been the large percentage of highly skilled newcomers with technical and professional expertise. Because of its wealth of educational institutions and knowledge-based industries, greater Boston has attracted more than its share of such new immigrants, who have increased their share of the city's foreign-born workforce from 18 percent in 1980 to 27 percent in 2010 (see fig. 11). By the twenty-first century, more than a third of recent immigrants to Massachusetts held a bachelor's or advanced degree, and roughly a quarter of the state's newcomers were admitted under skill preferences—compared with only 13 percent nationwide.[26]

The rising skill levels of the immigrant population began after World War II, when the United States granted refugee status to foreign-born scientists and intellectuals from communist-bloc countries—primarily from China and eastern Europe. Harvard, MIT, and other Boston area universities were attractive destinations for these talented newcomers, including computer and electronics developer An Wang (Chinese) and foreign policy specialist Zbigniew Brzezinski (Polish). During the Cold War, the Fulbright program and other international educational exchanges attracted growing numbers of foreign students to Boston area universities. Originating in Europe, but also from newly independent states in Asia, Africa, Latin America, and the Caribbean, these visitors helped initiate new streams of foreign students to local universities, some of whom would find work and stay permanently. Other professional and technical workers were admitted under the skill preferences of the 1952 and 1965 immigration acts.

Since the 1960s, the region's universities, hospitals, and high-tech industries have recruited many of these skilled workers. Federal funding spurred growth in all of these areas in the postwar era, creating new labor demands and preferences. The GI Bill and other postwar student aid programs helped expand enrollments and faculties at area universities, while brisk competition between the schools prompted them to look abroad for top professors and researchers. The establishment of Medicare and Medicaid in 1965 dramatically expanded demand for healthcare services, although American medical and nursing schools could not keep pace. To fill the gap, especially in the lower-paying urban public hospitals, foreign-trained medical students and nurses were recruited from countries such as the Philippines, Canada, Ireland, and India. Later, the growth of private health insurance plans, the rapid aging of the state's population, and the passage of a mandatory public health insurance program in Massachusetts in 2006 and the federal Affordable Care Act in 2010 have continued to fuel demand. The nursing shortage has been particularly acute; to facilitate the recruitment of foreign nurses, Congress passed bills in 1989 and 2006 providing qualified applicants with temporary work visas and easier access to green cards. Overall, the foreign born have filled much of the demand for new medical personnel in Massachusetts: by 2005, they made up more than half of all medical scientists, 40 percent of pharmacists, 28 percent of physicians and surgeons, and 10 percent of registered nurses.[27]

Finally, skilled immigrant workers have played a critical role in the region's high-tech electronics, computing, and information technology sectors. Like medicine and education, these industries benefited from federal funding during and after World War II as the government sought to develop sophisticated new communications, weapons, and data systems. During the 1970s and 1980s, tech firms recruited foreign-born (mostly Asian) engineering and computer science students from MIT and other universities, as well as hiring Soviet refugees with technical backgrounds. Still hungry for new talent and innovation, technology firms lobbied Congress to create a new category of H-1B visas under the 1990 Immigration Act. The H-1B program subsequently admitted tens of thousands of new computer programmers, engineers, physicians, and other highly skilled workers on a temporary basis.

Local computer technology firms used the program to recruit a large crop of Indian workers in the 1990s and 2000s. Some of these workers returned home after a year or two; others stayed and became permanent legal residents when employers sponsored their green cards.[28]

The government's newfound role in facilitating the migration of skilled foreign workers has been the target of criticism from some quarters. Some industry observers have claimed that alleged "shortages" of US engineers and programmers were exaggerated, and that employers were paying foreign workers less and assigning heavier workloads. In fact, between 2000 and 2007, the US Labor Department found that six Boston area companies were in violation of rules governing H-1B employment (requiring prevailing pay rates in the industry) and ordered back pay issued to those employees. Like trade union workers of an earlier era, many native-born tech workers resented these practices, charging that employers were using the H-1B program to create a class of "techno-slaves," thereby undercutting the pay and job security of American workers. Related complaints were common among nurses, who argued that hospitals were relying on quick fixes in the form of immigrant workers rather than addressing the larger problems of compensation, working conditions, and career development that were discouraging the native-born from pursuing nursing careers. Others observed that by relying on foreign-trained medical and nursing school graduates, the United States was effectively shirking its responsibility to provide adequate social investment in education.[29]

Criticism of foreign worker recruitment also centered on its impact on the migrants' home countries. During the Cold War, when doctors, scientists, engineers, and other professionals were being lured from developing countries, scholars dubbed this process "the brain drain." The loss of these valued and scarce workers was a blow to many hard-pressed regions of Africa, Asia, and Latin America, where their skills were desperately needed. Global integration scholars later challenged this view, suggesting that the migration of skilled labor also created a "brain-exchange" in which returning migrants brought new skills and experience back to their home countries and fostered an international exchange of ideas and services.[30] While the rise of transnational companies in the Boston area (especially Indian- and Chinese-owned firms) suggested that such brain exchanges were in fact occurring, the loss of professional talent from countries like Nigeria, Haiti, and the Philippines remained a serious problem.

In the Boston area, however, skilled immigrant workers did serve as an important engine for economic development by founding dozens of start-ups in fields like computer software, data systems, medical devices, and biotechnology. Between 1995 and 2005, 29 percent of all science and engineering firms in Massachusetts were founded by at least one foreign-born partner. A study of the local biotech industry in 2007 discovered that more than a quarter of biotech firms in the state were founded by immigrants, mainly from Asia, Europe, and Canada. Such ventures, concentrated in and around Cambridge and Route 128, contributed more than four thousand jobs to the local economy.[31]

MIT and other Boston-area universities have been fertile breeding grounds for such ventures, but ironically, some of the barriers that immigrants faced in the United States have also encouraged such entrepreneurship. Amar Sawhney, an Indian-born Sikh who founded two Boston-area medical device firms in the 1990s, explained how his lack of a green card moved him into a start-up. After finishing his master's degree in chemical engineering, he said, "I applied for thirty positions with companies that came to the campus and twenty-nine of them sent me a rejection letter. And the last one, when I went for the interview, they realized I didn't have a green card and they rejected me." He then decided to continue on for a Ph.D. and jumped at a chance to join a start-up a few years later. "If you have not much to lose," Sawhney said, "you take more risks and you try harder." Other immigrants noted that encountering "a glass ceiling" because of their race or religion convinced them to leave their jobs and start their own firms. As the region's manufacturing base continued to shrink, these immigrant-owned companies provided new jobs in a field that combined two of the region's leading knowledge industries—medicine and technology—in what has proved to be a key area of economic growth in the twenty-first century.[32]

THE BIMODAL ECONOMY

The concentration of immigrant workers at the top and bottom rungs of the urban economy is a reflection of what economists refer to as the "hourglass" or "bimodal" economy. In greater Boston, European and Asian immigrants—particularly those from India, Korea, Japan, and Taiwan—have been most concentrated at the top professional and technical end of the hourglass, while Latino, Southeast Asian, and Afro-Caribbean migrants have made up a disproportionate share of workers on the lower end. Prior educational achievements, English proficiency, and occupational skills have often determined where one lands in the new economy, so those from poorer countries with fewer educational resources have been at a distinct disadvantage. Racial bias and employer preferences—typically for European, non-Muslim Asian, or lighter-skinned Latino workers—have also shaped the workforce options of new immigrants, consigning many to low-paid, unorganized, and unstable sectors of the economy.[33]

The bimodal economy has thus produced divergent economic outcomes and prospects for the social integration of immigrants. In recent years, highly educated newcomers have enjoyed much more rapid social mobility and integration than those who arrived a hundred years ago. The proliferation of high-earning immigrant professionals has been a striking development that has diversified many Boston workplaces, schools, and neighborhoods and has laid the groundwork for continued prosperity and integration of the second generation. On the other end of the economic scale, however, the growth of low-income and often socially marginalized migrant populations has been a worrisome trend. Concentrated in some of Boston's poorer neighborhoods and in the region's older industrial towns and cities, low-income migrant workers have struggled to survive in a region where housing and living costs have been driven steadily upward by real estate and consumer markets geared to high-end workers of the knowledge economy.

Although the foreign born of greater Boston have had consistently high rates of workforce participation, the low pay, instability, and sometimes exploitative terms of that employment—combined with low levels of education and English proficiency among many immigrants—have resulted in lower wages and family incomes. In 2011, Boston's foreign-born employees earned approximately three-quarters the wages earned by the native born, and over the course of the preceding thirty years the median income of foreign-born families had fallen in comparison with that of the native born: in 1980, the median income of the city's foreign-born families was only 6 percent below that of the native born. That differential grew to 9 percent in 1990, 12 percent in 2000, and by 2010 was 17 percent. This growing inequality has resulted in part from the rapid growth of lower-paid service work among immigrants, but even among professional and managerial workers, average foreign-born income lags significantly behind.[34]

For many working-class immigrant families, these low incomes have produced severe economic pressures, requiring many to work multiple jobs to survive. Since many have also been responsible for supporting needy relatives back home, the hardships have been even greater. Furthermore, for those in hard-pressed older industrial cities, eroding tax bases and substandard education and services have posed critical obstacles to the educational and social advancement of their children. For the second generation, incorporation into American society has often meant joining a low-wage and predominantly nonwhite employment sector—with little likelihood of completing college or moving into the middle or upper ranks of the economy.

For some foes of immigration reform, these grim realities suggest that newcomers have harmed the US economy and lowered American living standards. In metro Boston, however, immigrant labor has been indispensible to the new service-based economy, at both the top and bottom ends. As in many older northeastern cities that saw steep population losses after World War II, the Boston area labor force and economy simply could not have grown and flourished without new immigrants. Moreover, the region's knowledge economy has not been a zero-sum game in which foreign-born workers simply took jobs from the native born. In ethnic businesses across the region, and particularly in the high-tech fields, immigrant entrepreneurs have added thousands of jobs to the local economy, contributing to the long-term revitalization of the metro area. The ongoing challenge of the bimodal economy, then, has been to find more equitable ways to train and integrate new immigrant workers and to promote—through more affordable housing, better labor laws and enforcement, and improved education—a more widely shared prosperity.

CHAPTER 5

Nativism, Violence, and the Rise of Multiculturalism

I n the summer of 1980, Hao Tan Lai was staying with friends in Boston before heading back to college. Originally from Nha Trang, Vietnam, Lai had arrived in the United States in 1977 along with thousands of other Vietnam War refugees. His friends had thrown a party for him, but a pleasant evening turned sour when a rock was thrown through the window of the Brighton apartment belonging to one of the Vietnamese celebrants. Lai and his friends set out to confront the vandals, who fled to nearby Oak Square. As the Vietnamese arrived in the square, a group of white teenagers pelted them with bottles and cans, and a melee ensued. Lai and his friend Dien Pham escaped down the street, but the white youths caught up with them. Moments later, Lai and Pham were beaten and stabbed. Pham was badly wounded; Lai died in the hospital the following day.[1]

Lai was the first of three Southeast Asian refugees who were killed by whites in the greater Boston area in the 1980s. Hundreds of others were the victims of assault, battery, arson, and other crimes as an epidemic of anti-Asian hate crimes swept the city's neighborhoods and inner suburbs. Boston was just one of several cities in which this resurgence of nativism and racism took place: Philadelphia, Los Angeles, New York, Washington,

DC, Houston, and several Gulf Coast cities all saw sharp increases in anti-Asian violence. Such attacks made national headlines in the late 1980s and became the subject of congressional hearings that led to the passage of federal hate crimes legislation.[2] This chapter explores the resurgent nativism of the 1980s and the campaigns against it in greater Boston.

Contemporary observers explained such violent acts as misdirected responses to the nation's trade war with Japan and to lingering resentments over the Vietnam War. Asian Americans also highlighted the United States' long history of anti-Asian racism, violence, and exclusion, seeing the attacks on new immigrants as merely the latest episode in this ongoing politics of prejudice. While there is much validity to these views, reexamining these events from a historical perspective exposes the origins and development of a larger anti-immigrant movement that has been gaining momentum in the United States since the 1980s. Historians have documented this new nativist movement as it emerged in California in response to growing Mexican and Central American immigration. But in East Coast cities such as Boston and Philadelphia, where Asians accounted for a large percentage of newcomers in the 1980s, anti-immigrant sentiment was particularly focused on those groups. Since many were Southeast Asian war refugees, a nativist discourse emerged in which the state was directly implicated. This new emphasis on the role of government in facilitating immigration and subsidizing migrant families would become a key tenet of the contemporary anti-immigration movement and would distinguish it from earlier waves of nativism in the United States.[3]

Focusing on Boston also allows us to better understand the economic and social context of older East Coast cities where many refugees and immigrants settled. Contemporaries noted the troubled economy and growing Asian competition as sources of white racial resentment, citing the murder of Vincent Chin as an emblematic case. Chin, a young Chinese American man mistakenly thought to be Japanese, was beaten to death in 1982 by two Detroit autoworkers who blamed him for layoffs in an ailing US auto industry. Unlike Detroit, however, Boston had a roaring economy for much of the 1980s, thanks to a high-tech boom that produced record high employment levels—the so-called Massachusetts Miracle. Indeed, the metropolitan area was at a pivotal juncture in its history, as it evolved from a declining manufacturing center to a growing knowledge- and service-based economy. But amid these shifting economic currents, the status of both immigrants and the region's native-born working class was profoundly unstable, prompting a variety of racial and class resentments. Although immigrants and native-born whites often came to blows, the violence also gave rise to new panethnic and community-based movements in which native-born activists allied with newcomers to combat racism and anti-immigrant bias. Those efforts marked the beginnings of a wider acceptance of multiculturalism and immigrant incorporation in the region—but also simmering nativist attitudes that blamed liberals and the state for encouraging and subsidizing the immigrant influx.

The genesis of violence in this period was rooted in the troubled economic and social landscape of Boston in the post–World War II era. With the decline of urban manufacturing industries, together with generous federal subsidies for home loans, highways, and higher education, a growing portion of the city's white ethnic working class moved to the suburbs and into middle-class occupations. As Boston's population plummeted, many of the city's remaining industries, retail establishments, and tax dollars followed.[4] In an attempt to stop the hemorrhaging and retool the urban economy, city leaders launched an ambitious redevelopment campaign to build a "New Boston" that would attract white-collar service industries and middle-class residents. As bulldozers razed poor and working-class neighborhoods in the South and West Ends, Chinatown, Roxbury, and Mission Hill, older residents were displaced by new office towers, highways, medical facilities, university buildings, and luxury housing. The growing pressure on Boston's remaining working-class areas aggravated long-standing ethnic and racial tensions in a city that was well known for its parochial neighborhoods and tribal turf battles. The dual forces of suburban white flight and urban redevelopment resulted in population shifts and racial transition in neighborhoods such as Roxbury, Dorchester, and Mattapan. White residents—subject to block-busting and real estate profiteering—bitterly resisted black and Latino settlement in the 1960s and 1970s. A spiral of racial animosity and violence followed, and mounting tensions exploded in 1974 when a federal court–ordered desegregation plan ignited a series of violent clashes in South Boston, Charlestown, and other neighborhoods. The Boston busing crisis enveloped the city for the next two years and served to harden racial battle lines in many poor and working-class areas (see chapter 7 for more on the impact of busing on immigrants and politics).[5]

It was into this profoundly tense and divided social landscape that the first wave of Southeast Asian refugees began arriving in the late 1970s. As previously discussed, voluntary agencies secured housing and sponsors for incoming refugees; typically they found vacancies in predominantly white working-class areas where the population had been declining—neighborhoods such as Dorchester, East Boston, and Allston-Brighton, as well as older suburbs like Quincy, Chelsea, Somerville, and Revere.[6] When the first refugees began arriving in Massachusetts in 1975, they confronted a grim economy in which relentless layoffs and factory closures resulted in double-digit unemployment and poverty rates well above the national average. By 1983, however, the state's economy was on the rebound as the new high-tech and service-based industries began to bear fruit. From 1983 to 1987, in fact, the Massachusetts economy was booming, with unemployment rates that were among the lowest in the country. As we saw in the last chapter, refugee organizations helped find newcomers low-paid assembly jobs at computer and medical equipment companies or service work in downtown office buildings, hotels, and restaurants. The low wages for these jobs, however, forced many refugees to share housing and resources, leading to overcrowding in what were often already large family households. Moreover, refugee agencies often settled newcomers in clusters of adjacent apartments, where they could offer each other financial and emotional support in what proved to be an increasingly hostile environment.

At the other end of the state's booming economy, the Boston area saw an expansion of highly skilled technical and professional jobs, both downtown and in the suburbs. This influx of highly skilled workers, often recruited through the region's bounty of colleges and universities, served to push housing prices up dramatically. During the 1980s, median housing prices in Boston grew from $36,300 to $161,400 (a whopping 180 percent increase in inflation-adjusted dollars), making Boston one of the most expensive housing markets in the country. This housing bonanza accelerated gentrification and condominium conversions in the city and drove median rents up from $189 to $544 per month in the 1980s (an 81 percent increase in real dollars). Such rent hikes did not keep pace with the wages of lower-income workers and put additional pressure on the region's struggling manufacturing industries, many of which finally shut down. Between 1984 and 1987—the peak years of the Massachusetts Miracle—the state lost 11.2 percent of its manufacturing jobs, the second highest rate in the country. Among the dozens of local plants that closed during the 1980s were Colonial Provision Company in Dorchester, P & L Sportswear and the Bethlehem Shipyards in East Boston, and Schrafft's Candy and Revere Sugar in Charlestown.

These plant closings produced painful dislocations for the city's blue-collar workers. As numerous economists pointed out, many of those laid off faced steep pay cuts, loss of union or company benefits, and longer commutes. "We look for work, but nothing pays what we were making," said one laid-off worker who had been earning $10.65 per hour at Colonial Provision, a meat processing plant in Dorchester. "The best you can get is $6, maybe $6.50 an hour. . . . These jobs won't cover people's mortgages." Although the state legislature established a fund for retraining workers who lost their jobs as a result of plant closures, the transition to the new high-tech/service economy proved difficult for many families. Unemployment also remained high among teenagers, particularly working-class youth who had limited mobility and skills. Meanwhile, rents in the city surged upward, pitting new and old residents against one another in the struggle for affordable housing. Buffeted by unemployment or falling wages on the one hand, and gentrification and rising rents on the other, some native-born white Bostonians vented their resentments on the closest target—their new immigrant neighbors.[7]

Following the 1980 murder of Hao Tan Lai, reports of vandalism, harassment, and assaults on Southeast Asian newcomers grew increasingly common. A report later compiled by the Asian American Resource Workshop indicated that the number of racially motivated crimes against Asians in Boston grew from fewer than five cases in 1979, to thirty-two in 1983, to forty-five in 1985. Moreover, the increase occurred at the same time as the overall number of civil rights–related crimes in the city saw a dramatic decline. While the victims were both Asian American and foreign born, newcomers from Vietnam and Southeast Asia made up a disproportionate percentage: well over half of all Asian cases from 1983 to 1987. Authorities noted that Southeast Asians were targeted in part because of their reluctance to contact police; a lack of knowledge about their rights and negative experiences with authorities in their home countries had made many distrustful of the state. In addition to Lai, two other refugees died in the violence—Anh Mai, a twenty-three-year-old from Vietnam was killed in Dorchester in 1983, and Bun Vong, a thirty-five-year-old Cambodian man was fatally beaten in Medford in 1985.[8]

This dramatic surge in anti-Asian violence peaked in 1985–1986, high-lighted by an explosion of attacks that ripped through two Boston neigh-borhoods on Memorial Day weekend in 1985. The first incident occurred in South Boston in the early morning hours of May 25, when a group of roughly thirty white men surrounded the home of three Vietnamese men, shouting racial epithets and bombarding them with bricks and bottles. After a window broke, one of the men crawled inside and opened the door to the crowd, who then attacked the residents. Two nights later, violence broke out in East Boston, when four Cambodian residents were chased and beaten by fifteen to twenty white teens brandishing hockey sticks and a lead pipe. Three of the Cambodians were hospitalized for their injuries. The series of violent incidents attracted widespread media attention and served to propel the issue into the public eye. On May 31, the *Boston Globe* ran an editorial condemning racial violence and calling on the city to take firmer measures, noting: "The lack of highly visible efforts by the city administration and by responsible citizens can only encourage the bigots who commit such acts."[9]

The violence, however, continued. A few weeks later, Bun Vong, a Cambodian refugee living in Lowell, was beaten to death by two white motorists in a roadside dispute a few miles north of Boston. Around the same time, the Cambodian refugee community of nearby Revere was tar-geted in a series of assaults and arson attacks that continued for months, leav-ing dozens homeless. Tensions were also rising in Quincy and Somerville, two older predominantly working-class suburbs where new Asian residents had their cars vandalized, rocks thrown at their homes, and arson attempts on their buildings. Extensive press coverage of these incidents, along with reports filed by community groups, provide important insights into the sources of the violence and the growing nativist resentments.

SOURCES OF VIOLENCE

As many noted at the time, the bitter legacy of the Vietnam War—which had ended just a decade earlier—figured prominently in the attacks. Lingering resentments over the nation's loss in Vietnam colored many Americans' atti-tudes toward Southeast Asians refugees, as well as a wartime experience that cast the Vietnamese enemy (and all those who resembled them) as treach-erous "gooks." Even though most refugees had fought against communist regimes in their home countries, they were often derided as communists by their new white neighbors. Ratha Yem, a Cambodian community leader in Chelsea and Revere, explained: "People believe that Southeast Asians fought against American soldiers in Vietnam . . . and they see us as a whole as the enemy." Asian American activist Peter Kiang also emphasized the lingering impact of the Vietnam War: "Lets face it, there's a great deal of hostility and racism left over from the Vietnam War. The 'gook' mentality is still very prevalent."[10]

Moreover, the anti-Asian violence of the mid-1980s was also a response to a new revisionist view of the war that was emerging during the Reagan years. As historians have argued, this revisionist perspective blamed US political leaders for the nation's military defeat and spawned popular revenge fantasies in which heroic Americans reconquered the country. The Memorial Day violence of 1985, in fact, broke out just as the latest Rambo movie opened in local theaters. The story of an ill-treated Vietnam veteran, *Rambo: First Blood II* featured an AK-47–toting Sylvester Stallone returning to Vietnam to rescue abandoned US prisoners of war. Captured and tortured by the Viet Cong, Rambo escapes through the jungle, killing dozens of faceless Vietnamese along the way. As Ric Kahn noted in the *Boston Phoenix*, thousands of local teens flocked to the film (often multiple times), fired up by Rambo's patriotic spirit and belated victory. Although the film was not the principal cause of the violence, it likely exacerbated a festering anti-Asian mood that manifested itself in angry cries of "Go home, Rambo is here" and "Cambo" graffiti sprayed on the homes and cars of local Cambodian refugees. Indeed, the string of violent incidents that burst forth over the long holiday weekend began just hours after the film opened on May 24.[11]

Although national media coverage sometimes highlighted the violent acts of traumatized veterans, most of the perpetrators in Boston tended to be male teens who were too young to have served in the war. Nevertheless, they sometimes shared the resentments of their working-class families, and several had served in the military more recently. As one fifteen-year-old in East Boston put it: "They fucked us up during the war, and we're still taking 'em in." Young people, who had long engaged in racial and ethnic turf battles in the city's neighborhoods, became the shock troops in these racialized struggles. As one former marine who had served in Vietnam explained, he had come to feel alienated in his Quincy neighborhood after many Asian refugees and immigrants settled there. He believed that much of the anti-Asian sentiment was spreading from veterans to their children: "you got a lot of vets here, and they harbor a lot of resentment. And the kids pick it up, and they play with it. It's a recap of twenty years. I think there's a second generation of hatred coming alive."[12]

The fact that many of these teens and their families faced some of the highest unemployment rates in the state meant that the refugees in their neighborhoods often became scapegoats for broader economic discontent. Such resentments were common among teenagers interviewed in East Boston following the Memorial Day violence of 1985. "I'm out looking for a job and I can't find no jobs," said one sixteen-year-old young man. "They [the Cambodians] take 'em for less pay." Some Southeast Asian newcomers agreed that job competition was fueling some of the violence. As one Vietnamese restaurant owner asserted in 1983: "The companies like to hire them [refugees] because they work hard for low wages. Maybe some people resent this, especially now because there are not so many jobs." Such comments were more common in the early 1980s (when unemployment rates were higher) and reflected long-standing nativist resentment toward immigrants who presumably undercut wages and working conditions for native-born workers. Some white residents, however, recognized that the better-paying jobs they and their family members once had were now in short supply. As one fifteen year old from East Boston explained: Cambodians "take the jobs the white people won't take. The garbage jobs." From this boy's perspective, the refugees were complicit in accepting the reduced wages and downward mobility that characterized the bottom end of the new Boston economy.[13]

Others focused on the unfair competition posed by refugees who clustered together in overcrowded triple-deckers. "It's hard to compete with people who live in a communistic sort of way. They all pool together. It's good for them, but that's not how we do it in America," said one unemployed glazier in North Quincy. "If I was to compete with those people next door, I'd have to be earning the salaries of four people. How are Americans not growing up like that supposed to compete?" His comment conjured up older stereotypes of Asian immigrants who huddled together and subsisted on rice and rats, while his view of them as "communistic" also suggested continued bitterness over the Vietnam War. At the same time, however, his statement was an accurate observation on the survival strategies of recently arrived refugees who initially shared homes and apartments and deployed multiple family wage earners in order to cope with the region's rising rents and high cost of living. Although very few refugees were communists, many relied on a set of traditional values that highlighted family unity and communal sacrifice as a means of creating a new life in America. This too was hardly a new phenomenon; generations of European immigrants had used similar strategies to survive in Boston's old immigrant quarters, and in some of the same neighborhoods and triple-deckers that the refugees now occupied.[14]

While liberals stressed the similarities between old and new immigrants (though ignoring the changed economic context), many white ethnics contrasted the noble struggle of their immigrant parents and grandparents with the dependency of Southeast Asian refugees. In fact, the issue of government support for newcomers—more so than job competition—proved to be the most salient feature of the anti-Asian discourse of the 1980s. Again and again, working-class whites claimed that Southeast Asian refugees benefited unfairly from government assistance that was not available to their own families. Sister Carole Rossi, a Catholic activist in East Boston, remembered that few of the area's Italian American residents saw parallels between their immigrant parents and the newcomers. "They'd say, 'Oh, it was different then, we weren't on welfare, we didn't ask for charity, we didn't expect to be taken care of, we took care of our own.'"[15] Such views, of course, obscured the fact that since the New Deal, the welfare state had become a more active presence in most Americans' lives, from Social Security, Medicare, and public housing to the postwar education and home loan programs that underwrote widespread suburban home ownership. But the refugees' experience seemed different, perhaps because they were fleeing the aftermath of an unpopular US-led war and because the federal government was providing funding for initial resettlement and services.

Soon, however, rumors circulated that refugees were getting even more, including low-interest loans for homes and cars, preferences in hiring, and permanent welfare benefits. In Quincy, where Vietnamese families had started buying homes in the late 1980s, some white neighbors charged that refugees were getting government loans that drove up housing prices, making them unaffordable for longtime residents. "I pay taxes, and we can't afford to buy a house," said one young white woman. "They come here and they get 1 percent loans. They come to this country and get everything on a silver platter." Similar charges were made in East Boston, where one local teenager said, "They don't do nothing and get welfare. . . . We've been here for so many years, and we don't get nothing from the government. They get a car and a house and money." Another Revere man echoed this idea, adding that Cambodian refugees were getting priority hiring for jobs and were now "driving around here in new cars while we're still walking. That ain't right." Cambodian refugee leader Ratha Yem confirmed the pervasiveness of such beliefs, noting that local whites in Chelsea and Revere "suspect that Asians are buying new cars and houses with welfare benefits they are not entitled to." Not surprisingly, refugees' cars (typically bought on credit and vitally needed to commute to jobs in the suburbs) stood out as symbols of their success and became the most popular targets of the widespread vandalism directed against them.[16]

The idea that refugees were welfare cheats was also part of a racialized discourse that grew out of the larger history of race and class relations in the city and nation. Since the War on Poverty in the 1960s, and the culture of poverty theories that accompanied it, urban black families had been stigmatized as pathological and welfare dependent. Such stereotypes were easily transferred to Latinos and Southeast Asians, and in the 1980s, Ronald Reagan's coded racial attacks on "welfare queens" suggested that blacks and immigrants were gaming the system through welfare fraud. White rumors that refugees were getting cars, housing, and preferential hiring were logical extensions of conservative attacks on welfare, public housing, and affirmative action and the (nonwhite) freeloaders who presumably took advantage of such programs.

These themes were especially powerful in Boston, where the racial violence of the busing crisis had consumed the city just a few years earlier. Some of the neighborhoods in which refugees were resettled—Dorchester and East Boston, for example—had been battlegrounds during the busing crisis, and white residents now rechanneled their neighborhood "defense" efforts toward Southeast Asian newcomers. When state authorities used civil rights laws to try to prosecute those perpetrating anti-Asian violence, some local whites charged that they were being harassed by federal marshals sent there to protect the refugees. Antipathy toward middle-class "outsiders" reflected the class tensions that had emerged during the busing crisis when working-class whites resented the interference of federal judges and liberal white politicians from the suburbs whose own communities remained largely unaffected by desegregation.[17] Similarly, in the case of the refugees, the burden of resettlement (as well as fighting the Vietnam War) was disproportionately borne by the city's working-class communities. The backlash against refugee resettlement, then, drew on a deep reservoir of ill will toward racial minorities who many believed benefited unfairly from government intervention, as well as a liberal political establishment that seemed to favor them over native-born white workers and their families.

Finally, violence against Southeast Asian refugees was also influenced by deeply rooted anti-Asian racism. As Asian American activists pointed out at the time, Boston's Chinatown dated back to the 1870s, and the city had a long history of anti-Chinese sentiment that had contributed to the national movement for Chinese exclusion. Those sentiments persisted in the twentieth century and gained new life with the renewed flow of Asian immigrants after 1965. White residents frequently called refugees "Chinks" and repeated both new and old racist stereotypes, saying that refugees ate dogs and rats, fought with swords and Kung Fu, and had sided with the Japanese in World War II. Southeast Asians were also subject to newer stereotypes of Asians as a model minority, a concept that emerged in the Cold War era as Chinese and Japanese Americans began to enter the US mainstream. Although some Asian Americans were economically success-ful and upwardly mobile, most Southeast Asian newcomers struggled to make ends meet. Cambodians in particular—who were targets of some of the worst violence—were often deeply traumatized and had poverty rates that were well above the state average. The popular idea that Southeast Asians were "taking over" had little basis in reality, but it stoked racial and economic resentments that helped fuel the violence.[18]

VIOLENCE AND PANETHNIC ACTIVISM

The violence directed at Southeast Asians in the 1980s perpetuated the city's reputation as a racially troubled city, but it also produced an impres-sive array of grassroots antiracist organizations. This crisis-driven activism gave rise to new panethnic groups and mobilizations that helped usher in a political commitment to multiculturalism on the state and municipal levels. Among the most significant organizing efforts of the 1980s was the East Boston Ecumenical Community Council, a church-based community group; Asians for Justice (AfJ), a regional Asian American organization; and a Cambodian-led community mobilization in Revere.

One of the earliest efforts to support refugees surfaced in East Boston, where the violence of the busing crisis had given birth to an ecumenical religious movement. East Boston had been an epicenter of racial violence in the 1970s, when local residents vehemently opposed busing and launched firebomb attacks against black families in the Maverick housing project. Led by Sister Carole Rossi, a Dominican nun based at Most Holy Redeemer Parish, a group of progressive clergy and lay people organized to protect black school children that were being bused to local schools. In 1978, a Latina resident of the Orient Heights housing project, Esmeralda Sanchez, came to the group asking for protection after a rock was thrown through her apartment window where her young son was sleeping. The incident was merely the most recent in a long pattern of harassment, and Sanchez had gotten no help from police. Rossi and her group quickly organized a march to the local precinct and staged a sit-in to demand police protection. The protest was successful, Rossi said, and "it was really a radicalizing moment for many of us." It proved to be the founding of what would become the East Boston Ecumenical Community Council (EBECC).[19]

Two years later, Don Nanstad took over as pastor of Our Savior Lutheran Church in Maverick Square and quickly joined forces with Rossi and her group. In 1982 a member of his church proposed sponsoring Southeast Asian refugees, and soon the basement of Our Savior became the headquarters of a neighborhood refugee assistance task force. Within months, however, white residents began harassing the Vietnamese and Cambodian newcomers, vandalizing their cars and homes, setting fire to their buildings, and assaulting refugees on the street. EBECC assisted the victims, including several families displaced by arson. But the violence continued, resulting in a stabbing and a street fight in the summer of 1984 and the aforementioned Memorial Day clash of 1985.

Following that incident, EBECC launched Project Welcome, an effort to protect the neighborhood's newcomers and encourage cross-cultural understanding. Rossi, Nanstad, and other project volunteers began organizing community meetings and block patrols and worked with the Community Disorders Unit (CDU—the Boston police unit in charge of civil rights enforcement) to deter and arrest offenders. According to Rossi and Nanstad, the group got terrific cooperation from the CDU: the officers attended meetings with community groups, used restraining orders to curb repeat offenses, and "were here when [we] needed them." Project Welcome also hired two Southeast Asian staff to do outreach to the refugee population, facilitate communications with the police, and accompany victims to court. To improve understanding across cultures, EBECC hosted an annual Festival of Unity, as well as cosponsoring a Cambodian New Year's celebration. By the late 1980s, EBECC had become one of the largest community organizations in East Boston, serving as both a gathering place for the neighborhood's diverse racial, ethnic, and religious communities and a bridge between those communities and the city.[20]

Meanwhile, in Chinatown, a different kind of organization was tackling many of the same issues. Asians for Justice was founded in 1983 as part of a nationwide pan-Asian organizing effort in response to the brutal murder of Vincent Chin in Detroit and the minimal sentences given to his killers. Many of its Boston members, including students, community workers, and professionals, came out of the Asian American movement that had flourished on college campuses in the late 1960s. In the 1970s they had organized to fight urban renewal in Boston's Chinatown and to promote low-income housing, healthcare, and other community services (see chapter 7). While many of the local activists were Chinese American, they embraced a broader pan-Asian identity and agenda that was influenced by the black power movement; in 1978, they helped found the Asian American Resource Workshop (AARW), an education and advocacy organization. In the summer of 1983, AARW activists had just organized a local Vincent Chin support committee when a Vietnamese refugee was murdered in north Dorchester.

Racial tensions had been growing in this area since the late 1960s, as African Americans and Latinos trickled into this predominantly white working-class section bordering Roxbury. Black families moving to all-white blocks were subject to vandalism, arson, and assaults, while some poorer whites remaining in the area became increasingly defensive and embattled. In the early 1980s refugee agencies began resettling Vietnamese and Cambodians in triple-deckers in and around Fields Corner, which was emerging as a center of Vietnamese settlement. They too got a chilly reception, suffering frequent assaults on the street and vandalism to their homes and cars (fig. 13).[21]

FIGURE 13. In the summer of 1982, Cambodian refugees in Fields Corner move out of their Westerville Street triple-decker after ongoing harassment and vandalism (note smashed car window in foreground). Photo courtesy of *Boston Globe*.

On July 24, 1983 a twenty-seven-year-old Vietnamese refugee named Anh Mai was stabbed to death in front of his home in Fields Corner; three of his roommates were also injured in the attack. Mai had arrived in the country in 1981 under the sponsorship of the International Rescue Committee. He had found a job as a hotel cleaner and secured the apartment in Dorchester that he shared with four other refugees. Mai and his roommates, however, soon encountered numerous problems with local white teenagers. On the night of the 24th, Mai's attempt to quiet several of the youth drinking outside his building led to an altercation in which Robert Glass Jr., a nineteen-year-old white marine, pulled a knife and stabbed several of the Vietnamese. One of Mai's roommates was permanently disabled in the attack, while Mai died of stab wounds the next day.

Asians for Justice immediately channeled their organizing efforts around the case. During Glass's trial in 1985, the group met with prosecutors to express their concerns, sent dozens of observers to court each day, and issued press releases describing the proceedings—highlighting the racial dimensions of the case. "We will be following this trial closely to ensure that the token 'justice' meted out for the Vincent Chin case is not repeated," they declared. AfJ also worked behind the scenes to find Mai's roommates—most of whom had left the state after the attack—to convince them to come back and testify. Two of the men did return and provided critical testimony. After two weeks, the jury returned a guilty verdict for first-degree murder, and Glass was sentenced to life imprisonment. The verdict was a victory for AfJ, whose organizing and publicity efforts had brought public attention and scrutiny to the case.[22]

On the same day the verdict was announced, a highly controversial arrest in Chinatown thrust AfJ members back into action—this time in a case of police violence. On May 1, a fifty-six-year-old Chinese immigrant and restaurant cook, Long Guang Huang, was beaten by an undercover vice officer in a Chinatown alley bordering the Combat Zone. In what was likely a case of mistaken identity, Officer Frank Kelly punched Huang repeatedly while arresting him for solicitation of prostitution and resisting arrest. Speaking no English, Huang said through an interpreter that he had tried to flee because he thought the plainclothes officer was a thief trying to rob him—a not uncommon occurrence in the crime-ridden Combat Zone. Huang sustained serious head injuries and was hospitalized for several days. Several witnesses—mainly white employees at nearby New

England Medical Center—said they saw Kelly pin Huang against a barrier and punch him two or three times. Two of the witnesses said that the prostitute involved yelled at the officer that Huang was "not the guy." Huang later explained that it was his day off and that he "was just out walking on the streets. I did nothing wrong."[23]

Huang's ordeal reverberated throughout Chinatown in part because of his plight as a newly arrived immigrant who had entered the country just a few months earlier, spoke no English, and worked long hours to support his family of four and a mother in China. His arrest for prostitution was especially galling for local residents who had long resented the city's placement of the Combat Zone, with its attendant vice and crime problems, immediately adjacent to Chinatown. Over the next month, Asians for Justice joined with other Chinatown groups to aid Huang. Representing Asian American groups across the political spectrum, the Committee to Support Long Guang Huang spearheaded his defense and called on the city to take disciplinary action against Kelly. Galvanizing hundreds of supporters, the committee organized bilingual community meetings, met with the mayor and police commissioner, organized press conferences, and staged a march on city hall (fig. 14). Grassroots mobilization was key to these efforts; the committee set up information tables in a local park, posted news bulletins about the case around Chinatown, and organized local restaurants to donate food for fundraisers. Ultimately, the committee collected more than five thousand signatures on a petition with eight demands: the dropping of charges against Huang and full compensation for his injuries, the suspension of Kelly without pay and a public investigation of his actions, the appointment of an Asian American police commander and bilingual officers in all precincts with large Asian populations, the establishment of an independent police review board, and the elimination of the Combat Zone. Key black leaders such as Mel King and Charles Yancey, whose constituents had a long history of fighting police abuses in their own communities, also voiced support for the committee's demands.[24]

Responding to the pressure, Mayor Ray Flynn and Police Commissioner Mickey Roache took a number of steps to reassure the Chinatown community. The mayor personally visited Huang and his family, bringing them groceries and escorting Huang to the hospital for additional medical care. In an unprecedented move, Commissioner Roache arranged for a disciplinary hearing of Kelly that was open to the public. The committee quickly

FIGURE 14. Organized by the Committee to Support Long Guang Huang, hundreds of supporters march on city hall in June 1985 to protest police brutality against a recent Chinese immigrant. Photo courtesy of Northeastern University Libraries, Archives and Special Collections Department.

mobilized hundreds of supporters to attend both the hearing and Huang's criminal trial. While Huang was quickly acquitted of all charges, Kelly's hearing proved to be a prolonged and astonishing display of racist bravado. Much of it centered around Kelly's Detectives Union attorney, Thomas C. Troy, who was a Korean War veteran and former police officer from East Boston known for his courtroom antics. Troy outraged Asian Americans attending the trial by his gratuitous references to December 7 (the day of the Pearl Harbor bombing), his insinuations that Huang was an illegal immigrant, a communist, and a Japanese collaborator, and his tendency to refer to Huang as "Long Wang" throughout the hearing. At one point, plainclothes police officers who attended the hearing wore identification badges that said simply "Kelly," and Asian attendees complained that some officers made racist remarks as they entered the building. On July 12, the support committee issued a blistering statement saying that Troy's behavior "offended the entire Asian American community" and criticizing the hearing officer's failure to control the proceedings. Saying the hearing had become "at best a waste of taxpayers' money and at worst a severe travesty of justice," the committee argued that the police department was incapable of policing itself.[25]

After numerous delays, the hearing finally ended on September 6. The presiding police superintendent found Kelly guilty of excessive force and filing a false report, and Commissioner Roache suspended him for a year without pay. Huang also filed a civil suit against the city and was awarded an $85,000 settlement in 1988. Unbeknownst to Huang and the support committee, however, the city also decided to settle with Kelly, who had appealed his suspension and sued the police commissioner. Rather than incur additional legal costs, the city settled with Kelly for $115,000—that is, $30,000 more than Huang had received. Huang's lawyer and the support committee roundly denounced the decision, saying that it "implicitly condones police misconduct."[26]

Although backers were dismayed by the city's reversal in the case, the committee's campaign to support Long Guang Huang was an important milestone in pan-Asian and immigrant organizing in Boston. The support campaign was the first successful effort to build a grassroots movement of Asian immigrants and Asian Americans that bridged political and ethnic lines. By unifying Chinatown's many groups, the movement effectively leveraged accommodations from the city in the wake of the Huang case, including the establishment of an Asian-language translation program for emergency services in 1986 and the appointment of Vietnamese and Cambodian liaisons to the mayor's Office of Neighborhood Services in 1987. Moreover, in an effort to "inform the entire city that [China]-town will not allow itself to be used as the vice den of the city," the support committee turned its attention to reclaiming the Combat Zone. Organizing community patrols in the fall of 1985, the committee sought to drive away johns and prostitutes by taking their pictures and recording their license plate numbers for publication. Soon after, Mayor Flynn announced the appointment of a Chinatown Neighborhood Council, one of five new community-based councils created to deal with development issues in the city, and Flynn himself would become instrumental in efforts to eliminate the Combat Zone.[27]

Just as Long Guang Huang's ordeal was galvanizing the Chinatown community, however, violence against Southeast Asians continued to spread. In July of 1985, a Cambodian refugee named Bun Vong was killed in a roadside dispute north of Boston, propelling Asians for Justice into another high-profile case. The two white suspects, Scott Arsenault and John Febbi of Somerville, were charged with the beating death of Vong, an aspiring Buddhist monk who lived in Lowell. Coming on the heels of the Glass verdict and the Huang beating, the case was widely publicized, particularly after Governor Michael Dukakis appeared at Vong's funeral and condemned the crime.[28] As the trial got under way, though, the judge ruled that the race issue could not be raised, since Vong's Cambodian companion did not understand English (and therefore could not testify as to whether racial epithets were used). AfJ denounced this approach, insisting that the incident be understood in the broader context of anti-Asian violence in the area. Once again, AfJ packed the courtroom and met with reporters and prosecutors, but this time the jury was not persuaded. They acquitted Febbe of manslaughter and deadlocked over Arsenault, causing the judge to declare a mistrial in the latter's case. Both were convicted on the lesser charge of assault and sentenced to a year in jail. The AfJ spokesperson Elaine Song called the verdict a disgrace: "It makes a statement that violence against Asians is acceptable and need not be punished—that an Asian life is cheap." With the glare of publicity on the case, however, the district attorney quickly retried Arsenault; in June he was found guilty of manslaughter and received a seven-to-twelve-year prison term.[29]

In both the Vong and Mai murder cases, AfJ proved to be a formidable force in demanding justice for the victims of racial violence. And as in the Vincent Chin case, AfJ's organizing around the Massachusetts cases mobilized a broader pan-Asian response. The violence issue galvanized Boston's Asian American community in powerful ways precisely because it affected the entire community, as Chinese and Japanese Americans were often mistaken for Southeast Asians and vice versa. As Peter Kiang explained in describing a 1985 attack on a Chinese American restaurant owner in Mattapan: "To her neighbors, she is still a gook. Cambodians in Revere are told to go back to Vietnam. Vietnamese in South Boston are told to go back to China." As AfJ member Elaine Song noted: "All Asians are subject to attack, regardless of culture, language or nationality." Drawing on the organizing expertise and professional skills of the Asian American community, AfJ established itself as a watchdog for Asian civil rights while seeking to build bridges to African American and Latino groups in the city. Following Vong's murder, AfJ also helped organize the Boston Area Refugee Coalition, a network of seven Southeast Asian mutual assistance associations. This coalition held a series of meetings and workshops on violence prevention, relations with police, and crisis intervention for victims.[30] The skills learned in these gatherings helped Southeast Asians organize in their own defense when violence struck, as it did in Revere that summer.

Located about 5 miles north of Boston, Revere was a run-down beach town populated mainly by working-class Italian and Jewish Americans. Site of the nation's oldest public beach and a popular amusement park, Revere Beach had been in decline since the 1950s, and many of its facilities had been destroyed in the blizzard of 1978. The older Jewish community around Shirley Avenue near the beach had been gradually leaving the area, replaced by lower-income whites and immigrants. Cambodian refugees began moving to Shirley Avenue in the early 1980s, when resettlement agencies secured housing there. Other Cambodian refugees followed, some of them fleeing the violence in Dorchester and East Boston. By 1985, there were roughly twelve hundred Cambodian residents. As their numbers increased, so did the harassment, which proved relentless. As the scholar and former Revere resident Shirley Tang explained: "Rocks thrown through windows, assaults on the street, racial slurs, spitting, and other forms of violence were daily occurrences."[31]

Restraining orders were filed against some of the perpetrators, but soon arson became the weapon of choice. In the summer of 1983, two buildings housing Cambodians were set on fire when burning newspapers were thrown on their porches; the following summer, another Cambodian-occupied building on the same street was firebombed. An even more damaging fire occurred in the summer of 1985, when a mattress was ignited under a triple-decker at 9 Walnut Place; thirty-six Cambodians were left homeless from the blaze. Suspicion focused on twenty-six-year-old Robert Lee Stephens who, a month earlier, had led several juveniles in pounding the same building with stones and bottles and had attacked two of its Cambodian residents. A few days after Stephens was arrested, the building was torched. A subsequent investigation led by the FBI and the Suffolk County District Attorney's office resulted in multiple indictments against Stephens, who was convicted and sentenced to seven to ten years in prison in 1986.[32]

In the wake of the arson at 9 Walnut Place, Revere mayor George Colella established a Human Rights Commission "to assure the rights and protections of all citizens." Noting that "we are all immigrants or children of immigrants to this great country," Colella led the commission's efforts to improve race relations in Revere and act as a liaison between the Cambodian community, refugee agencies, and the city. Although the creation of the commission was an important step in recognizing the city's racial problems, tensions and violence against Cambodians continued. On Christmas Eve in 1986, arson claimed another building at 50–52 Shirley Avenue (just three blocks from Walnut Place), displacing twenty-one Cambodian residents, including a pregnant woman and more than a dozen children. On Christmas Day, white teenagers looted one of the burned apartments, stealing victims' clothes and belongings.

Exasperated and outraged, Revere Cambodians organized a demonstration on January 10, the first Cambodian-led protest in US history. Carrying placards and banners saying "Enough Is Enough" and "No More Racist Arson," some three hundred Asian, white, and black demonstrators marched from Revere City Hall to the site of the fire-charred building on Shirley Avenue. There they unfurled a banner that read "We Want Peace in Our Neighborhood." Representing a new Cambodian-led coalition in Revere, Samath Chap and Kowith Kvet called on the city to improve civil rights enforcement and arson prevention programs and to provide replacement housing for the homeless families. Mayor Colella also addressed the crowd, pledging the cooperation of the city.[33]

For the next year or so, Revere Cambodians and their allies worked through the Human Rights Commission to combat racism and develop multicultural and bilingual programs. The city established a monitoring system for civil rights violations, and the Garfield School (an elementary school in the Shirley Avenue neighborhood) inaugurated a racial harmony and language arts program for students. The following summer, the school also hosted workshops for older students who produced a community mural incorporating Cambodian and other immigrant cultural themes. In 1987 the city opened an Office of Southeast Asian Affairs, whose full-time coordinator acted as a liaison between the Cambodian community and local agencies, while the police and a community healthcare clinic hired Khmer interpreters.[34]

As in Chinatown and East Boston, Asian newcomers and their native-born allies in Revere mobilized around the crisis of violence to demand protection, intercultural programs, and bilingual services. As outbreaks of violence spread to nearby suburbs such as Lynn, Chelsea, and Quincy, those communities responded with similar programs and initiatives. These efforts were supported at the state level, where the Dukakis administration established the Massachusetts Office of Refugees and Immigrants in 1985. The following year, the legislature approved the Gateway Cities program, which provided $14.7 million in state aid for more than two dozen "immigrant gateway" cities, including Boston, Lawrence, Lowell, Chelsea, Revere, Lynn, and Quincy. A number of these older industrial cities had experienced recent outbreaks of anti-Asian violence, while a white-Latino riot had erupted in Lawrence in 1984. The funding was intended to ease the stress and burden on those cities that housed a disproportionate share of the state's newcomers. For the next three years, Gateway Cities would support more than 330 local programs in job placement, ESL, interpreter services, housing assistance, intercultural programming, and other services. Among some native-born residents, however, such programs only served to confirm the belief that immigrants were getting preferential treatment from the government.[35]

At the same time, Asians for Justice and the Asian American Resource Workshop were working to document incidents of anti-Asian violence and the grassroots efforts to combat them. In 1987 they published a fifty-page report titled *To Live in Peace: Responding to Anti-Asian Violence in Boston*, which became part of the written testimony submitted before the US House of Representatives hearing on anti-Asian violence later that year. Led by Michigan representative John Conyers, the hearing was one of several conducted by the Judiciary Committee that resulted in the passage of the Hate Crime Statistics Act of 1990, requiring federal authorities to collect nationwide data on civil rights–related crime. AARW activists also went on to develop their own violence prevention program called SafetyNet. Building on the methods pioneered by Asians for Justice, SafetyNet included a telephone hotline for violence victims, bilingual advocacy within the criminal justice system, and training programs for social service and public safety professionals. In Boston, meanwhile, hate crime data indicated that racially motivated crimes against Asians had declined in the late 1980s and early 1990s; by 1993, such crimes had fallen to roughly half of their peak level in 1985.[36]

Although incidents of violence against Asians continued, the decline in reported cases suggests that the efforts of groups like AfJ, EBECC, and the Cambodian-led coalition in Revere were at least partially successful. But while these groups worked effectively with victims and law enforcement, they were less successful in convincing the public that racism was a root cause of such crimes. As the Bun Vong case had demonstrated, proving that a crime was racially motivated could be difficult for immigrant victims who spoke little English. But even in cases where juries did convict on civil rights violations—as in the trial of Robert Lee Stephens in Revere—some white residents remained resistant to acknowledging racism. As one juror in the case described the deliberations, "A powerful irony prevailed: Only by avoiding explicit discussion of racism were we able to convict Stephens of violating civil rights. As soon as the conversation veered into Stephen's motivation or into expressions of sympathy for the victims, the consensus was shattered."[37]

A similar de-emphasis of race and racism also characterized the local initiatives for multiculturalism. Although the civil rights movement and struggles around busing had profoundly influenced the founders of groups like AfJ and EBECC, many of the multicultural initiatives adopted in the late 1980s and early 1990s highlighted ethnicity, language, and culture rather than race as the basis of diversity. At a time when many whites were mobilizing against race-based programs such as school desegregation and affirmative action and were very defensive against charges of racism, pluralistic notions of diversity and multiculturalism seemed less controversial. In addition, the ethnic revival of the 1970s had made many white ethnics more inclined to embrace their families' immigrant heritage and culture. In the Boston area, where many white residents were second- or third-generation ethnics, the tendency to identify with new immigrants and compare them with one's own parents or grandparents had a powerful appeal that was used by political leaders like Mayor Colella in Revere (Italian American), Mayor Raymond Flynn of Boston (Irish American), and Governor Michael Dukakis (Greek American). The fact that African Americans were not a part of this immigrant pantheon was either ignored or quietly acknowledged; in fact, some older ethnics extolled the hard work and family values of new immigrants in contrast to the presumed indolence and pathology of the native-born black poor. Moreover, some Asian, Caribbean, and Latino immigrants eagerly embraced this new brand of multiculturalism and ethnic politics, while distancing themselves from native-born blacks and Latinos and the more controversial politics of race.[38]

The new politics of multiculturalism proved vulnerable, however, particularly after the economic "miracle" in Massachusetts collapsed in the late 1980s. One of the first casualties was the Gateway Cities program, which faced steep cuts in 1989 and was discontinued thereafter. Facing budget problems of their own, many cities had to pare down their newcomer services and lay off interpreters and bilingual workers. At the same time, pressure also grew to deny public health, education, and welfare benefits to unauthorized immigrants, an issue that featured prominently in the 1990 gubernatorial election. Such policies were favored by fiscally conservative Republicans but also by Democrats like Boston University president John Silber, a candidate in the governor's race who made immigrant welfare reform a key plank in his campaign. His claim that Massachusetts was a "welfare magnet" for immigrants, however, built on familiar undercurrents—namely, the widespread belief, evident in the earlier attacks on Southeast Asian refugees, that the state and federal governments were encouraging immigration and subsidizing migrants at the expense of native-born citizens. Although attempts to cut benefits did not succeed in Massachusetts at the time, this new current of state-centered nativism would soon result in federal and state legislation in the 1990s that further reduced refugee aid and made it more difficult to provide public assistance and services to unauthorized immigrants. As we will see in chapter 7, state aid to both undocumented and legal resident immigrants alike would plummet in Massachusetts.

This new role of the state in migration and settlement services has been one of the distinctive features of recent debates over immigration in Massachusetts and the United States more generally. The targeting of government services to immigrants was not surprising, given the growing role of the state since the New Deal, but it was also a product of the large-scale shift in the global and regional economy and the class and racial tensions it generated. In Boston, the outbreak of anti-Asian violence occurred amid wrenching changes as the region shifted to a suburban, high-tech, knowledge-based economy that boosted the state's income but ravaged many older working-class communities. Resentments over the Vietnam War, the civil rights movement, and busing aggravated that discontent and channeled it toward the latest newcomers from Southeast Asia. In such a climate, the liberal state emerged as a primary culprit; in the eyes of many native-born, working-class whites, the government was unfairly subsidizing refugees, forcing the integration of neighborhoods through resettlement programs, and protecting newcomers while persecuting hard-pressed white youth.

At the same time, groups that organized to defend the newcomers called on the state to extend its civil rights apparatus to Asian refugees and to provide culturally and linguistically sensitive services for newcomers. The multicultural programming that resulted, however, tended to downplay race and, as we shall see, did not entail a significant redistribution of political power, thus leaving these programs vulnerable to cutbacks. While the more horrific forms of violence receded after the 1980s, the class and racial resentments behind them continued to fuel the anti-immigrant movement and its efforts to exclude immigrants from the benefits of government protection and social welfare.

CHAPTER 6

Immigrant Religion and Boston's "Quiet Revival"

On Thanksgiving Day 1953, some forty Korean students met for worship services in Marsh Chapel at Boston University. Coming from BU, Harvard, MIT, and other universities around New England, the students gathered for prayer and fellowship over the quiet holiday weekend. The Reverend Park Dae Sun, a Methodist divinity student at BU, led the service and what would soon become the Korean Church of Boston (KCB). Over the next fourteen years, New England's first Korean church was led by a succession of Protestant ministers from Korea and moved to a series of temporary homes in Cambridge and Boston. Eventually, in 1967, the KCB found a permanent home in Brookline, sharing facilities with a local Presbyterian Church. The KCB grew rapidly over the next two decades, adding a Sunday School and Korean language classes for children and affiliating with the Presbyterian Church USA. As the membership of the mostly white mainline congregation dwindled, the more evangelical KCB took over stewardship of the Brookline church in 1997, fulfilling the Koreans' dreams of having their own church as the KCB approached its fiftieth anniversary.[1]

The story of the Korean Church is an early example of a broader transformation of Christianity in greater Boston that has been under way since the 1960s. At the time, the region was one of the most Catholic of all US metropolitan areas, a legacy of its Irish, French Canadian, and European immigrant past. It also contained sizable populations of Protestants and Jews, the former including growing numbers of African Americans. Particularly in Boston and its older industrial suburbs, however, many Protestant and Catholic churches faced downturns in the post-1965 era, as suburbanization, deindustrialization, and outmigration to the Sunbelt caused their congregations to shrink. In the coming years, though, new Asian, Latino, African, and Caribbean immigrants began to replenish and transform them.

This influx not only filled the pews but also infused these ailing churches with more dynamic religious styles from the migrants' home countries and more evangelical forms of spirituality—a development some have called "the de-Europeanization of Christianity." But this transition did not occur smoothly. Many immigrants initially encountered hostility or resentment from native-born Christians, or found themselves consigned to off-hours services in basements and annexes. With the dwindling and aging of many white native-born congregations, however, new immigrants gradually increased their presence and took possession of many urban churches. In the 1970s and 1980s, the Catholic Church benefited disproportionately from the arrival of Catholic refugees and immigrants in the Cold War era. By the end the century, however, the proliferation of new evangelical Protestant churches was outstripping that of Catholic parishes, particularly among migrants from Latin America and the Caribbean. Both Catholic and Protestant denominations welcomed the newcomers as a source of spiritual renewal for their congregations, but in the face of fiscal and clerical crises that struck the Boston Archdiocese especially hard, evangelicals were more successful in cultivating the immigrant faithful. Promoting what they called "the quiet revival," local evangelical organizations worked cooperatively with newcomers to accommodate new immigrant congregations and spiritual leaders. In Boston, one of the nation's most Catholic cities since the late nineteenth century, the quiet revival suggests that the city may be returning to a more Protestant cast via the influence of post-1965 immigrants and the de-Europeanization of Christianity.[2]

Among non-Christian groups, an even more obvious de-Europeanization of the religious landscape was under way. Since the 1990s, Buddhists, Hindus, Muslims, and others have built temples and mosques across the metropolitan region. While immigrant Christian congregations benefited from local Catholic and evangelical networks and assistance, non-Western religious groups relied more heavily on their own members and on transnational connections and funding. As more immigrants arrived, these new religious centers have also had to accommodate rapid demographic and physical growth and increasing ethnic and religious pluralism within their own ranks. Moreover, native-born perceptions of these new groups as alien and potentially dangerous—particularly in the wake of 9/11—have made for an ambivalent and at times hostile reception. These tensions, however, have fueled an assortment of interfaith efforts across ethnic and denominational lines, fostering a new brand of religious pluralism that is unprecedented in Boston's history.

IMMIGRANTS AND THE CATHOLIC CHURCH

Founded in 1915, St. Anthony's started as a mission church to serve a growing population of Italian immigrants in the fast-growing industrial suburb of Somerville. Run by the Missionaries of St. Charles (or Scalabrinians), the church grew into a vibrant ethnic parish just north of Cambridge. For decades, the Italian-language Mass continued on Sunday mornings, but its attendance dwindled as the original Italian parishioners died or moved away. After 1970 a new wave of Haitians, Portuguese, and Asians settled in Somerville and were soon followed by a surge of Brazilian arrivals in the late 1980s and 1990s. St. Anthony's held its first Mass in Portuguese for fifteen Brazilian parishioners in 1990, and two years later a Scalabrinian missionary from Brazil joined the parish and began ministering to several hundred Brazilian migrants and their families. His flock grew quickly. By the late 1990s, they made up the majority of the parish.[3]

The story of St. Anthony's illustrates the striking parallels in the religious development of the two great waves of immigration to greater Boston. Whether arriving in the 1910s or the 1990s, Catholic immigrants had the benefit of a vast transnational institution and hierarchy that had both physical and organizational resources and a long history of ministering to migrant populations. As noted in chapter 1, Italians and other second-wave immigrant groups had sometimes taken over city parishes

FIGURE 15. Father Fred O'Brien, the first director of the Hispanic apostolate in the Boston archdiocese, leads a class with Puerto Rican migrant workers at a farm in Concord in 1957. Photo courtesy of *Boston Globe*.

built by their Irish and German predecessors. Beginning in the 1980s, many of these same churches became home to the new wave of Latinos, Haitians, Vietnamese, Brazilians, and other groups settling in the metro area. Although in many ways a familiar story, the newcomers' encounter with the Roman Catholic Church was also characterized by some new problems and challenges that made for a more troubled reception: the shortage of clergy and religious personnel, the more diverse racial identities and settlement patterns of new immigrants, and the fiscal difficulties of urban parishes—problems that were aggravated by the clergy sex abuse scandal of the 1990s.

Outreach to Spanish-speaking migrants in the Boston Archdiocese first began in the 1950s, with the arrival of Puerto Rican agricultural workers in outlying communities. The church assigned Spanish-speaking priests to minister to these workers and set up community centers at local churches (fig. 15). As Puerto Ricans and Cubans settled in Boston's South End, the Cathedral of the Holy Cross began offering a Spanish-language Mass, and in 1957 Cardinal Richard Cushing established the Hispanic apostolate to coordinate Spanish-language Masses and pastoral services. That same year the archdiocese also founded El Centro del Cardenal in the South End as a social service center for the city's Latinos. Soon Spanish-speaking seminary students were working with Puerto Ricans at local parishes and staffing a travelers' aid service at Logan Airport.[4]

Outside of the South End, though, the church's response to new Latino arrivals was uneven at best. The first director of the Hispanic apostolate, Father Fred O'Brien, explained in a 1998 interview that the reception of Latinos depended mainly on the initiatives of local priests: "They left us on our own. Each city had a different experience. Priests working with Latinos were very creative. The Cardinal didn't have a policy. . . . In this country, the hierarchy doesn't know what to make of [Latinos] even now." His successor in the 1970s, Father Daniel Sheehan, added that financial pressures on aging urban parishes also limited institutional support, and that "few in the Archdiocese were willing to promote Latinos and to be prepared for the future." Nevertheless, local parishes responded piecemeal to the growing Latino population by adding Spanish Masses and clergy. In the 1980s, many became pan-Latino as new waves of Central Americans and Colombians arrived in the region. In 1988 the archdiocese appointed an auxiliary bishop, Roberto Octavio González, a Franciscan born in Puerto Rico, to represent the estimated 150,000 Hispanic Catholics in the region. By 2000, the Hispanic apostolate coordinated Spanish Masses and programs at thirty-six parishes in greater Boston.[5]

During these years, the Catholic Church extended a welcome to other migrants as well, including Haitians, Vietnamese, and Brazilians. Beginning in the 1960s, Haitian immigrants clustered around St. Leo's and St. Matthew's churches in South Dorchester and later expanded into St. Angela's in Mattapan and Our Lady of Pity in Cambridge. Vietnamese refugees built a large congregation at St. Peter's in Fields Corner, while the Allston-Brighton Vietnamese community attended St. Aidan's in nearby Brookline. These and other immigrant congregations were placed under the supervision of the Office of Ethnic Apostolates, established by the archdiocese in the late 1980s.[6]

Over the next decade, the Office of Ethnic Apostolates would coordinate new ministries for Brazilians, Africans, and other groups as well. As Portuguese speakers, Brazilian newcomers sometimes found a home with existing Portuguese churches, but different worship styles and tensions rooted in past colonial relationships made some Portuguese parishes unwilling to host the newcomers. The predominantly Portuguese parishes of St. Anthony's in Cambridge and St. Tarcisius in Framingham welcomed the Brazilians, but they soon established separate Brazilian Masses to accommodate their more lively liturgies and music. Meanwhile, new Brazilian congregations, such as St. Anthony's in Somerville, proliferated in the 1990s, and a Brazilian apostolate was established to supervise ministries in eight different parishes. Additionally, the archdiocese opened an African Pastoral Office in 1998 to tend to the religious needs of migrants and refugees from Cape Verde, Nigeria, and a half dozen other African countries.[7]

As in the case of St. Anthony's, most of these churches experienced a dramatic demographic transition. As the historian Thomas O'Connor described it: "Old gothic churches in depopulated urban areas where old congregations had either died off or moved away were often practically deserted, and devotional services that had once drawn thousands of faithful communicants now went largely unattended." As newcomers moved into these neighborhoods, they helped to revitalize dying parishes with young immigrant families whose baptisms, first communions, and weddings packed the pews each week. St. Anthony's, for example, conducted thirty-five baptisms and sixty-two funerals in 1988; by 1992—with a young and growing Brazilian congregation—the ratio reversed to sixty-one baptisms and forty-one funerals. Most Holy Redeemer, an East Boston parish where the Latino population skyrocketed, conducted nearly three hundred baptisms in 1992. This was almost as many as in 1858, at the height of the Irish migration around which the church had been built. The influx of new members no doubt pleased many church leaders. At St. Anthony's, the pastor praised the Brazilians as "a young, vibrant and active Christian community. . . . The Brazilian members have added a new, youthful and inspiring element to our parish."[8]

But not all Catholics were so sanguine; some longtime church members were ambivalent or even hostile to the new arrivals. At some formerly Irish and Italian American parishes, Haitian and Latino newcomers reported that they were ignored or shunned by white church members. "There was a time when the Americans would not say hello to us; when we sat next to them they would move to another pew," remembered Carmen Torres, an early member of the Latino community at St. Peter's in Dorchester. At nearby St. Gregory's, new Haitian arrivals remembered the hostile treatment they received from white parishioners who refused to shake their hands during the peace offering at Sunday Mass.[9]

While efforts at interethnic fellowship reduced conflict at some of these parishes, the expansion of separate foreign-language liturgies and ongoing demographic change helped accommodate newcomers. Catholic parishes that had retained their white ethnic members into the 1960s saw rapid outmigration in the last quarter of the century. As the wave of new immigrants reached a critical mass in the 1990s, many of the new ethnic apostolates "moved upstairs"—taking over the main sanctuaries or prime Sunday morning Mass times. Like the Portuguese and Italians who had once claimed older Irish Catholic parishes, the new immigrants inherited many of the city's historic churches. With them, however, came the burdens of aging urban parishes—leaky roofs, crumbling walls, ailing parochial schools, and mounting debt. This decaying infrastructure posed problems that earlier immigrants had rarely encountered, as they had arrived at a time when the church was strong and its parishes proliferating. In the late twentieth century, as parishes aged and the newer immigrant congregations struggled financially, the archdiocese began to close some of them in the 1990s. But decaying infrastructure was just one source of the problem; as in the Catholic Church more generally, the ethnic apostolates faced a critical clergy shortage. Between 1988 and 2004, the number of diocesan priests in the Boston Archdiocese declined by 37 percent, and the median age of those still active in 2004 was fifty-nine. This too was unprecedented. During the boom years of the earlier migration, the number of priests in the archdiocese had grown more than eightfold between 1866 and 1907.[10]

The shortage of priests was exacerbated by the need for bilingual clergy. Although the archdiocese began requiring new seminarians to study Spanish or Portuguese in the 1990s, there was a continuing shortage of bilingual priests. As in the earlier immigrant church, mission-oriented religious orders stepped into the breach, playing a critical role in the apostolates. One such group was the Society of St. James the Apostle, founded by Cardinal Richard Cushing in 1958. A missionary program that sent diocesan priests to serve in Ecuador, Peru, and Bolivia, the society had the added benefit of producing bilingual priests who served in the Hispanic apostolate on their return. Equally important were the Scalabrinians, a religious order founded in 1887 to serve Italian immigrants in North and South America. In the 1960s, the Scalabrinians broadened their mission to encompass migrants around the world and have been especially active in Latin American communities. Summoning priests from Brazil and neighboring countries, they have been actively ministering to both Latinos and Brazilians in Boston-area churches. Similarly, the Capuchin friars of the Franciscan Order, some of whom had worked as missionaries in the Cape Verde Islands, were frequently called on to run the Cape Verdean apostolate in Boston.[11]

For other groups, however, the archdiocese relied on formal partnerships with archbishops from sending countries who agreed to loan priests for three- to five-year periods. One such relationship was formed between Cardinal Bernard Law and the Archbishop of Daegu in South Korea, who agreed to send a local priest to serve the Korean Catholic Community of Boston every four years. At St. Benedict's in Somerville, Salvadoran parishioners contributed funds to help bring over several priests from El Salvador to say the Spanish Mass and renew connections with their homeland. Although such arrangements provided a new supply of bilingual and bicultural priests, the persistent turnover in church leadership resulted in a lack of continuity. Moreover, most foreign-born priests came with limited English and sometimes less knowledge of life in the United States than their own parishioners had. Their ability to provide seasoned, stable leadership for their congregations was thus limited, forcing parishes to rely on a rotating supply of priests, seminary students, nuns, and volunteers. To address this problem, Boston College began a certificate program in Hispanic Ministry in 2005, hoping to expand the ranks of both ordained and lay ministers.[12]

The personnel shortage was even more dire in the Catholic schools, which experienced a steady decline in numbers after the mid-1960s. For earlier generations of immigrant Catholics, the parochial schools of ethnic parishes were important vehicles of religious identity, Americanization, and social mobility. Such schools were often better alternatives to underfunded public schools and became feeders to a growing crop of Catholic high schools, colleges, and universities. Parochial schools have continued to serve this purpose for new immigrants, but for a smaller proportion. With growing fiscal pressures and a steep decline in the ranks of women religious who made up the teaching staff, the number of Catholic schools in the archdiocese declined from 474 in 1966 to 122 in 2010, with enrollment falling from more than 150,000 to under 43,000. This meant fewer schools and lower levels of enrollment for a fast-growing immigrant population, especially as the decline was greatest among the more affordable parochial and diocesan schools. As a result, new immigrant Catholic youth did not have the same access to parochial schools as had been available to earlier Catholic immigrants, schools that frequently offered better and safer educational environments than many troubled public schools. Indeed, the declining number of schools and parishes, combined with personnel shortages and fiscal pressures, has produced serious challenges for the Catholic Church's ability to serve new immigrants.[13]

Despite these handicaps, some ethnic apostolates developed innovative ways to build their congregations. Like most ethnic institutions, parishes relied on networks of family and friends to bring in new members, but they also developed an array of activities and services to welcome and assist newcomers. At Most Holy Redeemer, the church developed a tradition after Sunday Mass of having Latino newcomers stand before the Sacred Heart of Jesus statue, where they could meet church members and get leads on jobs or rooms for rent. In Somerville, St. Anthony's advertised its Portuguese Masses in the local Brazilian press, inviting newcomers for coffee and refreshments afterward. At that time, church leaders would introduce themselves, describe pastoral activities, and "assess any other personal needs that new arrivals may have." The church's Family Committee then followed up with the new arrivals to offer assistance with jobs, housing, or other matters. Similarly, during Masses at the Korean Catholic Community, newcomers and their families were called up and given a microphone to introduce themselves. They were then assigned to one of several small group fellowships, or *goo yuk*, that were geographically based in the various suburban communities where most Koreans settled. After the Mass there was a fellowship time when the *goo yuk* coordinators personally welcomed the newcomers to their group, which met once a month in local members' homes for dinner and Bible study. In this way, church members broke through the anonymity of large-group worship to offer a more personal welcome.[14]

Some of the early church-based efforts to assist newcomers eventually grew into sophisticated social service centers for the city's immigrant communities. Beginning in the late 1970s, members of St. Leo's in Dorchester began offering English classes for recent Haitian immigrants and soon branched out into job counseling, food and shelter programs, immigration services, and later, an AIDS outreach campaign. Incorporated into Catholic Charities in 1984, the Haitian Multi-Service Center was housed at St. Leo's for more than twenty years and became the "Plymouth Rock" of the Haitian community. An equally elaborate program evolved out of efforts to assist immigrants at Most Holy Redeemer Parish in East Boston, where Catholic church workers joined other local clergy to protect immigrants from racial violence in the 1980s (see chapter 5). Soon their group, known as the East Boston Ecumenical Community Council, established English classes, a food pantry, a clothing center, a job referral program, a family shelter, and a volunteer translator service. As one church leader noted, "We are, in effect, one of the major social service providers in the East Boston area." Although its early efforts centered mainly around Southeast Asians, the council later became one the principal community agencies for Boston Latinos.[15]

Some of the most important support services that Catholic churches provided for immigrants were those for children and youth. With both parents employed in many migrant families, a number of parishes started preschools for young children, as well as afterschool and summer camp programs to care for school-age youth. In neighborhoods that were perennially short of such services, immigrants relied on the church and sometimes became members as a result. A Haitian mother and hotel worker in Mattapan described the importance of such programs: "If we wanted our children to be safe after school and in the summer, the only people we could trust was the Church." Aware of the critical role of urban Catholic youth programs, local churches conducted regular outreach campaigns among immigrant parents, regularly inviting them to Sunday Mass and other church functions.[16]

Although many of these activities were reminiscent of how Catholic churches had appealed to earlier European migrants, more recent efforts have expanded to include immigration counseling and advocacy. These services were in high demand among parishioners wanting to bring over family members to the United States, but also with undocumented migrants who attended Mass but remained in the shadows for fear of detection or deportation. St. Anthony's in Somerville, for example, sponsored meetings with the Brazilian consul and with lawyers who could answer questions about visas and other immigration issues. Most Holy Redeemer Parish, where the congregation was roughly half Salvadoran in the late 1990s, provided space for community lawyers who aided undocumented parishioners seeking to apply for temporary protected status under federal law. At St. Tarcisius, Brazilian parishioners organized a beeper service that undocumented

church members could call when they needed assistance because of ill-
ness, family problems, or police or immigration issues. Nor was advocacy
in behalf of immigrants limited to the parish level; as federal authorities
stepped up immigration enforcement in the wake of 9/11, Cardinal Sean
O'Malley and other archdiocesan officials expressed strong support for
immigration reform and publicly opposed state laws denying drivers
licenses and in-state college tuition rates to undocumented immigrants.[17]

Addressing secular needs, however, was only one aspect of the church's
response to new immigrants; its primary goal was to uphold the Catholic
faith. As it had with earlier immigrant groups, the church offered linguistically accessible Masses and incorporated culturally distinct traditions
to meet the spiritual needs of the newcomers. But while such accommodations for earlier migrants had taken years to evolve, the Hispanic and
Ethnic apostolates moved quickly to embrace the cultural diversity that
Cardinal Law and other church leaders now regarded as "a gift." One of
the most obvious additions was the impressive array of Marian devotions
and processions brought by the immigrants. In many Dominican congregations, Our Lady of Altagracia occupied a central place; Vietnamese in a
Chelsea parish paid homage to Our Lady of La Vang; and Cape Verdeans
at St. Patrick's in Roxbury organized several thousand people in an annual
spring procession to honor Our Lady of Fatima. During the Christmas
season, Latino Catholics enacted *Las Posadas,* a Mexican novena and procession reenacting Mary's and Joseph's search for shelter in Bethlehem.
Celebrations of traditional saints days, such as Festa Junina (a Brazilian
feast honoring St. John the Baptist), also became regular events in many
parishes. Migrant parishioners sometimes had to convince local churches
to embrace homeland devotions and traditions, as was the case among
Salvadorans in Somerville. After several years of resistance, immigrants
from the town of Yucuaiquín convinced local priests at St. Benedict's to
celebrate their town's patron saint, San Francisco (St. Francis of Assisi), and
el baile de los negritos, a traditional dance done with colorful masks that is
a central part of the celebration.[18]

Distinctive cultural practices were also evident in the liturgy, reflecting
the Catholic Church's efforts to validate the culture and contributions of
Asian, African, and Latin American Catholics. Korean, Vietnamese, and
Ugandan churches, for instance, conducted special Masses to honor the
Catholic martyrs of their countries. Canonized by the church since the

1960s, these nineteenth-century Catholic believers had faced persecution and death at the hands of their rulers. Vietnamese Catholics in Boston have venerated the martyrs each November with colorful clothing, dances, and music preceding the Mass. Asian New Year celebrations have also been commemorated with special Masses and rituals. At St. James the Greater, a Chinese Catholic church in Chinatown, the New Year's Mass is dedicated to the ancestors of the parishioners, thus incorporating the religious folk traditions of Chinese Catholics. As immigrants introduced these new traditions and devotions to local parishes, they have helped to diversify and transform Catholicism in greater Boston, just as French Canadian, Italian, Portuguese, and other European immigrants did in an earlier era.[19]

Moreover, the church has also embraced the Charismatic movements and lively liturgy styles common among Hispanic, Haitian, and Brazilian migrants. Often several hours long, these groups' Masses are filled with music, singing, and testimony. In the late 1990s, for example, the Sunday evening Brazilian Mass at St. Tarcisius featured a twenty-person chorus accompanied by synthesizer, guitars, conga drums, and dramatic reenactments from the Bible. Father Roque Pattussi worked the crowd with a wireless microphone asking for stories and testimony amid laughter, tears, and applause. An equally dynamic Mass took place at St. Angela's, where a youth choir sang Haitian and French Gospel songs accompanied by congas and marimbas. Underscoring the importance of home-country music and liturgies, many churches imported missalettes and installed monitors on which they projected lyrics in the native language.[20] Most Latin American and Haitian churches also had active Charismatic prayer groups, where church members shared a personal relationship with the Holy Spirit, manifested through prophecy, glossolalia (speaking in tongues), faith healing, and saying the rosary.

The flowering of the Charismatic movement among immigrant Catholics was a prime example of the transnational flow of ideas, practices, and resources within the Catholic Church. Although the Charismatic movement originated with American college students in the 1960s, much of the energy behind immigrant spiritual renewal has come from places like Brazil, Haiti, and Korea, where Charismatics have been evangelizing since the 1980s. Latin American bishops welcomed this development, hoping to stanch the flow of Catholics to Pentecostal sects that were aggressively proselytizing and expanding. As immigrants from Brazil, Haiti, and other countries began immigrating to the United States, they brought the renewal movement back with them. The church has supported the movement through a traveling circuit of "healing priests" and lay preachers from the Caribbean and Latin America who lead retreats, Masses, and concerts in New England.[21]

Boston Catholics have thus had access to clergy and financial resources that crossed borders with relative ease. In addition to the clergy visits and rotations mentioned above, the archdiocese also hosted visits from foreign church leaders who celebrated special events with the ethnic apostolates. In 1996, for example, the archbishop from Daegu, South Korea joined Cardinal Law in a Mass to celebrate the twentieth anniversary of Boston's Korean Catholic Community. To celebrate the confirmation of its youth, the Brazilian apostolate invited bishops from the home country to celebrate a joint sacramental Mass with all of its churches. These and other local Masses were broadcast on television in Governador Valadares, the home state of many Brazilian immigrants, where viewers tuned in hoping to see their family and friends in Massachusetts. At the same time, immigrant Catholics in greater Boston collected funds to support construction of church facilities, social programs, and clerical education back home. A Brazilian church in Allston, for example, provided funds in the 1990s to support a seminary student in the Diocese of Governador Valadares as well as four ministries to street children.[22]

While the church's extensive global network and resources have facilitated transnational connections and cultural continuity for its migrant members, finding a stable physical home within the Boston archdiocese has been a vexing problem for many congregations. The demographic decline in many older parishes opened up space for the newer apostolates, but it also required different ethnic/racial groups to cooperate and negotiate arrangements for the sharing of space and expenses. The Korean Catholic Community is a case in point. Established in 1976 at a seminary in Milton, the group moved seven times in its first twenty-five years, in what one church member described as "a gypsy existence." Only in 2012—after thirty-six years of peregrinations—did the archdiocese establish a permanent parish in Newton for the Korean Catholic Community. Most of the other apostolates also moved around to different host churches. Such moves were prompted by a variety of factors: expanding congregations that outgrew the space, tensions with host congregations, or—most critically—fiscal problems that resulted in the closing or merging of parishes. In some cases, the closings struck at the heart of immigrant religious communities. In the late 1990s, for example, St. Leo's Church—the mother church of Boston's Haitian community—closed, as did Our Lady of Pity, the main Haitian church in Cambridge a few years later. Such closings caused wrenching disruptions for Haitian Catholics, many of whom had remained loyal to these parishes even after moving to the suburbs.[23]

Spatial dislocation of ethnic communities became even more critical with the massive reconfiguration of the archdiocese in the wake of the clergy sex abuse crisis. Financially pressed by the wave of lawsuits and settlements around abuse cases, Cardinal O'Malley in 2004 announced the closing of more than 80 of the archdiocese's 357 parishes. Long supportive of poor and immigrant Catholics, O'Malley gave preference to diverse parishes and insisted that financial issues alone not determine closures. As the process unfolded, there was little evidence that poorer parishes had been targeted; rather, the most vulnerable parishes tended to be those with low attendance and fewer sacraments performed. But it was also inevitable, given the dense network of parishes in the city's older neighborhoods and mill towns, that a disproportionate number of closures would come from those areas. Although ethnic apostolates had revitalized many of these declining urban parishes, their numbers alone could not sustain old Gothic churches designed for thousands. This was especially true for groups like the Haitians and Vietnamese, who had arrived in earlier decades and were now moving to the suburbs. Moreover, many of the old urban churches were in poor repair, and a good number were mission churches (built without schools) to accommodate earlier immigrants moving into the old zone of emergence. Since parishes without schools and those needing costly repairs were more likely to be closed, many ethnic congregations were forced to relocate.[24]

A survey conducted by the *Boston Globe* confirmed that a high percentage of urban and non-English-speaking parishes were affected. The archdiocese closed more than 27 percent of urban parishes, compared with 18 percent of suburban ones. Overall, 27 percent of parishes with foreign-language Masses were closed, compared with 19 percent of parishes with Masses only in English. Some of these churches were older French, Polish, and Lithuanian parishes, but they also included two Spanish-language parishes and eighteen other ethnic apostolate communities across the archdiocese. Several of these congregations, such as those of the Vietnamese communities in Dorchester, were consolidated, while others were relocated.[25]

As a result of the reconfiguration process, many of the ethnic communities found homes in large surviving parishes that housed multiple congregations. Parishes like St. Rose of Lima in Chelsea, Most Holy Redeemer in East Boston, and St. Joseph's in Lynn became multiethnic churches, with Masses in three or more languages. Developing a sense of community and avoiding balkanization was a challenge in these churches. While Masses and most other activities were conducted separately, pastors encouraged the ethnic communities to sponsor joint social events and attend multilingual liturgies several times a year. To promote joint governance, pastoral councils sought to include representatives from each of the ethnic communities, although some groups were better equipped or more inclined to participate than others. Ultimately, the pastor's leadership and skill in engaging diverse populations was critical in determining how cohesive and successful such parishes would be.[26]

A somewhat different type of multiethnic church emerged at St. Mark the Evangelist in South Dorchester, a parish that narrowly escaped closure in 2004. Prior to the 1980s, St. Mark had been one of Boston's largest and wealthiest parishes, with a largely Irish American, upper-middle-class congregation. During the busing crisis, racial tensions in the neighborhood intensified and whites began leaving the area for the South Shore suburbs. Meanwhile, African Americans and immigrants began settling on the western flanks of the parish. As the racial transition peaked in the late 1980s and early 1990s, immigrant parents began enrolling their children at St. Mark's school, and some newcomer families began attending the church. A new pastor, Father Daniel Finn, arrived in 1993 to find a heterogeneous but racially and ethnically fragmented parish. Finn, an Irish immigrant who had helped found the Irish Pastoral Center to aid Irish immigrants in the late 1980s, was determined to break down the social barriers. Along with other church leaders, Finn organized a series of one-on-one conversations between parishioners from different backgrounds who met each week to share their life stories and concerns. Later, they brought in trained community organizers to conduct house meetings to identify common concerns in the parish community. A number of parish-building initiatives came out of these meetings, including a voter registration drive, English and citizenship classes for immigrants, and church-sponsored afterschool and pre-K programs.[27]

Partly as a result of these efforts, the parish's diversity grew. By 2003 more than 70 percent of St. Mark's parishioners were immigrants and their

children, including many Vietnamese, Haitian, African, and Irish immigrants. All of these groups were represented in the parish building campaigns, and at least five languages were regularly spoken and translated at
church functions. Like other multicultural parishes, St. Mark sponsored
ethnic festivals and incorporated a variety of Marian devotions and litur-
gical styles that reflected its diverse membership. Interestingly, however,
most Masses continued to be conducted in English. This reflected parish leaders' desire for a nonsegregated congregation and a shared sense
of diversity that they feared would be eroded if ethnic groups established
separate worship services. St. Mark's brand of multicultural Catholic fellowship has been notably successful, but it remains to be seen whether
it will survive if the diversity of the neighborhood gives way to a more
homogeneous population.[28]

Ultimately, neither St. Mark's nor the more numerous multilingual
apostolate churches have mirrored the experience of the European ethnic
parishes of earlier generations. Except for a few of the panethnic Latino
congregations, most of Boston's ethnic apostolates have not possessed the
numbers or degree of geographic concentration to develop into de facto
ethnic parishes (as has occurred in the largest immigrant gateways, such
as New York and Los Angeles). Nor does the Catholic hierarchy endorse
such a system. Rather, it sees the apostolates as a temporary mission to
welcome newcomers, share their faith and cultural heritage, but ultimately
"foster full integration and participation of immigrants and refugees in
the life of the local parish and the Archdiocese." The sheer diversity of the
region's new immigrant population, combined with the fiscal and personnel problems of the archdiocese, has complicated this effort and made for
a sometimes troubled reception. In many cases, newcomers were shuffled
from church to church, relied on temporary or unstable leadership, and
depended on parishes and apostolates with dwindling financial resources.
Moreover, without strong youth programming, many of the second generation simply left the church as they got older.[29]

Some church leaders view this as a tragically missed opportunity—a
chance to repopulate and revitalize the church with a new wave of immigrants who were overwhelmingly Catholic in their home countries and
who were desperate for spiritual and social assistance. Instead, many have
gravitated to evangelical Protestant groups who proselytized intensely
both in Massachusetts and in the migrants' home countries. Indeed,

apostolate priests frequently voiced these concerns. As one local Haitian priest explained in 1993, his church desperately needed more resources "to counteract the inroads of members of cults and sects among non-churched or lapsed Catholics." But amid the financial, spiritual, and organizational crisis that beset the Catholic Church beginning in the 1990s, few resources were forthcoming.[30]

PROTESTANTS AND THE "QUIET REVIVAL"

Like Catholics, Protestants in greater Boston viewed the new immigration as an engine of religious renewal—an opportunity to put "new wine in old bottles." Like many urban Catholic parishes, most of the city's mainline Protestant churches had been in decline since the 1950s as white residents moved to the suburbs and joined new congregations closer to home. In the South End and Roxbury, African Americans took over some of these churches, but beginning in the late 1960s, Latino and Asian migrants also formed congregations that would become part of the city's new religious landscape. Many of these churches differed from their mainline predecessors not only in language but in cultural style and theology as well. A large proportion, in fact, was evangelical or Pentecostal. This transformation of urban Protestantism is often portrayed as a spontaneous development springing from the imported religious fervor of newly arrived immigrants. In reality, the process in Boston has been more organized and collaborative, as native-born evangelicals helped facilitate what they called "the quiet revival."

This incremental but powerful religious movement built on the city's historical traditions of evangelism and church networking. From its Puritan roots in the seventeenth century, the city had hosted a succession of evangelical revivals led by preachers such as Charles Finney in the 1850s, Dwight Moody in the 1870s, Billy Sunday in the 1910s, and Billy Graham in the 1950s. Through these waves of spiritual excitement, the Park Street Church—next to Boston Common—was a key site of support. A Conservative Congregational church, Park Street had a long history of evangelical fervor and reform, hosting preachers who supported abolition, women's suffrage, temperance, and foreign missionary work. After World War II, Park Street's pastor, the noted theologian Harold Ockenga, was one of the cofounders of the National Association of Evangelicals, a group

espousing an updated brand of evangelicalism that blended fundamental-
ist theology with a more socially engaged approach to modern life and culture. Together with Billy Graham, J. Howard Pew, and other "neo-evangel-
icals," Ockenga founded the Gordon-Conwell Theological Seminary north
of Boston and became its first president in 1969. The school would become
an important training ground for Latino and immigrant ministries and
would work with Park Street and other established evangelical churches to
spread the Gospel among the city's newcomers.[31]

Some of the earliest examples of evangelical cultivation of new immi-
grants occurred in the Chinese community. What would become New
England's largest Chinese Christian congregation, the Chinese Evangelical
Church, was founded in 1961 by the Reverend James Tan, who arrived in
Boston in the 1950s to serve at a Chinatown mission church established
by mainline Protestant groups. Raised as a Presbyterian in South China,
Tan had been influenced by evangelicals and Pentecostals working in rural
China. With his more popular evangelical style, he soon grew uncomfortable in the Chinatown mission and founded his own church in 1961. Baptists
with the Union Rescue Mission helped the new congregation secure a
worship space, while leaders of the Park Street Church helped them write
bylaws and navigate the legal incorporation process. As the church grew,
its members raised funds to erect their own building on Harrison Avenue
in 1979. Most of the early members were Cantonese-speaking laundry and
restaurant workers; after 1980, however, the church attracted a growing
number of Mandarin-speaking migrants from the mainland and added
Mandarin-language services in 1989.[32]

During the 1950s and 1960s, Christian student groups at local universities were the seedbed for new churches serving more highly educated
Asian immigrants. Much like the Korean Church of Boston, which started
at Boston University, the predominantly Taiwanese Chinese Bible Church
of Greater Boston had its roots in a Bible study group at MIT around the
same time. The church's founder, Peter Yen, was a student (and later faculty
member) at Harvard Medical School, a member of the MIT Bible Study
Group, and a deacon at the Park Street Church. In 1969 he organized an
independent church that initially met in his living room in Newton and
later at Grace Chapel in Lexington. In 1992 the group built a new sanctuary
nearby that attracted some five hundred members, mainly Chinese professionals from affluent western suburbs.[33]

Beginning in the 1970s and 1980s, local churches such as Park Street, Grace Chapel, and Cambridgeport Baptist developed special ministries for foreign students. Working with campus evangelical ministries like InterVarsity and International Student Ministries, local churches helped locate chaplains for various ethnic groups and offered English classes, sightseeing trips, intercultural workshops, and host family relationships for students and their families. Such activities appealed to newly arrived students while also introducing them to local churches, Bible study groups, and Sunday worship. Some students who remained in the area after graduation became permanent members of these churches or, like Peter Yen, sought evangelicals' assistance in establishing, or "planting," new ethnic churches. Since the 1990s, some of the larger Chinese and Korean churches have themselves started special ministries to appeal to Asian students at local universities.[34]

While the area's first Asian churches were opening their doors in the 1960s, an even more dramatic explosion of religious activity was taking place among Latino migrants. In the South End, Puerto Rican Pentecostals organized three new churches—Iglesia de Dios, MB (Mission Board); Iglesia de Cristero Misionera; and Asamblea de Iglesias Cristianos. Along with Canaan Defensores de la Fe, founded in Roxbury in 1966, these churches became the foundations of a dynamic Latino Pentecostal movement in Boston. The rapid proliferation of these churches followed the growing diaspora from Puerto Rico and the Dominican Republic, islands where Pentecostal denominations such as the Assemblies of God and the Pentecostal Church of God had strong followings. In some cases, church members called on their home churches to send preachers to Boston, where they then sought out storefronts or older churches to house their ministries.

Recognizing the dynamism of these new churches, Boston evangelicals sought to reach out and aid the migrant newcomers. Support was especially forthcoming from the Emmanuel Gospel Center (EGC), a nondenominational mission founded in 1938 to serve the impoverished population of the South End. Reflecting the new activism of the urban ministry movement of the 1960s, EGC gradually transformed itself from a neighborhood mission to a citywide service center providing support to churches in Boston's poorest neighborhoods—mainly those serving African Americans, Puerto Ricans, and increasingly, new immigrants. One of EGC's new initiatives was the Emmanuel Book and Record Shop, started in 1970 as a storefront resource center that provided Spanish-language religious materials, mentorship, and meeting space for new congregations. EGC also worked with Latino pastors to foster various cooperative ventures, such as evangelistic crusades, concerts, and parades. In the 1970s, for example, the crusade of Puerto Rican evangelist Yiye Avila resulted in the founding of the Pentecostal Church of God in Dorchester, a church that later spawned dozens of affiliates around New England.[35]

Over the next two decades, Latino Protestantism would experience extraordinary growth and mobility as new churches opened and older ones expanded and relocated. With the gentrification of the South End, many Latino congregations moved out to Roxbury, Dorchester, and East Boston, while new churches sprang up to serve growing Latino populations in Chelsea, Lynn, and Somerville. A 2000 survey conducted by the EGC found at least eighty-five Protestant Spanish-language churches in the city of Boston, most of them serving pan-Latino congregations. Many of these churches were Pentecostal, but there were also many other denominational churches that shared sanctuaries with dwindling white or black congregations. This was especially true in Jamaica Plain, where older Methodist, Presbyterian, and Baptist churches became predominantly Latino in the 1970s and 1980s. St. Andrews United Methodist Church, for example, became a mixed Anglo-Latino congregation in the early 1970s and initiated a Spanish-language ministry, the first among New England Methodists. Another new denominational church was Leon de Judá, a Baptist congregation that began meeting at the Emmanuel Gospel Center in 1980. With the help of a Baptist urban ministry group, the church relocated to Cambridgeport in 1982 but returned to Boston 1993 and began renovating an empty warehouse building in lower Roxbury. In its new home, Leon de Judá would become one of the largest Latino congregations in the metro area.[36]

Other immigrant groups also began to build evangelical churches during these years. Although most early Haitian arrivals were French-speaking Catholics, the more diverse wave that followed included a growing number of Baptists and Pentecostals. Beginning in 1969, the First Haitian Baptist Church began as a Bible study group in Dorchester, led by a young seminary graduate, the Reverend Verdieu Laroche. In 1978 the church purchased the former Blue Hill Avenue synagogue (Adath Jeshurun), where it would flourish for the next thirty years. Several other pioneer congregations formed in the 1970s, but a veritable explosion of new Baptist and

Pentecostal churches occurred in the late 1980s and 1990s to serve the new wave of Kreyol-speaking migrants. The number of Haitian Protestant congregations in greater Boston thus increased from one in 1970 to more than fifty in 2000.[37]

Arriving somewhat later, Brazilians and Africans also proved to be avid Protestant church-builders. Beginning in the mid-1980s, Brazilians formed dozens of Pentecostal and Baptist churches, including the burgeoning World Revival Church, led by Pastor Ouriel de Jesus. De Jesus arrived in Somerville in 1985 to serve the Brazilian Assembly of God congregation there. Under his charismatic (and controversial) leadership, the church expanded quickly and spawned new congregations across the state, breaking with the Assemblies of God and reorganizing as the World Revival Church. Most Brazilian churches, however, were smaller congregations that proliferated in Brazilian strongholds like Framingham, where dozens of Portuguese-language churches were operating by the early 2000s. Finally, some of the most recent additions to the Protestant network have been African churches, among which Pentecostal groups such as the Apostolic and Nigerian Aladura churches are well represented. West African Christians have also been increasingly visible in mainline denominations such as the Anglicans and Baptists, often joining native-born whites and blacks in English-language ministries.[38]

This spawning of new immigrant churches contributed to a doubling of the number of churches in the Boston-Cambridge area (from roughly three hundred to six hundred) between the late 1960s and 2000. Many of these congregations started out by sharing space with mainline Protestant churches. In surveys done by the EGC, it found that a quarter of all churches in this area were sharing quarters in the early 1990s, while more than a third were doing so a decade later. Some of the new groups found homes through cooperative arrangements with older churches of the same denomination, but EGC and other evangelical organizations also facilitated church planting and sharing as a deliberate strategy for religious renewal. After its founding in 1970, EGC provided meeting space for new congregations in the South End; by the 1990s it was acting as a clearinghouse for newer, mostly immigrant, congregations desiring to share space with struggling older churches. Organized officially in 2000, the EGC's Greater Boston Church Planting Collaborative facilitated space sharing while offering guidance and resources to potential church planters. Cooperating churches typically

offered their sanctuaries to the immigrant congregations on Saturday eve-
nings or Sunday afternoons, while the original congregations worshipped
on Sunday mornings. Some of the new groups later disbanded, but the most
successful flourished and built their own churches or purchased and renovated older synagogues and churches. This was especially common in aging
urban neighborhoods but also occurred in the suburbs. In the early 2000s,
for example, the New Covenant Church, a Haitian evangelical congregation that had outgrown its sanctuary in North Cambridge, purchased St.
Joseph's Catholic Church in Waltham, a formerly French Canadian parish
with a sanctuary that seated more than a thousand. Around the same time,
the Chinese Evangelical Church in Chinatown acquired the stately Central
Congregational Church in Newton as a satellite church to accommodate
its suburban members. Less prosperous immigrant groups planted their
churches wherever they could afford space—in storefronts, strip malls, former nursing homes, factories, and fraternal halls.[39]

Boston's older evangelical community saw the dynamism of new immigrant churches as a godsend for Christianity in New England, a place they
viewed as a mission field "especially in need of the gospel." Lamenting the
secularization of the region's native born, they praised immigrant church
planting as a "quiet revival" that could revitalize the older Christian community. "Euro-American churches may need a transfusion of vitality from
congregations of other cultures," the ECG explained. They could benefit from "the simple faith and Christ-centered lifestyle of the immigrant
churches while the latter might benefit from the leadership experience
of the older Euro-American churches." Some immigrant church leaders
shared this missionary outlook. "We feel that we can do something in the
United States," said the pastor of a Brazilian Baptist church in Framingham.
"We feel the churches here are looking for revival."

Ironically, many of the evangelical and Pentecostal movements embraced by Latino, Asian, and African immigrants were first introduced by
American missionaries working abroad in the early twentieth century. A
good example is the Church of the Nazarene, a holiness movement that
flourished in the Cape Verde Islands after the arrival of missionaries there
in the 1930s. Their work helped promote Protestantism on the islands, rein-
forcing an earlier missionary effort by Cape Verdean migrants who were
converted while working on whaling ships in New England. Despite persecution by Portuguese colonial rulers, the Church of the Nazarene became

the largest denomination on the islands and has been reinvigorated in Boston and southern New England through the church-planting efforts of recent migrants. Africans, in fact, have been particularly active in revitalizing local Nazarene, Apostolic, and other Protestant denominations. Even among mainline groups such as the Anglicans, Africans have promoted a more conservative brand of Christianity. After US Episcopalians appointed an openly gay bishop in New Hampshire in 2003, the archbishop of Nigeria founded an alternative Anglican network espousing a more conservative theology and invited US Episcopalians to affiliate. Attracting both African migrants and native-born Episcopalians alike, the newly formed Convocation of Anglicans in North America sought to push US Anglicanism in a more traditional direction.[40]

Immigrant churches have varied widely in worship style and beliefs, but most have practiced a more evangelical-style of Protestantism characterized by cultural styles and values brought from their home countries. Many Caribbean and Latin American churches featured long services (two to three hours) with a lot of lively singing, musical accompaniment on guitar, drums, or tambourine, and a highly expressive worship style. Asian churches have introduced a variety of religious styles, from more traditional Western-style liturgies to more contemporary evangelical services. Religious scholars, however, have noted that Confucian values such as family loyalty, humility, and saving face continue to shape religious practices among Asian Protestants. Like other evangelicals, most immigrant Protestants believe in the Bible as the ultimate source of religious authority, the need for a direct personal relationship with Jesus Christ, and a strict moral code that forbids drinking, drugs, and other vices. Those who are members of Pentecostal sects also practice glossolalia, faith healing, and other spiritual expressions.

Most important, many immigrant Protestant churches have been committed to evangelization via proselytizing, revivals, and church planting. The effectiveness of evangelical outreach is evident in an account by Elba Mireya Vasquez, a longtime member of Iglesia Bautista Central in Cambridge, explaining how she and her mother first joined the church in 1984. Arriving from Honduras in 1982, Vasquez's mother (a nominal Catholic) faced stress and depression as a single parent trying to adjust to life in the United States. Feeling isolated and being unable to speak English, she was eager to find a supportive community. One day while watching a

Christian evangelist on television, her mother asked Vasquez (who had learned English) to call the phone number on the screen and see if they had someone who could pray with her in Spanish.

> And so I called, they put somebody on the phone, and the person who actually spoke to her was the founding pastor of the church that we currently attend. . . . He took all my mom's information down. I think within that week, he and a couple of other people from his congregation came to our home and decided to visit us. And you know, they basically arranged so that—you know we didn't have any transportation to get to church—somebody could come pick us up. So we started attending Iglesia Bautista Central in Cambridge.[41]

Such assertive methods resulted in a profusion of new Protestant churches, a process that accelerated in the 1990s when the Boston archdiocese was closing parishes, combining apostolates, and consolidating community-based services for immigrants.[42]

Stepping into the breach, immigrant evangelicals sought to attract new adherents by addressing the social and emotional needs of migrant newcomers. Like some of the Catholic apostolates, Protestant churches welcomed prospective members with fellowship and social services. At St. Andrews Methodist Church in Jamaica Plain, Pastor Luis Benavides and his wife, Nancy, helped build a growing Latino congregation in part by offering family counseling services and a shelter for homeless families. In Dorchester, Puerto Rican Pastor Luis Aponte and his wife, Millie, started a drug treatment program at the Pentecostal Cristo El Rey Church. In Framingham, Brazilian evangelical churches were known for their elaborate welcoming services that helped newcomers find jobs, housing, and family counseling. While many such efforts were small scale and personalized—with aid administered via Bible study or cell groups—some immigrant churches developed elaborate social service delivery systems. In 1997, for example, the Latino Baptist Church, Leon de Judá, opened a four-story building housing social ministries that included ESL and computer classes, counseling, summer programs for children, and a higher education resource center. As Pastor Roberto Miranda explained, the congregation renovated an old warehouse in Lower Roxbury in order "to minister to the needs of the particularly Caribbean Hispanics who are usually the most affected by poverty and all the elements that impact our community negatively." In Chinatown, the Chinese Evangelical Church offered a similar array of programs for its members, as well as working with the city of Boston to provide affordable housing and to eliminate the Combat Zone. Although both Protestants and Catholics sought to address the needs of new immigrants, evangelical programs continued to grow in the 1990s, while funding for Catholic services at the parish level diminished in the face of the church's fiscal crisis.[43]

Evangelical Protestant churches came to have an even greater advantage in terms of church personnel and leadership. Oftentimes, economic pressures forced migrant preachers to work full-time jobs in addition to their ministries. As migrants working to survive in a new country, the ministers understood the struggles of their followers and developed their churches as outposts of emotional and spiritual support. But they often lacked formal theological training or the administrative skills necessary to run a successful church. To support these ministries, the Gordon-Conwell Seminary established the Center for Urban Ministerial Education (CUME) in Roxbury in the mid-1970s. CUME provided teachers who offered Spanish-language courses on theology, pastoral care, and administration. Unlike traditional seminary programs, CUME offered low-cost evening courses at a central location, including certificate programs for those with limited formal education. Over time, the program expanded, offering courses in Portuguese, Haitian Kreyol, French, and Khmer. Latino pastors also found support and training from the Confraternidad de Pastores Hispanos de Nueva Inglaterra (Fellowship of Hispanic Pastors of New England), a regional ministerial association founded in 2002. Working with the Emmanuel Gospel Center, the Confraternidad secured funding from the Lilly Foundation to launch the Institute for Pastoral Excellence, a program of workshops and retreats on pastoral leadership and administration that served fifteen to twenty pastors per year. Such programs helped build ministerial resources from the ground up and developed a local evangelical network for common religious, political, and social projects. Catholic institutions such as Boston College have developed similar lay ministry programs for Latinos in recent years, but they started decades after their evangelical counterparts.[44]

Finally, a number of immigrant Protestant churches also benefited from the leadership and expertise of women copastors (usually the wives of pastors). Particularly among Pentecostal churches, women pastors preached and led family or social service ministries in congregations that included a high proportion of women. Even in evangelical churches with generally conservative views on the role of women, such female copastors were publicly recognized as spiritual and institutional leaders whose skills were valued and respected.[45]

Protestant church leaders also fortified their migrant congregations by engaging directly in missionary and relief efforts in their home countries. With the support of the Southern Baptist Convention, the First Haitian Baptist Church inaugurated a missionary program in northern Haiti and worked with other Haitian evangelical churches to bring fiery preachers from the homeland to pulpits in Massachusetts. Since the 2010 earthquake, the local Haitian ministers' association has organized teams from their churches to provide medical assistance and relief. Local Asian, African, and Hispanic churches also engaged in missionary work and church planting in their home regions. Berkland (later Antioch) Baptist Church in Cambridge planted several new congregations in Japan, Korea, and other parts of Asia. Members of New Beginnings Church of God in Dorchester sponsored children in the Dominican Republic, while Canaan Defenders of the Faith in Roxbury planted three new churches in Puerto Rico. Although generally lacking the formal transnational networks of the Catholic hierarchy, evangelical mission work has involved more direct contact between church members in the United States and abroad, fueled by a passion for evangelization that has been central to Pentecostal and Baptist faiths.[46]

Perhaps the greatest challenge for immigrant evangelicals was keeping their own children within the fold. Like Catholic immigrants, first-generation Protestants saw their sons and daughters pulled in various directions—toward Euro American and African American churches or away from religion altogether. Immigrant church leaders responded by developing youth programs and separate English-language ministries targeted at the second generation. At the same time, some churches (especially Asian ones) launched native-language and cultural programs for children to encourage them to embrace and appreciate their cultural heritage. Such programs also served as a vehicle for attracting coethnic, non-Christian families to the faith. Just how effective these efforts have been at retaining the second generation is unclear, but they have provided a distinctive space and measure of autonomy for immigrant youth within ethnic churches that stands in contrast to the more assimilationist approach of Catholicism.[47]

Second-generation ethnics have also been key supporters of a small but growing number of multicultural congregations in greater Boston.

The Austin Baptist Church in Lynn, for example, hosts a mixture of Euro Americans, Cambodians, Latinos, and Africans. Here, denominationally loyal Liberians took the lead in integrating the English-language services and fostering a more multicultural approach. A similar transition has occurred at other denominational churches in which Africans and West Indians have integrated formerly white, native-born congregations. By the early 2000s, the once predominantly white Hyde Park Presbyterian Church in Boston had become a hybrid congregation of West Indians, Africans, and native-born whites and blacks. Like St. Mark Catholic Church in Dorchester, these heterogeneous English-speaking churches have actively embraced their diversity in neighborhoods undergoing rapid demographic change. Their existence suggests that the children of new immigrants may forge their own distinctive religious cultures in the future.[48]

WORLD RELIGIONS IN BOSTON

The de-Europeanization of Christianity in greater Boston is only one dimension of the sweeping impact that new immigrants have had on the region's religious life. Here, as in cities around the country, newcomers from Asia, the Middle East, and Africa have brought faith traditions that were sparsely represented prior to the 1970s. Indeed, the Pluralism Project's database on World Religions in Greater Boston indicates that several hundred religious centers with non-Western and immigrant origins have sprung up since 1960. These include a wide array of groups, including Hindus, Buddhists, Muslims, Sikhs, and many others.[49]

Compared with other parts of the United States, the Boston area has been a relatively hospitable environment for this flowering of religious pluralism. Boston's maritime history and its role as a key port in the nineteenth-century China and India trade encouraged a mutual, if unequal, exchange of culture and religious ideas. The local transcendentalists Ralph Waldo Emerson and Henry David Thoreau read and translated Hindu and Buddhist texts as early as the 1830s and helped introduce them to American intellectuals. By the 1880s interest in Buddhism had become widespread, and a group of Harvard professors known as "the Boston Buddhists" made the university a center for the study of Buddhism in the United States. In the 1950s, Harvard established a professorship in Buddhist Studies and created a Center for the Study of World Religions that would become a focal

point for the comparative study of religion, attracting international scholars and practitioners from diverse religious traditions.[50] Indeed, much
of the research for this section draws on the work of Harvard scholars,
and the three main traditions I discuss here—Hinduism, Buddhism, and
Islam—have all had some kind of connection with Harvard students, faculty, or visiting scholars in building their local congregations and centers.
The celebration of religious pluralism at Harvard and other local universities, however, has not always been the reality on the street, inasmuch as
anti-immigrant sentiments and religious tensions have periodically surfaced, particularly in the aftermath of 9/11.

Hinduism

By 2010 there were more than thirty Hindu temples and organizations in
greater Boston. Most of them were founded after 1990, when the area's
Indian and South Asian populations began to increase precipitously. While
a number of smaller temples took root in Boston and Cambridge, some of
the largest have sprung up in the suburbs west and north of the city where
many Indian migrants have settled. Often the founders of these temples
began by meeting in each other's homes or in local rented halls, and a few
later bought and converted old church buildings. But some of the largest
groups preferred to purchase land and build their own temples so that
they could design a space to suit their worship needs and to adhere to ritual citing and construction practices. These suburban temples have grown
rapidly, reaching out to new arrivals from South Asia and other parts of the
world and becoming more ethnically and culturally diverse in the process.[51]

A good example of this evolution is the Sri Lakshmi Temple in suburban Ashland. Located near the Ashland-Framingham border, the temple
traces its origins back to the 1970s, when eight local Indian families began
meeting in each other's homes. Mainly Tamils from South India, these
doctors, scientists, and engineers had come to Boston for professional
training and later found work and settled in the area. They soon began
gathering for *puja* (ritual offerings) and for various Hindu celebrations.
As they started raising families, they worried about how to preserve their
Hindu religion and cultural identity for the next generation. In 1978 they
incorporated as the New England Hindu Temple, and each donated $101 to
launch a building fund. For the next several years, they met in rented space
in a Knights of Columbus Hall in Melrose and later in a community center

in Needham. By 1981 they had raised $30,000 and decided to purchase a 12-acre parcel in Ashland for the construction of a new temple, which they named Sri Lakshmi, after the Goddess of Prosperity. As the official temple history explains, the founders decided to dedicate the temple to Lakshmi, "since most of us have come to this country in search of the prosperity and happiness bestowed by the grace of Mahalakshmi." Ultimately, the professional skills and affluence of the temple's membership would help ensure its success and expansion, but in the early 1980s the struggle to develop the Ashland site seemed immense.[52]

Indeed, it would take more than a decade, and a good bit of support from Hindus in the homeland, to complete the temple. First, Sri Lakshmi's planners commissioned an architect in India who sited and designed the temple according to ritual canons. To finance some of the construction costs, the temple secured a loan from Thirumaial-Thirupathi Devasthanam, a consortium of Hindu temples in southern India. In 1986 the main hall was opened for worship services, and two years later Sri Lakshmi appointed its first full-time priest, brought in from India. Meanwhile, construction of the ornamental towers continued as temple members raised more funds to hire artisans from India to craft and install the ornamentation for the towers and the interior. Finally, by 1990, the four towers had been completed and consecrated in a week-long series of ritual offerings and ceremonies that attracted thousands of participants and onlookers.[53]

Over the next decade attendance at Sri Lakshmi would continue to grow, while the temple added more priests and more religious and cultural programming. Beyond being a place of worship, the temple offered space for community activities, as well as classes where members' American-born children could study religion, classical Indian music and dance, Sanskrit, and other languages. The high-tech boom of the 1990s attracted many more Indian professionals to the area, while new Hindu migrants also arrived from Sri Lanka, Singapore, Malaysia, Nepal, and Trinidad. Meeting the needs of these groups meant that the temple had to provide services and meeting space for those with disparate Hindu traditions. Moreover, in 2009 the temple worked with refugee agencies to aid a newly arrived group of Hindu Bhutanese refugees, providing transportation to the temple on festival days, organizing clothes and appliance drives, and helping with job placement. Finally, the temple devoted considerable energy to public outreach to the larger community, opening its doors to local high school and college classes and also to other religious groups who came to learn about Hinduism.[54]

These continuing outreach efforts seemed to pay off. For the most part, the temple did not encounter serious obstacles in getting building permits, and—with only a couple of exceptions—residents of the Ashland-Framingham area were accepting of their new neighbor.[55] In this generally supportive climate, temple members went ahead and purchased nine more acres of adjacent land in 2010 and announced plans for a $2 million expansion, including space for more classrooms, a kitchen, and dining and function areas. The temple hoped that these facilities would better accommodate its growing and increasingly diverse membership, as well as the more than three thousand Hindus who came from throughout New England for major religious celebrations.[56]

Buddhism

Like Hindus, many newly arrived Buddhist immigrants had to build their temples and religious organizations from the ground up. Although Chinese migrants had been settling in Chinatown and other communities since the late nineteenth century, their practice of Buddhism had been limited to home altars and family shrines. In fact, as late as the 1980s there were very few Buddhist temples in greater Boston. The Cambridge Buddhist Association, founded by Harvard professors in 1957, was the first Buddhist organization in the region and would later offer space and support to new groups arriving from Tibet, Sri Lanka, and other parts of East and Southeast Asia. But the largest numbers of new Buddhist adherents came from China, Vietnam, and Cambodia, and it was they who would build the fastest growing new temples in the region.[57]

One of the first to emerge was the Thousand Buddha Temple in Quincy. The temple was founded by the Reverend Sik Kuan Yen, a Buddhist monk from Hong Kong who came to the United States to study at a monastery in New York in the mid-1980s. After visiting Quincy in 1989 and seeing that local Buddhists in the Pure Land tradition had no place of worship, she and her spiritual leader, the Reverend Sik Wing Sing of the Hong Kong Budhi Society, decided that she should stay and start a temple. Leading services in her residence in Wollaston where many new Asian immigrants were settling, Reverend Sik soon faced complaints and legal threats from her Quincy neighbors who disapproved of the crowds, chanting, and parking problems. Moreover, tensions between Asian newcomers and some of the native-born were still evident in Quincy, which had seen a spate of violent clashes in the late 1980s. Consequently, with the guidance of the city's new Committee on Immigrants and Refugees, the Reverend Sik and her followers purchased and renovated an old function hall in a mixed-use area of Quincy Point. The Hong Kong Budhi Society provided some initial funding for the project, but temple members—who included building trades workers, restaurant owners, and others—supplied much of the labor and materials. After several years work, the new Thousand Buddha Temple opened in 1996, featuring a large meditation hall lined with more than a thousand Buddha statues symbolizing the Buddha-nature to which all followers can aspire. Alongside the hall they built a large dining area and kitchen for communal meals and a meeting room, with a library upstairs. The dedication ceremony attracted more than five hundred people from around the region, as well as Buddhist venerables (ordained monks and nuns) from New York, Taiwan, and China. In a telling counterpoint to Quincy's recent history of ethnic tension and violence, Mayor James Sheets used the occasion to praise and celebrate the city's diversity, noting that "in diversity this city and this country [have] found [their] strength."[58]

The new temple provided much needed space for Buddhist worship, education, and other services. Regular Sunday services were conducted in both Cantonese and Mandarin, followed by a communal vegetarian meal in the dining hall. Members also attended classes and meditations to enhance their spiritual practice. To serve its immigrant members, the temple established committees of volunteers to coordinate additional services. One committee oversaw religious and cultural education for children; another organized visits and hospice care for the sick and elderly; and a third supervised charity and relief efforts. The latter has centered on both local efforts—such as the temple's participation in Interfaith Social Services (a multiservice program for needy families on the South Shore)—and international efforts, such as raising relief funds for victims of the earthquake in Sichuan Province and the cyclone in Myanmar in 2008. Temple members have also supported the resident and visiting monks with regular donations of food and clothing, a practice that helps subsidize operating expenses.[59]

Since its founding, the Thousand Buddha Temple has seen robust growth, from roughly fifty members in 1990 to the more than two thousand who received the temple's newsletter in 2012. Although a much smaller number

attend Sunday services, annual events such as Buddha's birthday, Chinese
New Year, and other celebrations bring in hundreds from as far away as
New Hampshire and Rhode Island. Many of the original members were
Chinese migrants from Hong Kong, but over time the temple has attracted
newcomers from across the mainland, as well as from Vietnam, Taiwan,
and Malaysia. To accommodate this increasingly diverse membership, the
temple began hosting venerables who speak several languages and live in
residence in the temple for up to two years. The venerables provided services and instruction in several languages, including English for the growing contingent of American-born children. The temple's Sunday school
program—offering religious instruction in Buddhism as well as classes in
Mandarin and Cantonese—has helped attract new members interested in
preserving their cultural heritage for their children. The growing popular-
ity of the youth education programs prompted the temple to raise funds to
build a new community building across the street, completed in 2008 with
the help of members' labor and donations.[60]

The growth and success of the Thousand Buddha Temple have been
repeated among Buddhists in Asian communities across the region. As
Quincy's Vietnamese population grew and spread to adjoining Braintree,
for example, two new Buddhist temples sprang up there in 2001: the Bode
Center, a temple that follows Zen teachings, and the Samantabhadra Center,
a former nursing home that was converted to a center for Vietnamese
Buddhism. The Samantabhadra Center grew especially fast, becoming one of the largest Buddhist centers in greater Boston. It joined older
Boston-based Vietnamese temples located in Dorchester, Roslindale, and
East Boston. To the north, Theravada Buddhists from Cambodia founded
temples in Revere, Lynn, Lowell, and North Chelmsford, anchoring growing refugee communities in those areas in the 1980s and 1990s. Koreans,
Tibetans, and Thais also founded Buddhist temples in Cambridge and
surrounding suburbs, including the massive NMR Meditation Center that
opened in Raynham in 2014, reportedly the largest Thai Buddhist temple
outside of Thailand. By the 2010s there were more than sixty Buddhist temples and centers in greater Boston, roughly half of them founded by new
immigrants.[61]

The vibrancy and diversity of these groups was evident in an interieth-
nic gathering of Boston-area Buddhists to celebrate Buddha's birthday in
May 2003. Spearheaded by the Greater Boston Buddhist Cultural Center in

Cambridge, followers of more than fifty Buddhist organizations—including Chinese, Japanese, Vietnamese, Thai, and Korean groups—gathered in Copley Square to commemorate the 2,547th birthday of the Buddha. Wearing brightly colored robes and dress from their native countries, representatives from sixteen delegations made offerings to a statue depicting the baby Buddha, followed by speeches, ethnic music and dance performances, and the ritual showering of the Buddha with water. A watershed event for local Buddhists, who typically marked the founder's birth in separate temple-based ceremonies, the highly public celebration attracted an estimated two to three thousand participants. Organizers saw the event as a way of fostering collaboration and communication between Buddhist organizations, but also as an opportunity to introduce Buddhism to the wider Boston community.[62]

Islam

Less than a mile east of the Thousand Buddha Temple, near the Quincy waterfront, is another landmark religious institution—the Islamic Center of New England (ICNE). Built in 1964, the ICNE is the oldest mosque in New England. Unlike local Buddhist and Hindu immigrants who had to build their temples and communities from scratch in the 1980s and 1990s, Muslim immigrants to the Boston area have built on the religious foundations of an earlier generation of Syrian and Lebanese settlers. While this support was a distinct asset for Muslim immigrants in the years after 1965, growing tensions between the United States and the Muslim world since the 1980s—and especially since 9/11—have created a more hostile climate.

Although the vast majority of earlier Syrian and Lebanese immigrants were Christian, a small number were practicing Muslims who struggled to build an Islamic community for themselves and their children. There were no mosques at the time in Boston's Little Syria in the South End, but a nascent Muslim community began to emerge among Arab migrants who moved to nearby Quincy to take jobs in the Fore River Shipyard during and after World War I. It was not until 1931, however, when Mohamed Omar Awad arrived from Lebanon, that the Quincy Point community began to organize itself as distinct from the local Lebanese Christian majority. Around 1934, a group of seven families came together under Omar's leadership to form the Arab American Banner Society, a Muslim cultural and charitable group that soon purchased a house near the shipyards for

Friday prayers, holiday celebrations, and religious and cultural instruction of their children. Despite attempts to hold on to their heritage, however, many of their children intermarried and moved to nearby suburbs, and almost none of the younger generation had ever entered a mosque.[63]

After World War II, the American-born generation, some of whom were now businesspeople and professionals, helped to reactivate the society in the hope of enhancing the religious identity of their children. With a new slate of officers, the society met monthly in a Lebanese-owned luncheonette to organize religious activities and begin plans to build a mosque. From 1957 to 1963 the society raised money through pledges from its members, donations from Muslim organizations in New York and Detroit, and from a host of community fundraising activities including picnics, raffles, auctions, dances, and card parties. In 1961, King Saud came to Boston for eye surgery, during which time members of the society attended a reception and visited him in the hospital. A few months later, the Saudi king donated $5,000 to the mosque's building fund. With forty-four members and $20,000 in cash, the society (now incorporated as the Islamic Center of New England) broke ground in 1963 on the site of the group's old meetinghouse on South Street. The new Islamic Center opened the following year, one of only a handful of mosques in the United States at the time.[64]

Despite their success in building the mosque, the Quincy Muslim community continued to struggle in the face of low membership, financial problems, and difficulties in engaging the younger generation. Within a few years, however, the empty edges of the prayer hall began to fill as students from the Middle East and South Asia arrived to study at local universities. As some found permanent employment and settled in the area, mosque membership tripled in the first decade, with members hailing from more than twenty-five countries. Soon the ICNE was bursting at the seams. As it raised more funds, the mosque expanded its facilities, adding a library, office space, and new classrooms to house its growing Sunday school programs. As with many non-Christian religious centers in the United States, members raised funds in their home countries, attracting donations from Iraq, Kuwait, Libya, and Saudi Arabia.[65]

In the 1970s and 1980s, the demographic and physical expansion of the mosque also led to growing pains for its increasingly diverse membership. As newer immigrants took up leadership positions in the mosque, they introduced more orthodox practices from their homelands, including weekly prayer schedules, ablution rooms (for ritual washing before prayer), and Friday sermons (*khubat*) in both English and Arabic. Instructing the older founders in the religious tenets of Islam, the newcomers also convinced them to discontinue certain fundraising practices that were deemed "un-Islamic." These included American-style raffles, card parties, auctions, and the annual picnic (which sold beer and was open to the wider Quincy community). Some older members of the ICNE left the mosque in protest, but most worked for an accommodation with the newcomers. In the late 1970s, the ICNE also experienced a series of policy disputes between the founders and some of the newer immigrant leaders over membership criteria. These ended with some of the newcomers leaving the mosque to found a new religious center in 1981, the Islamic Society of Boston (ISB) in Cambridge. The ISB drew its members mainly from the Muslim Students Associations at MIT, Harvard, and other local universities.[66] Paralleling the earlier history of Jewish synagogues, newly arrived Muslim immigrants founded their own religious institutions when they judged the local mosques of their predecessors to be too Americanized. And like some of the new evangelical Christian churches serving immigrants, the ISB got its start in the student lounges of local universities.

In Quincy, the ICNE sought to resolve some its internal tensions by bringing in a new imam from Lebanon when its founder, Mohamed Omar Awad, retired. Arriving from Tripoli in 1983, Imam Talal Eid helped build bridges between old and new members and would play an important role in interfaith activities and public outreach with the larger Boston community. This educational and public relations work became increasingly important as anti-Muslim sentiment grew in response to developments in the Middle East and rising Islamic extremism. Events such as the Iranian hostage crisis of 1979 and US interventions in Libya, Lebanon, and the Iran-Iraq War of the 1980s all heightened domestic fears of Muslims. Not surprisingly, then, ICNE members assumed the worst when a fire tore through the mosque one night during Ramadan in 1990. Although the cause of the fire was never determined, ICNE leaders believed it to have been arson, noting earlier incidents of rock-throwing and threats. The fire caused $500,000 in damage, but with financial assistance from Muslims and non-Muslims across the region, the mosque was soon rebuilt.[67]

Nevertheless, the ICNE could not accommodate its growing numbers and sought to build a sister mosque in the surrounding suburbs. In 1991,

its leaders located a 7-acre property in Milton owned by a Catholic religious order and made arrangements to purchase it. Soon, however, affluent
residents of the surrounding neighborhood expressed opposition to the
deal, claiming that the mosque would bring traffic, parking problems, and
incompatible architecture. Just three hours before the sale was to have been
finalized, the sellers accepted a bid from a group of five neighbors who had
organized to buy the parcel. "I just couldn't believe it," said ICNE president
Mian Ashraf. "We've tried to cooperate with the town during negotiations
because we felt the center would . . . add to Milton's strength. . . . But it
seems some people just didn't want us here."[68]

Although expansion efforts had failed in Milton, expressions of friend-
ship and interfaith support convinced the ICNE to build their new mosque
in the town of Sharon, 16 miles to the south. The idea first emerged when
Rebecca and Jerry Larason, who owned a 54-acre horse farm in Sharon,
read about the aborted land sale and contacted the ICNE, offering to sell
them their land. With the Larasons as allies, the ICNE worked closely with
the Sharon Clergy Association and Rabbi Barry Starr of Sharon's Temple
Israel to meet with and address the concerns of local residents. The Larasons
even held a house party and went door to door among their neighbors to
show a video about Islam and answer questions about the proposed mosque.
Concerns about traffic and zoning were widespread, but Rabbi Starr noted
that "there were obviously some people who were outright prejudiced and
fearful." In the end, the proactive interfaith effort succeeded, and the heavily
Jewish town welcomed the new mosque, which opened in 1995.[69]

The Sharon mosque was just one of dozens of new mosques and Islamic
organizations that sprang up in greater Boston during the 1990s. By the
end of the decade, there were at least twenty mosques in the region serving an estimated thirty-five to forty thousand Muslims from the Middle
East, Asia, Africa, and the United States. Like the Hindu temples, many
were located in the metrowest suburbs where immigrants employed in
the medical and high-tech sector had settled. Most started out as house
gatherings of local Muslim families, while others met in the basements
of local churches and synagogues. Unlike the earlier mosques, which
were all Sunni dominated, the new mosques represented a variety of
ethnic groups and Islamic traditions. They included two Shii'a mosques
in Hopkinton and North Billerica, an Ahmahdiyya mosque in Sharon,
and several predominantly African American mosques in Roxbury

and Dorchester that began serving growing populations of African and Caribbean immigrants.[70]

Many of the new mosques had faced battles over zoning and traffic, and a few had experienced serious threats of arson and vandalism; when the terrorist attacks of 9/11 occurred, that event dramatically heightened anti-Muslim fears across the country. Nowhere was this more evident than in the five-year controversy that emerged around the building of the new Roxbury mosque (the Islamic Society of Boston Cultural Center). The idea for the mosque dated back to the early 1990s, at which time the Cambridge-based Islamic Society of Boston was seeking to expand. Around the same time, a group of primarily African American mosques in Boston joined together to try to purchase a city-owned parcel of land in Roxbury Crossing that was part of a larger redevelopment project along the Southwest Corridor. Financial difficulties, however, prompted the Roxbury group to develop a partnership with the ISB, and the Boston Redevelopment Authority (BRA) subsequently designated the ISB as the main developer of the site. In exchange for the parcel, the society paid the city $175,000 plus pledges for an assortment of community benefits including a parking garage, library resources, and a lecture series for adjoining Roxbury Community College.[71]

As the ISB was planning the new mosque and cultural center, the terrorist attacks of September 11 shook the country. Two of the airliners and more than two hundred of the victims came from Boston, and these events had a profound impact on the city. As federal investigators combed the financial records of Muslim organizations and individuals, the months that followed proved disastrous for ISB fundraising. Nevertheless, the society held a groundbreaking ceremony in November 2002 and focused on building the mosque as "Phase I" of the larger complex. Within a few weeks of the groundbreaking, however, a trustee of Roxbury Community College began raising questions about the ISB and whether it might be linked to Islamic extremists. Over the next two years, the *Boston Herald* published a series of articles alleging ISB ties to extremists and reporting on anti-Semitic statements made by ISB leader Walid Fitaihi. In 2004, leaders of the David Project, an outspoken pro-Israel group, along with other mosque critics made additional charges of anti-Semitism and extremism against the ISB and cited alleged improprieties in the BRA's land sale. That fall a Mission Hill resident aligned with mosque opponents filed suit against the BRA and ISB, charging that the city had conveyed the land at significantly less than its market value and thus violated the separation of church and state. The ISB filed a countersuit in 2005, charging the *Boston Herald,* Fox Television, the David Project, and other mosque opponents with defamation.[72]

The controversy dragged on for two more years and brought construction of the mosque to a halt. It also deeply divided the local Jewish community, with some groups affirming the David Project's right to voice objections and others supporting the ISB and calling for interfaith dialogue. In 2006, the Interreligious Center for Public Life, an interfaith group started by Hebrew College and Andover Newton Theological School, initiated mediation in an attempt to settle the dispute out of court and later urged both the ISB and the David Project to drop their lawsuits. In early 2007, the court dismissed the suit against the BRA land deal; three months later, ISB leader Walid Fitaihi apologized to Jewish leaders for earlier anti-Semitic statements and the ISB agreed to drop its defamation suit. That September, on the eve of both Rosh Hashanah and Ramadan, a group of five imams, two rabbis, and several prominent lay leaders of local synagogues signed a joint statement denouncing "all forms of terrorism, racism, anti-Semitism, [and] anti-Muslim prejudice" and issued a call for dialogue and reconciliation.[73]

Although the David Project and other critics of the mosque refused to sign the statement and continued to protest the ISB, construction resumed and community allies organized interfaith expressions of support. When in 2009 the *Boston Phoenix* published a new series of articles criticizing the ISB, they received a prompt rebuke from twenty local religious and interfaith leaders. The Islamic Center of Boston Cultural Center held its inaugural celebration in July 2009, with some three thousand people in attendance, including Muslims, Christians, Jews, Mayor Thomas Menino, and other public officials (fig. 16). A small group of protesters gathered across the street, but the controversy was clearly fading.[74]

This episode would be replayed many times across the country in the years following 9/11. The best-known case was in New York City in 2010–2011, when plans to build a mosque near Ground Zero sparked angry protests that stalled construction of the project. Although the New York controversy garnered the most widespread media attention, similar protests occurred in Murfreesboro, Tennessee; Temecula, California; Sheboygan, Wisconsin; and other locations where Muslims attempted to build new mosques or cultural centers. As in Boston, they found allies among other faiths, including Protestant ministers, Catholic priests, rabbis, and other

FIGURE 16. Muslim men perform sunset prayers following the groundbreaking ceremony for the Islamic Society of Boston Cultural Center, a Sunni mosque that opened in Roxbury Crossing in 2009. The sex-segregated congregation reflects the diverse array of ethnic and class backgrounds of Boston's Muslim community. Photo courtesy of *Boston Globe*.

clergy. Many of those supporters noted the historical persecution faced by their own groups—Jewish and Catholic immigrants especially—whose synagogues and churches had faced opposition and vandalism.[75]

Muslims, along with Hindus, Buddhists, and other non-Western religious groups, have all faced challenges in establishing their faith traditions in greater Boston. Like earlier generations of Catholics and Jews, they have faced fear and distrust from the native born, rapid growth and widening diversity within their own ranks, and internal struggles over theological and institutional issues. These predictable problems, however, occurred amid a global crisis that created a particularly virulent climate for Muslim newcomers. Nevertheless, mosques and other Muslim religious organizations have continued to proliferate, with more than fifty centers in greater Boston in 2010.

These Muslim centers, together with dozens of Hindu and Buddhist temples and an assortment of other immigrant faith and folk traditions, have made for a far more diverse religious landscape than the Catholic-Protestant-Jewish cast that characterized the region in the early 1960s. This new pluralism has resulted in a de-Europeanization of religion in greater

Boston, a tendency that has been evident within Christian churches as well. The transformation of Catholicism and Protestantism was not simply the result of immigrants importing their distinctive religious cultures, but the fruit of a collaborative process in which native-born institutions have worked with new immigrant congregations to tap transnational religious connections and denominational and interdenominational networks. Evidence from greater Boston suggests that Protestant churches, particularly evangelical churches, have benefited more from this process than the Catholic Church, which has been mired in financial difficulties, a clerical shortage, and a painful and costly clergy abuse scandal. Church membership figures are notoriously unreliable, but the net growth in the number of churches in the city of Boston is telling. Between 1980 and 2000, the number of Protestant churches in the city more than doubled, from 203 to 412—the majority of which were foreign-language congregations; the Boston Archdiocese, meanwhile, experienced a net loss in the same period as ten of the city's parishes closed or merged. The net gain in new Protestant congregations continued through 2010 as the wave of Catholic parish closings and mergers accelerated following the clergy abuse crisis.[76] Catholic financial and personnel problems, however, have not been the only liability. Evangelical Protestants, in particular, adopted a grassroots church-planting strategy that promoted flexible partnerships and collaborations that have proven more nimble than the efforts of a more unwieldy and slow-moving Catholic hierarchy. With support from groups like the Emmanuel Gospel Center and its ethnic-based pastoral networks, small urban churches led by indigenous religious leaders seem to have been more able to respond to the shifting currents of migration and settlement and the social and spiritual needs of immigrant newcomers.

Once known as a center of American missionary activity, Boston has been at the receiving end of a vast wave of new religious influences that have been washing up on its shores via the immigrant faithful of the post-1965 era. Exactly how the balance of religious groups will evolve with the second and third generations remains to be seen, but it is clear that Boston's reputation as an Irish-Catholic city is no longer the reality and that new immigrants are transforming the religious landscape in ways that we have yet to fully appreciate.

CHAPTER 7

The New Ethnic Politics in Boston

While Boston's new immigrants have succeeded in transforming the region's neighborhoods, workplaces, and religious institutions, the process of political incorporation has been much slower. Newcomers have faced numerous barriers to political participation, and as with earlier generations of immigrants, it often took several decades and the emergence of the second generation to compete successfully for political power. Moreover, the process of immigrant political incorporation has changed over time and has varied not only by ethnic group but also between city and suburb and among different types of suburbs, making analysis complicated.

This final chapter does not pretend to tackle all of these issues but rather to explore how newcomers have been incorporated into state and local politics through a case study of the city of Boston, home to the region's largest and most diverse mix of immigrant residents and voters. Long a stronghold of ethic and especially Irish American politics, the city underwent dramatic social and political upheavals after World War II under the impact of urban renewal, civil rights, school desegregation, and the War on Poverty. New immigrants began arriving in the midst of these sweeping changes and the emergence of a new framework of ethnoracial politics fostered by the civil rights movement. Given that a majority of new immigrants have been people of color, how did these developments affect them, and what impact did they have on this new brand of ethnoracial politics?

Initially, newcomers became involved in politics not through party organizations and elections, as many earlier immigrants had, but through grassroots, community-based organizations. In the 1960s and 1970s, many new immigrants from Latin America and Asia found support among native-born Puerto Ricans and Chinese Americans who, like African Americans, founded new community-based organizations as part of the civil rights and antipoverty movements. These community groups became the seedbed of a new ethnoracial politics in the city and, in some cases, springboards into electoral politics. Over the years, growing numbers of Latino, Asian, and African-descent immigrants strengthened the forces of ethnoracial politics under the Voting Rights Act, fueling demands for representation through redistricting and organizing "rainbow" coalitions— such as the one supporting Mel King's mayoral campaign in 1983. While such efforts produced only limited political gains, they forced the mainstream political establishment to pay more attention to the voting power of New Bostonians by making more diverse administrative appointments and cultivating support in the city's new ethnic communities.

As immigrants became more engaged with local politics, however, they also brought new issues and concerns to the table. Whereas Latino and Asian leaders of the civil rights era pressed for bilingual programs, social services, and community control, ethnic leaders since the 1980s have prioritized immigrant rights in what has become an increasingly restrictive, repressive, and bureaucratic environment. Some immigrant organizations have also lobbied hard for English classes and citizenship programs to foster civic integration and empowerment of newcomers in this more unstable environment. New immigrants thus helped reshape the local ethnoracial political agenda, which a new generation of Latino, Asian, and Afro-Caribbean leaders would carry into the electoral arena of the twenty-first century.

COMMUNITY MOBILIZATION IN THE NEW BOSTON

A new brand of community-based ethnoracial politics first took shape in Boston in response to official efforts to redevelop and revitalize the city in the years after World War II. From the 1950s through the 1970s, Boston would experience a dramatic overhaul of its ailing infrastructure, using federal funding for "slum removal" and the building of new public housing after the war. After the passage of federal housing and highway legislation in the mid-1950s, however, urban renewal programs were increasingly geared toward downtown redevelopment that would attract more affluent whites back from the suburbs—a phenomenon later dubbed "gentrification." To stimulate new investment and attract new residents, the Boston Redevelopment Authority (BRA) planned a staggering array of new projects: metropolitan highways, high-rise office buildings, a civic center, a medical complex, university buildings, and luxury housing and shopping facilities. Such top-down schemes, which threatened to displace thousands of residents from their homes, did not sit well in Boston's poor and working-class areas. The conflicts that ensued would become the crucibles of powerful neighborhood-based movements across the city.[1]

During the mayoral administrations of John Hynes and John Collins, the campaign to build a New Boston got under way in the early 1950s with the demolition of the New York Streets, a poor multiracial section of the South End. A few years later, planners targeted the West End, a predominantly Italian American neighborhood near downtown where more than twenty-seven thousand residents were displaced and seven hundred buildings destroyed to make way for Government Center and a complex of luxury high-rise apartments. This time, however, the West Enders fought back with organized resistance and protests. While they did not prevail, their efforts to preserve the neighborhood echoed across other areas facing the bulldozer, including Charlestown, Roxbury, the South End, and Chinatown. In racially mixed neighborhoods, where many new migrants were settling, resistance to urban renewal would become intertwined with growing civil rights activism and movements for community control in the 1960s.[2]

But while government-imposed urban renewal helped generate racial- and ethnic-based resistance in Boston, federal and local efforts to calm those tensions provided support for new community-based organizations in the city's growing black, Latino, and Asian neighborhoods. Seeking to avoid the concerted resistance that challenged redevelopment in the West End, BRA director Ed Logue proposed a new approach of community outreach and "planning with people." He and Mayor Collins partnered with the Ford Foundation—which was then developing its Gray Areas program to address urban planning and social welfare concerns—to help create a new organization, Action for Boston Community Development (ABCD). Founded in 1962, ABCD soon became the bridge between the BRA and local neighborhoods, conducting social research and advocating for improved social services. Although the mayor envisioned ABCD as "the handmaiden of the BRA," the agency hired a raft of young community organizers, some of them African Americans and Latinos, who were as likely to challenge the BRA as champion its plans.[3]

The role of these young organizers expanded in 1964 when ABCD became the city's official antipoverty agency under President Lyndon Johnson's War on Poverty. Funded by the federal Office of Economic Opportunity, ABCD soon began administering community-based programs such as Head Start, Job Corps, and Legal Assistance. Through its Area Planning Action Councils, ABCD partnered with and funded community-based groups working on housing, education, healthcare, and youth services. One of their earliest achievements was the founding of the Roxbury Multi-Service Center, a neighborhood-based center for family, health, and employment services that opened in 1964. This decentralized style of community action and service delivery was designed to facilitate "maximum feasible participation of the poor," a guiding principle of the early War on Poverty.[4]

Before long, however, local activists moved beyond service delivery to challenge municipal policies and authority. In black, Latino, and Asian communities, this resistance grew in tandem with the civil rights and antiwar movements. Well attuned to the politics of race and power in the city, activists in several neighborhoods voiced opposition to urban renewal plans and helped to organize local tenants facing displacement. These grassroots movements served to reshape the city's redevelopment plans and often gave rise to more permanent community-based organizations (CBOs), many of them representing new urban migrants.

Changes in federal antipoverty programs in the late 1960s would influence the structure and strategies of these new community organizations. Alarmed by the militancy and conflict arising from some of the local community action groups, federal policymakers shifted power over programs and funding back toward city mayors under the Model Cities program of 1966. Around the same time, urban policymakers—including many at

Harvard and MIT—began to emphasize housing revitalization and small business development, encouraging the formation of nonprofit community development corporations (CDCs) as local partners in urban renewal. Mayor Kevin White, who took office in 1968, established a network of Little City Halls—neighborhood centers staffed by a municipal liaison—in the hope of diffusing the backyard revolution that was erupting around the city. During the next decade, the White administration worked uneasily with a growing phalanx of CBOs and CDCs that had sprung up in the neighborhoods. Particularly in the Latino and Asian American communities, these new organizations would provide a launching pad into city and state politics that offered the potential for greater inclusion and incorporation for the city's new migrants and their children.[5]

THE RISE OF LATINO ACTIVISM

The earliest Latino community mobilization occurred in the mid-1960s in the South End, where several thousand Puerto Rican migrants had settled amid widespread poverty and some of the worst housing conditions in the city. There, mostly black and Puerto Rican residents lived in run-down, vermin-infested buildings bordering trash-strewn lots. Absentee landlords did little to maintain the buildings, and arson was a constant threat. The BRA had targeted several parts of the neighborhood for urban renewal, including what they called Parcel 19 in the heart of the Puerto Rican settlement around West Newton Street.[6]

In the 1950s and early 1960s, local settlement houses and churches were gathering points for the growing Puerto Rican community. In particular, St. Stephen's Episcopal Church, a multiethnic church on the edge of Blackstone Square, recruited Spanish-speaking ministry workers who founded Centro de Acción in 1965. Funded partly by ABCD, Acción became an independent group that helped organize local tenants, pressured the city to clean up a local junk heap, spearheaded attempts to fight arson and delinquent landlords, and convened initial public meetings with the BRA about redevelopment.[7]

While Acción focused on housing issues, another Latino organization, Association to Promote the Constitutional Rights of the Spanish Speaking (APCROSS), worked to improve services for the community. This group was made up of young Puerto Ricans from the Cardinal Cushing Center and St. Stephen's, including Alex Rodriguez and Antonio Molina, who worked to turn out the Latino vote for Kevin White in the 1967 mayoral election. Soon after setting up a storefront in 1968, APCROSS called on ABCD to expand social services in the South End, arguing that antipoverty programs in Boston were concentrated in black areas and ignored Latinos. In fact, the geographically based antipoverty programs were initially designed to address the problems of African American communities; newly arrived Latinos, by contrast, found themselves increasingly dispersed around the city as redevelopment forced them out or away from the South End. To dramatize their demands for equity, APCROSS staged a sit-in of the ABCD director's office in 1968. Shortly afterward, the group won government funding to provide translation, job placement, youth work, and other services for South End Latinos.[8]

A similar struggle for services took place among Latinos in Roxbury, where growing numbers of Puerto Rican and Dominican migrants were settling alongside African Americans in the 1960s. The Roxbury Multi-Service Center provided many of the neighborhood's antipoverty services, but its programs were not equipped to serve Spanish-speaking populations. Frieda Garcia, a Dominican family worker at the Roxbury Center, was approached by ABCD in 1969 to conduct a study of the Latino population and service needs in the area. She soon discovered a group of teachers and church members around the Winthrop School who helped with the study and began pressing Model Cities officials for better services. When their initial appeals failed, they picketed the local Model Cities office to protest the lack of Latino staff and programming.

Calling themselves the Spanish Alliance, or La Alianza Hispana, the group received a planning grant from Model Cities in 1970 and opened a storefront office. With help from the Roxbury Multi-Service Center, they developed plans for a Latino multiservice center that was funded by Model Cities the following year. Soon afterward, the group began renovating an old police station on Dudley Street that became its new center. La Alianza Hispana would soon become the largest Latino service provider in Boston, working with growing communities in Roxbury, Dorchester, and Jamaica Plain.[9]

While the need for services was a major driver of early Latino mobilization, urban renewal proved an even bigger impetus. The most dramatic example occurred in response to the city's plan to redevelop the South End.

The BRA's 1964 plan called for the relocation of 3,300 families, the rehabilitation of 3,000 buildings, and the construction of 3,000 rental units, many of them luxury or market-rate. Most of those slated for displacement were low-income black and Puerto Rican families. Tenants' groups opposing displacement formed in several parts of the neighborhood, forging a coalition known as the Community Assembly for a United South End.[10]

In the area known as Parcel 19, St. Stephen's Church became the focal point of opposition to the renewal plan. Beginning in 1967, the church's Spanish-speaking pastor and seminarians arranged several community meetings with the BRA. Together with local residents, they went door to door alerting tenants to the BRA's plans and encouraging them to become involved. Alarmed at the looming displacement, local residents organized the Emergency Tenants Council (ETC) to help formulate a better rehousing plan. Initial plans called for St. Stephen's to be the developer of the new housing, and the church brought in professional planners and architects to meet with the community. Soon, however, the ETC pressed for direct control of the project and incorporated as a community development corporation in 1968.

Mobilizing hundreds of Puerto Rican residents under the rallying cry *no nos mudaremos de la parcela* (we shall not be moved from the Parcel), the ETC picketed city hall demanding an alternative housing plan. After months of public meetings and community pressure, in 1969 the ETC was named developer of Parcel 19. With the help of St. Stephen's and professionals from Urban Planning Aid, ETC worked with the BRA to develop a housing complex for the site and got federal funding for hiring a paid director and staff. Over the next several years, ETC would oversee construction of a subsidized housing complex of more than eight hundred units, known as Villa Victoria (honoring the victory of the community). Its innovative design reflected the communal plazas, sloping roofs, and pastel colors of Puerto Rican architecture, with new streets bearing Puerto Rican place names, such as San Juan and Aguadilla (fig. 17).[11]

But the ETC's role in community development did not stop with bricks and mortar. In 1974, it gave birth to a new organization, Inquilinos Boricuas en Acción (Puerto Rican Tenants in Action), that sponsored an array of on-site services, including a childcare center, an arts and cultural center, a bilingual clinic, and a family support department. By the early 1980s, Inquilinos Boricuas en Acción (IBA) had a staff of more than eighty

FIGURE 17. View of the newly completed Villa Victoria in 1984. The culmination of more than a decade of Puerto Rican organizing, Villa Victoria became the cultural and political center of Boston Latinos in the South End. Photo courtesy of *Boston Globe*.

people offering a variety of programs and services. But as federal funding contracted during the Reagan administration, IBA and other community-based organizations relied increasingly on state and local funds and grants from private foundations.[12]

Although IBA remained predominantly Puerto Rican, its influence among Boston-area Latinos was significant. Since its inception, IBA has identified its mission as "promoting and advocating for Latinos citywide and . . . perpetuating the rich Latino cultural and artistic heritage." Villa Victoria thus became a center for pan-Latino cultural events and a launching pad for the careers of its Latino leadership. As one of the largest Puerto Rican CDC's in the country, it became a model for other Latino tenant groups. One such group was the Cambridge Alliance of Spanish Tenants, which purchased and managed the Columbia Terrace housing project in East Cambridge in the 1970s. IBA was also instrumental in starting a satellite service organization in Lawrence called Centro Panamericano, founded in the wake of the white-Latino riot there in 1984.[13]

As Miren Uriarte has argued, IBA, La Alianza, and other early Puerto Rican community groups became the organizational crucible of Boston's

Latino communities. Providing housing and culturally accessible services were the twin purposes driving this early organizing, and these groups were the seedbed of many others. Community development corporations like ETC gave rise to social-service and cultural organizations like IBA, but the reverse was also true. The multiservice center of La Alianza later helped launch community development corporations like Nuestra Comunidad, a CDC founded in Jamaica Plain in 1981, and the Dudley Street Neighborhood Initiative, a multicultural CDC established in Roxbury in 1984. In the years that followed, such agencies promoted housing and economic development while providing Spanish bilingual services to a growing Latino population that included Dominicans, Salvadorans, Colombians, and others. In most cases, the organizations did not set out to establish separate Latino agencies but were responding to the larger reality of urban housing segregation and the lack of linguistically accessible services, circumstances that effectively excluded Latinos from the mainstream.[14]

It was from this initial network of community-based organizations that Latinos made their first forays into citywide and statewide politics. In the 1970s, activists from APCROSS, IBA, La Alianza, and other groups began joining forces to tackle broader problems, such as health and education. The first such coordinated effort began in the late 1960s to address the high percentage of Spanish-speaking children not attending school. Alarmed at that situation, a group of concerned parents and teachers had formed the Spanish Federation in 1968 to start ESL classes for migrant children. A task force of the federation also conducted a survey of Latino families in the South End and Roxbury, published in 1970, which revealed that nearly half of all Latino children had dropped out or had never enrolled in school. Securing grant money from an educational foundation, the federation challenged the Boston School Committee to match the funds and initiate a bilingual program. Under intense pressure, the school committee approved a plan that allowed the federation to organize bilingual classes in two schools in Roxbury and the South End. To lessen resistance in the future, the federation also began lobbying for a state law mandating bilingual education when needed. Facing busloads of Latino supporters during hearings at the statehouse in 1970, the Massachusetts legislature voted to approve the Transitional Bilingual Education Law, the first state in the country to adopt such legislation. Requiring mandatory bilingual classes for school districts that had at least twenty students from a single language group who were not proficient in English, the law established the framework for hundreds of bilingual classes across the Commonwealth for the next thirty years.[15]

As Latinos confronted problems of education, housing, and social services, their exclusion from urban- and state-level politics was hard to ignore. Although federal antipoverty funding had helped launch many of the Latino organizations of the late 1960s, control of most federal funds had shifted back to state and local officials by the 1970s. At the same time, Democratic mayors like Kevin White first acknowledged the potential power of Latino voters and worked to bring them into his camp. Alex Rodriguez and other members of APCROSS recognized this potential for political cooperation when they worked for White's 1967 campaign. Once in office, White appointed Rodriguez as his Hispanic liaison at city hall and in 1974 established a fifteen-member Mayor's Commission on Spanish Affairs. During these years, White's administration funded a number of initiatives, including an initial grant for APCROSS, funding for the annual Puerto Rican festival (which featured bilingual voter registration drives), and a Little City Hall with a Spanish interpreter to aid residents in accessing city services and filing complaints. On the state level, Governor Francis Sargent also appointed the first special assistant for Spanish Affairs beginning in 1969. These "liaison" appointments would constitute the main form of political representation for Massachusetts Latinos for more than a decade.[16]

Despite their growing political access, these early Latino leaders found it impossible to win elective office. Alex Rodriguez was the first to try in 1968 when he ran for state representative from the South End and lost. Afterward, he launched the Latino Political Action Committee of Massachusetts, an organization that registered Latino voters and rallied support for Governor Michael Dukakis, among others. Increased registration, however, did not result in victory for the next Latino candidate for statewide office, Carmen Pola, a Puerto Rican community leader from Mission Hill who ran for state representative in 1980. Winning on the municipal level was equally if not more difficult, as Felix D. Arroyo discovered the following year. A Boston public school teacher from Puerto Rico, Arroyo ran for the Boston School Committee—an at-large citywide race. He won in the primary but lost the general election, and did so again in 1983, despite registering several thousand new Latino voters.[17]

The weak showing of Latino candidates in Boston had become a major concern by the early 1980s. The Hispanic Office of Planning and Evaluation,

a newly formed coordinating council for the city's Latino organizations, conducted a major study of political participation in 1983. They identified several obstacles to electoral success rooted in demographic, cultural, and political factors. First, Latino migrants tended to be disproportionately young,
low income, and from limited educational backgrounds—factors that tend
to correlate with low voting rates. Many were highly transient, both within
the city and between the Caribbean and Massachusetts, making consistent
voter registration more difficult. Among Dominicans and other non–Puerto
Rican groups, many were not citizens and would remain ineligible to vote
until they could naturalize, assuming they had the documentation that
allowed them to do so. But even among those who were eligible, many felt
disaffected from American politics, which they found bland, uninspiring,
and disconnected from their concerns as Latinos. Unlike the neighborhood-
based ethnic political machines of earlier Irish immigrants, the reform-style
politics of postwar Boston offered little of the personal connection, patronage, and pageantry that was typical of pre–World War II Boston and that
continued to characterize politics in many parts of the Caribbean.[18]

Other obstacles to electoral participation, however, seemed more amena-
ble to change. Linguistic barriers were an obvious case, one that community
leaders had already begun addressing through interpreter programs and
ESL classes. Polling places, however, proved to be unfriendly territory for
many non-English speakers, whose voting rights were routinely challenged
and who had to negotiate voting procedures and materials with little assistance. Some became discouraged and gave up, while others were too intim-
idated to try. In later years, Latinos would join other civil rights activists in
challenging these discriminatory practices through the courts.[19]

At the time, however, the clearest obstacle to Latino empowerment was
the structure of the electoral landscape. On the municipal level, all elected
positions on the Boston City Council and School Committee were at-large
seats. Running for such citywide office was expensive and tended to dilute
the voting power of ethnoracial minorities. This structure was the legacy
of Progressive reforms that had eliminated an immigrant-dominated ward
system and replaced it with a council of nine at-large seats.[20] People of
color around the country challenged at-large systems in the 1970s, and
in Boston, a 1981 charter reform established a new council with nine districts and four at-large seats. While the creation of a new Roxbury district
made black representation a reality, Latinos were split between multiple

districts in part because of political maneuvering but also because of the growing dispersion of the Latino population across the city. As a result, Latinos would have no representation on the city council in the twentieth century. The situation was not much better on the state level. Although district-based seats encouraged Alex Rodriguez and Carmen Pola to run for the legislature, Latino voters were not a majority in either the Jamaica Plain or the Mission Hill district, and their bids failed. Indeed, no Latino candidate would win state office until a growing Latino population and subsequent redistricting would offer new opportunities in the future.[21]

ASIAN AMERICAN POLITICS: A NEW GENERATION

As in the Latino community, Asian American activism in Boston grew out of the community politics of the 1960s and 1970s. Although a small geographical area, Chinatown faced immense challenges as urban redevelopment threatened its land base and institutions while new immigration intensified demographic pressures and social ills. At the same time, the antiwar and civil rights movements profoundly influenced many young Asian Americans. After 1968, some became part of a growing Asian American student movement that started in the San Francisco area and spread to New York, Boston, and other cities. These Asian American students worked with African Americans and Latinos to press for ethnic studies programs on campus, while also taking up civil rights and antipoverty organizing in nearby Asian enclaves to extend those rights and benefits to their own communities.[22]

In Boston, some of these young activists were American-born Chinese from the suburbs; others had grown up in Chinatown, the children of post–World War II immigrants. Some of the younger, more radical activists came out of the Asian American movement, but a slightly older generation of working professionals was also active in mobilizing the community. Both groups had attended local universities in hopes of escaping the long hours of restaurant and garment work so common among their parents' generation. At the same time, their growing consciousness of racism and poverty made them painfully aware of the social dislocations affecting Boston's Chinatown. Challenging stereotypes of Asian passivity and the model minority, these activists became impatient with the insular and conservative style of politics practiced by Chinatown's older merchant leadership.

Originating in southern China, groups like the Chinese Consolidated Benevolent Association (CCBA) and the On Leong Merchants Association represented family, regional, and trade associations that had facilitated Chinese migration to New England since the late nineteenth century. They did so by providing lodging, jobs, and mutual aid for the mostly male immigrants of the pre–World War II era—and in some cases profiting from gambling and vice operations as well. The Merchants Association also provided credit and mediated disputes between local merchants, providing an insular form of support and regulation within the Chinese community. After 1949, CCBA and On Leong leaders allied themselves with the Chinese nationalists in Taiwan, and they functioned as Chinatown's de facto political representatives to the city. But as the forces of urban renewal and immigration shook the neighborhood in the late 1960s and 1970s, their leadership was challenged.[23]

These changes hit Chinatown with unprecedented force in the late 1950s and 1960s, when state highway building carved away large swaths of Chinatown's land base as the Southeast Expressway and Mass Pike Extension sliced through the neighborhood. Equally disruptive was the BRA's South Cove Urban Renewal Project, which demolished more than a hundred homes to make way for the expanded Tufts New England Medical Center in the late 1960s. By 1970, these redevelopment projects had resulted in the demolition of 418 buildings, 1,200 housing units, and 14 businesses, displacing hundreds of Chinatown families to the South End, Allston-Brighton, and other neighborhoods. During these same years, hundreds of new Chinese immigrants flocked to the neighborhood, seeking work in the area's restaurants and garment shops. Working long hours for low pay, these newcomers and their families had pressing social needs. They joined Chinatown's older community of families and an aging bachelor society—a group of older male migrants who lived together in cramped, overcrowded apartments with little access to healthcare or other social services.[24]

In face of such critical needs, the older Chinatown leadership seemed ineffectual to many younger Chinese Americans. The CCBA's memorandum of understanding with the BRA, signed in 1963 to protect the interests of the Chinatown community, did little to slow the ongoing process of demolition and displacement. In the meantime, new immigration and overcrowding contributed to some of the city's worst living conditions. By 1970, Chinatown had the highest population density, the lowest median family income, and the highest infant mortality and tuberculosis rates, as well as a critical shortage of educational, recreational, and healthcare facilities. Vice and crime were also on the rise along Washington Street, where the Combat Zone—a district of strip clubs and adult theaters—was emerging in the wake of the demolition of Scollay Square, an earlier BRA "slum clearance" project in the West End. Critically caught in the cross-currents of urban renewal, rising immigration, and desperate social needs, the younger generation of Chinese American activists began to stake out new priorities for the community.[25]

The first sign of this new activism came in 1967, when a group of mainly American-born Chinese from outside Chinatown started the Chinese American Civic Association (CACA). Caroline Chang was one of the founders and was typical of the new generation of leaders. Raised in Chinatown by immigrant parents, Chang and her family moved to the suburbs when their home was taken by eminent domain during the construction of the Massachusetts Turnpike Extension. A graduate of Boston University, Chang lived outside of Chinatown and worked for several years for a suburban defense contractor. She maintained close connections and involvement in Chinatown, however, and joined other young Chinese American professionals in founding the CACA. Starting mainly as a social organization, CACA quickly waded into the controversy surrounding the South Cove Urban Renewal Project. Criticizing the city's delays in building replacement housing and the lack of social services in Chinatown, CACA insisted that the city build a new community center. For the next two years, CACA's calls for reform eventually prompted the CCBA to arrange a community meeting with members of Mayor White's administration in 1969. With some two hundred people in attendance, Chinatown residents publicly aired their grievances over redevelopment, housing, services, and crime. This was an unprecedented occurrence, for as Caroline Chang later explained, "Some of us began to educate ourselves about our rights. We had to get over the idea that going outside the community was asking for handouts." As a younger college student put it more bluntly: "The older generation has just kept quiet while they were treated as second- and third-class Americans. . . . The blacks aren't keeping quiet, so why should we?"[26]

This more proactive approach brought stunning results. Following the meeting, the Mayor's Office of Human Rights established a Task Force for Resolution of Grievances in Chinatown and hired Caroline Chang to open a Little City Hall in the neighborhood. As the task force conducted its work, Action for Boston Community Development issued an eighty-eight-page study of Chinatown in 1970 confirming many of the problems raised at the meeting. Marshaling this data and organizing a conference with the help of a federal planning grant, CACA and other local leaders came together in the fall of 1971 to develop a master plan for the future of Chinatown.

Over the next several years, the fruits of these efforts would flower across the neighborhood. First, a Golden Age Drop-in Center that provided fellowship and Chinese-style meals for seniors was opened in 1971 under the auspices of Little City Hall. The center later expanded its services to include elder health programs and to sponsor the development of Hong Lok House, a housing project for the elderly in Chinatown. The CACA meanwhile reorganized as an ABCD-linked nonprofit and opened a Chinese multiservice center on Tyler Street the following year, offering English classes, interpreter services, job placement, and housing assistance—services critical for new immigrants. Young Chinatown activists also formed a taskforce to fight for linguistically and culturally accessible healthcare services. As Caroline Chang explained, even though the New England Medical Center occupied a central position in the neighborhood, "the community still had very little access to its services, in terms of being able to go in for service, and then once getting there, being able to find someone who could communicate in the right languages." Rather than relying on the NEMC, the taskforce tapped new federal funds for community-based healthcare and founded the South Cove Community Health Center, a bicultural and bilingual clinic that opened in 1973. "We finally realized, well, instead of waiting for New England Medical Center, we could do our own healthcare planning," Chang said.[27]

The health center, Little City Hall, and many of the other new services later found a home in the new Quincy School and Community Center that opened on Washington Street in 1976. The Quincy School Community Council, which helped design the complex, had battled the BRA for several years to gain a greater voice in planning the new school complex. Beyond the school itself, the council also developed an array of child, youth, and community services that were housed in the new center. Also pulling the community together, CACA started a bilingual newsletter in 1972 that would later become *Sampan*, Chinatown's bilingual community newspaper.[28]

Although Chinatown activists could not claim a landmark victory on

the order of Villa Victoria in the South End, the creation of a Chinese community center and social service network marked a major turning point for
the community. The social agencies founded by CACA and other activists
in the 1970s provided critical services to a growing immigrant population
and signaled the ascension of a younger, less traditional Chinese American
leadership that engaged with the larger city and challenged the more pater-
nalistic style of the old merchant elite. Like Latinos in the South End and
Roxbury, they made demands on the public sector, resulting in federal antipoverty funding for a host of new social agencies that would serve as a seedbed for nonprofit Asian American organizations. As new immigrant groups
arrived in the late 1970s and 1980s, CACA and South Cove Community
Health Center accommodated the newcomers by adding Vietnamese-,
Khmer-, and Mandarin-speaking staff. In 1979 CACA changed its name
to the Asian American Civic Association, reflecting its more diverse base.[29]

Like IBA and La Alianza Hispana, the Chinatown organizations would
later extend their service model to other growing Asian settlements. South
Cove Community Health Center, for example, opened a clinic in North
Quincy in 1995, while the Golden Age Center established a satellite center in Brighton in the 1980s and opened programs for seniors in Quincy
and Malden in the 1990s. The action organizations of 1970s Chinatown
thus spawned a regional network of ethnic service provision in the years to
come, serving immigrant populations across greater Boston.[30]

In both the Latino and Asian American communities, however, the service agencies that grew out of the War on Poverty faced devolution and
fiscal cutbacks in the 1970s and 1980s that forced them to rely more on state
and local funding. In Massachusetts, municipal funding was also reduced
after the passage of Proposition 2½ in 1980—a measure that limited local
property tax increases to 2.5 percent annually—a product of the conservative tax revolts springing up across the nation. Community groups
thus became more dependent on private foundations and grants for their
operating expenses. As nonprofit entities, they could not engage directly
in electoral politics, and foundations that funded them demanded professional credentials for their staff. Service agencies in both communities thus
became increasingly focused on professionalized service delivery, rather
than community mobilization. In Chinatown, however, a more leftwing
group of activists coalesced around the Chinese Progressive Association,
an advocacy organization founded in 1977 that focused on redevelopment

issues, garment factory closings, racial violence, and police misconduct. The CPA sometimes worked in coalitions with more conservative groups, such as the CCBA, as in the Long Guang Huang case discussed in chapter 5, but it was just as likely to challenge their leadership around economic issues of employment and urban redevelopment.[31]

Other former activists found their way to city hall, where they became key allies to Mayor Kevin White and his successors. Frank Chin, vice chairman of the 1971 Task Force on Chinatown, became city purchasing agent in 1974, serving as a key link between Chinatown and the mayor's office for the next twenty-two years. Frank and his brother Billy, who operated the China Pearl Restaurant in Chinatown, held fundraisers for Democratic candidates and helped deliver Chinatown votes in return for greater influence in housing construction, restaurant licensing, and neighborhood policing. The CPA and other neighborhood activists criticized Chin for failing to stop the expansion of the Tufts New England Medical Center and for his support of white city councilmen Jim Kelly and Albert "Dapper" O'Neill, who were infamous for their racist and anti-immigrant utterances. Known as "the powerbroker of Chinatown," Chin bears a striking resemblance to old-style ethnic political bosses of an earlier era.[32] But as in the Latino community, this liaison-style of politics did little to advance the electoral prospects of Asian or Asian American Bostonians; indeed, none were elected to any city or state office in the twentieth century.

THE LAST HURRAH OF GRASSROOTS ETHNIC POLITICS

While political insiders such as Frank Chin and Alex Rodriguez moved into city hall in the 1970s, community-based organizations among both Latinos and Chinese Americans continued to rely on grassroots mobilization as a means of political empowerment. In the mid-1970s, however, housing and social service issues were eclipsed by the controversy and chaos wrought by the busing crisis. Following years of African American struggle to desegregate the Boston Public Schools, a series of federal court orders in 1974–1975 called for mandatory busing of black and white students to comply with the state's Racial Imbalance Act of 1965. Massive white opposition to the court order in South Boston and Charlestown led to boycotts, riots, and assaults on black students. Black parents responded with their own boycotts, and black youth at times retaliated with violence. For the next two years, bitter racial unrest in Boston would make national headlines as city residents struggled to resist or adapt to the new system.[33]

Latinos and Asians found themselves awkwardly pitted in this ostensibly black-white conflict. For many Latinos, busing by race made little sense for families whose children did not fit easily into categories of black or white; indeed, some parents saw their light and dark-skinned children assigned to different schools. Moreover, for both Asians and Latinos, one of the cherished successes of 1960s community organizing was the creation of community-controlled bilingual schools: the Rafael Hernandez School in the South End and the Josiah Quincy Community School in Chinatown. Busing threatened to undercut these new programs, and in fact, the viability of bilingual education depended on a concentration of Spanish- and Chinese-speaking children. Activists such as Carmen Pola in Mission Hill and Suzanne Lee in Chinatown worked with their communities and with the federal court to ensure that the busing plan could accommodate the hard-fought bilingual programs. Still, desegregation and busing proved controversial in both communities, defining Asian and Latino children as "others" who might be used as "buffers" between hostile camps of blacks and whites.[34]

Busing was not the only issue that sometimes divided the city's Latino and Asian communities from African Americans. During the late 1960s and early 1970s, competition for antipoverty funding and the desire for bilingual services had fueled tensions between black and Latino action groups, even as black civil rights and calls for community control inspired Puerto Rican activism. In the late 1970s, black and Latino political activists joined forces to challenge the at-large election system for the Boston City Council and School Committee, but their success in creating several district-based seats in a 1981 referendum posed new problems. As the two groups quickly realized, their overlapping patterns of settlement posed different obstacles for each group. With their numbers dispersed across several neighborhoods, the voting power of Latinos was diluted. African Americans, by contrast, were highly segregated in the Lower South End and Roxbury and thus faced the problem of having their votes "packed" into two districts. This meant that Latino candidates had little chance of winning against African American competitors. If African American and immigrant communities came together, however, they might be able to elect mutually agreeable candidates through a coalition effort.[35]

One of the leaders of the redistricting effort was Mel King, a longtime community activist from the South End who led a historic effort to unite black, Latino, Asian American, and other identity-based communities in his run for mayor in 1983. King was the ideal person to build such an alliance. The son of West Indian immigrants, he grew up in the multicultural New York Streets section of the South End that was the first to be destroyed by urban renewal in the 1950s. He later became a settlement worker in the South End, where he engaged with both the Puerto Rican and black communities. As an antipoverty organizer in the late 1960s, he helped form the Community Assembly for a United South End (CAUSE), which fought for greater neighborhood control over BRA redevelopment projects. His leadership in the Tent City protests of 1968, in which South End residents camped out in a vacant lot to protest the destruction of housing for a parking garage, inspired both black and Puerto Rican organizing. As Latinos launched their own campaign for community control, King and CAUSE backed ETC's campaign to build Villa Victoria. King also worked with the United Community Construction Workers, a black group that in the late 1970s pressed for affirmative action hiring, but which moved toward a multiracial organizing strategy that included Latinos, Asian Americans, and Native Americans. King personified this multiracial style of politics during his ten years of service in the state legislature (1972–1982), where he fought for rent control, tenants' rights, limits on gentrification and redevelopment, education, affirmative action, and antidiscrimination policies.[36]

When Kevin White stepped down at the end of his fourth term, King announced he was running for mayor and set out to build a progressive multicultural coalition. After winning one of the top two spots in the mayoral primary—the first person of color ever to do so—King faced off against Ray Flynn, an Irish Catholic city councillor from South Boston. King and Flynn took similar positions on many economic issues: supporting rent control and tenants' rights, restrictions on condo conversions, and endorsement of the linkage policy—in which downtown developers would pay fees to support the building of affordable housing in hard-pressed neighborhoods. Where they differed was over social issues such as abortion, busing, and gay rights—all of which Flynn opposed. King, on the other hand, supported abortion and gay rights and had been a longtime advocate for desegregation. While both men aggressively reached out to new ethnic neighborhoods and constituents, King confronted issues of racism and inequality directly (drawing connections to South Africa, Central America, and other

FIGURE 18. The activist and mayoral candidate Mel King campaigns in Chinatown, 1983. Photo courtesy of Northeastern University Libraries, Archives and Special Collections Department.

international struggles), while Flynn ran a populist campaign that down-played race in favor of a broad-based, working-class coalition.[37]

In contrast to Flynn's populist strategy, King's approach was to build a "Rainbow Coalition" of African Americans, Latinos, Asians, and other iden-tity-based groups (a concept that Jesse Jackson borrowed for his 1984 presi-dential campaign). The King campaign established Latino and Asian sup-port committees that held community meetings in Chinatown and in Latino neighborhoods, published bilingual campaign literature, and organized can-didate dinners, neighborhood "Walks for Mel King," and voter registration drives (fig. 18). King was also prominently featured at the Puerto Rican and August Moon festivals. In Chinatown, King won the backing of Mike Liu, Suzanne Lee, and other activists with the Chinese Progressive Association who praised King's support for community control. In Jamaica Plain, King's Latino backers held a pig roast to support both Mel King and Felix D. Arroyo, who was running for Boston School Committee. As some of King's Latino supporters commented, "It was a social movement as much as a campaign." But Ray Flynn also won key supporters in these communities, including Carmen Pola in the Latino community and the Chin brothers in Chinatown.[38]

In the end, Flynn won decisively, with 66 percent of the vote and especially high totals among white voters. King, however, won by a landslide
among African Americans and had strong showings in both Chinatown
and in Latino precincts. The election saw record-high turnouts of over 69
percent, but with whites making up more than three-quarters of the electorate, Flynn's forces easily prevailed. In many ways, it was the last hurrah
of 1960s-style grassroots politics in the city's black and immigrant neighborhoods. But it was also an important beginning, as it helped establish
Latinos and Asian Americans as recognized players in the city's electorate
with whom Ray Flynn and future mayors would have to contend. Flynn
acknowledged as much by making a number of Latino and (to a lesser
extent) Asian American appointments: his prominent supporter Carmen
Pola became director of constituent services; Felix D. Arroyo (whose bid
for school committee had failed) was later named director of office personnel; and Consuelo Gonzales-Thornell was the first Latino and the first
woman appointed as a BRA commissioner. The Chinatown powerbroker
and Flynn supporter Frank Chin retained his job as purchasing agent, and
Flynn appointed other Asian Americans to the Transportation Department
and the Human Rights Commission.[39] By the late 1980s, city hall offices
were beginning to reflect some of the diversity of the city's new ethnic
communities.

The profusion of Latino appointments was not limited to city hall;
around the same time, Governor Michael Dukakis made numerous
Latino appointments in the wake of the strong support he had received
from Alex Rodriguez and the Latino Political Action Committee in the
1982 election. Dukakis appointed Rodriguez as chair of the Massachusetts
Commission against Discrimination, Manuel Carballo as secretary of
Human Services, and Jovita Fontanez as a metropolitan district commissioner. Equally significant was Dukakis's creation of new administrative
bodies concerned with Latinos and immigrants. In 1983, he signed a bill
creating a state Commission on Hispanic Affairs, which conducted a
major demographic study called *Hispanics in Massachusetts*. Two years
later, the Dukakis administration drew on federal funding to create the
state Office of Refugees and Immigrants to coordinate migration affairs
for the Commonwealth. Both offices would be headed by Latinos, Asian
Americans, or other immigrant group representatives.[40]

These new appointments were not simply political payback for electoral support but were the fruits of growing Latino and Asian political organization, mobilization, and legal action during the 1980s. In 1985, the Boston-based Latino PAC was joined by a new state-level organization, the Latino Democratic Committee, founded by Felix D. Arroyo and the Cuban American activist Yohel Camayd-Freixas. This new organization worked to define a Latino agenda and encourage Latinos to run for office, but it also sought to work jointly with other minority groups. Indeed, one of the legacies of the 1983 Rainbow Coalition was the growing political cooperation between Boston's African Americans, Latinos, and Asian Americans. In 1987, the Black Political Task Force joined forces with Latino and Asian American PACs to contest the recent redistricting for state legislative elections. Arguing that the state's plan created unequal districts that violated the Voting Rights Act, the multiracial coalition successfully sued in federal court, resulting in a new plan that included an additional minority district in the Roxbury–North Dorchester area. In the decades that followed, the 5th Suffolk district would prove to be an entry point for numerous immigrant and second-generation politicians of color in the city. At the time, Camayd-Freixas, Mel King, and others approached Nelson Merced, the former director of La Alianza Hispana, to run for this new seat.[41]

Merced was well positioned to run in this diverse new district, whose residents included Puerto Ricans, Dominicans, African Americans, as well as Haitians, Cape Verdeans, and Vietnamese. Born in New York City to Puerto Rican parents, Merced had moved to Boston in the 1970s and became director of La Alianza Hispana in 1971, overseeing major fundraising and expansion efforts. He was also a founding member of the multicultural Dudley Street Neighborhood Initiative, an organization established in 1984 to revitalize the devastated Dudley triangle. In short, his work in social agencies and community-based organizations provided a firm foundation for his 1988 campaign. "It was a great district," Merced explained. "It covered all of the La Alianza neighborhoods where I had worked and was known." Running a grassroots, multiracial campaign that echoed the Rainbow Coalition efforts of 1983, Merced won the election with the support of Latinos, African Americans, organized labor, and the gay community. He was the first Latino elected to the Massachusetts state legislature, where he served from 1988 to 1992.[42]

Merced's election marked a watershed in Latino politics in the city and state, but it did not prove to be a harbinger of further Latino victories.

Indeed, Latinos in Boston continued to face daunting obstacles to winning elective office. Despite the steady growth in the city's Latino population, it remained widely dispersed across six or more neighborhoods, and redistricting efforts to create a predominantly Latino city council district repeatedly failed. Like Merced, Latino candidates had to build multicultural coalitions, a task that became even more challenging as new immigrant groups arrived in the 1980s and 1990s. Latino candidates for city council thus consistently lost to African American challengers in District 7 (Roxbury) and District 4 (Mattapan) and to white candidates in other districts.

Asian American candidates were likewise excluded, since Chinatown was part of District 2, which included South Boston, the city's Irish American political stronghold. For twenty-three years (1984–2007), South Boston's high turnouts kept the irascible James Kelly in office, his racist utterances frequently offending his Asian and Latino constituents. Ironically, the only representation Asians and Latinos had on city governing bodies came when the Boston School Committee was rechartered as an appointive body following a public referendum in 1991. Mayor Flynn then appointed Felix D. Arroyo and George Joe of Chinatown to the school committee, giving Boston's Asian and Latino communities a long-sought voice in the Boston public school system. While these appointments were clearly a step forward and reflected the tireless organizing of the Latino and Asian communities, the interests of the two groups remained, as one observer put it, "almost totally dependent upon the enlightened goodwill of others."[43]

The disappointing showings of Latino and Asian candidates in these years did not mean that political interest was lacking or unimportant in the city's immigrant communities. As noted earlier, immigrant demographics, dispersed population patterns, connections to the homeland, and other barriers to immigrant voting made political mobilization difficult. As with earlier southern and eastern European immigrants, successful engagement in electoral politics was a long-term project that rarely occurred in the first generation.[44] In the meantime, however, ethnic community-based organizations and community development corporations continued to play an essential role in immigrant communities in the 1980s and 1990s, while their number and diversity grew to accommodate new immigrant and refugee groups.

Some of the larger of these new organizations were those serving migrants from the Caribbean and Vietnam. In Dorchester, a growing parish-based ESL program was reorganized as the Haitian Multi-Service

FIGURE 19. In the late 1970s, St. Leo's Parish began offering ESL classes and other services to a growing Haitian community in Dorchester. Incorporated into Catholic Charities in 1984, its programs became part of the new Haitian Multi-Service Center, shown here in 1987. Photo courtesy of *Boston Globe*.

Center in 1984. Under the auspices of Catholic Charities, the center offered a variety of educational and social services accessible to French and Kreyol speakers (fig. 19). As new arrivals moved south to Mattapan, Haitian health-care professionals organized the Haitian American Public Health Initiative in 1989 to meet the critical health and service needs of Haitians in that area. In another Dorchester neighborhood, the burgeoning Vietnamese com-munity of Fields Corner was initially served by the Vietnamese American Civic Association, a government-funded mutual assistance association for refugees. As the community grew, a younger group of leaders raised in Boston organized VietAID in 1994, a CDC that built affordable housing and encouraged small business development. Reminiscent of the Chinatown organizing of the 1970s, VietAID also raised funds to build a Vietnamese American Community Center, which opened in 2002, providing space for ESL classes, childcare, cultural and youth programs, and other services. In other neighborhoods, Boston's Brazilian, Irish, and African immigrants created similar community-based organizations.[45]

The profusion of ethnic-based CBOs was a sign of the growing organizational power of immigrants and the greater acceptance of multicultural politics growing out of the civil rights movement. But it also posed challenges for how such groups might work together—and with native-born neighbors—for common causes such as housing, education, and healthcare. Such fragmentation was especially evident in black neighborhoods, where African Americans lived interspersed with French- and Kreyol-speaking Haitians, English- and Spanish-speakers from the Caribbean, Portuguese Creole-speaking Cape Verdeans, and other African newcomers speaking a variety of languages. While some English-speaking Caribbean migrants and their children—who had a much longer history in the city—had been active participants and leaders in black civil rights struggles of the 1960s and 1970s, the non–English speaking groups that came later tended to organize separately and often experienced tensions with their native-born African American neighbors.

In Mattapan, for example, there was considerable conflict between Haitians and African Americans, especially in the 1980s, when Haitian migrants were widely and unfairly branded as backward "boat people" and carriers of HIV. As Haitians banded together to build their own community and church groups, some grew increasingly wary of their African American neighbors, whom they associated with crime, violence, and low educational achievement. While these tensions later subsided into what one local leader described as "a fragile peace," the two groups remained relatively isolated from each other. As Alix Cantave explained, the relationship between the two has been "marked by miscommunication, misunderstanding, and misconception. The two groups have not been able to build on a shared history of common struggle."[46] These misunderstandings and the conflict between racial and ethnic identities, then, were sometimes obstacles to broader community-based mobilization.

The new ethnic community organizations also experienced significant changes that affected CBOs and CDCs across the country after 1980. As federal funding for social programs was cut back dramatically during the Reagan years, community groups came to rely more heavily on state and municipal funding, and on grants from the private sector. The latter included a growing roster of local foundations such as the Boston Foundation, the Hyams Trust, and the Stearns and Barr foundations, as well as corporate donors from the financial and medical industries, which were flourishing in the New Boston. These funders provided critical financial support to the ethnic CBOs, but also shaped their priorities and demanded high standards of efficiency and professionalism. Community organizers of the 1960s and 1970s thus gave way to credentialed professionals who shared a common language and perhaps region of origin but often did not live in the communities where they worked. Moreover, the nonprofit tax status of the CBOs and CDCs (required for foundation funding) precluded many forms of political advocacy, serving to depoliticize these organizations, in comparison with the more radical community action groups that had preceded them.⁴⁷

Nevertheless, ethnic CBOs and CDCs benefited from the education and skills of new immigrants and their children, while also providing job opportunities and upward mobility for members of the second generation. Some organizations were directed and staffed by the immigrant graduates of local universities and professional schools who came in growing numbers after 1965. One example is Cheng Imm Tan, an ethnic Chinese immigrant from Malaysia who moved to Boston to attend Harvard Divinity School. She later became a Unitarian minister and organized the Asian Task Force Against Domestic Violence in 1992. Tan and other immigrant professionals constituted a new talent pool that simply did not exist in earlier immigrant flows. Drawn by the growing international appeal of Boston's universities and its knowledge economy, these newcomers made use of student visa programs and skill preferences that favored more educated newcomers. Second-generation ethnics were also important in building the CBOs, which provided an avenue of upward mobility for those who completed college degrees in fields such as social work, education, and healthcare. These were also fields in which women predominated, thus providing middle-class occupations and leadership roles for immigrant daughters. These professional leadership roles were historically unprecedented in offering at least some immigrant/ethnic women a degree of security, power, and recognition in their communities and reflected the changing climate for women more generally in the late twentieth century.⁴⁸

Ethnic CBOs and CDCs would also become launching pads into electoral politics and public administration. CBO leaders were in fact the pioneers among Latino and Asian elected officials. Whereas Nelson Merced, the former director of La Alianza Hispana, became the first Latino elected to statewide office in 1987, the Korean-born Sam Yoon, the former director of the Asian Community Development Corporation, would become the city's first Asian American elected official in 2005. CBO and CDC leaders were even more likely to be tapped for jobs in municipal and state administration. Launching their public service careers in ethnic organizations, these agency directors became de facto leaders of their communities, developing crucial organizing experience, contacts, and political skills. Just as many African American elected officials had cut their teeth in the 1960s antipoverty agencies, ethnic community organizations would serve as a pathway to politics for new immigrant and ethnic leaders in the late twentieth century.[49]

The growing network of ethnic community organizations became increasingly important in city politics under mayors Flynn and Menino. Unlike Kevin White, who had focused much of his attention on downtown redevelopment during his final two terms, Flynn made the neighborhoods his top priority. He did so in part through the linkage program, which made funding for affordable housing and community development available through fees levied on downtown developers. Flynn's newly created Office of Neighborhood Services housed the administration's liaisons to different ethnic groups and developed contacts with CBOs and CDCs that worked closely with the city. This flow of funding helped solidify Flynn's support in the city's immigrant communities, as it did for his successor, Thomas Menino. The ethnic CBOs and CDCs thus replaced the ward-based political machines that were once so prevalent in immigrant communities. In the new system, however, political support was less explicit and direct and was given in exchange for services and housing, rather than patronage jobs.[50] It was still a political machine, but without the rampant corruption that characterized the old ethnic ward associations.

Elected in 1993, Mayor Menino built on this successful formula with another initiative specifically targeted at new immigrants. Opening its doors in 1998, the Mayor's Office of New Bostonians (MONB) was a clearinghouse for immigrant services and organizations. Headed by the Reverend Cheng Imm Tan, the founder of the Asian Task Force against Domestic Violence, the MONB was not a service provider but rather, as Tan put it, "a catalyst, a convener, a facilitator, an advocate." Conferring with immigrant and ethnic organizations, MONB developed a network for immigrant information and referrals and identified a number of service priorities for the city. MONB then used municipal funds to leverage private sector donations for three initiatives: an English for New Bostonians program that expanded ESOL course offerings by local providers; free biweekly legal clinics for immigrants at city hall; and a New Bostonians Vote Campaign, an annual voter registration drive conducted through the community organizations. MONB thus provided local CBOs with additional funding and services while encouraging their clients to become active citizens and voters (who would presumably vote for Menino). MONB also sought to make city government more accessible to immigrants by sponsoring an annual New Bostonians Day at city hall and organizing a volunteer interpreter pool among city employees.[51]

The mayor's enthusiasm for MONB was not just politically motivated; as the city's first Italian American mayor, he regularly invoked his own family's immigrant experience and the vital role of newcomers in the city. To educate the larger community, MONB published data profiles on the city's major immigrant groups, demonstrating their significance to the local workforce, economy, and culture. It also published New Bostonian guides to city and local services in multiple languages. The Mayor's Office of New Bostonians was one of the first municipal offices of its kind in the nation, one that was emulated in New York, San Francisco, Houston, and elsewhere.[52] The rapid proliferation of such offices speaks to both the need for support and services among new immigrants and the willingness of migrant communities to repay that support with political backing.

Immigrant communities also gained attention at the state level, as Massachusetts allocated funding to create new ethnic studies institutes at the University of Massachusetts Boston. The Mauricio Gastón Institute, established in 1989 to study Latino community development, and the Institute for Asian American Studies, organized in 1993, provided a steady flow of research and policy analysis on new immigrant communities and their patterns of political participation. Many of the faculty were veterans of the grassroots community struggles of the 1960s and 1970s who then trained a second generation of Latino and Asian American students as they confronted new challenges in the late 1980s and 1990s.[53]

THE POLITICS OF IMMIGRANT RIGHTS

A series of foreign policy crises, changes in US immigration law, and a growing emphasis on national security following 9/11 put pressure on existing organizations to aid and protect new immigrants. In addition to providing basic health and social service needs, ethnic CBOs increasingly had to fight for immigrant rights in what was becoming a more repressive and complex immigration system. These growing pressures led to the formation of new community and statewide organizations that advocated for immigrants at the local, state, and national levels. By the twenty-first century, many of these groups would embrace a new agenda of immigrant integration that was notably different from the antipoverty / community control orientation of earlier ethnic community groups.

The civil wars and human rights crises in Central America sparked the first stirrings of the new immigrant rights organizing in the 1980s. Locally, Cambridge became the center of this movement as the Old Cambridge Baptist Church became a sanctuary for undocumented Salvadoran and Guatemalan war refugees. Other churches, such as St. Mary's, a Roman Catholic parish in Central Square where many Central Americans were settling, also struggled to support the newcomers. In 1981, Sister Rose Cummins, an outreach worker at St. Mary's, and human rights attorney Dan Kesselbrenner established a new organization to serve the needs of local Central Americans. Sister Rose described how the organization began:

> Salvadoran and Guatemalan communities began to come to Massachusetts in large numbers. . . . It was pretty overwhelming. There was no center that was dealing with their issues. All were undocumented. They told stories of things that had happened to them in their countries—stories that were unimaginable to me. It soon became evident that there was a need for legal services—because many of them had been arrested by Immigration. There was also a big need for social services and ESL classes. A group of Salvadorans and another friend and I decided we would try to create a place where Salvadorans and Guatemalans would feel safe and able to get the support and assistance they needed.

In addition to establishing these programs, that new organization—Centro Presente—worked with others to pass a resolution designating Cambridge an asylum city, and it became one of the plaintiffs in the federal *American Baptist Churches v. Thornburg* class action suit. The 1991 settlement of that case granted certain rights and benefits to Guatemalan and Salvadoran asylum seekers across the country. Initially a religious service organization led by native-born whites, Centro Presente evolved into a statewide Latino-led membership organization dedicated to community empowerment and leadership development. By 2006 it had more than twelve hundred members and had moved to larger quarters in Somerville, where many Central Americans had settled.[54]

Centro Presente was the first of dozens of local groups that were struggling to aid growing numbers of undocumented immigrants in the 1980s and 1990s. Outside the Central American asylum effort, other undocumented migrants got their first chance to adjust their status under the amnesty provision of the 1986 Immigration Reform and Control Act. By May 1988, more than ten thousand immigrants in greater Boston had registered for amnesty. To help coordinate this process and provide a voice for the newly legalized residents, a new statewide organization opened its doors in 1987 with office space and funding assistance from Action for Boston Community Development. Representing roughly fifty immigrant and refugee groups across the state, the Massachusetts Immigrant and Refugee Advocacy Coalition (MIRA) brought together ethnic CBOs, mutual assistance associations, faith-based groups, and labor unions working in their behalf on both Beacon Hill and Capitol Hill. In one of its early efforts, MIRA partnered with Centro Presente and local Haitian groups to press for legislation granting temporary protected status to those fleeing Central America and Haiti in the 1980s. With Ted Kennedy chairing the Senate's Immigration Subcommittee and Congressman Joe Moakley sponsoring asylum legislation in the House, MIRA proved to be an effective voice for the state's immigrant population. In the mid-1990s, however, growing public concerns about unauthorized immigration and a Republican resurgence in the 1994 midterm elections led to a spate of anti-immigrant legislation in Washington.[55]

MIRA's workload, staff, and membership grew dramatically in this period, especially after the passage of the welfare reform bill in 1996. Title IV of the Personal Responsibility and Work Opportunity Reconciliation Act was in fact a backdoor immigration measure designed to discourage the foreign born from coming to the United States, which some argued had become a "welfare magnet." Title IV thus denied many benefits—including cash assistance, food stamps, and Medicaid—to legal resident immigrants during their first five years in the United States, while barring the undocumented from nearly all government programs. The bill allowed states to provide some of these programs at their own expense, but only by passing laws that explicitly reauthorized them. MIRA and its allies successfully pressed the Massachusetts legislature for such reauthorization and worked with Ted Kennedy and the Massachusetts delegation on Capitol Hill to restore benefits to certain classes of legal residents—minor children, abuse victims, the elderly, and the disabled. After 2001, however, Massachusetts safety net programs were again threatened by budget cuts, which MIRA fought to restore with some success. Still, welfare reform effectively redrew the boundaries of public social provision, leaving many legal residents and undocumented immigrants ineligible for much-needed assistance and services for their families. Accessing those services thus became a more complicated process, with constantly changing eligibility rules that immigrants needed help navigating, as did the agencies that served them. MIRA sought to provide that help and worked to protect immigrant rights at the state level as the national climate for reform deteriorated.[56]

Moreover, since the late 1990s, immigrants have also faced critical challenges from anti-immigration policies in response to increased illegal immigration and the war on terror. The 1996 Illegal Immigration Reform and Personal Responsibility Act, a complex set of regulations designed to curb illegal migration, vastly increased the number of local detentions, deportations, and family separations. In the wake of 9/11, in which Boston was a key staging ground for the terrorist attacks, there were widespread anti-immigrant sentiments and violence, government round-ups of the foreign born, and increasingly harsh and abusive practices under the Patriot Act. "Now if you even *look* dark, you are asked in the street to give your green card," said Concilio Hispano director Sylvia Keeber in 2002. The stepped-up enforcement continued well past 2001, as Immigration and Customs Enforcement launched numerous raids, including one in March 2007 at the Bianco leather factory in New Bedford that caused a humanitarian crisis as hundreds of female workers across the region were separated from their children. The 2012 Secure Communities program, which mandated that local police report immigration violations to federal authorities, increased deportations and raised immigrants' fears of local law enforcement. MIRA took action on all of these issues, lobbying legislators and federal officials, working through the courts, and rallying people for demonstrations in behalf of national immigration reform in 2006 and 2010 (fig. 20).[57]

Although MIRA often worked in a defensive mode, it also spearheaded a proactive campaign for immigrant naturalization and integration. As immigrants saw their rights erode after 1996, MIRA encouraged newcomers

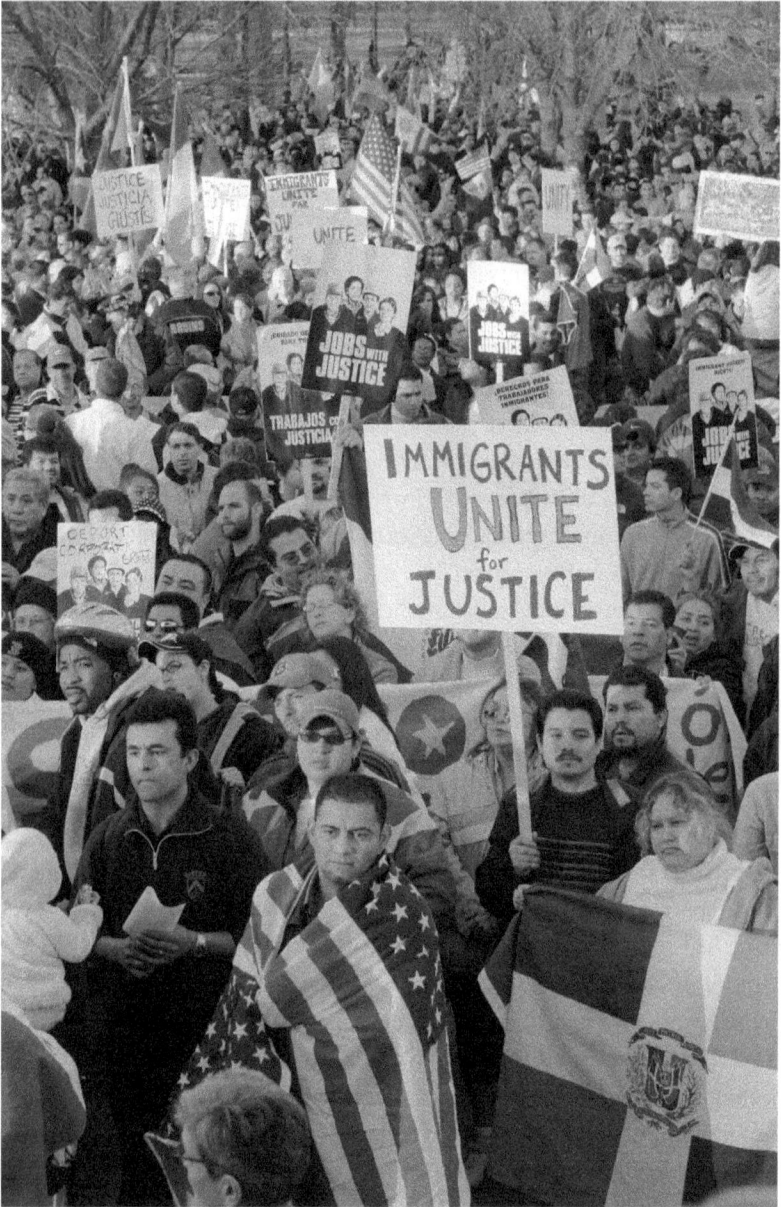

FIGURE 20. Thousands of immigrant rights supporters rallied on Boston Common in March 2006, one of hundreds of demonstrations across the country calling for immigration reform in the twenty-first century. Photo courtesy of *Boston Globe*.

to learn English and become citizens as a way of protecting their rights and showing their patriotism. Long backlogs in the naturalization process and long waiting lists for English and citizenship classes, however, made this difficult. MIRA thus led a campaign in the late 1990s to streamline the naturalization process while promoting a state-level Citizenship Assistance Program that provided $2 million in funding for additional ESL and citizenship classes at more than a hundred local organizations. Beginning in 2008, MIRA worked with Governor Deval Patrick and his staff on developing and implementing a New Americans Agenda, calling for immigrant integration in the Commonwealth. To this end, MIRA coauthored a comprehensive immigration report and agenda for the state and launched an Integration Institute to conduct research and pilot projects on immigrant entrepreneurship, recredentialing, and workforce development.[58]

MIRA's vision of integration was more culturally inclusive than the old model of assimilation but less militant and more patriotic than the vision of community control that had animated the ethnic politics of the 1960s and 1970s. "We see integration as a two-way process," explained MIRA's executive director, Eva Millona: "[It means] valuing what diverse newcomers bring with them, as well as emphasizing what is needed to ensure their success and their potential contributions." In practice, MIRA called on the government to do its part with better policies and resources while encouraging newcomers to learn English and the skills necessary to compete in the state's economy. Viewing immigrants as key drivers of a state workforce that would otherwise be shrinking, MIRA offered a pro-growth vision of multiculturalism that prioritized English and citizenship over older notions of bilingualism and community control. As in World War I and the 1920s, when immigrant organizations took up patriotic causes and hyphenated American identities, MIRA's brand of immigrant politics has been a pragmatic adaptation to a growing anti-immigrant climate and a shrinking public sector. Its pro-citizenship agenda and its efforts to promote voting and civic engagement, however, also reflect a long-term goal of changing the political climate, making it more conducive to immigrant rights and multiculturalism. "We wanted to empower new Americans to fight back by representing their own interests and those of their fellow immigrants at the ballot box," explained MIRA's organizing director, Marcony Almeida, about the coalition's 2012 efforts to register immigrant voters. This pragmatic approach to immigrant integration goes well beyond Massachusetts, with MIRA playing a leading role in the National Partnership of New Americans, a federation of twelve state coalitions working to build a national immigrant integration movement.[59]

MIRA and other immigrant rights groups also took strong positions supporting undocumented immigrants in their quest for human rights and fair treatment in Massachusetts. They supported efforts to grant driver's licenses to unauthorized immigrants and to allow undocumented youth (the so-called dreamers) to pay in-state tuition rates at Massachusetts-run colleges and universities—a benefit that was effectively discouraged under the Illegal Immigration Reform Act of 1996. In 2005, MIRA helped local high school and college students organize the Student Immigrant Movement (SIM), a group advocating for an in-state tuition bill and passage of the federal Development, Relief, and Education for Alien Minors (DREAM) Act. Becoming an independent organization in 2009, SIM formed support groups for undocumented students, organized online petition drives to get deferments for students facing deportation, met with state and federal legislators, and lobbied Boston-area college presidents to support the Dream Act. One of the most effective methods SIM used was a tactic borrowed from the gay rights movement—"coming out" about their undocumented status. By revealing their faces and names and publicly telling personal stories of their struggles and dreams, SIM members contributed to a nationwide effort that persuaded President Barack Obama to grant temporary Deferred Action for Childhood Arrivals in 2012. Soon afterward, SIM organized workshops with local attorneys to help youth fill out their applications and collect the necessary documentation.[60]

Students were just one group among the undocumented who began speaking up for fair treatment. The growing problems of immigrant workers, particularly the undocumented, also gave rise to new organizations known as worker centers. The Brazilian Immigrant Center (BIC) in Allston-Brighton was a good example, becoming one of more than 137 worker centers that had sprung up across the country by 2005. BIC was established in 1995 with the assistance of the Massachusetts Alliance of Portuguese Speakers (MAPS), an organization serving Portuguese immigrants founded in 1970. MAPS began in the Portuguese strongholds of Cambridge and Somerville but expanded into Allston in 1995 to serve the growing Brazilian population there. Helping immigrants find housing, English classes, and translation services, MAPS also encountered a growing number of Brazilian workers reporting labor abuses. The Brazilian Immigrant Center was established to deal with these more complex work-place issues, with MAPS providing a small office and help in securing a federal start-up grant. BIC soon became a separate organization that han-dled a steady stream of work-related complaints from a Brazilian commu-nity that included a high percentage of undocumented workers.[61]

One of the most common problems was employers who withheld wages or underpaid their workers. If the latter were undocumented, their employers sometimes threatened to report them to immigration author-ities. The threat of deportation thus kept many quiet, allowing unscrupu-lous employers to exploit migrants with impunity. BIC helped workers negotiate with employers to resolve individual cases while referring others to volunteer attorneys. In the most egregious cases, they referred employ-ees to the state attorney general's office or the US Labor Department as potential class action suits. In the process, BIC and other local worker centers encouraged the Massachusetts Attorney General's office to hire more bilingual attorneys, produce complaint forms in multiple languages, and refrain from asking about the legal status of complainants. BIC thus became a critical bridge between Brazilian immigrants and the legal sys-tem, protecting the rights of workers regardless of their documentation status.[62]

BIC has also led efforts to protect workers' health and safety. Concen-trated in the construction and cleaning industries, Brazilian workers have faced high rates of workplace accidents, often with no Workmen's Com-pensation insurance or other protection. BIC began workshops on worker rights and safety in the early 2000s and was awarded a federal grant in 2011 to run safety training programs. While such programs are commonly administered by labor unions, worker centers like BIC have taken up this role in an economy increasingly populated by nonunion companies rely-ing on immigrant labor. Since 2010 BIC has made domestic work a top pri-ority, organizing local Brazilian domestic workers—mainly women who face problems such as low pay, sexual harassment, workplace hazards, and long hours with no overtime pay or sick leave. BIC joined with other com-munity groups and unions to press for a Domestic Worker Bill of Rights in Massachusetts, which was signed into law in 2014. BIC has thus repre-sented immigrant workers in the mainstream political and legal systems, despite their marginalized, unorganized, and often unauthorized status.[63]

The rise of immigrant rights organizations such as the Brazilian Immigrant Center, the Student Immigrant Movement, Centro Presente, and the MIRA Coalition speaks to the changing political and economic climate for immigrants in the state and nation. The failure of national immigration reform and the piecemeal legislative measures that have characterized the period since 1986 have made for a complex bureaucratic system, while stepped-up enforcement and deportations have torn families apart and left immigrant communities confused and fearful. Immigrant rights organizations have thus become the new face of ethnic politics, focusing less on community control, bilingualism, and social service provision and more on immigrant rights, integration, and helping newcomers navigate the labyrinth of bureaucracy, regulations, and repression that have come to shape their lives. While some organizations, such as Centro Presente and the Brazilian Immigrant Center, continue to organize among particular ethnic and linguistic groups, others—like the Student Immigrant Movement—address the needs of multiethnic and multiracial constituencies for whom the label "undocumented" trumps other identities. The shifting functions, strategies, and identities of these new immigrant organizations reflect the changing role of the state in the post-1965 era—from service provider in the more prosperous civil rights era to agent of enforcement and deportation in an era of declining budgets and growing fears of terrorism and immigrant invasion.

The dramatic expansion of immigrant rights organizations since the 1980s and their growing impact on state and national issues suggest how significant new immigrants have been to the political life of greater Boston, the state, and the nation. This growing political influence came largely through nonprofit and service organizations, while immigrant representation in local electoral politics remained negligible. That reality, however, would begin to change in the twenty-first century as immigrant numbers and influence grew more visible, launching a new generation into the electoral arena.

Immigrants and the New Majority

orty years after the busing crisis broke out, State Senator Linda Dorcena Forry took the stage as emcee of the St. Patrick's Day breakfast in South Boston. The first non–Irish American to host this celebrated political roast, the Haitian American senator claimed the right to emcee the event, as senators from the first Suffolk district—often referred to as "the Southie seat"—had for decades. But that honor did not come automatically for Forry, who was elected with multicultural support from the Dorchester-Mattapan side of the district. Despite her victory and her marriage to a well-known Irish American newspaper publisher, some South Boston politicians insisted that only an Irish American representative could lead the breakfast, and they proposed an alternate host. Forry, however, stuck to her guns, and Mayor Menino and much of the city's political establishment, backed her up. The opposition conceded, and Forry became the first non-Irish pol—as well as the first woman and the first black—to preside over the breakfast.[1]

The dispute and its peaceful resolution spoke volumes about the social and political changes sweeping the city and the role of new immigrants in ushering in these changes. Despite the many challenges facing immigrants in the twenty-first century, there have been unmistakable signs of immigrant political ascendance in Boston as Latino, Asian, and Afro-Caribbean Americans have mobilized and won elective office. Shifting demographics have been partly responsible: by the time of the 2000 census, Boston had become a majority nonwhite city, thanks to fast-growing Latino, Asian, African, and Caribbean populations. But even more important was the realization among those communities that people of color were now the "New Majority" and that many American-born, second-generation ethnics were now of voting age.

After 2000, a number of new political groups and mobilizations formed to challenge the old guard, making it possible for some candidates representing new immigrant communities to compete successfully in the political system. In the wake of the 2000 census, which showed Latinos to be the fastest growing group in the state, Latino activists formed a new statewide political organization called Oíste [Have you heard], which sought to educate Latinos about electoral politics, register new voters, and groom a new generation for leadership roles. The Chinese Progressive Association, meanwhile, undertook similar activities in Chinatown and joined a coalition of organizations pushing for bilingual ballots. Oíste and the CPA also joined the Black Political Task Force in challenging redistricting at the state level in 2001, charging that a growing nonwhite voting population was being diluted or packed into a smaller number of Boston-area legislative districts. With support from these groups, the Black Political Task Force filed a successful lawsuit that later resulted in federal charges of obstruction of justice against Massachusetts speaker of the house Thomas Finneran, effectively ending his political career.[2]

In 2003, following a University of Massachusetts Boston conference on the city's new nonwhite majority, Oíste, the CPA, the NAACP, and other groups formed a New Majority Coalition to solidify cooperation between the city's black, Latino, and Asian American political forces. With the backing of the coalition that fall, Felix D. Arroyo won an at-large seat on the Boston City Council, the first Latino elected to that body.[3] During the 2003 primary elections, however, poll observers in Chinatown reported manipulation of voters by election workers and the turning away of at least seventeen registered voters. Such charges echoed similar ones by black, Latino, and Vietnamese complainants in the 2001 municipal elections. After the city failed to investigate these complaints, the New Majority Coalition

forwarded them to the Justice Department, alleging voting improprieties directed against limited-English-speaking citizens. These complaints
included poll workers requiring voters to produce identification, a lack
of trained bilingual election workers, absence of multilingual ballots (as
required by the revised Voting Rights Act of 1975), and political operatives
working inside polling places and filling out immigrants' ballots. In the
words of Lydia Lowe, the coalition's cochair and CPA's director, the New
Majority's call for a federal investigation followed "years of irregularities
and a pattern of practices which obstructs immigrant citizens' exercise of
their voting rights."[4]

After sending federal observers to the city's 2005 elections, the Justice
Department agreed, calling for specific remedies and federal supervision
of local elections. Accusing the city of "improperly influencing, coerc-
ing, or ignoring the ballot choices" of limited-English voters, the Justice
Department's lawsuit called for bilingual ballots for certain groups, impar-
tial translation services at polling places, and other remedies. Mayor
Menino's aides initially disputed these allegations, but the city later signed
a memorandum of understanding with the Justice Department. While
not acknowledging any wrongdoing, the city agreed to provide ballots
in Spanish, Chinese, and Vietnamese, to provide training for a sufficient
number of poll workers in those same languages, and to accept federal
oversight of elections for the next three years. The mayor also created a
task force to recruit and train new bilingual poll workers in time for the
fall 2005 elections.[5]

The conduct and outcome of the November municipal elections seemed
to please both sides. Election materials were made available in six foreign
languages (Spanish, Chinese, Vietnamese, Haitian Kreyol, Cape Verdean
Creole, and Russian), and more than 270 trained translators were on hand
to assist Spanish-, Chinese-, and Vietnamese-speaking voters. Mayor
Menino won re-election handily, as did incumbent city councilmember
Felix D. Arroyo. Perhaps most notable, however, was the third-place victory of Korean-born Sam Yoon to an at-large seat on the city council, the
first Asian American elected to municipal office in Boston.[6]

Arroyo and Yoon were just two of a growing crop of immigrant and
second-generation candidates who claimed city and state offices in the early
twenty-first century. One of the key early victories went to Marie St. Fleur,
a Haitian-born lawyer and state prosecutor who ran successfully for the

state legislature in the 5th Suffolk district of Roxbury/Dorchester in 1999 (formerly held by Nelson Merced). The first Haitian American to hold public office in Massachusetts, she served from 2000 to 2011. Another Haitian American, Linda Dorcena Forry, ran for the legislature in 2005 when Thomas Finneran stepped down. She too was elected, in this case with the support of a multiracial Dorchester coalition, cemented by her marriage into a prominent liberal Irish American family that owned the *Dorchester Reporter* and the *Boston Haitian Reporter.* She later went on to win a state senate seat in 2013. The victories of St. Fleur and Forry were a testament to grassroots organizing and network building in the Haitian American and Caribbean communities, which after years of settlement and a maturing second generation, were now strongly invested in local politics.[7]

Other ethnic groups also showed success in city and state politics. With the support of the Menino machine, Jeffrey Sanchez—the mayor's Latino liaison—won a state legislative seat representing Mission Hill and Jamaica Plain in 2002. Joining him on Beacon Hill was Jarrett Barrios, a Cuban American from Cambridge who was elected to the state senate that same year. Two years later, a Cape Verdean American woman, Andrea Cabral, won election as Suffolk County sheriff, the first woman and person of color to hold the office. In 2012, Governor Deval Patrick tapped her to be the state's secretary of public safety. Another Cape Verdean, the attorney Evandro Carvalho, won election to the state house in 2014 from the 5th Suffolk district, the Roxbury-Dorchester seat formerly held by Marie St. Fleur. At the municipal level, Felix D. Arroyo lost his re-election bid in 2007, but his son, Felix G. Arroyo, was elected to the council in 2009 and 2011. Michelle Wu, the city's first successful Chinese American city council candidate, won an at-large seat in 2013.[8]

Increasingly, then, immigrant and second-generation politicians have become more visible representatives of their communities and have become more integrated into the larger power networks of city and state politics. Unlike the first generation of black and Puerto Rican activists who came up through community-based struggles and organizations, the younger generation of immigrant political leaders have benefited from access to leadership-training programs, degrees from top universities and professional schools, and better access to mainstream political networks. Many of the New Majority generation, in fact, came up through the more traditional political and administrative ranks, working for district attorneys, in the mayor's office, or as legislative aides for both white and African American legislators. Although there has been some criticism that such alliances are a form of cooptation by the dominant white power structure, the recruitment of immigrant leaders into governing Democratic coalitions in fact speaks to the growing power that black, Latino, and Asian communities increasingly wield in the twenty-first century and a recognition that their voting power will only increase in the future.

There is little evidence in Boston that immigrant leaders have embraced an older notion of pluralist ethnic politics that ignores the problems of race. The New Majority Coalition and other less formal unity efforts suggest that Caribbean, Latino, and Asian American elected officials have been acutely aware of issues of racial inequality and their continued impact on Boston's schools, neighborhoods, and services. As different groups have faced different problems, though, they have not always agreed on strategies.[9] But the legacy of rainbow coalition building that grew out of Mel King's 1983 campaign has continued in campaigns for subsidized housing, statewide health insurance, school reform, and other common causes.

At the same time, immigrant leaders have brought new issues to the table—the plight of Haitian refugees, organizing relief for Haiti's 2010 earthquake, and the struggles of immigrants around documentation, deportation, work, and higher education. For the most part, immigrant leaders have been successful in generating support for such issues. During the 2006 immigrant rights march in Boston, when eight thousand people marched in support of immigration reform, the African American gubernatorial candidate Deval Patrick and the city's Black Ministerial Alliance expressed public support for the cause. Likewise, after Arizona passed its draconian immigration enforcement law in 2010, the Boston City Council voted unanimously for a resolution calling on the city to cut its business ties with the state of Arizona, a measure proposed by Felix G. Arroyo and supported by Mayor Menino.[10] For the most part, Boston-area Democrats across the city have lined up to support immigrant rights, waging battles at the state level with Republicans who have tried to cut social benefits for immigrants and who have so far succeeded in denying drivers licenses and in-state tuition to the undocumented. Because of these stands, the political incorporation of immigrants has occurred almost entirely within the state's Democratic Party and especially within Boston, where much of the immigrant voting power and advocacy work has been concentrated.

Progress has been notably slower in the suburbs. Except for a few of the older industrial cities and mill towns, the influx of new immigrants occurred somewhat later in the suburbs, and at-large voting patterns there have remained more prevalent. Nor do most of these towns and cities have a tradition of 1960s-era grassroots community mobilization that served as an important springboard for immigrant political engagement. Even in communities with high percentages of foreign-born residents—such as Quincy, Framingham, and Malden—new immigrants and ethnics have been largely absent from local governing councils and school boards. Local officials have made some efforts, though, to reach out to newcomers through translation and interpreter services, multicultural activities and festivals, and special constituent services such as Quincy's Asian Liaison's Office.

The Boston mayoral race of 2013 was a case in point. In that race, the Irish American contender Martin Walsh trounced the opposition, including Latino candidate Felix G. Arroyo and John Barros, a second-generation Cape Verdean. Although their defeat (along with that of African American candidate Charlotte Golar Richie) dampened the spirits of New Majority activists, it should be noted that Walsh himself is the son of Irish immigrants, and his runoff victory hinged on the support he assiduously cultivated among his black, Latino, and Cape Verdean competitors.[11] Although new immigrant communities have not yet put one of their own in the city's top office, the rise of a new nonwhite majority has offered them greater opportunities for political empowerment, increased participation in urban administration, and more equitable and multicultural political practices. Ultimately, though, the ability of new immigrant communities to win political leadership at the highest levels will depend on effective voter mobilization, turnout, and coalition building across the city.

Electoral politics, however, should not be the only yardstick by which we measure the impact of the new immigration. As Boston has once again become a major immigrant destination, newcomers have transformed the metropolitan area in a multitude of ways. That impact has been particularly evident in the region's economy, where immigrants first propped up ailing manufacturing industries in the 1960s and 1970s, and then became critical drivers of the medical, technical, and educational sectors that made up the new knowledge economy—as well as the lower-paid service industries that support it. During the long-term decline of the region's native-born population, immigrant newcomers have kept the metropolitan population and labor force growing and have contributed to the climate of innovation that has been so critical to Boston's new economy. The graying of the Massachusetts population—one of the oldest on average in the country—and the mass retirement of baby boomers that will occur over the next two decades suggest that immigrants will continue to play an essential role in replenishing the region's population and driving its economy.[12]

Immigrant settlement has likewise transformed the metropolitan landscape, revitalizing many of Boston's neighborhoods and its older industrial suburbs. From the 1960s to the 1980s, immigrants helped reinvigorate the old ethnic enclaves of Chinatown, the South End, and East Cambridge, though their efforts soon succumbed to gentrification and redevelopment. Since the 1980s, newcomers have gravitated to outlying urban neighborhoods such as East Boston and Dorchester, and to older industrial suburbs such as Quincy, Framingham, and Malden, where they purchased aging triple-deckers and created thriving ethnic businesses that have invigorated declining commercial areas. Their presence has also been evident in new religious congregations, which have repopulated old urban churches with new members, and in new religious styles and beliefs. This de-Europeanization of both Catholicism and Protestantism has constituted a "quiet revival" that has both revived and transformed Boston's religious landscape. Moreover, new immigrants have helped to diversify more affluent university communities and outlying suburbs, which in the 1960s were overwhelmingly white and native born. As immigrant suburbanization accelerated after 1980, even towns twenty miles or more from Boston had immigrant-owned shops and restaurants, ethnic associations, and centers for Islam, Buddhism, Hinduism, and other world religions.

Although immigrants have been vital to the transformation of greater Boston in the late twentieth century, there have been definite costs and dislocations associated with this process. In the 1980s, the wrenching turnover from a manufacturing to a service-based economy contributed to resentment and violence toward newcomers by native-born whites who blamed immigrants for their own declining fortunes. Nativism also fed this hostility, as it had toward earlier waves of immigrants, but racism and fears of terrorism have compounded the problem for recent arrivals hailing from the Caribbean, Africa, Latin America, Asia, and the Middle East. Since the 1990s, and especially after 9/11, anti-immigrant policies at the state and federal levels have made life more difficult for newcomers to the region as issues of documentation, policing, and deportation have become more vexing. Such concerns have forced immigrant advocates into a more defensive politics centered on protecting immigrant rights and retaining access to basic human services. If immigrants are to continue to play a central role in Boston's economic and metropolitan revival, there will have to be meaningful immigration reform that allows for the successful integration of newcomers.

We should also remember that the fruits of Boston's renaissance have not been equally shared, and that growing inequalities have accompanied the new economy that immigrants helped to build. The very success of immigrant neighborhood revitalization has led to gentrification and redevelopment that later displaced those same immigrant groups from areas like Chinatown, Jamaica Plain, Cambridge, and Somerville—to name just a few. Likewise, immigrants' contributions to the local labor force have sometimes been accompanied by exploitative practices by employers and contractors who have profited from weak labor regulation and enforcement, as well as minimum wage laws that have lagged far behind the cost of living. As a result, some newcomers, despite working long hours and multiple jobs, have ended up stuck in the region's most impoverished and troubled communities, where the urban crisis of earlier years has continued unabated. In the light of shrinking tax bases, troubled schools, and a host of unmet social needs, the prospects of upward mobility for the second generation in such areas have not been encouraging. Like the native-born poor, these families have faced a growing chasm between rich and poor and dwindling opportunities for better-paying jobs. With fewer rungs in the midsection of the social ladder, the rising cost of higher education, ongoing racial barriers, and new obstacles for the undocumented, the climb to middle-class status has become tougher than ever.

Some advocates of immigration reform argue that these problems could be alleviated by greater restrictions and tougher enforcement. This study of the new Bostonians, however, suggests that such a course would be ill advised for the region—an area where immigrants have been essential to the revival of the metropolitan economy and landscape. The same holds true for dozens of cities across New England and the Northeast, where newcomers have helped revive urban areas racked by years of deindustrialization, depopulation, and decline. But the prosperity that immigrants have helped to create in Boston and other cities—and that continues to attract newcomers from around the world—must be more widely shared. Improved wages and working conditions, more affordable housing, and a strong and effective system of public education that can address the special needs of immigrant children and youth, will be essential to reducing the social inequalities that disproportionately affect immigrants and people of color. As part of Boston's New Majority, immigrant labor and community leaders have emerged as vocal advocates for these issues, pressuring political leaders to be accountable to their increasingly diverse constituents. As the children of immigrants come of age and move into political leadership across the city and state, the potential for such egalitarian policies may be within reach.

Notes

∾

INTRODUCTION

1. The relationship between immigration and metropolitan revitalization is discussed more fully in the forthcoming volume edited by Thomas J. Sugrue and Dominic Vitello from the 2014 conference Immigration and Metropolitan Revitalization in the United States, Penn Social Science & Policy Forum, University of Pennsylvania.

2. Oscar Handlin, *Boston's Immigrants: A Study in Acculturation* (New York: Atheneum, 1973). This is a revised edition of the author's dissertation, originally published in 1941.

3. One of the most important works is Nancy Foner's study of New York's new immigration, which compares it to Jewish and Italian migrations of the early twentieth century; see Nancy Foner, *From Ellis Island to JFK: New York's Two Great Waves of Immigration* (New Haven: Yale University Press, 2001). Other city-level studies by social scientists of the new immigration include Enrique Ochoa and Gilda Ochoa, eds., *Latino Los Angeles* (Tucson: University of Arizona Press, 2005); Alejandro Portes and Alex Stepnick, *City on the Edge: The Transformation of Miami* (Berkeley: University of California Press, 1993); and Ayumi Takenaka and Mary Johnson Osirim, eds., *Global Philadelphia: Immigrant Communities Old and New* (Philadelphia: Temple University Press, 2010). A useful collection of essays on new immigrants in metropolitan areas is Audrey Singer, Susan Wiley Hardwick, and Caroline Brettell, eds., *Twenty-First Century Gateways: Immigrant Incorporation in*

Suburban America (Washington, DC: Brookings Institution Press, 2002). For some of the most recent historical work on the new immigration, see Marilyn Halter, Marilynn S. Johnson, Katheryn P. Viens, and Conrad E. Wright, eds., *What's New about the "New" Immigration: Traditions and Transformations in the United States since 1965* (New York: Palgrave Macmillan, 2014).

4. For MAPC criteria, see www.mapc.org. Some of these suburbs were small villages or farming communities in the 1960s and 1970s, and thus were not part of the metro area at the time.

5. Since the 1980s, the cities of Lawrence, Lowell, and Brockton and their respective suburbs have been included in the larger "Combined Statistical Area" for Boston, but they have also been classified separately as part of smaller "Primary Statistical Areas." The changing definitions and proliferation of metropolitan designations have made use of this metropolitan census data difficult at best. Moreover, these former mill cities have distinctive and fascinating histories that deserve separate treatment. See, for example: Llana Barber, "Latino Migration and the New Global Cities: Transnationalism, Race, and Urban Crisis in Lawrence, Massachusetts, 1945–2000" (Ph.D. diss., Boston College, 2010); Ramón Borges Méndez, "Urban and Regional Restructuring and Barrio Formation in Massachusetts: The Cases of Lowell, Lawrence, and Holyoke" (Ph.D. diss., MIT, 1994); Tuyet-Lan Pho, Jeffrey N. Gerson, and Sylvia R. Cowan, eds., *Southeast Asian Refugees and Immigrants in the Mill City* (Lebanon, NH: University Press of New England, 2007).

1. BOSTON'S "OLD" IMMIGRANTS

1. Benjamin Carp, *Rebels Rising* (New York: Oxford, 2007), 25.

2. Lemuel Shattuck, *Census of Boston, 1845* (Boston, 1846), 37; Commonwealth of Massachusetts, *Census of Massachusetts, 1865* (Boston, 1867), 76; Oscar Handlin, *Boston's Immigrants* (1959; repr., Cambridge: Harvard University Press, 2011), 91–92.

3. Kevin Kenny, *The American Irish: A History* (New York: Longman, 2000), 45–54, 89–91; Handlin, *Boston's Immigrants*, 29–34, 44–45.

4. Handlin, *Boston's Immigrants*, 52; Kenny, *The American Irish*, 142.

5. Stephen Puleo, *The Boston Italians*, 48–51; Nancy Foner, *From Ellis Island to JFK: New York's Two Great Waves of Immigration* (New Haven: Yale University Press, 2000), 19–20; US Immigration Commission, *Reports of the Immigration Commission*, vol. 26: *Immigrants in Cities*, part 5: Boston (1910), 436 (hereafter cited as Dillingham Report).

6. William Braverman, "The Emergence of a Unified Community," in *The Jews of Boston*, ed. Jonathan Sarna et al. (New Haven: Yale University Press, 2005), 65–86; Mary Antin, *The Promised Land* (Boston: Houghton Mifflin, 1912), 22; Alan Kraut, *The Huddled Masses* (Arlington Heights, IL: Harlan Davidson, 1982), 34–38; Foner, *From Ellis Island to JFK*, 20–21.

7. Braverman, "The Emergence of a Unified Community," 65–86; Kraut, *The Huddled Masses*, 34–38.

8. Leo Pap, *The Portuguese Americans* (Boston: Twayne, 1981), 22–23, 36–37, 56, 130–31.

9. US Census Bureau, *Census of Population and Housing*, 1910, vol. 4, Massachusetts, available at www.census.gov; Federal Writers Project, Works Progress Administration, *The Armenians in Massachusetts* (Boston: Armenian Historical Association, 1937), 27–34; Philip Kayal and Joseph Kayal, *The Syrian-Lebanese in America* (Boston: Twayne, 1975), 81.

10. Frederick Rudolph, "Chinamen in Yankeedom: Anti-Unionism in Massachusetts in 1870," *American Historical Review* 53.1 (October 1947): 1–29; Andrew Gyory, *Closing the Gate: Race, Politics, and the Chinese Exclusion Act* (Chapel Hill: University of North Carolina Press, 1998), 40–49; Boston 200 Corporation, *Chinatown* (Boston, 1976), 2–5.

11. Marilyn Halter, *Between Race and Ethnicity* (Urbana: University of Illinois Press, 1993), 1–4; John Daniels, *In Freedom's Birthplace* (New York: Arno Press, 1969), 172.

12. Violet Showers Johnson, *The Other Black Bostonians* (Bloomington: Indiana University Press, 2006), 7–8, 14, 20.

13. Quotation from Constantine M. Panunzio, *The Soul of an Immigrant* (New York: Macmillan, 1928), 61; Handlin, *Boston's Immigrants*, 47.

14. Johnson, *The Other Black Bostonians*, 7; Halter, *Between Race and Ethnicity*, 5, 69–70.

15. Handlin, *Boston's Immigrants*, 57–61; Kenny, *The American Irish*, 109–10.

16. Handlin, *Boston's Immigrants*, 93–94, 96–98; Paula J. Todisco, *Boston's First Neighborhood: The North End* (Boston: Boston Public Library, 1976), 19–22. South Cove—the area that today covers Chinatown, the Mass Pike Extension, the Leather District, and adjacent blocks to the south—was a landfill project built largely by Irish labor in the 1830s and 1840s to house the depots of the Boston & Worcester Railroad (now South Station). Nearby Fort Hill was later leveled by downtown business interests, displacing thousands of poor Irish residents. As the historian Nancy Seasholes notes, it was "Boston's first slum clearance project" and was likely motivated by Know Nothing politics of the 1850s. Irish workers were thus enlisted both to tear down their old neighborhood as well as to build their future one. Nancy S. Seasholes, *Gaining Ground: A History of Landmaking in Boston* (Cambridge: MIT Press, 2003), 61, 237–56.

17. On the transformation of the textile industry in Lowell, see Thomas Dublin, *Women at Work* (New York: Columbia University Press, 1993), 147; on the shoe-making industry in Lynn, see Alan Dawley, *Class and Community: The Industrial Revolution in Lynn* (Cambridge: Harvard University Press, 1976).

18. Rudolph, "Chinamen in Yankeedom," 1–29; Mass Moments, "Chinese Workers Arrive in North Adams," www.massmoments.org; Doris C. J. Chu, *The Chinese in Massachusetts: Their Experiences and Contributions* (Boston: Chinese Culture Institute, 1987), 44–47; *A Chinatown Banquet* (DVD), Asian Community Development Center, 2006, Part I, "Boston's Lower East Side."

19. US Census Bureau, *Census of Population and Housing*, 1910, 4:854–55; Chu, *The Chinese in Massachusetts*, 50–51.

20. Richard D. Brown and Jack Tager, *Massachusetts: A Concise History* (Amherst: University of Massachusetts Press, 2000), 202–9; Johnson, *The Other Black Bostonians*, 26–27; Stephen G. Mostov, "Immigrant Entrepreneurs: Jews in the Shoe Trades of Lynn, 1885–1945," in *The History of Boston's Jewish North Shore*, ed. Alan S. Pierce (Charleston, SC: History Press and the Jewish Historical Society of the North Shore, 2009), 32–36.

21. Todisco, *Boston's First Neighborhood*, 29–31, 33–35; Dillingham Report, 428–30.

22. Puleo, *The Boston Italians*, 91–93; Todisco, *Boston's First Neighborhood*, 34–35; Brown and Tager, *Massachusetts*, 209; Dillingham Report, 473–76.

23. Braverman, "The Emergence of a Unified Community," 76–78; Antin, *The Promised Land*, 193–95, 264; Robert A. Woods, *City Wilderness: A Settlement Study* (Boston: Houghton Mifflin, 1898), 40–48, 55–57.

24. For more on the zone of emergence concept, see Robert A. Woods and Albert J. Kennedy, *The Zone of Emergence: Observations of the Lower Middle and Upper Working Class Communities of Boston, 1905–1914* (Cambridge: MIT Press, 1969); and Sam Bass Warner, *Streetcar Suburbs: The Process of Growth in Boston, 1870–1900* (Cambridge: Harvard University Press, 1962).

25. Woods and Kennedy, *The Zone of Emergence*, 70–72, 183, 195–97; Howard Husock, "Rediscovering the Three-Decker House," *Public Interest* 98 (Winter 1990): 51–53.

26. Woods and Kennedy, *The Zone of Emergence*, 45, 51, 70–72, 75–76, 77, 100–104, 170, 174–77, 190, 201–2, 208–11, 213; Pap, *The Portuguese Americans*, 56.

27. Gerald Gamm, *Urban Exodus: Why the Jews Left Boston and the Catholics Stayed* (Cambridge: Harvard University Press, 1999), 25–26, 178–79, 198, 203.

28. Johnson, *The Other Black Bostonians*, 104; Chu, *Chinese in Massachusetts*, 56; Boston 200 Corporation, *Chinatown*, 6, 9–11. On the different suburbanization rates of Catholics and Jews, see Gamm, *Urban Exodus*.

29. Quincy Historical Society, *Four Centuries of New Americans* (brochure produced for the Massachusetts Memories Road Show, 2007); Stephen W. Herring, *Framingham: An American Town* (Framingham, MA: Framingham Tercentennial Commission, 2000), 155, 235–36; Massachusetts Bureau of Statistics of Labor, *Census of the Commonwealth of Massachusetts, 1905* (Boston, 1909), xliii–xliv. Ironically, during Boston's massive Central Artery / Tunnel project in the 1990s, work crews (including many immigrants) hauled millions of pounds of earth from the downtown excavation site to fill the old Quincy quarries. Robert Preer, "Into Quarry's Depths No More," *Boston Globe*, 18 October 2001, 1. On Big Dig workers, see Michael Hintlian, *Digging: The Workers of Boston's Big Dig* (Boston: Commonwealth Editions, 2004).

30. Thomas H. O'Connor, *The Boston Irish* (Boston: Northeastern University Press, 1995), 46–49; Thomas H. O'Connor, *Boston Catholics* (Boston: Northeastern University Press, 1998), 56–57, 63–67; Brown and Tager, *Massachusetts*, 174–75, 177.

31. Kenny, *The American Irish*, 116; Handlin, *Boston's Immigrants*, 201, 203; Brown and Tager, *Massachusetts*, 180–81; O'Connor, *The Boston Irish*, 73.

32. Gyory, *Closing the Gate*, 47–48; on the anti-Chinese movement in California, see Alexander Saxton, *The Indispensible Enemy: Labor and the Anti-Chinese Movement in California* (Berkeley: University of California Press, 1971).

33. K. Scott Wong, "'The Eagle Seeks a Helpless Quarry': Chinatown, the Police, and the Press: The 1903 Boston Chinatown Raid Revisited," *Amerasia* 22.3 (1996): 81–103; Erika Lee, *At America's Gates: Chinese Immigration during the Exclusion Era, 1882–1943* (Chapel Hill: University of North Carolina Press, 2003), 6–7, 230–31.

34. Puleo, *The Boston Italians*, 14–15, 53; James R. Green, *Boston's Workers: A Labor History* (Boston: Trustees of the Public Library, 1979), 60–61; William Whyte, "Race Conflicts in the North End of Boston," *New England Quarterly* 12.4 (December 1939): 631.

35. Vincent Cannato, "Immigration and the Brahmins," *Humanities* 30.3 (May/June 2009), available at www.neh.gov; Dale T. Knobel, *America for the Americans* (New York: Twayne, 1996), 219–21; Thomas H. O'Connor, *Bibles, Brahmins, and Bosses: A Short History of Boston* (Boston: Trustees of the Public Library of the City of Boston, 1984), 167–68.

36. Foner, *From Ellis Island to JFK*, 143–49; Puleo, *The Boston Italians*, 76–77; Lee, *At America's Gates*, 39.

37. Green, *Boston's Workers*, 60; Puleo, *The Boston Italians*, 108–9, 117–18, 127–28, 135, 153.

38. Roger Daniels, *Guarding the Golden Door* (New York: Hill and Wang, 2004), 134–39; Michael C. LeMay, *From Open Door to Dutch Door: An Analysis of US Immigration Policy since 1820* (Westport, CT: Greenwood Press, 1987), 87, 91.

39. US Census Bureau, *Census of Population and Housing*, 1910, 1920, 1930, 1940, and 1970, available at www.census.gov.

40. O'Connor, *Bibles, Brahmins, and Bosses*, 22–23; Ellen Smith, "Strangers and Sojourners: The Jews of Colonial Boston," in Sarna et al., *The Jews of Boston*, 24–25.

41. David Kaufman, "Temples in the American Athens: A History of Synagogues in Boston," in Sarna et al., *The Jews of Boston*, 168–70.

42. James O'Toole, "The Newer Catholic Races: Ethnic Catholicism in Boston," *New England Quarterly* 65.1 (March 1992): 119; O'Connor, *Boston Catholics*, 125. In 1865, the Boston diocese included Massachusetts, Rhode Island, and New Hampshire.

43. Kenny, *The American Irish*, 76–77, 113–14.

44. Kaufman, "Temples in the American Athens," 173. Not all synagogues followed this path, however; Mishkan Israel, for instance, maintained a more traditional style.

45. The parish later built a new church, St. Jean-Baptiste, in 1888. In 1993 the parish was reorganized as Nuestra Senora del Carmen, to serve the city's Latino population, but was then closed in 2004.

46. O'Connor, *Boston Catholics*, 162–65; O'Toole, "The Newer Catholic Races," 122–23.

47. O'Connor, *Boston Catholics*, 175–83; O'Toole, "The Newer Catholic Races," 117–18.

48. O'Toole, "The Newer Catholic Races," 119–20, 125, 130–31; Kristen A. Petersen, "Contested Bodies and Souls: Immigrant Converts in Boston," in *Boston's Histories: Essays in Honor of Thomas H. O'Connor,* ed. James O'Toole and David Quigley (Boston: Northeastern University Press, 2004), 144.

49. William M. Demarco, *Ethnics and Enclaves: Boston's Italian North End* (Ann Arbor: UMI Research Press, 1981), 95–99; O'Connor, *Boston Catholics,* 166–71; O'Toole, "The Newer Catholic Races," 132.

50. O'Toole, "The Newer Catholic Races," 124, 133; O'Connor, *Boston Catholics,* 309–10; Joseph O'Keefe and Aubrey J. Scheopner, "Catholic Schools: A Tradition of Responsiveness to Non-Dominant Cultures," in *Two Centuries of Faith: The Influence of Catholicism on Boston, 1808-2008,* ed. Thomas H. O'Connor (New York: Crossroad Publishing, 2009), 97.

51. Judith E. Smith, *Family Connections: A History of Italian and Jewish Immigrant Lives in Providence, Rhode Island, 1900–1940* (Albany: State University of New York Press, 1985), 129–30; Kaufman, "Temples in the American Athens," 177–79; Gerald H. Gamm, "In Search of Suburbs: Boston's Jewish Districts, 1843–1994," in Sarna et al., *The Jews of Boston,* 141.

52. See Susan Ebert, "Community and Philanthropy," in Sarna et al., *The Jews of Boston,* 211–37.

53. Kaufman, "Temples in the American Athens," 180–81, 184, 193; Gamm, "In Search of Suburbs," 131–32.

54. See Gamm, *Urban Exodus.*

55. Geoffrey Blodgett, "Yankee Leadership in a Divided City: Boston, 1860–1910," in *Boston 1700–1980: The Evolution of Urban Politics,* ed. Ronald P. Formisano and Constance K. Burns (Westport, CT: Greenwood Press, 1984), 92–99.

56. O'Connor, *The Boston Irish,* 115–18, 130–33.

57. Alan Rogers and Lisa Rogers, *Boston: City on a Hill* (Sun Valley, CA: American Historical Press, 2007), 108–9; O'Connor, *The Boston Irish,* 141–48.

58. O'Connor, *The Boston Irish,* 168–70.

59. Rogers and Rogers, *Boston,* 110–11; O'Connor, *The Boston Irish,* 170–78.

60. James J. Connolly, *The Triumph of Ethnic Progressivism: Urban Political Culture in Boston, 1900–1925* (Cambridge: Harvard University Press, 1998); Ellen Smith, "'Israelites in Boston': 1840–1880," in Sarna et al., *The Jews of Boston,* 59–60; Puleo, *The Boston Italians,* 20–25.

61. Connolly, *The Triumph of Ethnic Progressivism,* 61–66; Braverman, "The Emergence of a Unified Community," 79–82.

62. Connolly, *The Triumph of Ethnic Progressivism,* 56–61; Puleo, *The Boston Italians,* 101–4.

63. O'Connor, *The Boston Irish,* 175–91, 225; Rogers and Rogers, *Boston,* 112–15; Connolly, *The Triumph of Ethnic Progressivism,* 133–60.

64. Thomas H. O'Connor, "The Jewish-Christian Experience," in Sarna et al., *The Jews of Boston,* 337; Connolly, *The Triumph of Ethnic Progressivism,* 146–47.

65. William P. Marchione Jr., "The 1949 Boston Charter Reform," *New England Quarterly* 49.3 (September 1976): 374–77; Puleo, *The Boston Italians*, 185–88, 266.

66. Evelyn Savidge Stern, "Beyond the Boss: Immigration and Political Culture from 1880 to 1940," in *E Pluribus Unum: Contemporary and Historical Perspectives on Immigrant Political Incorporation*, ed. Gary Gerstle and John Mollenkopf (New York: Russell Sage, 2001), 33–66; Green, *Boston's Workers*, 77, 83, 91, 110; O'Connor, *The Boston Irish*, 96–98.

2. ROOTS AND ROUTES

1. US Census Bureau, American FactFinder, 2012 American Community Survey 5-year estimates, available at factfinder.census.gov (hereafter cited as 2012 ACS 5-year estimates).

2. Reed Ueda, *Postwar Immigrant America* (Boston: Bedford Books, 1994), 44–46, 159; Aristide Zolberg, "Immigration Control Policy," in *The New Americans: A Guide to Immigration since 1965*, ed. Mary Waters, Reed Ueda, and Helen Marrow (Cambridge: Harvard University Press, 2007), 30–31.

3. Jesse Hoffnung-Garskoff, "The Immigration Reform Act of 1965," in *The Familiar Made Strange: Iconic American Texts after the Transnational Turn*, ed. Brooke L. Blower and Mark Philip Bradley (New York: Cornell University Press, 2015), chap. 10.

4. Julio Morales, "Puerto Rican Poverty and Migration to Elsewhere: Waltham, Massachusetts, A Case Study" (Ph.D. diss., Brandeis University, 1979), 192, 206.

5. Ibid., 71–73, 76, 190; Michael Piore, "Immigration, Work Expectations and Labor Market Structure," in *The Diverse Society: Implications for Social Policy*, ed. Pastora S. J. Cafferty and Leon W. Chestany (Washington, D.C.: Association Press, National Association of Social Workers, 1976), 113–14; Uriarte, "Contra Viento y Marea (Against All Odds): Latinos Build Community in Boston," in *Latinos in Boston*, ed. Miren Uriarte et al. (Boston: Boston Persistent Poverty Project, Boston Foundation, 1992), 6–7; Deborah Pacini Hernandez, "Quiet Crisis: A Community History of Latinos in Cambridge, Massachusetts," in *Latinos in New England*, ed. Andrés Torres (Philadelphia: Temple University Press, 2006), 152; Maldonado quotation from Rachel Long and Richard Nightingale, "Latinos in the Economy of Cambridge," Final Report, Fall 2002, 17, Urban Borderlands Records, Tufts University, Digital Collections and Archives (TDCA), Medford, MA, available at http://dl.tufts.edu.

6. Uriarte, "Contra Viento y Marea," 9.

7. Peggy Levitt, *The Transnational Villagers* (Berkeley: University of California Press, 2001), 42, 47; Larry Rohter, "Flood of Dominicans Lets Some Enter US by Fraud," *New York Times*, 19 February 1997.

8. Miren Uriarte et al., "Salvadorans, Guatemalans, Hondurans, and Colombians: A Scan of Needs of Recent Latin American Immigrants to the Boston Area" (2003),

Gastón Institute Publications, Paper 134, pp. 5–6, available at http://scholarworks
.umb.edu.

9. Lexie McGovern, "Roberto Flores Interview Report," 2003; Cecilia Dos Santos,
    "Rosa Flores Interview Report," 2003, both in Urban Borderlands Records,
    TDCA, Fall 2003, box 001.

10. Uriarte et al., "Salvadorans, Guatemalans, Hondurans, and Colombians," 5–6;
    Hernandez, "Quiet Crisis," 161–62.

11. Alejandro Portes and Reubén Rumbaut, *Immigrant America: A Portrait,* 3rd ed.
    (Berkeley: University of California Press, 2006), 135; Uriarte et al., "Salvadorans,
    Guatemalans, Hondurans, and Colombians," 6–7; James P. Allen and Eugene
    Turner, "Boston's Emerging Ethnic Quilt: A Geographic Perspective," paper pre-
    sented at the annual meeting of the Population Association of America (Boston,
    2004), 4, 7; Hernandez, "Quiet Crisis," 165.

12. Uriarte, "Contra Viento y Marea," 5, 6; Uriarte et al., "Salvadorans, Guatemalans,
    Hondurans, and Colombians," 1; Irene Bloemraad, "The New Face of Greater
    Boston: Meeting the Needs of Immigrants," in *Governing Greater Boston,* ed.
    Charles C. Euchner (Cambridge, MA: Rappaport Institute for Greater Boston,
    2003), 80. Latino population data for Boston is from the *US Census of Population
    and Housing,* 1970 (Spanish language speaking) and from "Selected Social
    Characteristics in the United States," 2012 ACS 5-year estimates.

13. Maxine L. Margolis, *Goodbye Brazil: Emigres from the Land of Soccer and Samba*
    (Madison: University of Wisconsin Press, 2013), 52–54; Carlos Eduardo Siqueira
    and Tiago Jansen, "Updating Demographic, Geographic and Occupational Data
    on Brazilians in Massachusetts," 108–13; and Sueli Siqueira, "Emigrants from
    Governador Valadares: Projects of Return and Investment," 178, both in *Becoming
    Brazuca: Brazilian Immigrants to the United States,* ed. Clemence Jouet-Pastre
    and Leticia J. Braga (Cambridge: Harvard University Press, 2008); "ESL Students
    Reflect Changing Face of Immigration in MetroWest," *MetroWest Daily News,* 30
    September 2010.

14. Zhongxin Wang, "A History of Chinese Churches in Boston, 1876–1994" (Ph.D.
    diss., Boston University, 2000), 218–21; Jennifer Holdaway, "China: Outside the
    People's Republic of China," in Waters, Ueda, and Marrow, *The New Americans,*
    357; David Reimers, *Still the Golden Door: The Third World Comes to America* (New
    York: Columbia University Press, 1992), 21–22; Rose Hum Lee, *The Chinese in the
    United States of American* (New York: Hong Kong University Press, 1960), 90.

15. Paula Bock and Ken Brusic, *The Asians: Quincy's Newest Immigrants* (Quincy:
    [Patriot Ledger], 1989), 4, 25; Holdaway, "China," 357–58, 360–62; Ueda, *Postwar
    Immigrant America,* 45.

16. Xiao-huang Yin, "China: People's Republic of China," in Waters, Ueda, and
    Marrow, *The New Americans,* 342–44, 346; "Illegal Immigrants Flood Chinatown,"
    Boston Globe, 12 November 1994; Brigit Zinzius, *Chinese America: Stereotype and
    Reality* (New York: Peter Lang, 2005), 280.

17. Reubén Rumbaut, "Vietnam," in Waters, Ueda, and Marrow, *The New Americans,*

654; Commonwealth of Massachusetts, Office for Refugees and Immigrants (ORI), "1997 Demographic Update: Refugees and Immigrants in Massachusetts" (1997), 8, 16; ORI, "Refugees and Immigrants in Massachusetts: A Demographic Report" (1989), 4.

18. Patrick M. McGroarty, "A Lion in Fields Corner: Building a Vietnamese Community in the New Boston" (senior honors thesis, Boston College, 2006), 12–13; Karin Aguilar-San Juan, *Little Saigons: Staying Vietnamese in America* (Minneapolis: University of Minnesota Press, 2009), 18–20; Rumbaut, "Vietnam," 654; "Thieu Looks Back, Ahead, from Newton Exile," *Boston Globe,* 25 November 1992; "Nyugen van Thieu, 78, South Vietnam Leader," *Boston Globe,* 1 October 2001.

19. Bock and Brusic, *The Asians,* 7, 9, 11.

20. Karin Aguilar-San Juan, "Creating Ethnic Places: Vietnamese American Community-Building in Orange County and Boston" (Ph.D. diss., Brown University, 2000), 48–49, 76; Sucheng Chan, *Survivors: Cambodian Refugees in the United States* (Chicago: University of Illinois Press, 2004), 97, 98; Rumbaut, "Vietnam," 654; Nancy J. Smith-Hefner, *Khmer Americans: Identity and Moral Education in a Diasporic Community* (Berkeley: University of California Press, 1999), 8; Henry Schipper, "The Boat People of Boston," *Boston Magazine,* June 1980, 127; Commonwealth of Massachusetts, Office of Refugee and Immigrant Health, *Refugees and Immigrants in Massachusetts: An Overview of Selected Communities* (1991), 1.

21. Aguilar-San Juan, "Creating Ethnic Places," 49; Rumbaut, "Vietnam," 654, 658; Bock and Brusic, *The Asians,* 10; "Amerasians Reach for Opportunity," *Boston Globe,* 8 July 1991.

22. Paul Watanabe, Michael Liu, and Shauna Lo, "Asian Americans in Metro Boston: Growth, Diversity, and Complexity" (2004), *Institute for Asian American Studies Publications,* Paper 16, pp. 4, 5, 17, available at http://scholarworks.umb.edu; Bloemraad, "The New Face of Greater Boston," 83; "Ethnic Journal's Time to Make Choices," *Boston Globe,* 6 November 2005; Nancy Foner, *From Ellis Island to JFK: New York's Two Great Waves of Immigration* (New Haven: Yale University Press, 2000), 25.

23. Andrew Sum et al., *The Changing Face of Massachusetts* (Boston: MassINC, 2005), 8; Watanabe et al., "Asian Americans in Metro Boston," 4; *US Census of Population and Housing,* 1970; 2012 ACS 5-year estimates.

24. Regine O. Jackson, "The Uses of Diaspora among Haitians in Boston," in *Geographies of the Haitian Diaspora,* ed. Regine O. Jackson (New York: Routledge, 2011), 141–44; Boston Redevelopment Authority, Research Division, *Imagine All the People: Haitian Immigrants in Boston* (Boston: BRA, 2007), 1–3.

25. Gina Sánchez Gibau, "Contested Identities: Narratives of Race and Ethnicity in the Cape Verdean Diaspora," *Identities: Global Studies in Culture and Power* 12 (July 2005): 410; census data from 2012 ACS 5-year estimates (figures are for "black or African American alone" and do not include those who selected multiple race categories).

26. BRA, *Gateway City: Boston's Immigrants, 1988–1998* (Boston: BRA, 1999), 15–16; ORI, "1997 Demographic Update," 18; Bloemraad, "The New Face of Greater Boston," 83; "Illegal Irish Fear Deportation," *Boston Globe,* 24 August 1987.

27. Ella Kagan, "The Russian-Jewish Experience," in *Short Stories of a Long Journey: An Oral History of Russian Jewish Resettlement North of Boston,* ed. Bernice Kazis (Swampscott, MA: Hand-in-Hand Oral History Project, 2002), 8–9; Marilyn Halter, "Ethnicity and the Entrepreneur: Self-Employment among Former Soviet Jewish Refugees," in *New Migrants in the Marketplace,* ed. Marilyn Halter (Amherst: University of Massachusetts Press, 1995), 44–46; ORI, "1997 Demographic Update," 18.

28. Morales, "Puerto Rican Poverty and Migration to Elsewhere," 71–73, 76, 190; Uriarte, "Contra Viento y Marea," 6, 7; Levitt, *The Transnational Villagers,* 38–44; Peggy Levitt, "Dominican Republic," in Waters, Ueda, and Marrow, *The New Americans,* 399–401.

29. Portes and Rumbaut, *Immigrant America,* 18; Foner, *From Ellis Island to JFK,* 24–25.

30. Luis Eduardo Guarnizo and Marilyn Espitia, "Colombia," in Waters, Ueda, and Marrow, *The New Americans,* 374; Teresa Sales, *Brazilians away from Home* (New York: Center for Migration Studies, 2004), 25–27; Zolberg, "Immigration Control Policy," 36.

31. Rubén Rumbaut, "Origins and Destinies: Immigration to the United States since World War II," in *New American Destinies: A Reader in Contemporary Asian and Latino Immigration,* ed. Darrell Y. Hamamoto and Rodolfo D. Torres (New York: Routledge, 1997), 27–28.

32. Levitt, *The Transnational Villagers,* 38–44; Levitt, "Dominican Republic," 399–401; Uriarte, "Contra Viento y Marea," 7.

33. Uriarte, "Contra Viento y Marea, 7; Lisa Konczal and Alex Stepnick, "Haiti," in Waters, Ueda, and Marrow, *The New Americans,* 448.

34. Portes and Rumbaut, *Immigrant America,* 26; Rumbaut, "Origins and Destinies," 27–28; BRA, *Gateway City,* 30.

35. In a few migrant groups, such as Puerto Ricans, working-class newcomers blazed the trail for some of the more educated professionals who came later. "They Came, They Saw, They Stayed to Help," *Boston Globe,* 9 May 1977; Foner, *From Ellis Island to JFK,* 28. On migrant homeland clusters, see Levitt, *The Transnational Villagers,* 2; Sales, *Brazilians away from Home,* 17–18; Sebastián Chaskel, "From Yucuaiquín to Somerville: Religious Beliefs and Traditions of a Transnational Community," final project report, Urban Borderlands, Tufts University, Fall 2004, 22–24, available at http://dl.tufts.edu.

36. "New Irish Leaving Boston as Economy Slows," *Boston Globe,* 5 February 1990; Jackson, "The Uses of Diaspora among Haitians in Boston," 155–57 (Haitian quotation); *Middlesex News,* "The Changing Face of Framingham" (reprints from the Middlesex News Diversity Series, April 1995), 13 (Latina quotation).

37. "Saigon to Massachusetts—Danger Rode with Boat People," *Boston Globe,* 15 July 1979; Schipper, "The Boat People of Boston," 94–97, 127–34; Bock and Brusic, *The Asians,* 7, 9.

38. David W. Haines, "Refugees," in Waters, Ueda, and Marrow, *The New Americans,* 56–58, 66; "'Gateway' Opens for Refugees," *Boston Globe,* 7 July 1986; "Cutbacks in the Promised Land," *Boston Globe,* 12 August 1989.

39. Quotation from June Namias, ed., *First Generation: In the Words of Twentieth Century American Immigrants* (Boston: Beacon Press, 1978), 206; Jean Larson Pyle, "Public Policy and Local Economics: The Phenomenon of Secondary Migration," in *Southeast Asian Refugees and Immigrants in the Mill City,* ed. Tuyet-Lan Pho, Jeffrey N. Gerson, and Sylvia R. Cowan (Burlington: University of Vermont Press, 2007), 19–38; Chan, *Survivors,* 102, 104. Secondary migration to Boston was also common among Somali refugees in the 1990s; see "Somali Community Sinks Roots in Hub," *Bay State Banner,* 3 August 2000.

40. Piore, "Immigration, Work Expectations and Labor Market Structure," 114; Uriarte, "Contra Viento y Marea," 7; "Hispanics in Massachusetts Face Uphill Battle," *Boston Globe,* 15 January 1978; "Haitians in Boston," *Boston Globe,* 29 August 1971.

41. Uriarte et al., "Salvadorans, Guatemalans, Hondurans, and Colombians," 9; "Refugee Policy Considered," *Boston Globe,* 17 March 1984; "Hearings Are Sought on Refugees Status," *Boston Globe,* 3 April 1984; "Many Haitians in Boston Area Ruled by Invisibility, Isolation," *Boston Globe,* 9 February 1986. Most Salvadorans became eligible for Temporary Protective Status (TPS) in 1990, a provision that allowed them to stay in the country legally until the end of hostilities in El Salvador.

42. Enrico Marcelli et al., *(In)Visible (Im)Migrants: The Health and Socioeconomic Integration of Brazilians in Metropolitan Boston* (San Diego, CA: Center for Behavioral and Community Health Studies, San Diego State University, 2009), 8, 15–16; and Marcelli et al., *Permanently Temporary? The Health and Socioeconomic Integration of Dominicans in Metropolitan Boston* (San Diego, CA: Center for Behavioral and Community Health Studies, San Diego State University, 2009), 9, 16.

43. "Illegal Irish Fear Deportation," *Boston Globe,* 24 August 1987; "INS Officials Question 11 Irish Nationals in Smuggling Probe," *Boston Globe,* 18 October 1987; "Illegal Immigrants Flood Chinatown," *Boston Globe,* 12 November 1994; "4 Charged in Smuggling Chinese Immigrants Were Headed for Massachusetts," *Boston Globe,* 20 November 1996; "Testimony Details Hardships of Crossing," *Boston Globe,* 30 April 1997.

44. Portes and Rumbaut, *Immigrant America,* 358–60; Blanca Alvarado, "Exploitation in the Shadows: Unauthorized Latina Migrants Tell Their Stories" (Ph.D. diss., Boston University, 2007), 60–61, 81–104, 112.

45. "Migrants Going North Now Risk Kidnappings," *New York Times,* 17 October 2009; "A Slip Ends American Dream," *MetroWest Daily News,* 19 December 2006.

3. THE METROPOLITAN DIASPORA

1. "Deepening Roots: Like the Irish and Italians before Them, Eastie's Latinos Are Forsaking Homeland Dreams to Move from Renting to Owning," *Boston*

Globe, 1 December 2002; Ramón Borges-Méndez, "East Boston," in *Immigrant Entre-preneurs and Neighborhood Revitalization*, ed. Ramón Borges-Méndez, Michael Liu, and Paul Watanabe (Malden, MA: Immigrant Learning Center, 2005), available at www.ilctr.org.

2. Miren Uriarte, "Contra Viento y Marea (Against All Odds): Latinos Build Community in Boston," in *Latinos in Boston: Confronting Poverty, Building Community* (Boston: Boston Foundation Persistent Poverty Project, Boston Foundation, 1992), 7; Felix V. Matos Rodriguez, "Saving the Parcela: A Short History of Boston's Puerto Rican Community," in *The Puerto Rican Diaspora*, ed. Carmen Teresa Whalen and Victor Vazquez-Hernandez (Philadelphia: Temple University Press, 2005), 204, 209; Mario Small, *Villa Victoria: The Transformation of Social Capital in a Boston Barrio* (Chicago: University of Chicago Press, 2004): 22–23.

3. Deborah Pacini Hernandez, "Quiet Crisis: A Community History of Latinos in Cambridge, Massachusetts," in *Latinos in New England*, ed. Andrés Torres (Philadelphia: Temple University Press, 2006), 152, 159, 162; Andrew Hara, Ariana Flores, Galen Maze, and Radhika Thakkar, "The Evolution of the Latino Community in Cambridge, Massachusetts," Final Report, Spring 2002, Urban Borderlands Records, Tufts University, Digital Collections and Archives (TDCA), Medford, MA, available at http://dl.tufts.edu; "Cambridge Votes to Be a Sanctuary," *Boston Globe*, 9 April 1985. In subsequent years, Brookline, Somerville, and Chelsea would also vote to become sanctuary cities.

4. Ferreira, quoted in Daniel B. Becker, "The Brazilian Immigrant Experience: A Study on the Evolution of a Brazilian Community in Somerville and the Greater Boston Area," Fall 2006, 48, Urban Borderlands Records, TDCA, available at http://dca.lib.tufts.edu; "A Tradition Called the Hudson Portuguese Club," *Boston Globe*, 24 March 1979; Leo Pap, *The Portuguese Americans* (Boston: Twayne, 1981), 100.

5. Regine O. Jackson, "After the Exodus: The New Catholics in Boston's Old Ethnic Neighborhoods," *Religion and American Culture* 17.2 (Summer 2007): 192, 195, 197–98.

6. Zhongxin Wang, "A History of Chinese Churches in Boston, 1876–1994" (Ph.D. diss., Boston University, 2000), 222–24; Jennifer Holdaway, "China: Outside the People's Republic of China," in *The New Americans: A Guide to Immigration since 1965*, ed. Mary Waters, Reed Ueda, and Helen Marrow (Cambridge: Harvard University Press, 2007), 368–69; Karen Aguilar-San Juan, *Little Saigons: Staying Vietnamese in America* (Minneapolis: University of Minnesota Press, 2009), 56, 134.

7. Henry Schipper, "The Boat People of Boston," *Boston Magazine*, June 1980, 97, 128; Don Nanstad, interview by author, 9 June 2010; "East Boston Negotiates Its Own Ethnic Truce," *Boston Globe*, 17 April 1991.

8. "Agencies Accused of Dumping Refugees," *Boston Globe*, 1 July 1980; "Hub's Asian Refugees: Some Given a Hard Time," *Boston Globe*, 31 May 1983.

9. Irene Bloemraad, *Becoming a Citizen* (Berkeley: University of California Press, 2006), 128–30.

10. Nancy Smith-Hefner, *Khmer Americans: Identity and Moral Education in a Diasporic Community* (Berkeley: University of California Press, 1999), 25–26.

11. Bernice Kazis, *Short Stories of a Long Journey* (Swampscott, MA: Hand-in-Hand Oral History Project, 2002), 10, 11, 16–18, 65–66.

12. Ibid., 23–29, 77–79.

13. "Haitians in Boston," *Boston Globe*, 29 August 1971; "Hub's Haitians: A People Apart," *Boston Globe*, 11 December 1980; "Mattapan Square Thrives Long after Supposed Demise," *Boston Globe*, 2 March 1985; Gina Sánchez Gibau, "Contested Identities: Narratives of Race and Ethnicity in the Cape Verdean Community," *Identities: Global Studies in Culture and Power* 12 (July 2005): 411–12. For more on BBURG, see Hillel Levine and Lawrence Harmon, *The Death of an American Jewish Community: A Tragedy of Good Intentions* (New York: Free Press, 1992); and Gerald Gamm, *Urban Exodus: Why the Jews Left Boston and the Catholics Stayed* (Cambridge: Harvard University Press, 1999).

14. Boston 200 Corporation, *Chinatown* (Boston: Boston 200 Neighborhood History Series, 1976), 12; "Chinatown Fights on Many Fronts," *Boston Globe*, 2 April 1979; "Chinatown Is at a Crossroads," *Boston Globe*, 2 August 1987; "The Fight for Chinatown," *Boston Globe*, 23 October 1994.

15. Jeffrey P. Brown, *Profile of Boston's Chinatown Neighborhood* (Boston: BRA, 1987); "Boston's Chinese Face Severe Job Problems," *Boston Globe*, 25 November 1970; "Chinatown Fights on Many Fronts," *Boston Globe*, 2 April 1979; "Chinatown Is at a Crossroads," *Boston Globe*, 2 August 1987; Boston Redevelopment Authority (BRA), *New Bostonians 2005* (Boston: Mayor's Office of New Bostonians, 2005), 26; BRA, *New Bostonians 2012* (Boston: Mayor's Office of New Bostonians, 2012). For a detailed, insightful analysis of redevelopment in Boston's Chinatown, see Thomas C. Chen, "Remaking Boston's Chinatown: Race, Place, and Community in the Postwar Metropolis" (Ph.D. diss., Brown University, 2014).

16. Small, *Villa Victoria*, 27–42; Rodriguez, "Saving the Parcela," 211–13; Uriarte, "Contra Viento y Marea," 15; "Villa Victoria: Where Families Stay," *Boston Globe*, 16 April 1982.

17. Hernandez, "Quiet Crisis," 153–55; "MIT Leaves behind a Rich History in Tech Square," *MIT News*, 17 March 2004, available at http://web.mit.edu; Nelson Salazar, interview by Andrew Hara, Maira Perez, and Marisela Perez, March 2002, p. 18, Urban Borderlands Records, TDCA, 2002, box 001.

18. Michael Liu, "Allston Village," in Borges-Méndez, Liu, and Watanabe, *Immigrant Entrepreneurs and Neighborhood Revitalization*, 8.

19. Uriarte, "Contra Viento y Marea," 16; Peggy Levitt, *The Transnational Villagers* (Berkeley: University of California Press, 2001), 48–50; Hernandez, "Quiet Crisis," 159; BRA, "Boston's Population—2000," report no. 555, May 2002, B4; "More Hispanics Are Taking Root in Roxbury," *Boston Globe*, 9 September 1996.

20. Miren Uriarte et al., "Salvadorans, Guatemalans, Hondurans, and Colombians: A Scan of Needs of Recent Latin American Immigrants to the Boston Area" (2003), *Gastón Institute Publications*, Paper 134, p. 14, available at http://scholarworks.umb.edu.

21. "Chao from Dot. Ave," *Boston Globe,* 12 September 1993.

22. Aguilar-San Juan, *Little Saigons,* xvi–xvii; Patrick Michael McGroarty, "A Lion in Fields Corner: Building a Vietnamese Community in the New Boston" (senior honors thesis, Boston College, 2006), 17, 65–66; BRA, "Imagine All the People: Foreign Born in Boston" (Boston: Mayor's Office of New Bostonians, 2007), 13; "Q & A with Long Nguyen on Building the First Vietnamese Center," *Boston Globe,* 18 July 1999.

23. BRA, "Imagine All the People," 13; BRA, *New Bostonians 2005,* 28.

24. BRA, *New Bostonians 2005,* 7; Nancy McCardle, "Race, Place, and Opportunity: Racial Change and Segregation in the Boston Metropolitan Area, 1990–2000" (2003), available at http://civilrightsproject.ucla.edu.

25. 2012 ACS 5-year estimates; US Census Bureau, *Census of Population and Housing 1910,* vol. 4, Massachusetts, 869, 893–94, available at www.census.gov. Although not part of this study, similar patterns of immigrant settlement have characterized the old mill cities of Lowell, Lawrence, and Brockton. Interestingly, these outlying communities have developed their own distinctive ethnic profiles. Lawrence became predominantly Dominican and Latino; Lowell attracted a heavily Cambodian and Southeast Asian population, while Brockton became home to Cape Verdeans, Haitians, and other immigrants of African descent. Such profiles suggest that once ethnic beachheads were established, kin-based networks have been central to mill town settlement patterns.

26. "Escalating Rents Drive Immigrants out of Boston, City Officials Say," *Boston Globe,* 25 March 1989; Leslie Bauman and Chelsea Commission on Hispanic Affairs, *Chelsea Hispanics: Who Are They? A Demographic Portrait* (Boston: Center for Community Planning and Collaborative for Community Service and Development, College of Public and Community Service, University of Massachusetts Boston, 1990), 16.

27. Beth Siegel, Barbara Baran, and Suzanne Teegarden, "Small Cities, Big Problems: Urban Economic Development Is Tougher outside the Metropolis," *Commonwealth* (Spring 2001), available at www.commonwealthmagazine.org; Miren Uriarte and Ramón Borges-Méndez, "Tales of Latinos in Three Small Cities," *Color Lines Conference: Segregation and Integration in America's Present and Future, August 29–September 1, 1983, Harvard University* (Cambridge, MA: Civil Rights Project, 2003), 2.

28. Barry Bluestone and Mary Huff Stevenson, *The Boston Renaissance: Race, Space, and Economic Change in an American Metropolis* (New York: Russell Sage, 2000), 93.

29. Institute for Asian American Studies, *Chinese Americans in Massachusetts* (Boston: University of Massachusetts Boston, 2006), 7–8; American FactFinder, 2010 Demographic Profile Data for Lexington, available at http://factfinder. census.gov; James P. Allen and Eugene Turner, "Boston's Emerging Ethnic Quilt: A Geographic Perspective," paper presented at the Annual Meeting of the Population Society of America (Boston, 2004), 5; and *Boston Globe* articles:

"International Influx of Students Hits Some Schools," 25 March 1990; "Moving Out and Moving Up: Asian Americans Establish Growing Presence in Suburbs," 19 May 1991 (Ho quotation); "Vibrant New Look of Western Suburbs: Immigrants Alter Region Culturally and Economically," 28 November 1999 (Indians quotation); "A High-Tech Home for Indians," 22 July 2000; "An Educated Move," 7 May 2001; "Driven to Prosper: A Growing Immigrant Enclave Makes Its Mark on the City," 23 September 2006.

30. Bluestone and Stevenson, *The Boston Renaissance*, 93, 99; Massachusetts Advisory Committee to the US Commission on Civil Rights and the Massachusetts Commission against Discrimination, "Route 128: Boston's Road to Segregation," Joint Report, 1975, 37–39, 42, 44–46.

31. Tom L. Chung, "Asian Americans in Enclaves—They Are Not One Community: New Modes of Asian-American Settlement," *Asian American Policy Review* 5 (1995): 78–94.

32. H. Hobart Holly et al., *Quincy's Legacy* (Quincy, MA: Quincy Historical Society, 1998), 11, 13–14, 134, 138–39; Atlantic Junior High School, "An Ethnic History of Quincy," 1976, and Louis A. George, "The Contributions to the City by Citizens of Lebanese Descent," 1961, both located in box 5, shelf 106, Quincy Historical Society.

33. Holly, *Quincy's Legacy*, 14–15, 86, 94, 119, 140; Anthony F. Sarcone and Lawrence R. Rines, "A History of Shipbuilding at Fore River," Thomas Crane Public Library, http://thomascranelibrary.org; "Asian Influx Helps Raise City Census by 3,178," *Patriot Ledger*, 7 August 1985.

34. "Asian Influx Forging a New Community in Historic Quincy," *Boston Globe*, 8 March 1998; "Asian Influx Helps Raise City Census by 3178," *Patriot Ledger*, 7 August 1985; Paula Bock and Ken Brusic, *The Asians: Quincy's Newest Immigrants* (Quincy: [Patriot Ledger], 1989), 19; *US Census of Population and Housing*, 1960, 1980.

35. Chi-kan Richard Hung, "Separate but Connected: Challenges amid Progress for Chinese American Enclaves in Boston," paper presented at New Immigrants in Urban New England Conference, Brown University, 16 April 2004), 5–6, available at www.brown.edu; "Asian Influx Forging a New Community in Historic Quincy," *Boston Globe*, 8 March 1998; "City's Growing Asian Population Keeps a Low Profile," *Patriot Ledger*, 18 March 1988; Bock and Brusic, *The Asians*, 7–8, 17, 19.

36. "Lutheran Church to Help Asians," *Patriot Ledger*, 27 February 1988; "Ministering to Newcomers," *Patriot Ledger*, 12 May 1988; Bock and Brusic, *The Asians*, 7–8; Hung, "Separate but Connected," 7; Shauna Lo, *Chinese Americans in Massachusetts* (Boston: Institute for Asian American Studies, University of Massachusetts Boston, 2006), 5.

37. Paul Watanabe, Michael Liu, and Shauna Lo, "Asian Americans in Metro Boston: Growth, Diversity and Complexity," paper prepared for the Boston Equity Initiative of the Harvard Civil Rights Project, May 2004, 3; "Immigrants from India in a Growing Community in Quincy," *Patriot Ledger*, 2 July 2003; "Arab Americans: A Family Tree of Immigrants with Deep Community Roots," *Patriot Ledger*, 29–30 September 2001.

38. "Chinatown South: Many Anticipate Quincy Is Becoming the Next Chinatown," *Patriot Ledger,* 28 June 2003; "Flushing: A Model for Quincy? NYC's Other Chinatown Could Be a Pattern for Quincy," *Patriot Ledger,* 29 June 2003.

39. Wei Li, *Ethnoburb: The New Ethnic Community in Urban America* (Honolulu: University of Hawaii Press, 2009); Bock and Brusic, *The Asians,* 6, 12.

40. Stephen W. Herring, *Framingham: An American Town* (Framingham, MA: Framingham Historical Society, 2000), 155, 212–13, 235–36, 295; Gloria Vollmers, "Industrial Home Work of the Dennison Manufacturing Company of Framingham, Massachusetts, 1912–1935," *Business History Review* 71.3 (Autumn 1997): 446.

41. Herring, *Framingham,* 308, 317, 356–57.

42. Ibid., 313–15, 322–23.

43. Ibid., 328, 353–54.

44. Middlesex News Diversity Series, *The Changing Face of Framingham* (1995), 7, 12, 13, 19, available at Framingham Public Library; 2012 ACS 5-year estimates.

45. Teresa Sales, *Brazilians away from Home* (New York: Center for Migration Studies, 2003), 133; Joel Millman, *The Other Americans: How Immigrants Renew Our Country, Our Economy, and Our Values* (New York: Viking, 1997), 229–30; Herring, *Framingham,* 359–60; Teresa Sales and Márcia Loureiro, "Between Dream and Reality: Adolescent and Second Generation Brazilian Immigrants in Massachusetts," in *Becoming Brazuca: Brazilian Immigration to the United States,* ed. Clemence Joüet-Pastré and Leticia J. Braga (Cambridge: Harvard University Press, 2008), 296.

46. Carlos Eduardo Siqueira and Tiago Jansen, "Updating Demographic, Geographic, and Occupational Data on Brazilians in Massachusetts," in *Becoming Brazuca,* 114–15; Sales, *Brazilians away from Home,* 54; Herring, *Framingham,* 360; Middlesex News Diversity Series, *The Changing Face of Framingham,* 29; "North of the Border," *Boston Globe,* 14 April 2005; "Like Long-Lost Friends: Brazilian City Mayor Tours Framingham as Part of Partnership," *MetroWest Daily News,* 3 December 2004. A 2007 study of Brazilians in Metro Boston said that about 70 percent of migrants surveyed were undocumented and estimated the total migrant population at 64,000, a percentage that is 29 percent higher than the 2000 census figures. Enrico Marcelli et al., *(In)Visible (Im)Migrants: The Health and Socioeconomic Integration of Brazilians in Metropolitan Boston* (San Diego, CA: Center for Behavioral and Community Health Studies, 2009), 42; "ESL Students Reflect Changing Face of Immigration in MetroWest," *MetroWest Daily News,* 30 September 2010.

47. Ruth Randall, *Malden: From Primitive Past to Progressive Present* (Malden, MA: Malden Historic Society, 1975), 50, 87, 90, 101; Richard Klayman, *The First Jew: Prejudice and Politics in an American Jewish Community, 1900–1932* (Malden, MA: Old Suffolk Square Press, 1985), 9, 50, 59; Richard Klayman, *A Generation of Hope* (Malden, MA: Old Suffolk Square Press, 1987), 79; Daniel A. Farbman, "Between Classes: A Cultural History of American High School Students, 1955–1980" (Ph.D. diss., Brown University, 1999), 57.

48. Massachusetts Historical Commission, "MHC Reconnaissance Survey Town Report: Malden" (1980), 10, available at www.sec.state.ma.us.

49. Randall, *Malden,* 119–26, 136, 138; "Malden: A City Restored," *Boston Globe,* 6 April 1972; Farbman, "Between Classes," 60.

50. Watanabe, Liu, and Lo, "Asian Americans in Metro Boston," 5; Hung, "Separate but Connected," 6; Sheryl Dong, "The Lines of Migration," typescript, Quincy Public Library, 2, 4, 7.

51. "A Place Where All Belong, Immigrants Transforming Malden Anew," *Boston Globe,* 23 December 2009; 2000 and 2010 census figures from American FactFinder.

52. Watanabe, Liu, and Lo, "Asian Americans in Metro Boston," 5; Becker, "The Brazilian Immigrant Experience," 49; 2012 ACS 5-year estimates.

4. IMMIGRANTS AND WORK IN THE NEW ECONOMY

1. Barry Bluestone and Mary Huff Stevenson, *The Boston Renaissance* (New York: Russell Sage, 2000), 54; "The Maynard Web: A History of the Mill," http://web.maynard.ma.us.

2. Bluestone and Stevenson, *The Boston Renaissance,* 59–66.

3. Aviva Chomsky, *Linked Labor Histories* (Durham, NC: Duke University Press, 2008), 152; Lake Coreth, "Chelsea under Fire: Urban Industrial Life, Urban Crisis, and the Trajectory of Jewish and Latino Chelsea" (senior honors thesis, Boston College, 2011), 60.

4. Ramón Borges-Méndez, "Urban and Regional Restructuring and Barrio Formation in Massachusetts: The Cases of Lowell, Lawrence, and Holyoke" (Ph.D. diss., MIT, 1994), 115–16; Chomsky, *Linked Labor Histories,* 16, 152, 164–65; Peggy Levitt, *The Transnational Villagers* (Berkeley: University of California Press, 2001), 48–49; Julio Morales Jr., "Puerto Rican Poverty and the Migration to Elsewhere: Waltham, Massachusetts: A Case Study" (Ph.D. diss., Brandeis University, 1979), 222 (Suncha quotation).

5. Margarita C. Lam, "Chinese Immigrant Women in the Garment Industry in Boston, 1965–1985" (honors thesis, Harvard College, 1991), 2, 17–18, 46–47, 52–53, 60–63.

6. Lam, "Chinese Immigrant Women in the Garment Industry," 66–68, 72–73; "Boston Garment Industry Workers Being Retrained," *Boston Globe,* 26 September 1986; "Laid-Off Garment Workers Celebrate Retraining Benefits Won after Fight," *Boston Globe,* 2 November 1986; Paula Bock and Ken Brusic, *The Asians: Quincy's Newest Immigrants* (Quincy: [Patriot Ledger], 1989), 33 (Seto quotation).

7. Joan Cuozzo, *Hispanics in Chelsea: Income and Employment* (Boston: University of Massachusetts Boston and Chelsea Commission on Hispanic Affairs, 1990), 28–29; Miren Uriarte, "Contra Viento y Marea (Against All Odds): Latinos Build Community in Boston," in *Latinos in Boston,* ed. Miren Uriarte et al. (Boston: Boston Persistent Poverty Project, Boston Foundation, 1992), 11–12; Ramón Borges

Méndez and Miren Uriarte, "Tales of Latinos in Three Small Cities," *Color Lines Conference: Segregation and Integration in America's Present and Future,* August 29–September 1, 1983, Harvard University (Cambridge, MA: Civil Rights Project, 2003), 8. On recruitment of Asian workers by high-tech firms, see Sucheng Chan, *Survivors: Cambodian Refugees in the United States* (Champagne: University of Illinois Press, 2004), 103; Bock and Brusic, *The Asians,* 30; untitled report on Jobs for Americans program, box 2, folder 1, Indochinese Refugee Foundation Papers, Center for Lowell History, Lowell, MA.

8. Andrew Sum et al., *The Changing Face of Massachusetts* (Boston: MassINC, 2005), 27.

9. Barbara Ehrenreich and Arlie Hochschild, eds., *Nannies, Maids, and Sex Workers in the New Economy* (New York: Macmillan, 2002), 20; Chomsky, *Linked Labor Histories,* 10; *US Census of Population and Housing,* 1970; 2012 ACS 5-year estimates.

10. Cindy Rodriguez, "Janitors' New Voice," *Boston Globe,* 12 January 2002; Cynthia Cranford, "Economic Restructuring, Immigration and the New Labor Movement: Latina/o Janitors in Los Angeles," UC San Diego, Center for Comparative Immigration Studies, 2000, available at http://escholarship.org; Tom Beadling et al., *A Need for Valor: The Roots of the Service Employees International Union, 1902–1992* (Washington, DC: Service Employees International Union, 1992).

11. "Life's No Fare for Struggling Cabdrivers," *Boston Globe,* 14 December 1992; Chris Berdik, "Fare Game?" *Boston Magazine,* September 2004, available at www.bostonmagazine.com; Gintautus Dumcius, "City Cab Drivers Rally for Fair Play," *Boston Haitian Reporter,* July 2007, 9; "Hard Hit by Gas Prices, Taxi Drivers Demanding Pay Hikes," *Boston Haitian Reporter,* July 2008, 9 (Chando quotation); "A World of Fares and of Grinding Unfairness," *Boston Globe,* 31 March 2013.

12. "Haitian Nursing Assistants Seek Workplace Respect," *Boston Globe,* 9 November 2003; "Healthy Outlook: Haitian Emigres Flock to Job Training," *Boston Globe,* 31 December 2001; Ramón Borges-Méndez et al., "Immigrant Workers in the Massachusetts Health Care Industry: A Report on Status and Future Prospects" (2009), *Center for Social Policy Publications,* Paper 1, pp. 11, 12, 13–15, available at http://scholarworks.umb.edu.

13. "For Ethiopian Parking Jobs Held Key to American Dream," *Boston Globe,* 25 April 2002.

14. Bock and Brusic, *The Asians,* 34; "Shift from Farm Work Yields Few Gains," *Boston Globe,* 29 May 1997; "Shadow Work Force Faces a Daily Grind: Illegal Immigrants Rely on Temp Jobs," *Boston Globe,* 24 October 1999; "Undocumented, Not Invisible," *Boston Globe,* 25 February 2001; "Undocumented and Unprotected: An Underground Economy of Improperly Classified Workers Cheats Labor and Taxpayers Alike," *Boston Globe,* 16 November 2006; "Fake IDs are Rife at State Job Sites," *Boston Globe,* 18 June 2006; "The Illegals," *Patriot Ledger,* 22 October 1988; "No Man's Land," *Patriot Ledger,* 27 July 2002; Miren Uriarte et al., "Salvadorans,

Guatemalans, Hondurans, and Colombians: A Scan of Needs of Recent Latin American Immigrants to the Boston Area" (2003), *Gastón Institute Publications,* Paper 134, p. 43 (Colombian quotation), available at http://scholarworks.umb.edu.

15. "Constitutional Battle in Immigration Court," *Boston Globe,* 11 December 1989; "Plant Depicted as "Sweatshop," *Patriot Ledger,* 7 March 2007; "350 Are Held in Immigration Raid," *Boston Globe,* 7 March 2007.

16. Uriarte et al., "Salvadorans, Guatemalans, Hondurans and Colombians," 44; "The Illegals," *Patriot Ledger,* 22 October 1988; "No Man's Land," *Patriot Ledger,* 27 July 2002; "Living in America, Toiling in a New Land," *Patriot Ledger,* 22 May 2004. On women workers, see "Immigrant Women Emerge from Shadow of Abuse," *Boston Globe,* 22 February 1992 (Philbin quotation); "Dream Is Shattered for Salvadoran Woman," *Boston Globe,* 17 November 1997.

17. Boston Redevelopment Authority, *New Bostonians 2012* (Boston: Mayor's Office of New Bostonians, 2012), 30.

18. Michael Liu and Paul Watanabe, "The Rise of Asian-Owned Businesses in Massachusetts: Data from the 2002 Economic Census Survey of Business Owners" (2007), *Institute for Asian American Studies Publications,* Paper 8, pp. 6–7, available at http://scholarworks.umb.edu; "Essential Shuttle Serves Chinatown," *Boston Globe,* 9 March 1997; "Chinese Workers Decry Conditions in Hub," *Boston Globe,* 3 September 1998.

19. "Vietnamese Activists Look Past Nails, Floors," *Boston Globe,* 1 August 2005; Karen Jung Wan Chai, "Protestant-Catholic-Buddhist: Korean Americans and Religious Adaptation in Greater Boston" (Ph.D. diss., Harvard University, 2000), 5; Nathan James Bae Kupel, "Profiles of Asian American Subgroups in Massachusetts: Korean Americans in Massachusetts" (2010), *Institute for Asian American Studies Publications,* Paper 24, p. 4, available at http://scholarworks.umb.edu.

20. Alvaro Lima and Carlos Eduardo Siqueira, "Brazilians in the US and Massachusetts: A Demographic and Economic Profile" (2007) *Gastón Institute Publications,* Paper 50, p. 11, available at http://scholarworks.umb.edu; BRA Research Division, *Imagine All the People: Brazilian Immigrants in Boston* (Boston: BRA, 2006), 5.

21. Joel Millman, "Immigrant Group Puts New Spin on Cleaning Niche," *Wall Street Journal,* 16 February 2006; Joel Millman, *The Other Americans: How Immigrants Renew our Country, Our Economy and Our Values* (New York: Viking, 1997), 232–36.

22. Teresa Sales, *Brazilians away from Home* (New York: Center for Migration Studies, 2003), 179; Millman, "Immigrant Group Puts New Spin on Cleaning Niche"; "Co-op Has a Deal for Cleaners' Helpers; Brazilian Immigrants See New Business Model," *Boston Globe,* 22 March 2007; Enrico Marcelli et al., *(In)Visible (Im)Migrants: The Health and Socioeconomic Integration of Brazilians in Metropolitan Boston* (San Diego, CA: Center for Behavioral and Community Health Studies, 2009), 21–22.

23. Millman, *The Other Americans,* 248; "Brazilians Build Business Base in City," *Boston Globe,* 21 July 2002; "Brazilians Add a Touch of Home; Throughout Region New Immigrants Are Reshaping Their Communities," *Boston Globe,* 5 January 2006.

24. "Hard-Working Hispanic Merchants Make Hyde Square a Success," *Boston Globe*, 14 July 1975; Ramón Borges-Méndez, Michael Liu, and Paul Watanabe, eds., *Immigrant Entrepreneurs and Neighborhood Revitalization* (Malden, MA: Immigrant Learning Center, 2005), 3, 18–26, 28–41, available at www.ilctr.org.

25. Karin Aguilar-San Juan, "Creating Ethnic Places: Vietnamese-American Community Building in Orange County and Boston" (Ph.D. diss., Brown University, 2000), 119. "Boston's New Geography: Vietnamese Edge into Chinatown, Transforming an Enclave," *Boston Globe*, 1 February 1993; Borges-Méndez, Liu, and Watanabe, *Immigrant Entrepreneurs and Neighborhood Revitalization*, 5.

26. Sum, *The Changing Face of Massachusetts*, 28; Irene Bloemraad, "The New Face of Greater Boston: Meeting the Needs of Immigrants" in *Governing Greater Boston: Meeting the Needs of the Region's People*, ed. Charles C. Euchner (Cambridge, MA: Rappaport Institute for Greater Boston, 2003), 101.

27. David M. Reimers, *Still the Golden Door: The Third World Comes to America* (New York: Columbia University Press, 1985), 99–102; Ramón Borges-Méndez et al., "Immigrant Workers in the Massachusetts Health Care Industry," 11, 12, 13–15.

28. Robert A. Nakosteen and Andrew Sum, "Immigration's Impact on the Commonwealth," *Massachusetts Benchmarks* 4 (Spring 2001): 14; "Foreign-born Grads Stymied by Work Visas Quota," *Boston Globe*, 27 April 2007; "Congress Asked to Review IT Field Engineers Group Upset over H1-B Visas, Job Losses," *Boston Globe*, 23 July 2002; Paul Chakravartty, "Symbolic Analysts or Indentured Servants? Indian High-Tech Migrants in America's Information Economy," in *The Human Face of Global Mobility: International Highly Skilled Migration in Europe, North America and the Asia-Pacific*, ed. Michael Smith and Adrian Favell (New Brunswick, N.J.: Transaction Publishers, 2006), 159–80.

29. "Five Mass Firms Ordered to Pay Back Wages, Foreign Workers Were Underpaid, Labor Department Says," *Boston Globe*, 21 March 2000; "Firm Underpaid Foreign Workers, Owes Them $2.4m," *Boston Globe*, 8 June 2007; Hal Salzman, "Will Science and Engineering Now Be a Good Career?" *Education Week*, 11 November 2009, 32; Megan Flaherty, "Nurses with Visas," *Nurseweek*, 15 March 1999, available at www.nurseweek.com.

30. Yingchan Zhang, "The Experiences of Immigrant Nurses in Lowell, Massachusetts: A Case Study" (Ph.D. diss., University of Massachusetts Lowell, 2009), 18–22. For more on the brain drain vs. brain exchange debate, see Lucie Cheng and Philip Yang, "Global Interaction, Global Inequality, and Migration of the Highly Trained to the United States," *International Migration Review* 32 (1998): 626–94; Devesh Kapur and John McHale, *Give Us Your Best and Brightest: The Global Hunt for Talent and Its Impact on the Developing World* (Washington, DC: Brookings Institute, 2005); and Michael Peter Smith and Adrian Favell, eds., *The Human Face of Global Mobility* (New Brunswick, NJ: Transaction Publishers, 2006).

31. Daniel J. Monti, Laurel Smith-Doerr, and James McQuaid, *Immigrant Entre-

preneurs in the Massachusetts Biotechnology Industry (Malden, MA: Immigrant Learning Center, 2007), 1–2, available at www.ilctr.org.

32. Amar Sawhney and Mahmud Jafri, interviews by Immigrant Learning Center, available at www.ilctr.org.

33. Alan Clayton-Mathews, Faye Karp, and Paul Watanabe, *Massachusetts Immigrants by the Numbers: Demographic Characteristics and Economic Footprint* (Malden, MA: Immigrant Learning Center, 2009), 25, available at www.iaas.umb.edu; Michael Liu, Thao Tran, and Paul Watanabe, "Far from the Commonwealth: A Report on Low-Income Asian Americans" (2007), *Institute for Asian American Studies Publications,* Paper 10, p. 26, available at http://scholarworks.umb.edu; Uriarte et al., "Salvadorans, Guatemalans, Hondurans and Colombians," 35.

34. Data on wages from BRA, "Briefing Book: Labor Market Trends in Metro Boston," 3–4, available at www.cityofboston.gov; data on median income between 1980 and 2010 was calculated from Steven Ruggles, J. Trent Alexander, Katie Genadek, Ronald Goeken, Matthew B. Schroeder, and Matthew Sobek, *Integrated Public Use Microdata Series: Version 5.0* (Minneapolis: University of Minnesota, 2010).

5. NATIVISM, VIOLENCE, AND THE RISE OF MULTICULTURALISM

1. Two seventeen year olds, Robert J. McGowan and James Smith, were convicted on manslaughter charges in Lai's death and sentenced to fifteen years in prison. See *Boston Globe* articles: "Vietnamese Man Killed in Brighton," 31 August 1980; "Gang Fight Stabbing Death Investigated in Brighton," 1 September 1980; "Gang Fight Is Denied in Brighton Killing," 1 September 1980; "Communication Trouble in Brighton Death Probe," 2 September 1980; Mike Barnicle, "A Viet Son Who Came Here to Die," 3 September 1980; "Brighton Youths Sentenced," 23 January 1980.

2. For general accounts of anti-Asian violence in the 1980s, see House Judiciary Committee, Subcommittee on Civil and Constitutional Rights, *Anti-Asian Violence: Oversight Hearing before the Subcommittee on Civil and Constitutional Rights,* 100th Cong., First Sess., November 10, 1987; Patricia Wong Hall and Victor M. Hwang, eds., *Anti-Asian Violence in North America* (Walnut Creek, CA: Altamira Press, 2001). On a related topic in Philadelphia, see Scott Kurashige, "Pan-ethnicity and Community Organizing: Asian Americans United's Campaign against Anti-Asian Violence," *Journal of Asian American Studies* 3.2 (June 2000): 163–90.

3. On comparisons of old and new nativism, see Charles Jaret, "Troubled by Newcomers: Old and New Attitudes and Action during Two Eras of Immigration to the United States," *Journal of American Ethnic History* 18.3 (Spring 1999): 9–39; Nancy Foner, *From Ellis Island to JFK: New York's Two Great Waves of Immigration* (New Haven: Yale University Press, 2000), 142–68; George Sanchez, "Face the Nation: Race, Immigration and the Rise of Nativism in Late Twentieth Century America," *International Migration Review* 31.4 (Winter 1997): 1009–30.

4. Barry Bluestone and Mary Huff Stevenson, *The Boston Renaissance* (New York: Russell Sage Foundation, 2000), 16, 59–61.

5. Ibid., 81–88; Thomas H. O'Connor, *Building a New Boston* (Boston: Northeastern University Press, 1993); Lawrence W. Kennedy, *Planning the City upon a Hill* (Amherst: University of Massachusetts Press, 1992), chaps. 7–8. On racial tensions in Dorchester, see Gerald Gamm, *Urban Exodus: Why the Jews Left Boston and the Catholics Stayed* (Cambridge: Harvard University Press, 1999); on the busing crisis, see Ronald P. Formisano, *Boston against Busing* (Chapel Hill: University of North Carolina Press, 1991).

6. Irene Bloemraad, *Becoming a Citizen: Incorporating Immigrants and Refugees in the United States and Canada* (Berkeley: University of California Press, 2006), 127–32; Commonwealth of Massachusetts, Office of Refugee and Immigrant Health, *Refugees and Immigrants in Massachusetts: An Overview of Selected Communities* (1991), 1; copy available at the Boston Public Library.

7. See *Boston Globe* articles: "State Economy: From Bust to Boom," 2 September 1984; "New England Shoe Factory Workers Face Up to Dwindling Jobs," 1 September 1985; "State Jobless Rate in '85 a Record Low," 9 January 1986; "The Economy's Hot but Some Still Left Out in the Cold," 6 April 1986 (Colonial Provision worker quotation); "76,000 Jobs in Mass Industry Vanish, 11.2% Drop Has Economist Worried," 17 April 1988; "A Miracle It Was," 23 May 1989.

8. Elaine Song, *To Live in Peace . . . : Responding to Anti-Asian Violence in Boston* (Boston: Asian American Resources Workshop, 1987), 10–12, 21; Jack McDevitt, "The Study of the Character of Civil Rights Crimes in Massachusetts, 1983–1987," research report for Boston Foundation / Northeastern University (1989), 9–10, available at http://eric.ed.gov. African Americans and Latinos were sometimes responsible for these attacks, but 86 percent of the reported assailants were white at a time when whites made up only two-thirds of the city's population.

9. Song, *To Live in Peace,* 13–14; "Gang Breaks into Home in South Boston and Attacks Three Vietnamese," *Boston Globe,* 26 May 1985; "New Attack on Asians Probed," *Boston Globe,* 30 May 1985; "Brawl Renews Concerns about Race Relations," *East Boston Community News,* 4 June 1985; "An Anti-Asian Climate," *Boston Globe,* 31 May 1985 (editorial quotation).

10. "Tattered Dreams Once in America, Some Asians Find Bigotry, Violence," *Boston Globe,* 31 March 1986 (Yem quotation); "Asians Look to Trial to Prove Refugee's Worth as Hub Citizen," *Boston Herald,* 14 April 1985 (Kiang quotation).

11. "Into the Fray: Rambo's Double Whammy in Boston," *Boston Phoenix,* 11 June 1985; Song, *To Live in Peace,* 8. For more on *Rambo* and other Vietnam films of the 1980s, see A. J. Bacevich, *The New American Militarism: How Americans Are Seduced by War* (New York: Oxford University Press, 2005), 112–13; and Gregory Waller, "*Rambo:* Getting to Win This Time," in *From Hanoi to Hollywood,* ed. Linda Ditmar and Gene Michaud (New Brunswick, NJ: Rutgers University Press, 1990), 113–28.

12. Ric Kahn, "Strangers and Fiction," *Phoenix,* 18 June 1985, 8 (teenager quotation);

Paula Bock and Ken Brusic, *The Asians: Quincy's Newest Immigrants* (Quincy: [Patriot Ledger], 1989), 52 (marine quotation).

13. Kahn, "Strangers and Fiction," 7–8 (East Boston quotations); "HUB's Asian Refugees: Some Give a Hard Time," *Globe*, 31 May 1983 (Vietnamese quotation).

14. Bock and Brusic, *The Asians*, 48 (glazier quotation). For a more complete analysis of Vietnamese family strategies, see Nazli Kibria, *Family Tightrope: The Changing Lives of Vietnamese Americans* (Princeton: Princeton University Press, 1995), 99–103; on earlier European immigrant family strategies, see Judy Smith, *Family Connections: A History of Italian and Jewish Immigrant Lives in Providence, 1900–1940* (Albany: State University of New York Press, 1985).

15. Sister Carole Rossi, interview by author, 9 June 2010.

16. Bock and Brusic, *The Asians*, 13 (Quincy woman quotation); Kahn, "Strangers and Fiction," 7–8 (East Boston quotation); Art Jahnke, "The New Racism," *Boston Magazine*, December 1983, 255 (Revere quotation); "Tattered Dreams Once in America, Some Asians Find Bigotry, Violence," *Boston Globe*, 31 March 1986 (Yem quotation); Song, *To Live in Peace*, 7; Shirley Suet-ling Tang, "Enough Is Enough: Struggles for Cambodian American Community Development in Revere, Massachusetts" (Ph.D. diss., University of Buffalo, 2002), 41.

17. Don Nanstad, interview by author, 9 June 2010; "Brawl Renews Concern about Race Relations," *East Boston Community News*, 4 June 1985. On class and race in the busing crisis, see Formisano, *Boston against Busing*. The Reagan administration did in fact send observers from the Justice Department to investigate racial and anti-immigrant violence in the mid-1980s, but there is no indication that they undertook any prosecutions. Their records can be found in RG 379, Department of Justice, Community Relations Service, Significant Case Files, 1974–1994, National Archives, Waltham, MA.

18. Song, *To Live in Peace*, 6–7; "Asians Look to Trial to Prove Refugee's Worth as Hub Citizen," *Boston Herald*, 14 April 1985; Peter Nien-chu Kiang, "Why the Asians," *Boston Phoenix*, 18 June 1985, 7; Jahnke, "The New Racism," 255. For Asian American income and poverty rates, see Paul Watanabe, "Asian Americans in Metro Boston," *New England Journal of Public Policy* 20.1 (September 2004): 149–65, available at http://scholarworks.umb.edu.

19. Rossi interview.

20. Nanstad and Rossi interviews; Song, *To Live in Peace*, 13–14, 26; "Brawl Renews Concern about Race Relations," *East Boston Community News*, 4 June 1985; "Youths Battle on East Boston Streets," *East Boston Times Leader Free Press*, 5 June 1985; "An Open Letter to the Community," *East Boston Community News*, 18 June 1985.

21. Song, *To Live in Peace*, 12; Jahnke, "The New Racism," 182–83; "Vietnamese Family Forced from Burning House," *Boston Globe*, 19 July 1981; "Civil Rights Incident Cited in Dorchester," *Boston Globe*, 28 July 1982.

22. Press Statement for Anh Mai Trial (quotation), 1984, Committee to Support Long Guang Huang (CSLGH) folder, Chinese Progressive Association (CPA) Papers, Northeastern University Archives; Jahnke, "The New Racism," 181–82; "Vietnam

Immigrant Slain, 3 Others Hurt," *Boston Globe*, 25 July 1983; "The Death of a Dream," *Boston Globe*, 27 July 1983; "Asians Look to Trial to Prove Refugee's Worth as Hub Citizen," *Boston Herald*, 14 April 1985; "A War That's Always There," *Boston Globe*, 15 April 1985; "Marine Gets Life Term in Stabbing," *Boston Globe*, 2 May 1985.

23. "Suit Eyed against Hub Officer," *Boston Globe*, 4 May 1985; "Immigrant Beaten in Chinatown Is Escorted to Hospital by Mayor," *Boston Globe*, 7 May 1985; "Huang Worries about Health, Family" *Sampan*, 8 May 1985 (Huang quotation); "Roache Finds Sufficient Evidence for Hearing Alleged Beating Case," *Sampan*, 22 May 1985; "Police Beating Victim Was Struck in Face," *Boston Herald*, 22 August 1985; "Officer Nabbed Wrong Man—Witness," *Boston Herald*, 23 August 1985.

24. CSLGH press statement, 13 May 1985, CSLGH files, CPA Papers; Michael Liu, "Campaign for Justice: The Case of Long Guang Huang," *Eastwind* (Spring 1987): 33–35; Peter Kiang, "Community Strategies: Fighting Back in Boston," *CALC Report* 13.5 (1986): 22–23; Song, *To Live in Peace*, 23–24; "Asian Americans Urge Officer's Suspension," *Boston Globe*, 10 May 1985; "Asian Group Prepares List of Demands to Give to Flynn," *Globe*, 14 May 1985; "Committee Lists Demands," *Sampan*, 22 May 1985; "Petitions Presented to Flynn," *Sampan*, 5 June 1985; "200 March to City Hall Plaza to Protest Alleged Brutality against Chinese Immigrant," *Boston Globe*, 19 June 1985.

25. Quotations from CSLGH press statement, 12 July 1985, and CSLGH letter to WBZ Radio, 24 October 1985, both in CSLGH files, CPA Papers; "Immigrant Beaten in Chinatown Is Escorted to Hospital by Mayor" *Boston Globe*, 7 May 1985; "Injunction Move Suspends Police Hearing," *Boston Globe*, 12 July 1985; "Huang Supporters Angered by Defense's Tactics," *Sampan*, 17 July 1985; "Police Probe Postponed," *Sampan*, 14 August 1985; "Huang Describes Shock at Being Chased, Arrested," *Boston Globe*, 30 August 1985; "Testimony Ends in Kelly Case," *Boston Globe*, 4 September 1985; "Kelly's Attorney Stirs up a Memorable Storm in Hearing," *Sampan*, 11 September 1985; "Thomas Troy, Flamboyant Lawyer, Defended 'Boston Strangler' at 70," *Boston Globe*, 15 February 2000.

26. CSLGH letter to Mayor Ray Flynn, 4 April 1988, CSLGH files, CPA Papers; "Detective Gets Year's Suspension," *Boston Globe*, 7 September 1985; "Hub Officer Faces $1M Brutality Suit," *Boston Globe*, 16 January 1987; "Suspension of Officer Who Hit Suspect Is Reversed," *Boston Globe*, 11 March 1988; "2-Way Settlement Ends Police Suit," *Boston Globe*, 15 July 1985; "City Settlements Send Mixed Signal to Asians," *Sampan*, 2 August 1989.

27. Quotation from "Watch Orientation & Checklist," 19 October 1985, CSLGH files, CPA Papers; "Combat Zone," *CPA Newsletter*, October 1985, newsletters file, CPA Papers; Liu, "Campaign for Justice," 35; "Asian Officer Expected to Be Named by October," *Sampan*, 31 July 1985; "Flynn Appoints 21 to First C-T Neighborhood Council," *Sampan*, 6 November 1985; "Program Will Recruit Interpreters to Aid Asians in Dealing with Police," *Boston Globe*, 11 June 1986; "Two New Liaisons Are Hired by City Hall to Serve the Southeast Asian Community," *Sampan*, 15 July 1987.

28. "Dukakis, at Lowell Wake, Condemns Local Attacks," *Boston Globe*, 17 August 1985.

29. See *Boston Globe* articles: "Somerville Men Arraigned in Medford Beating Death," 16 August 1985; "Defendant: Fatal Blows Thrown in Self Defense," 26 April 1986; "Tattered Dreams Once in America, Some Asians Find Bigotry, Violence," 31 March 1986; "Mistrial, Acquittal in Refugee Assault Trial," 2 May 1986; and "Man Convicted of Manslaughter Gets 7–12 Years," 27 June 1986. "Mistrial Is Declared in Bun Vong Case," *Sampan*, 7 May 1986.

30. Kiang, "Why the Asians," 40 (quotation); Kiang, "Community Strategies," 23–24; Song, *To Live in Peace*, 27–29 (Song quotation).

31. Tang, "Enough Is Enough," 28–31, 43–44.

32. For general accounts of the Revere violence, see Song, *To Live in Peace*, 15–16; and Tang, "Enough Is Enough," 43–46. On Walnut Place violence, see David de Milo, "Jury Duty," *Boston Magazine*, November 1986, 206–7, 302; *Commonwealth vs. Robert Lee Stephens*, 25 Mass. App. Ct. 117, 1987; "To Promote Racial Harmony, Human Rights Commission," and "Editorial: Support Needed," *Revere Journal*, 24 July 1985; see also articles in the *Boston Globe*: "Foreign Briefing; Refugees Assert Their Rights," 27 August 1983; "36 Cambodians Homeless in Revere Fire, Arson Suspected," 17 July 1985; "Revere Problem: Racism or Overcrowding," 18 July 1985; "Revere Panel to Address Attacks on Refugees," 24 July 1985; "In Revere, a Tense Street Scene after Sentencing in Racial Attack," 18 April 1986.

33. "Families Lose All in Blaze; Looters Hit after Fire Is Put out in Revere," *Boston Globe*, 26 December 1986; "300 March in Revere against Violence toward Cambodians," *Boston Globe*, 11 January 1987; "March Protests Acts of Violence," *Revere Journal*, 14 January 1987; "Revere City Response to Fire Victims Questioned Despite Mayor's Pledge," *Boston Globe*, 22 January 1987; "To Promote Racial Harmony, Human Rights Commission," and "Editorial: Support Needed," *Revere Journal*, 24 July 1985.

34. Tang, "Enough Is Enough," 45–46; "Asian Refugees, Conflict in a New Land: Burden of Arrival Is Felt by All," *Boston Globe*, 22 January 1989.

35. Bock and Brusic, *The Asians*, 57–60; "Gateway Opens for Refugees," *Boston Globe*, 7 July 1986; "$2.7 Million for Program to Aid Immigrants," *Boston Globe*, 20 March 1987; "Two New Liaisons Are Hired by City Hall to Serve the Southeast Asian Community," *Sampan*, 15 July 1987; "1,000 Protest Planned," *Boston Globe*, 12 May 1988.

36. See Song, *To Live in Peace*; and House Judiciary Committee, Subcommittee on Civil and Constitutional Rights, *Anti-Asian Violence*. On SafetyNet, see "A Place to Turn for Victims of Hate," *Boston Globe*, 26 June 1994.

37. De Milo, "Jury Duty," 298.

38. Scholars have commented on this phenomenon among both Vietnamese and Haitian immigrants in Boston; see Karin Aguilar-San Juan, *Little Saigons: Staying Vietnamese in America* (Minneapolis: University of Minnesota Press, 2009), 52; and Regine O. Jackson "Haitians in Boston: New Immigrants and New Blacks

in an Old Immigrant City," paper prepared for "New Immigrants in Urban New England" workshop, Brown University, 2004, 21, available at www.brown.edu.

6. IMMIGRANT RELIGION AND BOSTON'S "QUIET REVIVAL"

1. New England Centennial Committee of Korean Immigration to the United States, *History of Koreans in New England* (Seoul: Sun-Hak Press, 2004), 94–95, 112–13; First Presbyterian Church in Brookline, "About Us: History," available at www.fpcbrookline.org.

2. On de-Europeanized Christianity, see R. Steven Warner, "The De-Europeanization of American Christianity," in *A Nation of Religions: The Politics of Pluralism in Multireligious America,* ed. Stephen Prothero (Chapel Hill: University of North Carolina Press, 2006), 233–55; and Jenna Weissman Joselit, Timothy Matovina, Robert Suro, and Fenggang Yang, "American Religion and the Old and the New Immigration," *Religion and American Culture* 22 (Winter 2012): 24. Yang stresses the de-Europeanization of Christianity over the "new religious pluralism" of emerging nonwestern faiths discussed by Diana Eck in *A New Religious America* (San Francisco: Harper, 2002). I find, however, that both of these formulations make sense in greater Boston, with immigrants' new religious identities affecting both Christianity and the larger array of faith traditions. This diversification and transformation has been less evident, however, among Jews. The relatively small numbers of Jewish immigrants from the former Soviet Union have not had a major impact on local synagogues, as many migrants have remained secular. The one exception has been the orthodox Lubavitcher/Hasidic community, which has historically focused on outreach to nonobservant Jews. In 1989, the Boston Lubavitch founded a synagogue and school specifically for Russian Jews. The school, which has an advanced mathematics program, has been popular with Russian Jewish parents, many of whom work in high-tech fields. See Rita J. Simon and Melanie Brooks, "Soviet Jewish Immigrants' Adjustment in Four United States Cities," *Journal of Jewish Communal Service* 60 (November 1983): 62; Bernice Kazis, Elaine Bakal, and Zelda Kaplan, *Short Stories of a Long Journey: An Oral History of Russian Jewish Resettlement North of Boston* (Boston: Hand-in-Hand Oral History Project, 2002), 121–42; Jewish Russian Center and Synagogue of Greater Boston, "About Us," available at www.russianboston.org.

3. Parish Visitation Reports for St. Anthony Parish, 1993 and 1999, RG III.N Chancellor's Office, Office of Planning and Research, Archdiocese of Boston Archives, Braintree, MA (all subsequent Parish Visitation reports cited are from these files). A mission church was not a parish, but an expansion church founded by the archdiocese or a local parish to serve growing (typically new immigrant) populations.

4. Julio Morales, *Puerto Rican Poverty and Migration* (New York: Praeger, 1986), 85; "Seminarian Forges Ties between City, Spanish-Speaking," *Boston Globe,* 2 May 1971.

5. Jeffrey N. Gerson, "Latino Migration, the Catholic Church, and Political Division, Lowell," in *Latino Politics in Massachusetts,* ed. Carol Hardy Fanta and Jeffrey N. Gerson (New York: Routledge, 2002), 134–35 (O'Brien and Sheehan quotations); "Bienvenido Boston Gives Hearty Welcome to Bishop with Hispanic Beat," *Boston Globe,* 4 October 1988; "Keeping the Faith in Spanish," *Boston Globe,* 29 April 2000.

6. Regine O. Jackson, "After the Exodus: The New Catholics in Boston's Old Ethnic Neighborhoods," *Religion and American Culture* 17.2 (Summer 2007): 198–200; "St. Leo's Was Spiritual Home for Waves of Dorchester Families," *Dorchester Reporter,* 9 March 2006; "Brookline Parish Becomes Refuge for Vietnamese," *Boston Globe,* 16 December 1985; "Keeping Faith with Change at St. Peter's in Dorchester," *Boston Globe,* 26 October 1992.

7. Parish Visitation Reports for St. Anthony, Somerville (1993, 1999), St. Anthony, Cambridge (1993), and St. Tarcisius (1997); Joel Millman, *The Other Americans* (New York: Viking, 1997), 224; "Question and Answer with Sister Anne Malone of the African Pastoral Center," *Boston Globe,* 11 January 1998; Sister Mary Corripio, interview by author, 6 June 2011. The archdiocese also ran smaller ministries for incoming Irish, Chinese, Cambodians, and Koreans, as well as older ministries for Italian, Polish, Lithuanian, and Eastern Rite groups.

8. Thomas O'Connor, *Boston Catholics: A History of the Church and Its People* (Boston: Northeastern University Press, 1998), 309; Parish Visitation Reports for St. Anthony, Somerville (1993, 1999) and Most Holy Redeemer (n.d.).

9. "Keeping Faith with Change at St. Peter's in Dorchester"; Parish Visitation Report for St. Peter (1994); Jackson, "After the Exodus," 201.

10. Gerald Gamm, *Urban Exodus: Why the Jews Left Boston and the Catholics Stayed* (Cambridge: Harvard University Press, 2001), 276–78; James O'Toole, "Boston's Catholics and Their Bishops," in *Two Centuries of Faith: The Influence of Catholicism on Boston, 1801–2008,* ed. Thomas H. O'Connor (New York: Crossroad Publishing, 2009), 254–56.

11. Hoffsman Ospino, "Latino Catholics in New England," in *Latinos in New England,* ed. Andrés Torres (Philadelphia: Temple University Press, 2006), 213; "Text of Archbishop O'Malley's Speech on Church Finances," *Boston Globe,* 5 February 2004; "History of St. Anthony Parish," in Parish Visitation Report for St. Anthony, Somerville (1993); Charles Radosta, "History of St. Anthony of Padua Parish [Everett]," available at www.parishesonline.com; Ray Almeida, "The Church and the People of Cape Verde," available at www1.umassd.edu; "Capuchin Brothers Assume Parish Responsibilities" *Boston Pilot,* 1 June 2007.

12. Ospino, "Latino Catholics in New England," 213; Karen Joun Won Chai, "Protestant-Catholic-Buddhist: Korean Americans and Religious Adaptation in Greater Boston" (Ph.D. diss., Harvard University, 2000), 110–11, 117; Nora Martin-Cooley et al., "On Common Ground: Latino Immigrant Community-Building in Somerville," final report, Fall 2003, 27–28, Urban Borderlands Records, Tufts University, Digital Collections and Archives (TDCA), Medford, MA, available at http://dl.tufts.edu;

Hispanic Ministry and Theology at BC—Past, Present and Future, available at
http://libguides.bc.edu.

13. Joseph O'Keefe and Aubrey J. Scheopner, "Catholic Schools: A Tradition of
Responsiveness to Non-dominant Cultures," in *Two Centuries of Faith*, 97–98;
Joselit, Matovina, Suro, and Yang, "American Religion and the Old and New
Immigration," *Religion and American Culture* 22 (Winter 2012): 18. Catholic
school statistics are from *The Official Catholic Directory, 1966 and 2010* (New
Providence, NJ: P. J. Kenedy and Sons, 1966 and 2010).

14. "Faith in Numbers—East Boston Church Swells with Influx of Latino Immigrants,"
Boston Globe, 18 March 2001; Parish Visitation Report for Saint Anthony (1999);
Chai, "Protestant-Catholic-Buddhist," 163–64; Thomas Curry, "A Korean Catholic
Experience: St. Philip Neri Parish in the Archdiocese of Boston," *US Catholic
Historian* 18 (Winter 2000): 121.

15. "St. Leo's Was Spiritual Home for Waves of Dorchester Families"; Parish Visitation
Report for Most Holy Redeemer (n.d.).

16. Quotation from Jackson, "After the Exodus," 199–200; Parish Visitation Reports
for St. Leo (n.d.), St. Peter (1994), and St. Tarcisius (1997). Catholic immigrant
groups differed in the degree to which they patronized the parochial schools. For
example, those from Haiti, where there was a weak system of public schooling but
a high regard for education, enrolled in large numbers. By contrast, those from
Central America were underrepresented, in part because of their low incomes
and inability to afford the tuition.

17. Parish Visitation Report for St. Anthony (1999); "Faith in Numbers"; Millman,
The Other Americans, 226. On the hierarchy's support for immigration reform,
see *Boston Pilot* articles: "Local Religious Leaders Rally for Immigrants," 20 April
2007; "The Catch 22 for Haitian Refugees," 21 January 2010; and "The Catholic
Church and Immigration," 26 November 2010.

18. "Law Tells Vietnamese They're a Gift," *Boston Globe*, 25 December 1985;
"Parishes Replenish from Other Shores," *Boston Globe*, 29 July 2003; Almieda,
"The Church and the People of Cape Verde"; Ospino, "Latino Catholics in New
England," 209; Parish Visitation Report for St. Ambrose (1995) and St. Anthony
(1999). Holiday celebrations took an ecumenical turn in 2008 when Catholics
joined Protestants in performing *Las Posadas* around Boston Common to dra-
matize the plight of immigrants. See "Las Posadas: Biblical Journey Reflects
Immigrant Experience," available at www.ethnicnewz.org. For an excellent
account of the origins and significance of *el baile de los negritos*, see Sebastián
Chaskel, "From Yucuaiquín to Somerville: Religious Beliefs and Traditions
of a Transnational Community," final report, Fall 2004, Urban Borderlands
Records, TDCA, available at http://dl.tufts.edu.

19. Parish Visitation Reports for St. Williams (1993), "Parishes Replenish from Other
Shores," "Feast of Ugandan Martyrs Celebrated in Waltham," *Boston Pilot*, 11 June
2004; Emmanuel Gospel Center (EGC), *New England's Book of Acts* (Boston,
2007), 57, available at http://neba.egc.org.

20. Ospino, "Latino Catholics in New England," 212; Chai, "Protestant-Catholic-Buddhist," 123; Parish Visitation Reports for St. Anthony (1999) and St. Leo (n.d.).

21. Andrew Downie, "Behind Brazil's Catholic Resurgence," *Time*, 8 May 2007; Monte Reel, "Brazil's Priests Use Song and Dance to Stem Catholic Church's Decline," *Washington Post*, 14 April 2005; Susan A. Maurer, *The Spirit of Enthusiasm* (Lanham, MD: University Press of America, 2010), 4, 58–59; Ospino, "Latino Catholics in New England," 212.

22. Chai, "Protestant-Catholic-Buddhist," 116–17; Parish Visitation Report for St. Anthony (Somerville, 1999) and St. Anthony (Allston, 1997); Peggy Levitt, *God Needs No Passport* (New York: New Press, 2007), 117.

23. Chai, "Protestant-Catholic-Buddhist," 134–35; "New Korean Parish Set to Welcome Cardinal O'Malley," *Boston Pilot*, 20 December 2013; Curry, "A Korean Catholic Experience," 114, 122; Jackson, "After the Exodus," 202–3, "St. Leo's Was Spiritual Home for Waves of Dorchester Families."

24. "Church Closings Alarm Immigrants," *Boston Globe*, 9 May 2004; "In Cuts, Archdiocese Is Seen as Sharing Burden," *Boston Globe*, 26 May 2004; "10 More Parishes to Close This Year," *Boston Globe*, 6 August 2004.

25. "In Cuts, Archdiocese Is Seen as Sharing Burden"; "Facing Millions in Repairs, St. Peter's Parish Ponders Future," *Dorchester Reporter*, 4 May 2006; Archdiocese of Boston, "Reconfiguration Report, Part II: The Plan of Reconfiguration," available at www.boston.com.

26. Parish Visitation Reports for Most Holy Redeemer (n.d.) and St. Angela (1999); Ospino, "Latino Catholics in New England," 214–15; Rudy Mitchell, "A Portrait of Boston's Churches," in *Christianity in Boston* (Boston: Emmanuel Gospel Center, 1994), 11–12; Corripio interview.

27. Wendy Jane Wyche, "We Are the World: A Parish Struggles to Embrace Diversity and Become a Multiracial and Multicultural Community" (M. Div. thesis, Harvard Divinity School, 2005), 31–32, 42–55; "Diverse Parish Looks in Mirror and Learns," *Boston Globe*, 9 February 2000; "Ballot Brigade: St. Mark's District Struggles to Regain Its Voting Voice," *Boston Globe*, 15 November 2000.

28. Wyche, "We Are the World," 11, 80. Leaders from a cluster of Dorchester parishes recommended that St. Mark be closed in the 2004 reconfiguration. Dismayed at the scuttling of their hard work in rebuilding the parish, St. Mark's parishioners successfully appealed the decision. The parish's diversity was no doubt important in sparing the church.

29. "Many Latinos Switching to Evangelical Churches," *Boston Globe*, 2 June 2005. On the apostolates' mission, see www.catholicdiversity.org.

30. Quotation from Parish Visitation Report for St. Leo (1993); Ospino, "Latino Catholics in New England," 215. One sign of the waning influence of the Hispanic apostolate was the loss of the auxiliary bishop for Hispanic ministries, a position that remained vacant after Bishop Gonzales left for another post in the late 1990s.

31. Garth M. Rosell, *The Surprising Work of God: Harold John Ockenga, Billy Graham, and the Rebirth of Evangelicalism* (Ada, MO: Baker Academic, 2006); Rudy

Mitchell, "History of Revivalism in Boston," *Emmanuel Research Review* 24 (January–February 2007), available at www.egc.org.

32. Erika Muse, *The Evangelical Church in Boston's Chinatown: A Discourse of Language, Gender and Identity* (New York: Routledge, 2005), 1–2; Zhongxin Wang, "History of Chinese Churches in Boston, 1876–1994" (Ph.D. diss., Boston University, 2000), 145, 179–80.

33. EGC, *New England's Book of Acts,* 2:65; Wang, "History of Chinese Churches," 227–30, 231–45, 260–62.

34. EGC, *New England's Book of Acts,* 2:97–100, 122; Chai, "Protestant-Catholic-Buddhist," 238; "The Story of the English Speaking Asian-American Ministries (EM) in Greater Boston," in *Boston's Book of Acts* (Boston: EGC, 9 November 2002).

35. EGC, *New England's Book of Acts,* 2:6–8, 10.

36. EGC, *New England's Book of Acts,* 2:9–11; EGC, *The Boston Church Directory: Millennium Edition* (Boston, 2001), 361–62; "CLJ: A Brief History," available at http://leondejuda.org.

37. Soliny Védrine, "The History of the Haitian Church in Boston: 1969–2002," *Emmanuel Research Review,* no. 1 (March 12, 2004), available at http://egc.org/err1; Gamm, *Urban Exodus,* 252–53.

38. EGC, *New England's Book of Acts,* 2:12–14, 48–50, 120–21; "Newcomers Lead a Spiritual Revival," *Boston Globe,* 2 March 1997; "Many Latinos Switching to Evangelical Churches," *Boston Globe,* 2 June 2005. The World Revival Church was later reorganized as the Revival Church of the Nations.

39. Mitchell, "A Portrait of Boston's Churches," 14, 16; EGC, *New England's Book of Acts,* 2:38; 3:7–8, 35; "Believing in Each Other: Many Churches, Facing Dwindling Membership, Decide to Join Forces," *Boston Globe,* 18 December 1999; "Prayer Central: Known for Its Curries and Live Music, One Cambridge Neighborhood Is Home to Nearly 60 Congregations," *Boston Globe,* 4 November 2000; "BCEC Newton Campus," available at www.bcec.net.

40. EGC, *New England's Book of Acts,* 2:44–50; "Group Quits Episcopal Church over Gay Bishop," *Boston Globe,* 17 October 2004.

41. Elba Mireya Vasquez, interview by Elizabeth Butler, spring 2003, Urban Borderlands Records, 2002–2003, Box 001, TDCA.

42. EGC, *New England's Book of Acts,* 2:32–33; Chai, "Protestant-Catholic-Buddhist," 249; Muse, *The Evangelical Church in Boston's Chinatown,* 174; "Many Latinos Switching to Evangelical Churches," *Boston Globe,* 2 June 2005.

43. EGC, *New England's Book of Acts,* 2:10–11; "Newcomers Lead a Spiritual Revival," *Boston Globe,* 2 March 1997; Pastor Roberto Miranda (León de Judá), interview by Kerry Biggs, 16 April 2003, Urban Borderland Records, 2002–2003, Box 001, TDCA; Muse, *The Evangelical Church in Boston's Chinatown,* 2; Wang, "History of Chinese Churches," 184.

44. Mitchell, "A Portrait of Boston's Churches"; EGC, *New England's Book of Acts,* 2:7; Bob Wells, "Boston Program Helps Hispanic Pastors Build New Foundation for Ministry," available at http://faithandleadership.com.

45. For examples of such copastorates, see the lists of pastors at EGC's Boston Church Directory, available at www.egcbcd.com. See also Ann M. Detwiler-Breidenbach, "Language, Gender and Context in an Immigrant Ministry: New Spaces for the Pastor's Wife," *Sociology of Religion* 61.4 (2000): 455–59.

46. ECG, Haitian Ministries International, available at www.egc.org; Védrine, "History of the Haitian Church"; EGC, *New England's Book of Acts,* 2:10–11, 52, 59; Antioch Baptist Church, "Missions," available at www.antiochboston.org.

47. EGC, *New England's Book of Acts,* 2:17, 39–40; EGC, "The Story of the English Speaking Asian-American Ministries (EM) in Greater Boston"; Wang, "History of Chinese Churches," 184, 194, 198, 204, 257–60; Védrine, "History of the Haitian Church."

48. EGC, *New England's Book of Acts,* 2:54, 118–121; 3:9.

49. See Pluralism Project's database for "World Religions in Greater Boston," available at http://pluralism.org.

50. Pluralism Project, "World Religions in Greater Boston: Hinduism in Greater Boston" and "Buddhism in Greater Boston," both available at http://pluralism. org; Harvard Divinity School, Center for the Study of World Religions, "About: History," available at http://cswr.hds.harvard.edu.

51. See Center Profiles for Hindu Temples in Massachusetts at the Pluralism Project, available at http://pluralism.org.

52. Quotation from Sri Lakshmi Temple History, available at www.srilakshmi.org; Eck, *A New Religious America,* 88; Pluralism Project, "World Religions in Greater Boston: Hinduism," available at http://pluralism.org; "Ashland Center Rises as Center of Spiritual Community," *Boston Globe,* 5 March 1995.

53. Sri Lakshmi Temple History; Eck, *A New Religious America,* 89–90; Diego Ribadeneira, "A Hindu Haven in Ashland," *Boston Globe,* 19 August 1996.

54. "For Hindus, Room to Grow," *Boston Globe,* 6 December 2010; "Embracing Their Hindu Brethren, New Immigrants Find Welcome at Ashland Temple," *Boston Globe,* 29 March 2009.

55. A noted exception occurred in October 2003 when a local youth spray-painted racial epithets on a large rock outside the temple. Following a tip from a high school staff member, police arrested a seventeen year old who was charged and convicted of vandalism and a civil rights violation. See "Teen Charged with Painting Epithets at Hindu Temple," *Boston Globe,* 30 November 2003.

56. "For Hindus, Room to Grow"; "Temple Pays $330,000 for 9-Acre Parcel on Rte. 135," *MetroWest Daily News,* 21 November 2008; "Ashland Hindu Temple Hopes to Proceed with Expansion," *MetroWest Daily News,* 25 November 2010; Pluralism Project, "World Religions in Greater Boston: Hinduism."

57. Pluralism Project, "World Religions in Greater Boston: Buddhism," available at http://pluralism.org.

58. Rev. Sik Kuan Yen, interview by author, 20 August 2012; "House of Worship, Former Montello's Now a Buddhist Temple," *Patriot Ledger,* 13 January 1996; "Quincy Common," *Patriot Ledger,* 27 July 1996; "A Buddhist Blessing, Hundreds

Celebrate Temple Dedication," *Boston Globe,* 29 July 1996; Pluralism Project, "Center Profile: Thousand Buddha Temple," available at http://pluralism.org.

59. Sik interview; "Disaster Aids, Quincy Events to Fund China Relief Efforts," *Patriot Ledger,* 16 May 2008.

60. Sik interview.

61. Pluralism Project, "World Religions in Greater Boston: Buddhism"; "Thai Buddhist Temple Dazzles in Raynham," *Boston Globe,* 16 June 2014. See also Pluralism Project's directory of religious centers, available at http://pluralism.org.

62. "Research Report: United Celebration of the Buddha's Birthday 2003," available at http://pluralism.org.

63. Mary Lahaj, "Building an Islamic Community in America: History of the Islamic Center of New England" (M.A. thesis, Hartford Seminary, 1992), 4–5, 9, 11.

64. Lahaj, "Building an Islamic Community," 15–18; "New England Islamic Center Builds Quincy Mosque," *Boston Globe,* 9 June 1963.

65. Lahaj, "Building an Islamic Community," 20–21, 28–29; Mary Lahaj, "The Islamic Center of New England," in *Muslim Communities in North America,* ed. Yvonne Y. Haddad (Albany, NY: SUNY Press, 1994), 303.

66. Lahaj, "Building an Islamic Community," 21, 26, 29, 33–36, 46; Pluralism Project, "World Religions in Greater Boston: Islam in Greater Boston," available at http://pluralism.org.

67. Lahaj, "Building an Islamic Community," 36–37, 42–43, 47; "Arson Suspected in Mosque Blaze," *Boston Globe,* 31 March 1990; Eck, *A New Religious America,* 228–30.

68. Asraf quoted in "Milton Neighbors Snatch away Site for Mosque," *Boston Globe,* 1 August 1991; Eck, *A New Religious America,* 230; Lahaj, "Building an Islamic Community," 47.

69. "Islamic Center Finds Acceptance in Sharon," *Boston Globe,* 30 August 1992; Eck, *A New Religious America,* 230–31.

70. Some of the African American mosques were affiliated with the Nation of Islam, which Malcolm X once led in Boston. Since the late 1960s, however, a number of them have moved toward mainstream Islam. See Pluralism Project, "World Religions in Greater Boston: Islam in Greater Boston"; "Muslims Answer Call to Prayer; Islamic Population Increases in Region," *Boston Globe,* 17 January 1999; "A Mosque in Methuen Reflects Growth among Area's Religions, Congregations," *Boston Globe,* 13 August 2000; "Building Faith, Community at New Mosque," *Boston Globe,* 21 October 2004.

71. Pluralism Project, "Center Profile: Islamic Society of Boston Cultural Center," and "Islamic Society of Boston Cultural Center—Timeline," available at http://pluralism.org.

72. Pluralism Project, "ISBCC Timeline"; see also these *Boston Globe* articles: "Group's Website Challenges Mosque," 5 October 2004; "Channel 25, Herald Face Libel Suit," 12 May 2005; "Islamic Society Expands Libel Suit," 1 November 2005; "Judge Allows Suit Charging BRA's Sale of Land for Mosque," 22 November 2005; "Praised as Beacon, Mosque Project Stalls Amid Rancour," 18 December 2005.

73. Pluralism Project, "ISBCC Timeline"; and *Boston Globe* articles: "Muslims, Jews Spar in Ads over Mosque," 5 January 2006; "In Dispute, Cultures Meet," 1 March 2006; "Mediating the Mosque Dispute," 4 July 2006; "Schools Try to Patch Rift in Mosque Project," 30 December 2006; "Islamic Society Drops Lawsuit," 30 May 2007; "With Holidays, a Vow for Better Jewish, Muslim Relations," 12 September 2007.

74. "Menino's Mosque," *Boston Phoenix*, 24 November 2008; "Letters to the Editor: Building a Dialogue," *Boston Phoenix*, 5 December 2008; "A Call to Prayer, a Long Quest Fulfilled; Mosque to Open after Years of Controversy," *Boston Globe*, 26 June 2009; "Dissent Greets Mosque Opening," *Boston Globe*, 27 June 2009; Dennis Hale and Charles Jacobs, "Leaders Are Extremist" (op-ed), *Boston Globe*, 5 July 2009.

75. "Debate Heats Up about Mosque near Ground Zero," *New York Times*, 20 July 2010; "Interfaith Group Rallies on Beacon Hill v. Anti-Muslim Rhetoric," *Boston Globe*, 8 September 2010; "Across the Nation, Mosque Projects Meet Opposition," *New York Times*, 7 August 2010.

76. EGC, *The Boston Church Directory: Millennium Edition*, 324, 326; Steve Daman, "What Is the Quiet Revival?" *Emmanuel Research Review*, no. 94 (December 2013–January 2014), available at http://egc.org/err94; Archdiocese of Boston, "Suppressed and Merged Parishes," available at www.bostoncatholic.org. It is unclear whether the number of immigrants attending Catholic churches in the Boston archdiocese has actually declined, but the closing of numerous parishes, including several that once served local immigrant neighborhoods, is suggestive—especially in comparison with the rapid growth of local Protestant immigrant congregations. Of course many of the new Protestant groups have not survived, but the sheer number and variety of new congregations reflects a grassroots dynamism and flexibility that stand in contrast to the overall contraction and consolidation of Catholic parishes and programs.

7. THE NEW ETHNIC POLITICS IN BOSTON

1. Thomas H. O'Connor, *Building the New Boston* (Boston: Northeastern University Press, 1993), 124; Lawrence W. Kennedy, *Planning the City upon a Hill* (Amherst: University of Massachusetts Press, 1992), 159, 173; Jim Vrabel, *A People's History of the New Boston* (Amherst: University of Massachusetts Press, 2014).

2. Vrabel, *A People's History of the New Boston*, 12–15; Kennedy, *Planning the City upon a Hill*, 162; O'Connor, *Building the New Boston*, 135–39.

3. Stephan Thernstrom, *Poverty, Planning, and Politics in the New Boston: The Origins of ABCD* (New York: Basic Books, 1969), 22, 31; Kennedy, *Planning the City upon a Hill*, 188–89.

4. Thernstrom, *Poverty, Planning, and Politics*, 188–90; Annelise Orleck, "Introduction: The War on Poverty from the Grassroots Up," in *The War on Poverty: A New Grassroots History, 1964–1980*, ed. Annelise Orleck and Lisa Gayle Hazirjian

(Athens: University of Georgia Press, 2012), 10–11; Roxbury Multi-Service Center Finding Aid, Northeastern University Archives, available at www.lib.neu.edu.

5. Orleck, "The War on Poverty from the Grassroots Up," 14–18, and "Conclusion," 440–41; Eric A. Nordlinger, *Decentralizing the City: A Study of Boston's Little City Halls* (Cambridge: MIT Press, 1972), 51–54; G. William Domhoff, "The Ford Foundation and the Inner City: Forging an Alliance with Neighborhood Activists," available at www2.ucsc.edu.

6. Mario Luis Small, *Villa Victoria: The Transformation of Social Capital in a Boston Barrio* (Chicago: University of Chicago Press, 2004), 30–31.

7. Miren Uriarte-Gaston, "Organizing for Survival: The Emergence of a Puerto Rican Community" (Ph.D. diss., Boston University, 1988), 5, 130–34; Small, *Villa Victoria,* 36–37.

8. Uriarte-Gaston, "Organizing for Survival," 183–92; "Boston Puerto Ricans List 15 Demands for Mayor, BU," *Boston Globe,* 28 January 1969; "Puerto Rican Sit-in Protests ABCD Aid," *Boston Globe,* 4 February 1969; "How Boston's Spanish Speaking Hope to Emerge," *Boston Globe,* 20 December 1970; Community Affairs Department, "More Information about Boston's Spanish Speaking: A Report Submitted to the Boston Globe," 27 September 1971, 21–23, in Boston Globe Clipping Files (hereafter referred to as Globe Spanish Report).

9. Globe Spanish Report, 33; Uriarte-Gaston, "Organizing for Survival," 195–204; "Organizational History: Pilgrimage to Empowerment," box 10, folder 8, La Alianza Hispana Papers, Northeastern University Archives; "Spanish Group Awarded Quarter Million US Grant," *Boston Globe,* 17 May 1972; "Tutors Open New World to Hispano Women," *Boston Globe,* 24 July 1973; "La Alianza Hispana," *Bay State Banner,* 6 May 1971; and "Spanish Alliance Wins Station 9," *Bay State Banner,* 18 May 1972.

10. Small, *Villa Victoria,* 33–34; John H. Mollenkopf, *The Contested City* (Princeton: Princeton University Press, 1983), 184–86; Vrabel, *A People's History of the New Boston,* 112–16.

11. Félix V. Matos-Rodriguez, "Saving the Parcela: A Short History of Boston's Puerto Rican Community," in *The Puerto Rican Diaspora: Historical Perspectives,* ed. Carmen Teresa Whalen and Víctor Vázquez Hernández (Philadelphia: Temple University Press, 2005), 211; Vrabel, *A People's History of the New Boston,* 112–16; Small, *Villa Victoria,* 35–37; Uriarte-Gaston, "Organizing for Survival," 150–53, 161–74.

12. Small, *Villa Victoria,* 45; "In the South End, a Housing Project That Works," *Boston Globe,* 4 August 1983; "IBA: History," available at www.iba-etc.org.

13. "Housing Dream Comes True," *Boston Globe,* 21 May 1971; Llana Barber, "Latino Migration and the New Global Cities: Transnationalism, Race and Urban Crisis in Lawrence, Massachusetts (Ph.D. diss., Boston College, 2010), 335.

14. Miren Uriarte, "Contra Viento y Marea (Against All Odds): Latinos Build Community in Boston," in *Latinos in Boston: Confronting Poverty, Building Community,* ed. Miren Uriarte et al. (Boston: Boston Persistent Poverty Project,

Boston Foundation, 1992), 18–22; La Alianza Hispana, Inc., 1984 Annual Report, box 4, folder 14, La Alianza Hispana Papers.

15. Uriarte-Gaston, "Organizing for Survival," 222–36; Matos-Rodriguez, "Saving the Parcela," 214–15; Task Force on Children Out of School, *The Way We Go to School* (Boston: Beacon Press, 1970); "The Children Who Don't Go to School," *Boston Globe,* 14 December 1969.

16. Uriarte-Gaston, "Organizing for Survival," 185–87; Carol Hardy-Fanta, *Latina Politics, Latino Politics* (Philadelphia: Temple University Press, 1993), 107; Nordlinger, *Decentralizing the City,* 55, 221; "Seven Spokesmen for Hispanic-Americans," *Boston Globe,* 20 December 1970; Carol Hardy-Fanta with Jaime Rodriguez, "Latino Voter Registration Efforts in Massachusetts: Un Pasito Más," in *Latino Politics in Massachusetts,* ed. Carol Hardy-Fanta and Jeffrey Gerson (New York: Routledge, 2002), 246.

17. Hardy-Fanta, *Latina Politics, Latino Politics,* 105–6; Ramon Olivencia, "Multiracial Coalitions in the Election of the First Latino Legislator," in Hardy-Fanta and Gerson, *Latino Politics in Massachusetts,* 52–54; "School Board Veterans Run Strong," *Boston Globe,* 16 November 1983; "Changing Ingredients in the Political Mix," *Boston Globe,* 17 June 1984. One of the winners in the 1983 BSC election was Grace Romero, a college administrator and immigrant from Spanish Honduras who won with the support of Roxbury's black community. She became the first Latino elected to public office in Boston, and only the second in the state's history, but was not widely recognized as a representative of the Latino community.

18. Yohel Camayd-Freixas and Russell Paul Lopez, "Gaps in Representative Democracy: Redistricting, Political Participation and the Hispanic Vote in Boston" (Boston: Hispanic Office of Planning and Evaluation, 1983); Hardy-Fanta, *Latina Politics, Latino Politics,* 178–81.

19. Hardy-Fanta, *Latina Politics, Latino Politics,* 169–72.

20. Boston first instituted at-large city council elections in 1909. It then shifted to district-based elections after 1923 but returned to an at-large system in 1949.

21. Olivencia, "Multiracial Coalitions," 52–54; Camayd-Freixas and Lopez, "Gaps in Representative Democracy," 119–21.

22. Michael Liu, *The Snake Dance of Asian American Activism: Community, Vision, and Power* (Lanham, MD: Lexington Books, 2008), 46–49, 69–76.

23. Ling Arenson, "Beyond a Common Ethnicity and Culture," in *Asian America: Forming New Communities, Expanding Boundaries,* ed. Huping Ling (New Brunswick, NJ: Rutgers University Press, 2009), 71–73; Michael Chung-Ngok Liu, "Chinatown's Neighborhood Mobilization and Urban Development in Boston" (Ph.D. diss., University of Massachusetts Boston, 1999), 38.

24. Liu, "Chinatown's Neighborhood Mobilization," 32–33; Charles Sullivan and Kathlyn Hatch, *The Chinese in Boston* (Boston: ABCD, 1970), 18–21, 72; Andrew Leong, "The Struggle over Parcel C," Institute for Asian American Studies paper, University of Massachusetts Boston, 1997, 2–3, available at http://scholarworks.umb.edu.

25. Sullivan and Hatch, *The Chinese in Boston*, 22, 44, 49, 53, 64; "Boston's Chinese Joining the Cry for a Better City," *Boston Globe*, 8 December 1969.
26. Thomas C. Chen, "Reconstructing Boston's Chinatown: Race, Place, and Redevelopment after World War II," paper presented at the Organization of American Historians, Atlanta, 13 April 2014; "Chinatown Given Housing Promise," *Boston Globe*, 13 June 1967; "One Woman's Crusade to Bridge the Gap for Minorities," *Boston Globe*, 21 June 1987 (Chang quotation); "An Exotic Front, But Chinatown Suffers," *Boston Globe*, 11 December 1969 (college student quotation).
27. "Conference Plans Future of Chinatown," *Boston Globe*, 24 October 1971; Caroline Chang, interview by Ai-Li-Chin, 22 October 1995, Chinese American Women Oral History Project, Radcliffe Institute for Advanced Study, Harvard University, Schlesinger Library, Cambridge; Greater Boston Chinese Golden Age Center, "About: History," available at www.gbcgac.org; "Center Aids Chinese with New Language," *Boston Globe*, 3 November 1972.
28. "Chinatown Finds a New Voice," *Boston Globe*, 7 January 1979; Liu, "Chinatown's Neighborhood Mobilization," 54; Adam Smith, "Forty Years of History at Boston's AACA," *Sampan*, 16 February 2007. The Quincy School Community Council would become the Boston Chinatown Neighborhood Center in 1997. See BCNC, "About Us: History and Accomplishments," available at www.bcnc.net.
29. Smith, "Forty Years of History at Boston's AACA."
30. "Asian Health Center Opens Branch with Celebrations," *Patriot Ledger*, 21 September 1995; Greater Boston Chinese Golden Age Center, "About: History," available at www.gbcgac.org.
31. Uriarte, "Contra Viento y Marea," 23–24; Chinese Progressive Association, "About Us," available at http://cpaboston.org.
32. Mike Liu, "Grass Roots Politics and Boston's Asian Community," *Radical America* 17.6 and 18.1 (joint issue, November 1983 / February 1984): 82; "New Voices, Voters Empowering Chinatown; Mediator's Clout Yields to Activism," *Boston Globe*, 25 June 2007; Liu, "Chinatown's Neighborhood Mobilization," 41.
33. For more on the busing crisis, see Ronald Formisano, *Boston against Busing* (Chapel Hill: University of North Carolina Press, 1991).
34. Sara Melendez, "Hispanos, Desegregation and Bilingual Education: A Case Analysis of the Role of El Comité de Padres in the Court-Ordered Desegregation of the Boston Public Schools" (Ed.D. diss., Harvard Graduate School of Education, 1981); "Community Organizing Paid Dividends for Suzanne Lee," *Bay State Banner*, 27 December 2012; Carmen Pola Biographical Information and Timeline, 1979–2007, box 1, folder 5, Carmen Pola Papers, Northeastern University Archives; "Spanish-Speaking Residents Protest Desegregation Order," *Boston Herald*, 20 January 1975; "Confusion, Fear Reported Hurting Hispanic Schooling, Bilingual Program," *Boston Globe*, 11 September 1975.
35. Uriarte-Gaston, "Organizing for Survival," 199–203; Camayd-Freixas and Lopez, "Gaps in Representative Democracy," 3–4.

36. James Green, "The Making of Mel King's Rainbow Coalition: Political Changes in Boston, 1963–1983," *Radical America* 17.6 and 18.1 (joint issue, November 1983 / February 1984): 17, 23; Mel King, *Chain of Change* (Boston: South End Press, 1981), 70–71, 185–94.

37. Green, "The Making of Mel King's Rainbow Coalition," 10–12, 19, 25.

38. Melania Bruno and Mauricio Gaston, "Latinos for Mel King: Some Reflections," *Radical America* 17.6 and 18.1 (joint issue, November 1983 / February 1984): 69–79; and in the same issue, Liu, "Grassroots Politics and Boston's Asian Community," 81–86.

39. "Flynn Wins in a Big Way," *Boston Globe*, 16 November 1983; Green, "The Making of Mel King's Rainbow Coalition," 13; Hardy-Fanta, *Latina Politics, Latino Politics*, 47; "Changing Ingredients in the Political Mix," *Boston Globe*, 17 June 1986; "Hispanic Woman to be Appointed to BRA, Flynn Aid Says," *Boston Globe*, 16 January 1989; City of Boston, *Municipal Register for 1990–91*.

40. Hardy-Fanta, *Latina Politics, Latino Politics*, 47; "Changing Ingredients in the Political Mix"; "Latinos Seeking Political Clout, They Have the Numbers but Lack Organization," *Boston Globe*, 3 August 1986. Dukakis also appointed the first Asian American judge in Massachusetts when he named Richard J. Chin to the Boston Municipal Court in 1989; see "A Judicial First: Asian American Slated for Nomination," *Boston Globe*, 17 August 1989.

41. Olivencia, "Multiracial Coalitions," 52–54; "Opponents Offer Redistricting Plan," *Boston Globe*, 17 February 1988; "Mass Hispanics Urged to Become a Force in Local, State Government," *Boston Globe*, 29 October 1989.

42. Olivencia, "Multiracial Coalitions," 55–57; Hardy-Fanta, *Latina Politics, Latino Politics*, 108–9; "Latino Scales Beacon Hill, Merced Bears the Hopes of an Ethnic Community," *Boston Globe*, 6 December 1988 (quotation).

43. Liu, "Grass Roots Politics and Boston's Asian Community," 81; "Profiles of Members of the New Panel," *Boston Globe*, 15 December 1991; Camayd-Freixas and Lopez, "Gaps in Representative Democracy," 1 (quotation).

44. Evelyn Savidge Sterne, "Beyond the Boss: Immigration and American Political Culture from 1880 to 1940," in *E Pluribus Unum: Contemporary and Historical Perspectives*, ed. Gary Gerstle and John Mollenkopf (New York: Russell Sage Foundation, 2001), 35–43.

45. "A Center of Division: Haitians Spar with Catholic Charities over a Place of Their Own," *Boston Globe*, 26 November 2003; Haitian American Public Health Initiative, "Profile," available at www.haphi.org; Patrick M. McGroarty, "The Lion in Fields Corner: Building a Vietnamese Community in the New Boston" (senior thesis, Boston College, 2006), 54, 59–60; "Q&A with Long Nguyen, on Building the First Vietnamese Center," *Boston Globe*, 18 July 1999.

46. Alix Cantave, "Incorporation or Symbiosis: Haitians and African Americans in Mattapan," *Trotter Review* 19 (January 2010): 115–21, available at http://scholarworks.umb.edu; see also Regine O. Jackson, "Black Immigrants in the New Urban Landscape: The Case of Haitians in Boston," paper prepared for Woodrow Wilson International Center for Scholars, Washington, DC, 2005, 25–26.

47. Uriarte, "Contra Viento y Marea," 23–24; Nicole P. Marwell, "Privatizing the Welfare State: Nonprofit Community-Based Organizations as Political Actors," *American Sociological Review* 69 (April 2004): 267–68, 271; Glenn Jacobs, "Service versus Advocacy: A Comparison of Two Latino Community-Based Organizations in Chelsea, Massachusetts," *Trotter Review* 19 (January 2010): 81–106, available at http://scholarworks.umb.edu.

48. Hardy-Fanta, *Latina Politics, Latino Politics,* 24–27; Uriarte, "Contra Viento y Marea," 22; Rev. Cheng Imm Tan, interview by author, 3 August 2012.

49. Sam Yoon, "An Interview with Sam Yoon," interviewed by P. J. Kim, *Asian American Policy Review* 15 (2006): 1–2; "City Council Candidate Is the First Asian to Run," *Boston Globe*, 24 September 2004; Frances Fox Piven and Richard Cloward, *Regulating the Poor* (New York: Pantheon, 1971), 275–76.

50. Peter Drier, "Ray Flynn's Legacy: American Cities and the Progressive Agenda," *National Civic Review* 82 (Fall 1993): 380–403; Marwell, "Privatizing the Welfare State," 270; Els de Graauw, "Nonprofit Organizations: Agents of Immigrant Political Incorporation in Urban America," in *Civic Hopes and Political Realities*, ed. S. Karthick Ramakrishnan and Irene Bloemraad (New York: Russell Sage Foundation, 2008), 321–50.

51. Tan interview; "City Names Minister to Direct Bureau to Assist Immigrants," *Boston Globe*, 27 October 1998; "New Bostonians Vote Campaign," *Boston Globe*, 17 November 2002; "On a Waiting List for the American Dream," *Boston Globe*, 19 September 2004; "Tapping New Voters in City Races; Candidates Make Appeals to Naturalized Citizens," *Boston Globe*, 12 July 2005; Thomas Menino, "Helping Haitians and Other Immigrants Get English Skills," *Boston Haitian Reporter*, 31 May 2002.

52. Tan interview; "Tapping New Voters in City Races," *Boston Globe*, 12 July 2005. For demographic reports published by MONB, see Mayor's Office of New Bostonians, "Publications," available at www.cityofboston.gov.

53. "UMass Institute to Study Woes of State's Hispanics," *Boston Globe*, 6 December 1989; "Center Taps into the Asian Community," *Boston Globe*, 15 May 1994.

54. Sister Rose Cummins, e-mail interview by Andrew Hara, April 2002, and Elena Letona interview transcription, March 2002, both in Urban Borderlands Records, Spring 2002, box 001, TDCA; Shoshana Grossman-Crist, "Centro Presente: Building Community and Awareness of Rights among the Latin American Immigrant Population in Massachusetts," final report, Fall 2006, TDCA, available at http://dca.lib.tufts.edu.

55. MIRA, *Many Voices Joined for Justice: MIRA 25th Anniversary* (Boston, 2012); see also *Boston Globe* articles: "Amnesty Deadline Extension Urged," 6 November 1987; "A Flawed Immigration Act," 11 November 1988; "Flynn Hits Repatriation: Kennedy Urges It Be Suspended," 29 March 2000.

56. Eva Millona, interview by author, 2 July 2013; Michael Fix and Jeffrey S. Passel, "The Scope and Impact of Welfare Reform's Immigrant Provisions," Washington,

DC, Urban Institute, 2002, available at www.urban.org; "Injustice to Immigrants," *Boston Globe,* 29 March 2000; "10,000 Lose Health Coverage This Week," *Boston Globe,* 10 August 2003; "Massachusetts Cuts Back Immigrants' Health Care," *New York Times,* 31 August 2010. In Massachusetts, the undocumented retained access only to emergency medical care and a few basic services to protect public health and safety.

57. Sylvia Saavedra Keeber interview by John Keogh and Kathleen Flahive, Urban Borderlands Records, 2002, box 001, TDCA; Millona interview; MIRA, *Many Voices Joined for Justice,* 5–6, 8; see also *Boston Globe* articles: "On Common, 2,500 Rally for Immigrants," 28 March 2006; "Troopers Can Arrest Illegal Immigrants in Romney Deal," 3 December 2006; "US Judge Halts the Removal of More Detainees from the State," 10 March 2007; "Advocates Criticize Federal Roundups," 30 August 2007; "Deportees with No Criminal Past Grow; Advocates Alarmed by Trend in Region," 12 January 2008; "Family Life a Complex Affair for Immigrants; Illegal Status Creates Fault Lines," 11 May 2009; Eva Millona, "Immigration Program Threatens Community Safety" (Op-ed), 26 May 2011; "Illegal Immigrant Scrutiny Tightens in Mass.," 9 May 2012.

58. Millona interview; MIRA, *Many Voices Joined for Justice,* 4, 6, 8; "Patrick to Focus on Change for Immigrants," *Boston Globe,* 17 November 2010.

59. Millona interview; MIRA press release, "Four Thousand Americans Registered to Vote," 17 October 2012.

60. "Case by Case, Activists Fight Deportations," *Boston Globe,* 7 September 2009; "Students Here Illegally Rally in Hope of Living the American Dream," *Boston Globe,* 26 May 2010; "Illegal Immigrant Students Tell of Lost Opportunities," *Boston Globe,* 26 November 2010; "Learning to Apply for Their Dream," *Boston Globe,* 16 August 2012. For a detailed treatment of the SIM, see Thomas Piñeros Shields, "DREAMers Rising: Constituting the Undocumented Student Movement" (Ph.D. diss., Brandeis University, 2014). The 1996 Illegal Immigration Reform and Immigrant Responsibility Act barred states from offering in-state tuition benefits to undocumented residents unless they also offered the same benefits to US citizens who are not state residents. Those states that do offer this benefit have generally instituted requirements that students graduate from and attend a high school in that state for several years. Under such rules, a small group of legal resident graduates who no longer live in that state are eligible for the in-state tuition benefit. National Immigrant Law Center, "Basic Facts about In-State Tuition," available at www.nilc.org.

61. Brazilian Immigrant Center, "A Glimpse of Our History," available at www.braziliancenter.org; "Brazilian Haven Gets a Reprieve," *Boston Globe,* 2 August 1998. For more on worker centers, see Janice Fine, *Worker Centers: Organizing Communities at the Edge of the Dream* (Ithaca, NY: Cornell University Press, 2006).

62. Brazilian Immigrant Center, "A Glimpse of Our History"; "State Wage Laws Also Protecting Illegal Workers," *Boston Globe,* 29 December 2008. One of the

best-known cases surfaced in 2009 involving the Upper Crust Pizza chain, which worked its mainly Brazilian kitchen staff seventy to eighty hours per week without paying overtime. The owners were ordered to pay $341,000 in back wages but ultimately declared bankruptcy. The Harvard Square franchise was then purchased by the employees' lawyer, who helped to reorganize it as a company with employee ownership shares. "Pizzeria Chain May Face New Wage Case," *Boston Globe,* 22 July 2010; "Upper Crust Staffers Land at New Shop," *Boston Globe,* 30 May 2012.

63. "Immigrants Hurt at Work Face Hurdles," *Boston Globe,* 28 November 2003; Brazilian Immigrant Center, "Initiatives and Accomplishments since May 1, 2010," available at www.braziliancenter.org; Sheila Bapat, "Refocusing Our Lens: Domestic Workers' Rights Are a Neglected Feminist Issue," available at www.braziliancenter.org; "Governor Patrick Signs Domestic Workers Bill of Rights into Law," *Boston Globe,* 3 July 2014.

EPILOGUE. IMMIGRANTS AND THE NEW MAJORITY

1. "After the Backlash, St. Patrick's Roast Dispute Is Over, Easy," *Boston Globe,* 7 September 2013; "Guess Who's Coming to Breakfast," *Bay State Banner,* 11 September 2013; David Bernstein, "Don't F*ck with Linda," *Boston Magazine,* July 2014.
2. "Putting Latinos in the Loop," *Boston Globe,* 8 April 2001; "Blacks, Latinos Push for Districts, Want Voting Lines to Reflect Growth," *Boston Globe,* 11 February 2001; "Designing Districts to Give Minorities More Pull at Polls," *Boston Globe,* 17 June 2001; "Report Urges Overhaul of Boston's Election Procedures," *Boston Globe,* 24 October 2001; "Value of Restraint," *Bay State Banner,* 18 January 2007.
3. Arroyo first ran in 2001 but narrowly lost with a fourth-place finish. But when one of the top three vote getters resigned, Arroyo was seated. The 2003 election was thus the first outright win for a Latino candidate to the council.
4. For more on the New Majority and the 2003 elections, see *Boston Globe* articles: "A Unified Agenda for Minorities Eyed," 19 October 2003; "Councilors Keep Seats," 5 November 2003; "Coercion of Voters Reported in Chinatown," 26 September 2003; "Hearing Explores Inequities in Northeast Voting," 11 February 2001; "Justice Department Accuses City of Voting Rights Violations," 30 July 2005; "To Build Vote Bias Case, US Sought Reports," 2 August 2005; "The Struggle for Voting Rights Turns to Boston," 4 August 2005; and Lydia Lowe, "Groups Press City to Settle Voting Rights Suit," *Bay State Banner,* 18 August 2005.
5. "City Agrees to Accept Election Monitoring," *Boston Globe,* 16 September 2005; "Menino Names Voting Panel," *Boston Globe,* 4 August 2005.
6. "Trying for a Big Finish, Candidates Race to Get Out Vote for Mayor and City Council," *Boston Globe,* 8 November 2005; "A Fourth Term for Menino, Hennigan Falls; Flaherty, Arroyo, Yoon, Murphy Top Council Race," *Boston Globe,* 9 November 2005. Although often regarded as a tool to monitor and punish southern states, the Voting Rights Act proved critical in helping break down racial

barriers in Boston politics. With the Supreme Court's invalidation of section 4 of the Voting Rights Act in 2013, that tool is no longer available.

7. "A Lively Fight in Dorchester," *Boston Globe*, 20 May 1999; "Two Special Rep Races Draw Crowds," *Boston Globe*, 6 February 2005; "Now Haitian Americans Take Root in Local Politics," *Boston Globe*, 26 March 2005; "Dorcena Forry Beats Ureneck in Senate Race for 'Southie Seat,'" 29 May 2013.

8. "The Menino Factor Key in Sanchez' Win," *Boston Globe*, 29 September 2002; "Activists Encouraged by Turnout of Latinos," *Boston Globe*, 9 November 2002; "Arroyo Win Hailed as Political Bellwether," *Boston Globe*, 6 November 2003; "Gaining from Arroyo's Loss," *Boston Globe*, 9 November 2007; "City Top Vote Getter Upends Old Patterns," *Boston Globe*, 10 November 2011; "Andrea Cabral Sworn in as Secretary of Public Safety and Security," *OJornal*, 23 January 2013; "Women Top Ticket in Race for At-Large Council," *Boston Globe*, 6 November 2013.

9. The most notable controversies surrounding new ethnic candidates have been their alliances with powerful white political leaders. Marie St. Fleur was criticized for her support for State House Speaker Thomas Finneran in 2002, while newly elected City Councilor Michelle Wu faced sharp resistance for her backing of South Boston's Bill Linehan for council president in 2013. "Lawmakers Charge Retaliation in Finneran's Committee Choices," *Bay State Banner*, 13 February 2013; Yvonne Abraham, "Michelle Wu Is Stumbling out of the Blocks," *Boston Globe*, 12 December 2013.

10. "Politicians Court Immigrants at Tuesday's State House Event," 6 April 2006, and "Immigrant Marchers Roll through Boston," 13 April 2006, both in the *Bay State Banner*. "Council Calls for a Boycott of Arizona," *Boston Globe*, 6 May 2010.

11. "Minority Voters Were Key in Victory," *Boston Globe*, 7 November 2013; "From the Inside: How Walsh Came Out on Top," *Boston Globe*, 10 November 2013.

12. Andrew Sum et al., *The Changing Workforce: Immigrants and the New Economy in Massachusetts* (Boston: MassINC, 1999); Alicia H. Munnell et al., *The Graying of Massachusetts: Aging, the New Rules of Retirement, and the Changing Workforce* (Boston: MassINC, 2004).

Index

Page numbers in italics refer to illustrations or charts.

MARILYNN S. JOHNSON is a professor of history at Boston College. She is the author of several books, including *Street Justice: A History of Police Violence in New York City* and *The Second Gold Rush: Oakland and the East Bay in World War II*. She lives in Brookline, Massachusetts.

www.ingramcontent.com/pod-product-compliance
Lightning Source LLC
Chambersburg PA
CBHW020338270326
41926CB00007B/229